CW00622169

COMMUNITY CONT
MANAGEMENT, F
TRANSFORMATION

COMMUNITY CONFLICTS IN NIGERIA: MANAGEMENT, RESOLUTION AND TRANSFORMATION

Edited by
Onigu Otite
Professor of Sociology
University of Ibadan
and
Isaac Olawale Albert
Research Fellow in Social History
and Development Studies
Institute of African Studies
University of Ibadan

Spectrum Books Limited
Ibadan
Abuja • Benin City • Lagos • Owerri

Published by
Spectrum Books Limited
Spectrum House
Ring Road
PMB 5612
Ibadan, Nigeria

in association with
Safari Books (Export) Limited
1st Floor
17 Bond Street
St Helier
Jersey JE2 3NP
Channel Islands
United Kingdom

Europe and USA Distributor
African Books Collective Ltd.
The Jam Factory
27 Park End Street
Oxford OX1, 1HU, UK

© Academic Associates PeaceWorks

First published, 1999

Reprinted, 2001

All rights reserved. This book is copyright and so no part of it may be reproduced, stored in a retrieval system, or transmitted, in any form or by any means, electronic, mechanical, electrostatic, magnetic tape, photocopying, recording or otherwise, without the prior written permission of the copyright owner.

ISBN: 978-029-105-9

Printed by Kenbim Press Ltd.

Acknowledgements

Academic Associates PeaceWorks (AAPW) acknowledges with thanks the key role which the British Council and Department for International Development (DFID) UK played in providing the initial funding for our work from 1994 to 1999. They funded conflict management at a time when this was virtually an unknown field in Nigeria. DFID also provided financial support for the publication of this book and partial support for the launch in 2000. The United States Agency for International Development provided funding for three of the case studies in this book.

Special thanks to all the authors of the various chapters in the book. These authors are not paid academics, but rather, concerned people who have a real interest in seeking solutions to the conflicts which they studied. Fortunately, further activities by either AAPW or other conflict management practitioners have resulted in resolution of a number of the conflicts described in this book.

Further thanks go to Maj. Gen. Ishola Williams (Rtd.) who worked with me on all of these case studies in their initial stages, and made positive contributions to both the improvement of the studies and the interventions which followed. We are also appreciative of the efforts of the two authors, especially Prof. Onigu Otite, who was my teacher in the early 1970s and later became a friend and colleague.

Judith Burdin Asuni PhD
Executive Director

with best wishes to
Mr. Hafiz Galadima

Contents

Preface

Conflict is perceived in most parts of the world, including Nigeria, as something abnormal, dysfunctional and therefore detestable. Yet, conflict is a fact of life and could be a precursor of positive change. Every plural society is bound to experience one form of conflict or the other. What makes a society an ideal polity is the extent to which the conflicting interests and needs in a society are constructively managed so that violence does not threaten its continued existence. Conflict challenges the rational man to think of alternative ways of meeting contesting human needs and interests. What is to be emphasised, therefore, is not conflict *per se* but the ways man responds to it. Conflict need not follow a negative course. If constructively handled, it can become an agent of growth and development for all parties. To this extent, conflict is not to be demonised but confronted with efficient procedures for co-operative problem-solving.

The twelve essays contained in this volume, with three exceptions, were originally written to inform constructive conflict management in Nigeria. Violent community conflicts are a regular feature of social life in the country, especially since the 1960s. These conflicts result from different value systems, aggressive competition for land, water and political resources, and the unhealthy competition of some community leaders. There is hardly a year when there is no major violent community conflict in Nigeria. Not much has however been published on these violent conflicts. The few published works are in learned journals that are not easily accessible to scholars and the general reader. It is hoped that the essays in this volume will correct this situation.

The essays provide relevant information for understanding how most of the community conflicts arose and degenerated to violent stages as a result of poor conflict handling styles. They deal with specific community conflicts in Nigeria. The causes, courses and effects of the conflicts are discussed with a view to informing conflict managers about appropriate actions to take in dealing with the problems.

The essays, except the first two and the last, were commissioned between 1996 and 1998 by Academic Associates PeaceWorks [AAPW] with funding from the Overseas Development Agency, British High Commission in Lagos, the British Council office in Lagos; and the United States Agency for International Development. AAPW, a non-governmental organisation based in Lagos, engages in community peacemaking, peacebuilding and preventive diplomacy. It has worked in all communities mentioned in the chapters. In the course of intervening in various communities in Nigeria, AAPW implemented some of the recommendations in this book.

The present volume does not claim to be exhaustive of all that has to be said on community conflicts in Nigeria. The conflicts included in the volume are limited to those in respect of which AAPW did some practical conflict management work. Other equally important ones, like the problems in the Niger Delta, are not included. This is practically inevitable in a field that is both disparate and very large. AAPW has started work on the Warri crisis. With time and more resources, the organisation also intends to work on other important conflicts that are not reflected in the present volume.

The twelve chapters contained in the book are, expectedly, unequal in quality, being produced by a mixed group of specialists and amateur field practitioners with various academic backgrounds in conflict management, resolution and transformation. The authors sourced their data from observations, oral interviews and local archives. They tried as much as possible to base their work on the communities' perceptions of their conflicts and their responses to them, without distorting the feelings of the parties involved. In order to avoid any misunderstanding or misinterpretation, fictitious names are used in chapters 4, 8, 9 and 11 to conceal the identity of some individual actors.

The editors thank all the contributors for their work, realising that it took time and a great deal of effort to put each of the papers together. We are equally thankful to Major-General Ishola Williams [Rtd.] and Dr. Judith Burdin Asuni for their invaluable suggestions to improve the contents of the book. Last but not the least we thank the various international organisations, especially the British Council, for supporting the fieldwork leading to the production of the book.

University of Ibadan,   Onigu Otite
Nigeria.   Isaac Olawale Albert
May 1999

Chapter 1

Onigu Otite

On Conflicts, Their Resolution, Transformation, and Management

Conflicts arise from the pursuit of divergent interests, goals and aspirations by individuals and, or groups in defined social and physical environments. Changes in the social environment, such as contestable access to new political positions, or perceptions of new resources arising from development in the physical environment, are fertile grounds for conflicts involving individuals and groups who are interested in using these new resources to achieve their goals. By thus recognising the inherent nature of conflicts in heterogenous and competitive situations, people, more or less compellingly, sustain their societies as ongoing social systems through the resolution, transformation and management of conflicts.

One of the most quoted traditional definitions of conflict regards it as "a struggle over values and claims to scarce status, power and resources in which the aims of the opponents are to neutralise, injure, or eliminate their rivals" (Coser 1956: 8). In this sense, conflict may be conceptualised as a way of settling problems originating from opposing interests and from the continuity of society. Thus, Park and Burgess argue that "conflict is designed to resolve divergent dualism (and achieve) some kind of unity even if it be through the annihilation of one of the conflict parties" (1921: 574).

Conflict may therefore not be regarded only in a negative light of dysfunctional or dysjunctive process, and a breakdown of communication as some scholars tend to suggest (See for example Lundberg 1939: 275; Wilson and Kolb 1949: 714). Conflict is a conscious act involving personal or group contact and communication. Together with, though distinct from competition, struggle, and contest etc, conflict is a normal process of interaction particularly in complex societies in which resources are usually scarce. Although conflicts may generally exist "whenever incompatible activities occur" (Deutsch 1973: 156) and may result in a "win-lose" character, the resolution, transformation and management of conflicts may produce a "win-win" situation.

Hence Coser's elaborated definition of conflict becomes a useful clarification:

> Social conflict may be defined as a struggle over values or claims to status, power, and scarce resources, in which the aims of the conflicting parties are not only to gain the desired values, but also to neutralise, injure, or eliminate their rivals. Such conflicts may take place between individuals, between collectivities, or between individuals and collectivities. Intergroup as well as intragroup conflicts are perennial features of social life (1968).

Conflict can hardly be discussed outside the concept of pluralism. As Smooha (1975: 69) points out, both pluralism and conflict are related in complex ways J.S. Furnivally, a Dutch economist, is the reputed originator of the pluralism school in social science literature. His original formulation of a "medley of peoples" in societies in Burma and Java, where Europeans, Chinese, Indians and indigenes were perceived to "mix but do not combine," depicts a situation of co-existing diverse and basic compulsory institutional and cultural arrangements involving dominance and subordination in the same social setting. This idea of pluralism was picked up for systematic and serious analysis by several scholars, for example Kuper and Smith (1971) and their various contributors. Recent and current ideas of pluralism regard it as multidisciplinary and multidimensional, and defined in the context of cultural diversity and social segmentation of an encapsulating society. A plural society is thus characterised by co-existing but distinct cultural diversities and compulsory social institutions which determine and guide the individual and group behaviours of the incorporated peoples. As we shall examine later in this book, Nigeria, the country-setting for the essays presented in this book, is a plural society.

Here, there are group intercultural encounters in the process of fostering specific interests and aspirations in view of the limited common resources. In Nigeria, like in other plural societies, it is necessary to direct the analysis of conflicts to involve various cultures and strategic social institutions in the search for meanings conveyed through different lenses, logic, and grammars. In this way, we can more comfortably and assuredly assist parties in conflict to identify and eliminate systemic problems in the cause of the resolution, transformation and management of conflicts. Conflict and consensus are thus not polar opposites: rather competition, co-operation and consensus are parts of the same process of conflict identification and their resolution, transformation and management.

Although divergent interests and values may restrict concessions and co-operation among members of different ethnic groups, yet there are generally some political, economic and social ties that unite members of different ethnic groups in a plural society. However, it has been pointed out that " if these linkages come into competition with those of local or state-wide sentiment, the solidaristic nature of intimate group loyalties is likely to take precedence over other claims" (Rothchild 1969: 605).

As the social and physical environments are always changing because of one reason or the other, such as the establishment of new local government councils and the location of new headquarters, it is perhaps appropriate to focus attention on the interdependence of component ethnic groups and on their change of original positions when in conflict situations. Thus a conflict may be perceived to embrace hints and the necessity for its resolution or transformation. Conflict involves situations in which differences are expressed by interdependent peoples in the process of achieving their needs and goals (Donohue and Kolt 1992: 3), and it "arises when a difference between two (or more) people necessitates change in at least one person in order for their engagement to continue and develop. The differences cannot co-exist without some adjustment" (Jordan 1990: 4).

The question may still be raised in the minds of some readers as to why we bother to study conflicts. It should be noted that whether we view conflict as normal or abnormal, it is a recurring natural or even pathological fact, depending on the perspective of the analyst. It is inherent in all kinds of social, economic, or political settings and in business management jobs, etc. characterised by ethnic, religious and other forms of pluralism. Conflict is the very essence of most formal and informal social organisations and processes, such as ethnic groups as well as state and local government councils and headquarters where appointments and promotions are made. The location of sites and facilities, such as markets and grazing lands, generates conflicts and when these are not resolved or transformed, their negative consequences are felt beyond the immediate environment of the parties in conflict. For example, conflicts generated by the location of a local government council headquarters may have effects beyond the immediate locality and even the state. They may cause social instability which may retard or prevent development. In such a case, the federal government may be compelled to set up panels or commissions of enquiry to examine the conflicting claims of the parties involved and suggest solutions.

Conflicts have their objective bases in society. The concept is validated daily over access to a variety of limited resources which are created and distributed within defined establishment and locations: chairmanship position, power and status, grassland, market, water spots for animals and pasture-routes, jurisdiction of chiefs and kings, leadership of political parties etc. Conflicts are real, and serve in the above circumstances in the achievement of goals or the maintenance of claims. Thus, individuals and groups define a situation of conflict with reference to objective considerations.

A conflict is a dynamic phenomenon, which consists of five stages: initiation, escalation, controlled maintenance, abatement, and termination/resolution (Sandole 1993: 6). In this process, peace is the ultimate target or result of conflict, or even violence. Thus the aim of an individual or group in a conflict may not necessarily be achieved but it may be subdued by the conflict through negotiated settlement.

Karl Marx and Max Weber are well-known theorists in the sociology of conflict. Although it is apparent that Karl Marx is more celebrated in conflict sociology, Max Weber's contribution is more comprehensive (See Coser 1956). Both authorities are too well known to go into details here. Briefly stated in the context of this book, Marxist sociology emphasises two points: human societies are wholes or systems of interrelated parts - institutions, beliefs, etc., and that human societies are always changing largely through internal contradictions and conflicts (See Bottomore 1968, Bottomore and Rubel 1963). Marx emphasised the factor of the economy which he elaborated to formulate two different classes - those who own the means of production and those who sell their labour and are exploited by the owners of these means of production. Conflict is perceived to be inherent in the relations between these classes. This basic theme or scheme has influenced many thinkers since it was formulated with the general analysis that, basic to the structure of societies and of most, if not all, human relations, is the economic factor. Economic resources are of course scarce at least in many developing countries, such as Nigeria, and the competition for them between groups and individuals is an open source of conflict.

On the other hand, Weber dealt with the legitimation of power, and how order prevails in society through its use. Thereby, a conflict situation is created when a person or group attempts or succeeds in carrying out its will by overcoming the resistance of other groups or persons and their interests in a situation of scarcity of resources. Max Weber also devoted attention to the theory of action and the social conditions and consequences of economic behaviours (see R. Bendix 1968). Weber was concerned not only with group formation on the basis of material interest but also with the economic associations based on market and business interests. He defined social classes in the context of material interests. These matters, particularly those dealing with competition for political and economic power and resources, have important bearings on conflict studies in countries, such as Nigeria, defined by pluralism.

Arising from the above light shed by Marx and Weber, and by several well-known scholars in the field of conflict, it should be noted that some of the most noticeable social spheres in which conflicts are endemic are in industrial organisations, factories and bureaucratic set-ups. Class and workers-employers conflicts are well known perennial events which labour unions and employers' associations have encountered. Conflict resolution, transformation and management, like collective bargaining, corporate strategies and trade union management, are broad confrontational areas of social relations engaging the attention of labour law experts and specialists in industrial relations. In order to promote productivity, industrial peace, and stable fruitful activities in government or public and private sectors of the political economy, institutional arrangements are provided to reduce or manage conflicts ensuing between individuals, occupational groups, political-economic associations and unions, contesting divergent views and goals.

We will now examine closely the three concepts used in this chapter, that is, resolution, transformation and management.

Conflict Resolution

Conflicts do not normally result in the destruction of the societies in which they occur. Instead, as we noted in the preceding section of this chapter, they follow their own courses and stages, and usually terminate in the reconciliation of the communities concerned. They restore society to at least some degree of order which permits it to continue to exist in a changed form.

Although conflict resolution has been part of human experience for centuries, Burton (1993) argued that the concept is comparatively recent in academic discourse. He drew attention to the term "dispute" which some scholars interchange with conflict. For him, "settlement refers to negotiated or arbitrated outcomes of disputes, while resolution refers to outcomes of a conflict situation" (1993: 55). We thus have "dispute settlement" and "conflict resolution". However, dispute and conflict operate on the same principles and although they may refer to different conditions and scope of social relationships, they may, like the concepts of settlement and resolution, be used interchangeably.

Conflict resolution is essentially aimed at intervention to change or facilitate the course of a conflict. Other problem-solving techniques are known generally as "problem-solving workshops", "interactive problem-solving", "third party consultation", or "collaborative analytical problem-solving" (Mitchell 1993: 78). In general, conflict resolution provides an opportunity to interact with the parties concerned, with the hope of at least reducing the scope, intensity and effects of conflicts. During formal and informal meetings, conflict resolution exercises permit a re-assessment of views and claims as a basis for finding options to crises and to divergent points of view. Those who organise conflict resolution exercises or workshops usually constitute the third party in a triangular arrangement and consist of traditional rulers, modern sectoral leaders, outstanding opinion leaders and experienced key members of the public capable of producing new ideas and reconciliative conditions and actions.

Workshops organised to tackle conflicts are, according to Mitchell (1993: 82), expected to alter the perceptions, images and attitudes of the parties in conflict and widen their range of options. Participants at such workshops are expected to take specific conflict-deescalating proposals and ideas home to members of their groups.

Conflict resolution in plural societies can be quite complex, principally because of the determinate effects of culture and language symbolism. Hence, as Avruch and Black (1993) point out, it is quite dangerous to relegate culture to the background in conflict resolution. Although culture is a marker of social differences, it should not be regarded as an obstacle to conflict resolution in multi-ethnic/multi-cultural societies. Perceiving conflicts through divergent cultural lenses is natural. People interpret social action and social reality through their indigenous conceptions and knowledge. Understanding the local indigenous theories of conflicts is essential to their solution. Avruch and Black (1990; 1991; 1993: 132) argued that utilising what they labelled "ethnoconflict theories" is crucially important in conflict resolution. Decoding their cultural grammar is an important key to conflict resolution because it reveals the value placed on resources and the strength and centrality of symbols associated with their use.

Culture also determines the information processing as well as the use of metaphors and language in the bargaining and debating process. It is by paying attention to the intricate culture questions that even those apparently unresolvable conflicts can be broken down. The cultural question can muddle up and compound conflicts and make them appear impossible to resolve.

Wilmot and Hocker (1998) discussed several modes of intervention. These include facilitation, mediation, counselling and therapy, organisational development, conciliation, quasi-political procedures, informal tribunals, arbitration of several types and criminal and civil justice systems. In practical terms, a combination of these modes is often used to resolve conflicts. Also, elements and actors from the indigenous societies and "modern" socio-political set ups, are normally combined in Nigeria and other plural non-western societies.

The above points pose a special difficulty in conflict resolution, that is how to "delink" cultural values and philosophical or ideological positions from contemporary divergent interests and processes in conflict resolution. Recent research on this issue shows that "(a) conflicts of interests linked to differences in ideology are more difficult to resolve than conflicts that do not derive from contrasting ideological orientations, and (b) the more polarised the parties in ideological orientation, the more difficult it is to resolve a related conflict of interest" (Sandole 1993: 28; also see Zechmeister and Druckman 1973). The importance of this observation rests on the fact that the many inter-ethnic conflicts in Nigeria are based on historical grounds, ethno-philosophy, and even myths surrounding original and settler claims to land, water and grazing resources in the contemporary situation of local government council jurisdiction and activities.

Nader (1968) has reminded us of the three major structural levels at which most conflicts occur: intra-family, intra-community,, and inter-community. This anthropological insight also indicates that conflicts may occur in forms including physical attacks or verbal aggression, (also see Levine 1961). Third parties operate to resolve conflicts through arbitration, mediation, compromise, and adjudication. There are also institutional means for conflict resolution even in local settings such as elders' councils (see Richards and Kuper 1971). As the celebrated work of Fortes and Evans-Pritchard (1940) demonstrated, conflict resolution in non-western societies is not necessarily identified with specialised political offices. Nader points out in this connection that other means or agents of resolving or regulating conflicts in indigenous "stateless" societies include the diviner, shaman, as well as the roles of chief priests and headmen. Town or village councils represent accepted procedures and opinions, and when seated according to designated order, they make pronouncements which shift rapidly from political to judicial and to conflict resolution at the local level (see Otite 1973).

Conflict resolution performs a healing function in societies. It provides opportunity for the examinations of alternative pay-offs in a situation of positioned disagreements, and restores normalcy in societies by facilitating discussions and placing parties in conflict, in situations in which they can choose alternative positive decisions to resolve differences.

Failure to resolve conflicts over access to commonly valued scarce resources, and over divergent perceptions of socio-political situations, has the high potential of degenerating into genocide or fratricide as it occurred among the Ife-Modakeke Yoruba and the Tiv-Jukun of Nigeria (as shown later in this book), and the Hutu-Tutsi of Burundi and Rwanda (Lemarchand 1989). Conflict resolution promotes consensus-building, social-bridge reconstructions, and the re-enactment of order in society. As we noted earlier in this chapter, conflicts hardly breakup societies. On the other hand, they function ultimately to educate people on how different actors and social units play or should play their roles to reconcile society.

Conflict Transformation

Experiential situations and conflict workshop experiences tend to query the use of the term, conflict resolution. The questions are; can we ever resolve conflicts? Is conflict resolution a realizable goal? Or is it an ideal situation to which we may strive? The word resolution suggests that conflict is a bad social phenomenon which should be removed because of its assumed destructive outcomes. Conflict energizes and motivates social change, and since its resolution may not always be possible, or at times even necessary, some scholars prefer to use the concept of conflict management or conflict transformation.

As Galtung points out, "in a conflict there is, somewhere, a contradiction. And in a contradiction there is, somewhere, dynamism" (1994 : 89). Conflicts that are formed by actors with perceived goals in mind, are, in fact, dynamic situations marked by contradictions, incompatible elements, and compromises. Social and situational transformations are thus always taking place. In this sense every conflict has its complexity, and any approach towards understanding its transformation requires a multidimensional non-unilinear perspective.

A practical problem-solving workshop is probably one of the best ways of transforming conflicts. Here, dealing with quick solutions would be of secondary importance, as focus is placed on the overall conflict process (Rupesinghe 1995). In this respect, there must be sincerity, adequate consultation and communication amongst actors, and, where discussions and talking are open-ended, conflicts have the tendency to "wax", "wane" and transform themselves. Rupesinghe observes in this regard that

"In a broad sense, openness to change, flexibility, the ability to peacefully modify approaches and learn from processes is what conflict transformation is all about" (1995: 77). It is a situation with the potential for developing constructive dialogue, cultures and practices of tolerance, negotiations and the trading and rebalancing of interests, in the process of changing the nature and intensity of conflict. Any conflict is thus inherently dialectical and it can hardly ever be static as community actors continue to interact. Conflict transformation involves a movement, as well as changing roles or functions in the process of negotiating a settlement of issues in a conflict. It may also involve interventions and mediation through legislative and judicial or coercive approaches (see Moore, 1996).

Conflict transformation is a summary term for a complex web of interdependent factors - the parties concerned, social relationships, the changing positions and roles of interveners, and the moderation of planned and unintended consequences. It is in this sense that we can admit the viewpoint of Lederach that "conflict transformation represents a comprehensive set of lenses for describing how conflict emerges from, evolves within, and brings about changes in the personal, relational, structural, and cultural dimensions, and for developing creative responses that promote peaceful change within those dimensions through non-violent mechanisms" (1997: 83). What Lederach calls "constructive transformation of conflicts" (1997: 85) and peacebuilding require shared vision of new patterns of sustainable relationships, which go beyond "resolving" or "ending" particular conflicts.

Conflicts may be aggregated as one, and the evolution or emergence of a particular conflict may constitute, only one dimension of the totality of problems between two communities. For example, conflicts over land and over imposed rule of a traditional king, though interdependent, are analytically distinct. And although we may succeed in resolving the conflict over land, that of traditional overrule may remain. It may require two or more different problem-solving workshops to transform the phenomena of conflict between the communities.

AAPW is inclined towards conflict transformation, realizing from the Nigerian experience that conflict can hardly be resolved finally. The Ife-Modakeke conflict is a clear example in which workshop participants go through peacebuilding sessions and shake hands rejoicingly, only to revert to their conflict situations on returning to their home settlements. However, channels of communication are maintained, and politico-economic and socio-cultural resources are mobilized in an effort to reconvene and continue the process of peacebuilding by transforming the situation of conflict. Such resumed process of conflict transformation normally includes the use of face-saving tactics as a means of increasing flexibility and developing the culture of negotiation and interdependence during problem-solving workshops. Here, we may recall the point of naivety made earlier, if we assume the once-and-for-all resolution of conflicts after obtaining the signatories or thumb marks of kings as traditional rulers, modern elite, and youth leaders on prepared communique and agreement documents. (See also Galtung, 1994: 89).

Conflict Management

Definitions of conflict, for example by Jordan (1990: 4), as we noted earlier, indicate that differences and conflicts can not continue to exist without some adjustment in the positions held by the parties in conflict. Although both conflict resolution and conflict transformation, especially the latter imply changes in the relations between communities, the former is often regarded as a short term activity to deal with a particular issue. A conflict resolution may in fact be no more than frantic response or indeed a fire brigade approach to violent conflict or social upheaval.

Conflict management, on the other hand, may be perceived as a wider concept, involving conflict resolution and transformation when necessitated, and it is more of a long-term arrangement involving institutionalised provisions and regulative procedures for dealing with conflicts whenever they occur. People must learn to manage conflicts productively, otherwise the risks to society and its development are overwhelming. In some respects the concepts of conflict resolution, conflict transformation and conflict management overlap both in content and in practice.

In their "short course on conflict management", for instance, Wilmot and Hocker (1998: 48 - 49) identify some ideas for dealing with conflicts. These include clarification of communication and the checking of perceptions which in turn involve the following:

speaking out what is in one's mind or heart, listening carefully, expressing strong feelings appropriately, remaining rational, asking questions, maintaining a spirit of give and take, avoiding harmful statements, asking directly what is going on, telling others one's opinion, looking for flexible "shades of gray" solutions, recognising the power of initiating a co-operative move, identifying conflict patterns, and engaging in negotiations of agreements and settlements. Appropriate communication skills and channels are crucial in conflict management.

Conflict management must occur in a polite atmosphere and context. Yet conflicts do not generally follow the demands of politeness. Hence, conflict managers must be skilful to overcome the generally chaotic and disorderly scenes associated with the behaviour of parties in conflict. Emotions or sentiments and irrationality must be controlled. Simple common language and the use of metaphor normally make positive contributions to conflict management. Conflicts need not be portrayed as warfare or violence.

It promotes the success of conflict management if parties in conflict are portrayed as interdependent citizens, and if anger and strong emotions are minimised. Conflict management can also involve the mobilisation of cultural expectations, if not imperatives, such as African hospitality, commensality, reciprocity and belief systems. (Also see Uchendu 1965 and Anigbo 1988.) Kola hospitality and commensality are cultural instruments in Nigeria and elsewhere, that can be utilised to settle at least intra-family and intra-ethnic conflicts in the open glare of an attentive audience in town or village squares, or at the shrines of common deities, ancestors and predecessors.

Hence, by including both the living and the dead, together with their spirit world, indigenous African systems of conflict management may have even stronger potency of handling conflicts with more lasting effects than modern ones. Both adjudication and mediation reduce protracted conflicts and enhance everyone's satisfaction with decisions. They also reduce the re-occurrence of conflicts. As in modern-westernised situations (see Wilmot and Hocker 1998: 249), those involved must be capable of demonstrating patience, sincerity, wit, physical endurance, wisdom and probing skills. Whereas these attributes involve trained specialists in some cases, the African conflict management profile generally involves almost everybody with authority in several areas of life in the social structure.

In some African societies, some functionaries whom we may ordinarily regard as innocuous, may be the ones holding the key in tradition to conflict management. For example, among the Nuer of Sudan, the "leopard skin chief", a specialist with ritual power and capacity, is the one to deflate the balloon of an impending intergroup feud, violence and conflict, by allowing his house to function as a culturally prescribed sanctuary for those who committed the serious offence of intended or unintended murder, while he mediates and negotiates compensation, restitution, reconciliation, sacrifices, ritual cleansing and atonement (Evans-Pritchard 1940). Such indigenous functionaries and methods for managing conflicts are found elsewhere in Africa. In the case of the Nuer, it was observed that "the Leopard-skin chief does not rule and judge, but acts as mediator through whom communities desirous of ending open hostility can conclude an active state of feud. The feud including the role played in it by the chief, is thus a mechanism by which the political structure maintains itself" (Evans-Pritchard 1940:293). In this sense conflict management, as an institutionalised activity, can be properly described as a near-equilibrium - restoring instrument in society.

But African societies are not now constituted by the indigenous or modern-westernised sector alone. Both sectors co-exist. Hence conflict management must not ignore the importance of various and sometimes conflicting loyalties in the same setting. There is thus an intricate web of relationships in which the same people depend on one another for many things and reasons, while custom and culture define the identity and individuality of different symbols and relationships within the whole setting. The need to involve and mobilise state and local government functionaries, kings, chiefs, and modern forms of the "leopard-skin chief" as well as universalistic religious administrative personnel in modern conflict management structures and processes, can hardly be overemphasised in plural and multi-ethnic settings. This viewpoint perhaps helps to clarify the issue that although conflict management may appear co-terminous with conflict resolution/conflict transformation, the former, better than any of the latter, describes the structural and processual dimensions which deal with issues of conflict.

Conflict Situation as a State of Affairs and as a Process

The discussions above indicate that conflict resolution or conflict transformation is, analytically, both a state of affairs and a process. As a state of affairs, each is theoretically static, as a snapshot to enable us observe and deal with a particular conflict situation depicting interacting variables, for example anger, conflict scars such as damaged houses and crops, slaughtered cattle and other animal stock, bullet marks on walls, blocked or broken bridges and water passages, refusal to compensate or apologize etc.

Such a "state of affairs" is often an illusion, however sound it may seem theoretically. Most conflicts can hardly be finally or permanently resolved or transformed. The nearest to this "finality" or "perfection" of conflict settlement may be found in those African societies and communities in which divine or supernatural intervention is made part of conflict resolution or transformation. The atmosphere is believed to be spiritualised, and the fear of supernatural sanctions impels or compels the communities involved to adhere to mutually agreed terms of conflict resolution or transformation as a matter of collective conscience.

Generally, however, it is more realistic to regard conflict resolution or transformation as a process. This process may entail some of the eight steps, such as creating and recreating positive atmosphere, clarifying perceptions, generating options, etc. which Weeks (1994: 68 ff) enumerated. The variables in the snapshot picture indicated above are always interacting, a dialectical condition which produces social change between communities.

As a process, conflict resolution and conflict transformation come to about the same changing phenomenon, defined by several planned and unforeseen intervening variables which require an equally dynamic phenomenon of conflict management. This viewpoint indicates that conflict, as a process, is managed to avoid its escalation, and reduce instances or degrees of anger and criminal misconduct. And if conflict is so managed to produce peace, such a built-up peace may not be a permanent condition, especially if such a particular conflict was a symptom or part of a larger aggregate of conflicts, existing between two communities.

Peace is a relative condition, not a permanent one. It may be regarded as a condition of tranquilised conflict. Peace is required for social and politico-economic development such as the creation of Local Government Councils and the establishment of the position of Chairmen of Councils for administrative effectiveness. This development, as this books shows, has led to strife and competition for access to, and control of such a high position, often regarded as a socio-economic asset, involving contraposing inter and intra-community groups in the same local setting. Thus, because there is hardly any permanent peace or permanent resolution or transformation of conflicts, it may be more appropriate to speak of conflict management as a means of coping with the processes of resolving or transforming conflict.

The discussion in the preceding paragraphs indicate that conflicts arise from actions, interactions, and reactions between persons, groups and communities. Conflicts do not derive from a mere plurality of goals *per se*. They arise when people or communities pursue those goals in which others have interests and interfere as multiple users or utilisers.

This point may lead us to accept an updated reformulation of the traditional definition of conflict as "the interaction of interdependent people who perceive incompatible goals and interference from each other in achieving those goals" (Folger, Poole and Stutman, 1997: 4: also see Hocker and Wilmot, 1985). The discussions also indicate that even at the local community level, "a theory of conflict is as indispensable for development studies as it is for peace studies. The same is true of peace, but peace also has that emphasis on violence-reduction and non-violent transformation" (Galtung, 1994: 70). A theory of conflict is intimately connected to contemporary theories, such as those of human needs, verbal aggression, social influence and reciprocity etc. (See Folger, Poole and Stutman, 1997: 49-68).

Some Preliminary Notes on Conflict Perspectives by AAPW

Academic Associates Peace Works (AAPW), a non-profit, non-governmental organisation founded in Lagos by Dr. Judith Burdin Asuni in the early 1990s, is committed to contributing to the building of a world of peace through conflict transformation and peacebuilding. This book is AAPW's first publication of conflict case studies.

AAPW perceives conflict as a natural and inevitable phenomenon in the interactive social systems which people are not often prepared to acknowledge and deal with. AAPW focuses attention on raising peoples' awareness and acknowledgement of conflict and equipping them with skills to deal with it constructively. Peace is not regarded as an end in itself; it represents a positive condition for socio-economic development, progress, and a stable political order. This standpoint may not necessarily be reduced to harmony or equilibrium model of society which in practical terms is unreal. AAPW acknowledges that conflict is endemic in contemporary societies as communities and individuals compete for access to the limited political and economic resources available. Hence there is an emphasis on not merely identifying the causes and stages of conflict, but also undertaking activities towards its resolution, transformation and management. AAPW's peacebuilding and peace education activities represent guided attempts to cultivate orientations which forestall violence and conflict, while striving for social justice.

Cultural lenses and communicative acts receive attention through a deliberate programme of conflict management workshops in different socio-cultural areas and ecological zones, in Nigeria`s complex setting. The training of personnel as formal and informal mediators is one method of inundating the population with peace workers drawn from different cultures. With time at least in Nigeria, the present country of concentration for various obvious reasons, prompt interventions would reduce the range and minimise the instances of conflict.

Conflicts must be resolved, transformed or managed to ensure social justice and peace between individuals and groups having divergent interests. Such activities constitute some of the prerequisites of the social dimensions of development. If not resolved or properly managed, conflicts, especially ethnic conflicts, as Rothchild (1969: 598) has pointed out, have a clear chance of following the path to a serious imbalance or disjuncture between order and development at any level of the social structure. As we shall find later in this book, AAPW's approach consists of the identification and analysis of conflicts and their prevention, resolution, transformation and management, through various agents and programmes in relation to peace and development at several levels and spheres of societies.

Further Discussion

There is an obvious need to study and understand conflicts, their causes and consequences, and their inevitability in our social reality. Although conflicts have negative connotations, they constitute an essential creative element for changing societies and achieving the goals and aspirations of individuals and groups. Thus as Sandole (1992: 6) points out, there is nothing inherently wrong with conflicts. Or perhaps we should say that we need conflicts as catalysts for development, and as means of removing dullness and monotony from society. Yet conflict resolution, transformation and management aim at reducing or removing conflicts on the continuum towards consensus. This point suggests that neither conflicts nor consensus characterises society to the exclusion of the other. Both phenomena are two aspects of the same social reality. In order to achieve stable development, society needs a judicious mixture and control of these two natural phenomena, with a net balance of consensual over conflictual relationships to ensure the continuity of society. Or to put this idea differently, "a certain amount of discord, inner divergence and outer controversy, is organically tied up with the very elements that ultimately hold the group together" (Simmel 1908 - 1955). Similarly, it is well known that earlier social thinkers and theorists argued that political and other forms of conflict cannot be excluded from social life. Peace and conflict studies thus deal with the same nature of man in society. Man's multiple affiliations and social networks enable him to participate in a variety of social situations as allies and as antagonists.

When individuals or groups are in conflict, there could be two main outcomes, what Druckman (1992: 26) called "zero-sum outcomes" and "positive-sum outcomes". Whereas the former refers to a situation where one's losses equal another's gains, the latter describes a situation where both sides in a conflict gain. Between these two positions those in conflict normally compete and co-operate, and are left with various degrees of loss or gain. This situation of conflict entails Sumner's early distinction between "ingroup" and "outgroup" with opposing interests in intergroup relations. Without conflict, within and between groups, man could hardly have incentives towards peacebuilding.

With reference to any one group, it has been observed "how men quarrel in terms of certain of their customary allegiances, but are restrained from violence through other conflicting allegiances which are also enjoined on them by custom. The result is that conflicts in one set of relationships over a wider range of society or through a longer period of time, lead to the re-establishment of social cohesion" (Gluckman 1965: 2).

The Nigerian Context as a Social System

Although the name Nigeria was coined after the River Niger by the *London Times* of 8 January, 1897, it did not have British government official approval until July, 1899 (Otite 1971: 301 - 1). The country as a state came into being in 1914 with the amalgamation of the Northern and Southern Protectorates under Lord Lugard as a British colonial creation. Thus the state came into being before the society which was an encapsulation of pre-colonial independent nations, both renowned and relatively unknown states, as well as of peoples with uncentralised political systems and pastoral social formations.

The country is located between Latitudes $4^0 20'$ and 14^0 North and between Longitudes 3^0 $20'$ and 14^0 $30'$ East. Nigeria's geographical space of 923, 768 square kilometres, with a coastline of over 700 kilometres and a distance of 1,040 kilometres straight from the coast to the northern limits, consists of great diversities of vegetations, ecologies, economies and occupations. The swampy mangrove on the coastal areas changes to evergreen rain-equatorial forests and thins off into savanna grassland, and desert-like conditions at the northern limits. Nigeria's population is currently over 120 million people.

Nigeria is a plural society, defined by cultural-institutional diversities of the ethnic groups of various populations, and with people practising three main religions - Christianity, mainly in the South and Middle Belt; Islam, mainly in the North, and traditional religion in every part of the country. There have been various statements about the extent of Nigeria's ethnic pluralism, from the 250 mentioned by colonialists, and even half that number by superficial observers, to the figure of 374 ethnic groups which we found from our updated research (see Otite 1990). Admittedly, Nigeria is a very complex country with the behaviour and relationships of individuals and groups determined by the imperatives of cultural symbols and strategic social institutions. Different people are predisposed to conceptualise scarce political and economic resources and the access to them in divergent ways through their own coded lenses.

As from 1914, education and colonial legislative and administrative arrangements were used to reformulate the erstwhile independent nations and peoples as one entity. In 1939 (Ikime 1986), the Southern Protectorate was split into two - the West and the East, and in 1947, under the Richards Constitution, Nigeria was made a formal federation of three regions - North, West and East. This remained through the 1960 independence constitution until 1963 when the Mid-West region was created out of the Western Region. As a result of subsequent demands for more political-administrative units under the military regimes which began in 1966, twelve states were created in 1967, nineteen in 1976, twenty-one in 1987, thirty in 1991 and now as from 1996, thirty-six states. There are also 774 local government councils with different jurisdictional areas in Nigeria as shown in the Appendix.

Nigeria's constitutional, political, and administrative developments have thus created and recreated exclusive interests of regionalism, followed by those of "statism". Within each of the thirty-six states, exclusive interests of local government councils have been maintained even as people, especially nomads or pastoralists, move across often disputed boundaries, grazing animal stock across farmlands.

The Premise of Conflicts

It is obvious from the preceding paragraphs that Nigeria's social structure is inherently prone to generate conflicts from diverse ethnic-cultural interests and goals, and from the political and economic necessities of survival, as individuals and as identifiable autonomous social groups struggle for advantages. Crucial in this respect, especially amongst rural people, is the world of work to achieve subsistence in the economic order and the sphere of material and physical resources.

Seven main factors are identified as sources of conflict. The first is the land space and the resources available. Different people within and across the boundaries of local government council areas lay claim to land as original settlers or "aboriginals" and therefore, on this basis, fight off those regarded as intruders. The former may voluntarily or involuntarily allow strangers to settle as tenants with or without some periodic symbolic payments as recognition and re-enactment of tenancy. Farmers and pastoralists, fishermen and pond owners, foresters and timber loggers, etc. have clashed throughout Nigeria over controverted uses or exploitation of land and water resources. And since the 1960s, and particularly from the 1990s, communities in Nigeria's deltaic areas have clashed with one another over claims in territories in which oil exploration companies operate and for which royalty and amenities and development projects are expected.

The second factor is the disputed jurisdiction of certain traditional rulers and chiefs. When a king of one ethnic or sub-ethnic group claims rulership over peoples belonging to another ethnic group, his action often generates conflicts. The town of Warri is an example. Here, the Olu (King) of the Itsekiri ethnic group is labelled Olu of the whole of Warri in Delta State, owned and inhabited by members of Ijaw, Itsekiri and Urhobo ethnic groups. The situation arose when the Delta State Government enacted Edict No 1 of 1999 (Traditional Council and Chiefs Edict 1998 vol. 9) and appointed three other traditional rulers of equal status in Warri, two for the Urhobo kingdoms of Okere and Agbassa (Agbarha-Ame) and the third for the Ijaw of Warri. In the case of Ile-Ife in Osun State, the Modakekes' claims to the ownership of their settlement and farmland have been strongly resisted by the Ooni (King) and people of Ife. In these cases, many people have been killed as a result of violent conflicts.

The creation of local government councils and the locations of their headquarters is the third factor generating conflicts. This was evident in the two cases of Ife and Warri referred to above. The creation of the local government councils in their respective areas was the responsibility of the federal government. But conflicts arose when sections of the areas opposed such creation or their inclusion in the "wrong" council. Also, government's location and shifting of the headquarters from one place to another, following conflicts and oppositions, merely exacerbated the conflicts in many parts of the country, including Ife and Warri.

Similarly, ethnic claims over new headquarters and new

markets are a source of conflicts, for example, Zangon Kataf and Tafawa Balewa town in Kaduna and Bauchi States respectively.

The fourth factor is the normal one of ethnic and individual or sectional competition over access to scarce political and economic resources. The creation of states and local government councils means the availability of more political and administrative positions in the localities. There are, for example, positions of state commissioners and local government chairmen and councillors. These positions are limited. Contestants mobilise members of their ethnic groups for support in the competition to hold such positions through election (soliciting votes) or appointment. Naturally, divergent interests and inter-ethnic or sub-ethnic and town conflicts occur. It is generally assumed under such circumstances that the winner in any competition, and thus the incumbent of any high office, represents and promotes the interests of his people. He is expected to bring political goods home and promote the interests of his people in matters of conflict and contested local development programmes.

The fifth factor derives from the micro and macro social structures in Nigeria. Nigeria is a segmented society with varieties of conflicting cultural interests, values and preferences. Claims to the control of the commonwealth, and to national political positions and economic resources, as well as the divergent perceptions of co-existence in the same country-setting provide grounds for conflict. The opposing views which ethnic groups have of one another, such as the Jukun have of the Tiv and vice versa, also predispose people to conflicts. The exploited co-existence of cultural and religious differences amongst people in the same polity is itself inherently conflictual.

The sixth and last factor is population growth and expansionist tendencies to sustain ethnic-bound occupations. This is particularly important amongst users of land resources. The migration of the Tiv who are well known farmers has been a source of conflict in the territories of their neighbours, for example the Jukun in Wukari area. In these circumstances, mythology and migratory histories as well as descent and inheritance claims are manipulated to assert new ownerships in foreign territories and, in the process, create conditions of conflicts and bloody clashes and violence. It is important to note that the way different people perceive a resource is relevant in conflict generation and management. A resource in this sense may be defined as "an opportunity in the environment that has been identified and appraised by a population of potential users" (Meier 1968; in Mabogunje 1972: 30).

The seventh sphere of conflicts is the perception of disregard for cultural symbols and the "pollution" of cultural practices. Where an individual of one neighbouring or immigrant group threatens the cultural trait of another group, such an act could very easily be interpreted as that of an entire group, and consequently, the penalty imposed on the offender according to the hosts' culture is also often interpreted in terms of intergroup rather that interpersonal relations. For example, the killing and eating of a dog, or crocodile, etc. within a community that respects or worships it as a totem or symbol, or the destruction of a community's central shrine of a protective god or deity, could flare up emotions and impel men to violent action. Such central aspects of a people's cosmology or symbolism manifested in their relationships with certain deified animals or spiritualised house-shrines are surrounded with powerful charges which quickly impel people to violent revengeful action or placatory redresses. The most recent example of this kind of interethnic conflicts in Nigeria occurred in July 1999 when the Yoruba of Sagamu performed the night rites associated with *Oro* festival, during which time women are forbidden from coming out of their houses. However, when two Hausa women violated this ancient cultural practice, they were immediately apprehended. One of them was killed and the other that managed to escape reported the incident to the Hausa immigrant community. A violent and bloody conflict ensued, resulting in the loss of several lives and property on both sides.

This event was reported in Kano and other Hausa cities in the northern part of Nigeria by fleeing Hausa people. This sparked up retaliatory attack on the Yoruba in Kano resulting in the loss of many more lives and property, inspite of the efforts of the Police and the temporary closure of Kano market. The Federal Government despatched a team of ministers and other important personalities to Sagamu to reconcile the two warring ethnic groups. Also, appeals were made to the "combatants" by traditional rulers, religious leaders and pressure groups to stop the unnecessary mutual killings. Preventive measures were taken in other cities to avoid the escalation and spread of the conflict to other Nigerian towns and cities.

In turn, the seven factors mentioned in the preceding paragraphs are partly the products of:

(i)   the encapsulation of ethnic identities defined by language and cultural symbolism which predated Nigeria's colonial artificial boundaries,

(ii) persisting attachment to the symbols and sentiments of colonial administrative Regions and the post-colonial State and Local Government boundaries,

(iii) Socio-territorial and politico-economic inequalities and disabilities, and

(iv) the politicisation of religious pluralism and the fanatism of religious practitioners.

As we noted earlier in this chapter because societies are ongoing social systems, they may be described in terms of what has been indicated in Cuff and Payne (1979: 56) as composing of "men's clashing interests" and "men's shared agreements". Thus conflict and consensus as descriptive labels for life-processes in plural societies such as Nigeria are not diametrically opposed; rather although they have much in common, their differences represent two distinct sociological perspectives. In creating situations of consensus and conflict in plural settings, myths are given a mental life and symbols are strengthened. But "it is the very essence and potency of symbols that they are ambiguous, referring to different meanings, and are not given to precise definitions" (Abner Cohen 1979: 87). Thus, the use of symbols to maintain identities used for exclusive claims to territorial and other resources, also permits their use to maintain common interests at other levels and spheres of social relations.

Although the above points can often be exploited to promote conflict resolution, transformation and management amongst ethnic groups, for example those living within the same or adjacent local government council areas, such as those in which the Jukun and Tiv are found, certain key symbols cannot be shared or overstretched. Thus, for instance as Abner Cohen (1968: 362) points out, a threat to the position of the king, such as the Aku

Uka of the Jukun, is conceived of as a threat to the very essence and continuity of the Jukun as a distinct group. Such an act is often a source of inter-ethnic conflicts, despite the ambiguity normally associated with symbols. We may thus agree that in most socio-cultural settings, "some minimal consensus is necessary, then, for inter-ethnic bargaining to be present. Unless collectivities are aware of their interdependence as well as of their distinctiveness, an acknowledged negotiation situation seems out of the question" (Rothchild 1969: 611). In order to achieve successful conflict resolution, transformation and management in these situations in many parts of Nigeria, different networks and social action-sets involving kings, chiefs and other actors in the indigenous social system, as well as local government councillors and chairmen, party politicians, state governors and commissioners, must all be mobilised, as appropriate, in different circumstances and levels of social conflict. It is observed that panels and commissions of inquiry have been set up by governments towards the transformation or resolution of conflicts in different states of the Nigerian federation.

The Essays

This book deals with internal conflicts involving commuities within the State boundaries of Nigeria. Here, communities with separate multidimensional identities and multiple users of resources as well'as aspirers to high office engage in conflicts over access to limited economic and political resources within the territorial boundaries of Nigeria. As Rupensinghe (1995), Kriesberg (1989), and Azar (1986) have observed, such conflicts are not often single-issue conflicts. They are multiple conflicts which may be tackled simultaneously. These conflicts may arise from a single cause or grievance, and may escalate to demand enormous energies and a lot of the scarce resources of the local communities, the Local Government Councils and the State government(s) involved.

Against a variety of academic backgrounds in different disciplines, the contributions of the essays in this book have been generally descriptive, analytical, and or narrative in their presentations. The essays also vary in quality while dealing with the causes, stages and social complications of conflicts, their resolution, transformation and management in different geo-political zones and cultural areas in Nigeria. Although some critics may feel that the essays generally lack indepth presentations of interlocking variables in their social structures as contexts for viewing conflicts, yet, together in one volume, they enrich our perceptions of the complexity of conflicts, their resolution, transformation and management in a manner never before attempted in Nigeria.

While chapter two by Isaac Olawale Albert deals generally with AAPW's activities and contribution to peacebuilding through practical workshop sessions and communities leaders' training programmes, chapters three to ten are concerned with specific case studies by different researchers-authors who are involved with AAPW on a full or part-time basis.

Albert's chapter contains an analysis of AAPW's new direction in conflict resolution and management activities in several parts of Nigeria as detailed in some of the remaining ten chapters. It demonstrates the organisation's concern with practical issues in peacebuilding involving inter-ethnic and intra-ethnic groups in Nigeria. The aims and workshop programmes of AAPW's community leaders training and practical interventions in the management of conflicts between communities are exhaustively dealt with, to illustrate the organisation's commitment to peacebuilding in Nigeria.

In chapter six, Isaac Olawale Albert presents, professionally, a periodized historical account of the Ife-Modakeke conflict in Oyo State. Contemporary analysis and approaches to the solution of the Ife-Modakeke crisis may find it essential to rely on this historical account. The chapter is enriched by an analysis of the essential variables in the conflict such as kinship and kingship, dominance and defiance, migratory patterns of settlement, landlords and tenants, population increase etc; and how the traditions of origin and perceived political and economic gains informed changing alliances despite shared ethnic-cultural symbolism. Contemporary political party organisations, local government council creations and locations, as well as government processes by key functionaries including governors, are also analysed to present a good understanding of conflicts in the area.

The account of Tafawa Balewa by Akinteye, Wuye and Ashafa

in chapter eleven involves cultural differences and religion-based alliances and conflicts. Essentially, conflicts arose from contested claims on the ownership of Balewa town, the local administrative and political capital, differences in political cultures and aspirations at the local level, desire to create and maintain autonomous chiefdom, and the struggle for economic resources for survival.

Operating initiatives as well as suggested strategies for conflict resolution, transformation and management are described along with the involvement of key individuals and interest groups in both the generation and the handling of conflicts.

In chapter nine, Best and Abdulrahman describe conflicts over farmlands in the Mangu/Bokkos area of Plateau State that arose only after the 1980s. New political boundaries of the Mangu and Bokkos local government council areas and the individual and group competitions were sources of conflicts. Although Christianity helped to cement the relationships between the Ron and Mwaghaval peoples, government's delays or inactivity in setting up commissions of inquiry or in taking decisive actions on the recommendations of inquiries, delayed settlements among peoples living on the plateau in respect of the 1992 and 1995 conflicts. The authors identified the following as key causes of conflicts: farmlands and certificates of occupancy, claims derived from chieftaincy institutions, party politics and the creation of local government councils (Bokkos), as well as petty jealousy and the survival demands of the local political economy. Several panels of enquiry, stake-holders, and AAPW etc. participated in identifying the causes of conflicts and in formulating policies and strategies for their solution.

Williams, Muazu, Kaoje and Ekeh in chapter seven deal with the perennial problems of order and conflicts between the pastoralists and agriculturists in the north-eastern part of Nigeria. Claims and counter-claims over the ownership and use of land resources are key factors in inter-ethnic and inter-occupational group conflicts in the area. Perception of proneness to violence is also an issue in agriculturists-pastoralists' problems of peaceful co-existence in the same physical environment. The chapter deals with practical problems and issues and with inputs in conflicts, their resolution, transformation or their management. It is a good example of conflict studies involving several, in this case, five main groups of multiple users in four states - Bauchi, Borno, Jigawa and Yobe. Williams *et al* identified the five users of the limited resources as pastoralists, agro-pastoralists, farmers, fishermen, and woodcutters. Rainfed upland and irrigated territories - Fadama, draught, and the management of water resources, bush burning and increasing population pressures on land resources etc. produced and exacerbated ethnic and inter-user conflicts. Several agents such as those of the state government, security (police and army officers) and non-governmental organisations were involved in managing specific conflicts. Several recommendations are made including those for conflict avoidance.

In chapter four, Best, Idyorough and Shehu analysed communal conflicts and their resolution with special reference to the Tiv-Jukun conflicts in the Wukari Local Government Council area of Taraba State. The position and jurisdiction of the king, Aku Uka, under whose territory the Tiv lived and survived as farmers, was a source of conflict between the two ethnic groups. The Tiv opposed their label as settlers rather than land owners. The key factors involved in conflicts included contested appointment of a Tiv to the chairmanship of the Wukari Local Government Council and another Tiv as state commissioner in Gongola State in 1983 etc., changing "ethnic" electoral victories of the Tiv and Jukun in respect of the Federal House of Representatives, membership and local and national leadership of the political parties such as the Northern Peoples Congress (NPC) and the United Middle Belt Congress (UMBC), threats of modern political party power on the traditional territorial claims of the Jukun, and mutual perception of aggressive tendencies, especially with reference to the 1990-1992 conflicts. Other issues in the conflict included contested attempts regarding Tiv representations in Wukari Traditional Council, practices of shifting land cultivation and acquisition, and the use of land by elites and capitalist absentee-farmers, and mounting population pressures. The authors examined the issues for negotiation and the need for intervention, despite socio-political and parochial stake-holder obstacles.

Akinteye, Wuye and Ashafa, in chapter eight analysed the publicised Zangon Kataf crisis in Kaduna State. Of central importance here was the Kachia Local Government Council decision to relocate the Zangon market from its old site to a new one which was considered to be more spacious and accessible. The main factors in the conflict were the posting of district head from Zaria royal family to administer the indigenous southern Kaduna peoples, the consequent (excessive) tax collection activities imposed on the indigenes of the administered area, inter-ethnic conflicts between the Hausa and the Atyap (Kataf) communities, demand for local autonomous chiefdom and selfdetermination by the Kataf, ethnic-bound socio-economic disparity and status, the Hausa being perceived as rich traders/administrators while the Kataf were farmers, and the contested ownership of Zongo town. The authors examined the strategies of conflict resolution or transformation in the concluding part of the chapter.

In analysing the ethnic and religious conflicts in Kano in chapter ten, Albert refers to the phenomenon of colonialism in the creation of Sabon Gari as settlement for strangers who were also Christians in Kano. The walled city of Kano (the Birni) remained under the Emir and was reserved for the Muslim indigenes. The settlement pattern and the ensuing relationships was a reminder of Furnwall's segmented society. Here there were inter-ethnic as well as intra-ethnic and religious conflicts. There were religious intolerance and fanaticism practised by believers from inside the Kano area and from outside Nigeria such as Cameroon and Chad Republic and from North Africa. Albert concludes his chapter with suggestions for facilitating interventions including inter-religious dialogue, positive conflict management roles of committees of community elders and ward leaders, and government educational and economic programmes for destroying "street culture" among Kano youths.

In chapter three, Oka Martin Obono concentrated on the 1992 war in Yakurr society, a classic double descent society. Obono shows how the structure and settlement pattern encouraged and limited conflicts between the Ugep (the largest Yakurr unit), and Idomi (the smallest unit). He outlined the Yakurr social structure and examined demographic variables, changing war technology, and factors in the political economy dominated by farming. The Yakurr now form part of the new local government council and new political arrangement in Nigeria.

Chapter five, by Akin Akinteye shows how the settlement history and socio-political structure of Igbo-Ora determined conflicts over the overall government-recognised kingship institution and the assertion of sectional identities within the single polity. Several local and national conflict resolution initiatives were made. These included the efforts of the Christian Association of Nigeria (CAN) and the Stimulus Wits of Igbo-Ora. Further, a public lecture was organised, and conciliatory meetings and Peace Education workshops were held with stake holders. Steering committee meetings of Corps of Mediators designed intervention and mediation strategies which led to community leaders' workshops. The Igbo-Ora case study demonstrated how AAPW and other initiatives can be directed towards sustainable peace.

The book is concluded in chapter twelve which deals with reflections on conflicts in general and in the specific case of Nigeria, as well as with theoretical and practical issues and policies concerning conflict resolution, transformation and management.

Nigeria, with a population of over 120 million people and bewildering complexities in cultures and social organisations, is naturally prone to instances of community conflicts. Expectedly, only a few of these conflicts have been dealt with in this book. Other conflicts not contained in the book include those in the Niger Delta area, and those involving Udawa herdsmen from the Republics of Niger, Chad and Cameroon as well as Nigerian pastoralists in search of green pastures for their livestock in the dry season. During this period they encounter oppositions from settled farmers in all of the northern states, extending to Kwara, Oyo, and Benue etc. southwards. There are also (in 1999) several land-based conflicts among Aguleri and Umuleri communities in Anambra State, and among the Chamba-Kuteb communities in Takum Local Government Area of Taraba State; as well as the Ngizim-Karaikarai community conflicts over territory and the position of traditional rulership. Although this book is thus limited by its selective coverage, yet its contents illustrate sufficiently the major trends and theories in conflict resolution, transformation, and management.

The purpose of the book is achieved. It is a refreshing and stimulating account of conflicts, which other researchers and readers will find useful, away from the deadly and violent scenes and theatres of conflict. The book will be useful to academics for the purpose of analysis and comparison. It will also be helpful to members of the communities studied and others with similar conflicts, as well as to those government officials who are trying to manage conflicts within their areas of jurisdiction. Finally, the book is of interest to those who simply want to better understand the reality of social interactions and community relationships in Africa and elsewhere in the fields of conflict resolution, transformation, and management.

References

Anigbo, O. A.C.1988. "Commensality, the kolanut and the strangers in an Igbo Community", pp 31-40 in *Ugo the Anambra State Festival of Arts and Culture.* vol. 1 No. 6 Nov.

Avruch, K. and P. Black 1990. "Ideas of Human Nature in Contemporary Conflict Resolution Theory", pp 221-228 in *Negotiation Journal* vol. 5.

Avruch, K. and P. Black. 1991. "The Culture Question and Conflict Resolution", pp 22-45 in *Peace and Change,* vol. 16.

Avruch, K. and P. W. Black 1993. "Conflict Resolution in Intercultural Settings: Problems and Prospects", in D. J. D. Sandole and H. van der Merwe (eds), *1993 Conflict Resolution Theory and Practice, Integration and Application,* Manchester University Press.

Azar E. 1986. "Management of Protracted Social Conflicts in the Third World". Paper presented at the fourth ICES Annual lecture, Columbia University. June 1986. Mimeo-Centre for International Development and Conflicts Management, University of Maryland.

Bendix, R. 1968. "Weber, Max", in *International Encyclopaedia of the Social Sciences* edited by David L. Sills. New York: The Macmillan Co & The Free Press.

Bottomore, T. B. 1968. "Marxist Sociology" in *International Encyclopaedia of the Social Sciences* edited by David L. Sills. New York: The Macmillan Co & The Free Press.

Bottomore, T. B. and M. Rubek (eds) 1964. *Karl Marx, (1844-1875). Selected Writings in Sociology and Social Philosophy,* 2nd edition, New York: McGraw Hill.

Burton, J. W. 1993. "Conflict Resolution as a Political Philosophy" in D. J. D. Sandole and H. van der Merwe (eds), *Conflict Resolution Theory and Practice Integration and Application*. Manchester University Press.

Cohen, Abner 1968. "The Politics of Mysticism in Some Local Communities in Newly Independent African States", in M.J. Swartz (ed), *Local Level Politics Social and Cultural Perspectives* Chicago: Aldine.

Cohen, Abner 1979. "Political Symbolism", *Annual Review of Anthropology* 8, pp 87-113.

Coser, L. A. 1956. *The Functions of Social Conflict*, Glencoe III. The Free Press.

Coser, L. A. 1968. "Conflict-social Aspects", *International Encyclopaedia of the Social Sciences,* D.L. Sills, (ed) New York: The Macmillan Co. and The Free Press.

Cuff, E. C. and G. C. E. Payne 1979. *Perspectives in Sociology*, London. George Allen and Unwin.

Deutsch, M. 1973. "Conflicts: Productive and Destructive", in *Conflict Resolution Through Communication* , F.E. Jandt (ed), New York Harper and Row.

Donohue, W. A. and R. Kolt. 1992. *Managing Interpersonal Conflict*. Newbury, Park Calif. Sage Publications.

Druckman, D. 1993. "An Analytical Research Agenda for Conflict and Conflict Resolution", in D. J. D. Sandole and H van der Merwe (eds), *Conflict Resolution Theory and Practice Integration and Application*. Manchester University Press.

Evans-Pritchard, E. E. 1940. "The Nuer of the Southern Sudan", pp 272-296, in M. Fortes and E. E. Evans-Pritchard (eds) *African Political Systems*. London, Oxford University Press.

Folger J.P Poole. MS and Stutman 1997. *Working Through Conflict; Strategies for Relationships, Groups and Organisations* Addison. Wesley Educational Publishers Inc.

Fortes, M. and E. E. Evans-Pritchard 1940. *African Political Systems*. London Oxford University Press.

Furnivall, J. S. 1948. *Colonial Policy and Practice, A Comparative Study of Burma, Netherlands and India*. Cambridge, Cambridge University Press.

Galtung, J 1994. *Peace By Peaceful Means, Peace and Conflicts*

Development and Civilisation. Sage Publications.

Gerth, H. H. and Wright Mills, C. (eds) 1946. *From Max Weber, Essays in Sociology*, New York: Oxford University Press.

Gluckman, M. 1965. *Customs and Conflict in Africa*, Oxford: Basil Blackwell.

Hocker J.L and Wilmort WW 1985. *Interpersonal conflicts* Dubugue I.A. Wm C. Brown.

Ikime, O. 1986. "Towards Understanding the National Question" *Africa Events* vol. 3, No. 6, June.

Jordan, 1990. "Courage in Connection Conflict, Compassion Creativity", in *Works in Progress*, Stone Centre working paper series. Wellesley College, Mass, Stone Centre.

Kriesberg L et al (Eds) 1989. *Intractable Conflicts and Their Transformation*. Syracuse. Syracuse University Press.

Kuper, L. and M. G. Smith (eds) 1971. *Pluralism in Africa*, Berskeley University of California Press.

Lederach, J.P. 1997. *Building Peace, Sustainable Reconciliation in Divided Societies*. United States Institute of Peace Press Washignton D.C.

Lemarch R. 1989. "Burundi: The Killing Fields Revisited", pp 22-28, in *ISSUE, a Journal of Opinion*, vol. 18, No. 1.

Levine, R. A. 1961. "Anthropology and the Study of Conflict: An Introduction", *Journal of Conflict Resolution*, vol. 5 pp 3-15.

Lundberg, G. A. 1939. *The Foundation of Sociology*, New York: The Macmillan Co.

Mabogunje, A. L. 1972. *Regional Mobility and Resource Development in West Africa*. Keith Callard Lectures. Centre for Development Area Studies, Mcgill University.

Meier, R. L. 1968. "Resource Planning", in *International Encyclopaedia of the Social Sciences*.

Mitchell, C. R. 1993. "Problem-solving Exercises and Theories of Conflict Resolution", in D.J.D. Sandole and H. van der Merwe (eds). *Conflict Resolution Theory and Practice, Integration and Application*. Manchester University Press.

Moore, C.W. 1996. *The Mediation Process. Practical Strategies for Resolving Conflicts*. San Francisco: Jossey - Bass Publishers.

Nader, L. 1968. Anthropological aspects of Conflict. *International Encyclopaedia of the Social Sciences*. (ed), David L. Sills New York. The Macmillan Co. & The Free Press.

Otite, O. 1971. "On the Concept of a Nigerian Society", pp. 299-311, *The Nigerian Journal of Economics and Social Studies*, vol. 13, No. 3 Nov.

Otite, O. 1973. *Autonomy and Dependence: The Urhobo Kingdom of Okpe in Modern Nigeria*. London C. Hurst and Evanston, Northwestern University Press.

Otite, O. 1990. *Ethnic Pluralism and Ethnicity in Nigeria*, Ibadan: Shanesson C.I. Ltd.

Park, R. E. and E. W. Burgress 1921. *Introduction to the Science of Sociology*. University of Chicago Press.

Richards, A. and A. Kuper. 1971. *Councils in Action*, Cambridge University Press.

Rothchild, D. 1969. "Ethnicity and Conflict Resolution", *World Politics*, vol. 22 Oct.

Rupensinghe, K. (ed.) 1995, *Conflict Transformation*, London, St. Martin's Press.

Sandole, D. J. D. 1993. "Paradigm, Theories, and Metaphors in Conflict and Conflict Resolution: Coherence or Confusion", pp 3-24, in D. J. D. Sandole and H. \ ınder Merwe (eds) *Conflict Resolution Theory and Practice, Integration and Application*, Manchester University Press.

Simmel,. 1908 (1955). *Conflict, The Web of Group Affiliations*, Glencoe, III. Free Press.

Smooha, S. 1975. "Pluralism and Conflicts: A Theoretical Exploration", in *Plural Societies*, vol. 6 No. 3, pp 69-89.

Uchendu, V.C. 1965. *The Igbo of Southwestern Nigeria*, New York : Holt, Rinehart and Winston.

Weber, Max 1957. *The Theory of Social and Economic Organisation*. Translated and edited by A. M. Henderson and Talcott Parsons Glencoe III. The Free Press.

Weeks, D 1994. *The Eight Essential Steps To Conflict Resolution*. New York: Putnam's Sons.

Wilmot, W. W. 1998. *Interpersonal Conflict*, Boston: McGraw Hill.

Wilson, L. and W. L. Kolb 1949. *Sociological Analysis*, New York: Harcourt, Brace.

Zechmeister, K. and D. Druckman 1973. "Determinants of resolving a conflict of interests: A simulation of political decision-making", pp 63-88 in *Journal of Conflict Resolution*, vol.17.

Chapter 2

Isaac Olawale Albert

New Directions in the Management of Community Conflicts in Nigeria: Insights from the Activities of AAPW

Introduction

Conflicts are responded to in three possible ways in any society: by avoidance, confrontation and problem-solving. "Avoidance" means a situation where a group alleging injustice or discrimination is literally ignored or denied recognition by those being accused and those who have the capacity for helping to redress the injustices done to the group. Avoidance, as Wilmot and Hocker [1998: 114] observed, is characterised by "denial of the conflict, equivocation, changing and avoiding topics, being non-committal, and joking rather than dealing with the conflict at hand." This kind of response to a conflict situation compounds problems as the party that is "avoided" will later seek other means of getting listened to. Such people usually resort to violence. Writing on the disadvantages of avoidance, Wilmot and Hocker [1998: 116] noted that it "allows conflict to simmer and heat up unnecessarily rather than providing an avenue for improving it. It keeps one from working through a conflict and reinforces the notion that conflict is terrible and best avoided. It allows partners to each follow their own course and pretend there is no mutual influence when, in fact, each influences the other. It usually preserves the conflict and sets the stage for a later explosion or backlash."

The more a group is ignored, "avoided" or "denied" attention, the more it becomes confrontational [issuing threats, getting verbally aggressive, resorting to litigation or even physical violence] with a view to getting a win-lose outcome.

Almost all case studies in this volume on community conflicts in Nigeria have to do with the use of confrontation [especially physical violence] by the parties involved. As we will see in each of the cases, violence hardly resolves a conflict; it rather compounds the conflict situation. How then do we deal constructively with conflict? The best approach is by what is technically referred to as "problem-solving".

Problem-solving refers to the situation in which the parties to a conflict, either by themselves or through the assistance of a third party, find solutions to their problems in a cordial environment. Problem-solving procedure is non-judgemental and highly participatory in character. It promotes co-operation between antagonists who jointly analyse the structure of the conflict and carefully work out strategies for reconciling with each other. The dominant question in a problem-solving setting is: "How can the parties to a conflict peacefully work together in the community they both own and share with one another? How do the groups develop relational empathy? Or to be more specific, how do the two cultures merge into the production of a "third culture"? "Third culture" as Broome [1993: 104] noted can only occur in a conflict situation "through interaction in which participants are willing to open themselves to new meanings, to engage in genuine dialogue, and to constantly respond to the new demands emanating from the situation". It is an essential prerequisite for conflict resolution. Writing on how the third culture manifests, Casmir and Asuncion-Lande [1989: 294] noted:

> Though beginning with contrasting perceptions and behaviours, two individuals, through their interaction, create a unique setting for interaction. In the conjoining of their separate cultures, a third culture, more inclusive than the original ones, is created, which both of them now share. Within that third culture, the two can communicate with each other more effectively. Thus a third culture is not merely the result of the fusion of two or more separate entities, but also the product of the "harmonisation" of composite parts into a coherent whole.

This approach is popularly considered to be the best method of dealing with conflict as its outcomes are usually self-supporting in the sense that it is advantageous to all parties in the dispute. The essence of the problem-solving procedure is that:

> ...representatives of the parties in a dispute should meet in the presence of a small panel of disinterested consultants, professionally qualified in the social sciences, in order to analyse and possibly also to resolve their conflict, in conditions of total confidentiality. The parties should be enabled by the panel to negotiate not by bargaining in the conventional manner, but by collaborating in the

solution of their joint predicament through the discovery of accommodation affording net advantages to all concerned. Their joint predicament is the problem to be solved [de Reuck 1990: 183].

Problem-solving approaches "...empower the parties, meet their vital needs for identity and security, and lay the foundation for a stable, cooperative relationship consistent with the welfare and development of each party. Such changes imply some redistribution of power, as well as the gradual creation of a new culture shared by the former adversaries without, of course, abandoning their separate cultures" [Kelman p.xi]. The method borrowed a lot from psychology, counselling, psychotherapy, management theories, philosophical assumptions, group dynamics, communication theory, peace research, decision theory, traditional approaches to conflict management and several theoretical models from the social sciences.

With a view to differentiating between this approach and other methods for dealing with conflict situations, Burton [1969] called our attention to two important peace terms: *settlement* and *resolution*. Settlement implies a situation in which the conflict is dealt with on terms dictated by a third party such as a court or any judicial panel. It could be some suggested terms of compromise resulting from circumstances beyond their control. Resolution on the other hand implies a solution freely accepted by all parties, one that does not sacrifice any of their important values, one that parties will not wish to repudiate later.

Differentiating between the two, de Reuck [1990: 185] noted:

> Settlement merely reduces the level of intensity of conflict behaviour, possibly to zero; whereas resolution removes the very ground of conflict, and eliminates or transforms the conflict situation. Only when conflict is resolved, as distinct from settled, is the outcome self-supporting in the sense that it is positively advantageous to all concerned.

Problem-solving procedures make better meaning within the framework of the latter. Resolution promotes co-operation rather than a mere cessation of hostilities and this is the main goal of the problem-solving procedure. In their joint search for solution to their problems, the antagonists are divested of their roles as adversaries and made to perceive the conflict as a shared predicament that must be solved. They are consequently offered some alternative roles of analysts of the problems and challenged to become partners in problem solving.

Avoidance and Confrontation as Conflict Management Styles in Nigeria.

The proliferation of community and governance conflicts in Nigeria stems from the fact that Nigerians generally favour avoidance as a style of conflict management. At community and national levels, groups that feel aggrieved about certain issues complain very loudly about their predicaments but hardly get listened to by their adversaries or those that have the statutory responsibility to give them attention. The ignored groups soon take to violence and immediately get recognised by everybody. This has been the dominant style and tactic in Nigeria. All the papers in this volume graphically illustrate the point being made. Most of the violent conflicts in this volume occurred as a result of the aggrieved groups being avoided for a long period of time either by the other party against whom they have some grievances, or by the government which refused to take the necessary action at resolving the conflicts. The Ife-Modakeke crisis, the crises in Takum and Wukari, the Zango Kataf and Tafawa Balewa crises etc.- all started in the form of "strangers" vs "hosts" confrontation. A group usually starts by alleging some irregularities in the communities. As nobody takes appropriate action on their complaints, they gradually become confrontational. Most of the nine conflicts considered in this book started that way. None of them occurred suddenly. They were preceded by some "warning signals" which nobody took seriously.

Once a community becomes violent in Nigeria the first thing government does in line with its constitutional duty of maintaining law and order is to deploy some policemen to keep the peace in the area. Once the violence dies out, the police withdraws from the area based on the assumption that the conflict is over. In many cases, the violence escalates few days, weeks or months after the departure of the police. In some desperate situations, the government permanently stations a contingent of "peace-keeping" policemen and even soldiers in the conflict-prone area.

Cessation of physical violence in the feuding communities in Nigeria is usually followed by the setting up of commissions of inquiry to look into the civil disturbance. Such a commission would take evidence from all parties to the conflict. The report of the commission is presented to government at a widely publicised occasion and the people never hear anything after that until another round of violence breaks out in the area. As members of the public wait endlessly for the report of the panel to be released, those who want to keep the conflict alive would go to town once again with an analysis of "insider knowledge" of the content of the report. The party that considers itself to have been disadvantaged by the report will therefore start once again to mobilise towards redressing the "injustice" done to them. This popular way of responding to conflict shows that not much attention is given to problem-solving procedures by the Nigerian government. For Nigeria to experience sustainable peace, it has to change its attitude to conflicts.

Our main goal in this chapter is to map out the problem-solving strategies for responding to conflicts and discuss how this pattern of conflict management has been practised by Academic Associates PeaceWorks - a Nigerian non-governmental organisation based in Lagos.

Approaches to Problem Intervention

Problem-solving procedures can be introduced into a conflict environment using three main approaches. We need to know these as a way of generating ideas on how best to reach the parties in the conflict. The three approaches are top-down, middle-range and grassroots [Lederach 1997]. Each of these needs to be given a more detailed explanation.

Top-down Approach

The peacemakers and peace-builders in the top-down model are usually eminent personalities with public profiles. The work of these people are usually backed by the government or international organisations like the United Nations considered to be a neutral party in the conflict. The peacemakers or peace builders in this kind of setting shuttle between the top-level leaders of the conflict believing that any agreement reached with these people will trickle down the line. In most cases, the objective of this kind of approach is to facilitate cessation of physical hostilities between the "warring" parties as a first step to other peace efforts. This kind of peace work is usually subjected to close media scrutiny. This approach only works in a situation where those considered to be leaders of conflicting communities are their true leaders. In present-day Nigerian society, those in charge of community conflicts are youth leaders rather than the traditional rulers with whom a top-down peacemaker might want to strike an agreement. This is why most of the peace overtures of government agents, especially when dealing with community conflicts, hardly yield positive dividends despite their robust media coverage. Those consulted by top-down operators are usually not those in charge of the insurgencies but the "leaders" of the conflicting communities.

This is not to suggest however that the top-down approach is totally inappropriate. It works only when community leaders are in effective control and command the absolute respect of the gladiators in the conflict. For example, the violent youth in the Niger Delta area of Nigeria operate independently of some of their traditional rulers who are considered to be "sell outs". To the average youth in the Niger Delta, the traditional ruler or elders of his community is easily compromising or has been "settled" either by the government or the oil-producing companies operating in his community. If any peace agreement has to be worked out with the people of the area, he prefers to be included in the process rather than being represented by any local leader. We can see the same trend even in a pre-colonial situation in Yoruba land. The peace accord that was struck between the Ooni of Ife (Abeweila) and the Modakeke people in the late 1830s and 1840s was rejected by the Ife people. It was on this account that the Ooni was killed by his people. He too was considered a sell-out (see the Ife-Modakeke case in this volume) as the peace terms did not accommodate the interests of those who actually championed the hostility.

Middle Range Approach

The middle range approach to peace-making and peacebuilding is based on the understanding that those who lead community conflicts belong to the middle range and that if properly integrated in the peace process, might be very instrumental in facilitating sustainable peace. This approach is the one favoured by the protagonists of the problem-solving model of conflict management. This approach can be operationalised in three different ways: through conflict-management training, problem-solving workshops and establishment of peace commissions or committees. The closest Nigeria has moved to this approach to conflict intervention is the occasional constitution of panels of inquiry into community conflicts. The recommendations of these commissions are hardly implemented by the government. The establishment of National Reconciliation Committee (NARECON) was another useful initiative within this mould but the administration of General Sani Abacha which established the commission did not allow it to do any useful work until it was scrapped in 1998.

The advantage of the middle-range approach consists in the fact that those involved in the peace process can easily liaise with the high-level leaders of the conflict as well as the grassroots population about peace terms available to their society.

Grassroots or "Bottom-up" Approach

The grassroots population in any society usually has an intimidating numerical strength. Peace initiatives developed from this point could be intimidating to leaders of a conflict. Peace initiatives come directly from the people either because they are tired of fighting or because they can no longer cope with the costs of continued hostility. The best way to sustain a grassroots peace agreement is to follow it up with a problem-solving workshop or conflict-transformation training for the affected parties on how to respond constructively to future conflicts.

Problem-Solving Workshops and the Middle Range Approach

As could be seen above, the establishment of peace commissions, conflict-mangement training, and problem-solving workshops constitutes three major components of the middle-range and grassroots approaches to conflict intervention. The last two are different from each other and therefore need to be given better explanation. Whereas conflict-management training can be organised for any member of the conflicting group, problem-solving workshops are usually for those that could significantly change the course of the conflict (local government officials, local chiefs, journalists etc.) after their training.

Problem-solving workshops are known to some scholars as "inter-active problem solving" (Kelman 1986), "third party consultation" (Fisher 1983) or "collaborative, analytical problem-solving" (Banks and Mitchell 1991.) This method, which Mitchell (1993: 78) referred to as "the epitome of practicality within the field of conflict research" was introduced by John W. Burton. (Montville 1993: 114; Mitchell 1993: 78). The workshop, except those organised within a train-the-trainers context which could span a longer period, is usually a week-long affair under the management of three to five facilitators (who also double as "conveners of the meeting", moderators and sources of ideas for the trainees). The basic aim of such workshop is to enable representatives of a conflict group "to interact in an analytical rather than coercive manner as well as giving scholarly insights into the parties' mutual predicament" (Mitchell 1993: 78). A main thrust of the approach is to destroy negative stereotypes held by parties in conflict situations against each other and help to re-humanise their relationships. By learning together how to respond to conflict, the parties to the community conflict, or even international conflict, are made to realise that they can actually work together at solving their problems. They are helped to gain a realistic understanding of what conflict is and what it is not; they are made to have a better understanding of the costs of violent conflicts.

The trainees are assisted to analyse the conflicts in their community and encouraged to develop alternative courses of action to continued use of force. At the end of many problem-solving workshops, many participants step out of the erstwhile combative roles, drop their "unyielding" stereotypes and assumptions about the other party, having realised "for the first time" that the conflict that ravaged their community for that long can be resolved and that the other party is after all human (and thus can be talked to and listened to) as different from the beast that he or she was assumed to be. The participants thus take on the challenge of "change agents" at the workshop by accepting the responsibility for passing the message of reconciliation to others.

Some problem-solving workshops often end up becoming what Foltz (1977) described as "process promoting workshops". The main objective of the two is to impart practical skills to the participants for dealing positively with conflict. The latter is however different from the former in the sense that participants in such workshops are powerful opinion leaders or those close to decision makers in the conflicting communities. The objective of a "process promoting workshop" therefore is that of using the workshop participants to bring about immediate change in the conflict situation and promote longer-term peace objectives. Such a workshop, as Foltz (1977: 203) noted " gradually takes on the appearance of a negotiating session but one characterised by considerably more openness and willingness to examine radical solutions than is usual."

Conflict Management, Training and Problem-Solving Workshops in Nigeria: The Experiences of AAPW

AAPW is a Nigerian non-governmental organisation (NGO). Broadly defined, an NGO should be said to be any organisation that is not part of government but which operates in civil society. Ball and Dunn (1996: 20) see NGOs as " organisations which are not serving the self-interests of members, but are concerned in one way or another with disadvantage and or the disadvantaged, or with concerns and issues which are detrimental to the well-being, circumstances or prospects of people or society as a whole". This definition makes it easily possible for us to situate NGOs within development industry. They are usually distinguishable from other organisations in civil society in seven ways: they are voluntary, financially independent, managed by independent volunteer board of directors elected periodically by the membership, have a clearly defined constituency and are accountable to that constituency, have formal legal status, have permanent headquarters and employ professional or volunteer staff, are self-serving but geared towards humanitarian objectives and programmes (Agbola 1994: 60).

The leading objective of any NGO is to cause positive changes in the lives of its targeted population by providing them with those essential services that the government finds difficult or unwilling to provide. Generally speaking, NGOs operate on the principle that members of civil society have the right to shape their lives the way they want, independent of the government (SINA 1996). Writing on the importance of NGOs Ball and Dunn (1996: 9-10) observed,

NGOs are also an expression of people's belief that through their own initiative they can better fulfil their potential by working together, and in doing so reduce the opportunity gap which exists between the advantaged and disadvantaged in society. This means involving and empowering people, rather than either leaving them to fend for themselves or consigning them to the role of the helpless client of institutions. Between the global trends towards powerful institutions and individualism, NGOs thus represent a third force, for collectivism.

NGOs play four major roles in conflict management around the world: conflict resolution, conflict resolution training, peacebuilding and preventive diplomacy. All these problem-solving approaches to conflict management are covered by the work of AAPW. The main thrust of the organisation's activities are on peacebuilding and preventive diplomacy through conflict-resolution training and problem-solving workshops. The organisation's primary goal is to empower Nigerians with the necessary skills for non-violent conflict resolution and by so doing, contribute towards promoting and sustaining democratic governance in the country. Building a culture of peace in a society characterised by violent conflicts requires far-reaching re-education programmes. Training therefore remains a core activity of AAPW and forms the base of most of its programmes.

The aims of the organisation, as reflected in its Constitution, are as follows:

(i) To create awareness about the inevitability of conflicts in our society and promote, strengthen and undertake programmes aimed at attaining peace and stability in our society.

(ii) To undertake, encourage and support organisations and bodies (National and International) to implement and enforce laws, policies, treaties and programmes designed for conflict management, mediation and resolution in our society.

(iii) To encourage, promote, educate and support all peace initiatives, arbitration, mediation and transformation aimed at bringing peace and stability in our society and to carry out research, study and build a culture of peace in Nigeria and the world at large.

(iv) To serve as resource group of experts, advisers and consultants on conflict management and resolution to attain peace in the society.

(v) To curb, reduce and assist in the eradication of violence, strife, wars, conflicts and disputes in our society.

(vi) To organise congresses, workshops, seminars, meetings, print and prepare journals, pamphlets, bulletins, memoranda and undertake other forms of public enlightenment through the media and other means of communication, information transfer for the purpose of enhancing and achieving the objectives of the organisation in its quest to eliminate and reduce conflicts in our society.

(vii) To identify, strengthen and promote existing machinery, resources and facilities within and outside government and non-governmental organisations and give necessary technical, professional and specialised assistance in conflict management and resolutions.

(viii) To create and promote public awareness about the activities and programmes of Academic Associates PeaceWorks as an organisation incorporated under the laws in Nigeria.

(ix) To do such things and advance programmes and activities members consider will foster and enhance the aims and objectives of the organisation and its affiliates.

AAPW started work in the area of conflict management in 1992. Before this period, the organisation, which was initially known as Academic Associates (AA) (until 1997 when it became Academic Associates PeaceWorks), was running cross-cultural programmes for American students and other visitors to Nigeria. In 1992, AA tried to organise an educational tour for Nigerian university students to visit various conflict management centres along the eastern seaboard of the US. It was then decided that rather than taking the students abroad and risk having them stay in the US, it was better to run such programmes in Nigeria. Dr. Judith Burdin Asuni, the founder and Executive Director of AA, therefore shared her ideas with General Olusegun Obasanjo who gave permission for his African Leadership Forum (ALF) to be used for conducting the training. The first conflict management workshop organised by AA was therefore hosted by ALF at Ota in January 1993. All the facilitators of the programme offered free services; none of them was paid any honorarium. One of the trainers, Mr. Richard Salem, the Director of Conflict Management Initiatives in Illinois, USA who had previous working relationship in South Africa, paid his own way from America to participate in the training. The participants in the training programme were drawn from six Nigerian universities.

Salem returned to Nigeria in 1994 for two weeks as an academic specialist sponsored by USIS. The visit was planned and co-ordinated by A.A. He gave lectures and seminars to staff and students of the Obafemi Awolowo University in Ife; and organised a two-day seminar on conflict management for staff and students of Lagos State Polytechnic and Lagos State College of Education. This was followed by a one-day training-of-trainers for representatives of the institutions and a conflict management workshop for staff of Mayflower School, Ikenne, and another training-of-trainers for staff of the school. During the visit, Salem and some local experts also trained seventeen eminent Nigerians on how to respond to conflict. These people later constituted themselves into a peace group known as "Corps of Mediators". A member of the Corps contributed actively to the resolution of the ethnic and religious conflicts in Jos in 1994. An intervention programme planned for the crisis in Rivers State during the year could not take off due to the strike of petroleum workers. Thereafter the Conflict Management Network was also established with ALF, AA and AFSTRAG as the original members. The network was later joined by SEMA Ltd., a consultancy firm based in Kaduna.

The second in the series of conflict management workshops for Nigerian universities was organised by ALF and AA in July 1995 and was funded by the Friedrich Naumann Foundation. In 1996, the British High Commission in Lagos started to support the peace works of AA and SEMA Ltd. ALF could no longer participate in the training programmes due to the incarceration of General Obasanjo. AA has been enjoying the support of the British High Commission and technical support of Responding to Conflict in Birmingham since then for its university, secondary school, community and media training programmes. The organisation has also been supported on a few other occasions by USAID, ODA, Action Aid, USIS.

The community conflict management programmes of AAPW took a more definite shape following the two-and-half-week short course on conflict handling skills conducted in Lagos for twenty-one change agents drawn from Nigeria, Ghana and Sierra Leone from 19 May to 6 June 1996. The programme was facilitated by Steve Williams of Responding to Conflict, Dr. Judith Asuni and Mr. Samie Ihejirika, the Director of SEMA Ltd., an organisation with which AAPW was in partnership up till 1997. The short course produced a generation of local resource persons now being used by AAPW for conducting its conflict management-training and problem-solving workshops. Two of those trained at the forum Imam Mohammed Nurayn Ashafa and Pastor James Movel Wuye, veterans of the Zangon Kataf and Kaduna crises of 1992, now run the Muslim-Chiristian Youth Dialogue Forum in Kaduna and have trained several hundreds of youth leaders on how to de-escalate religious conflicts in northern Nigeria. As a result of the uniqueness of their works to peacebuilding in northern Nigeria, these two young men have been further trained in Britain, South Africa and America on managing conflict. They are now in charge of AAPW's religious programmes.

In all, AAPW has nine major programmes in the field of transforming community conflicts.

* Peace Education/Peer mediation training for secondary school students and staff.
* Conflict management training for students and staff of Nigerian universities;
* Conflict Transfomation-training and problem-solving workshops for community (traditional, local government, youth and religious) leaders;
* Problem-solving workshops on pastoralist-farmer conflicts;
* Documentation of case studies of community conflicts.
* Training of journalists on conflict reporting.
* Socio-cultural activities focussed on peacebuilding
* Mindset change and empowerment workshops for youths from highly politicized areas, especially the Niger Delta.

Time, space and the focus of this book will not allow us to go into the details of all these training programmes. For now, we will limit ourselves to those programmes pertaining to community conflicts.

Training Methods

The various community conflict transformation and

peacebuilding programmes are geared towards constructive transformation of conflict and building sustainable peace in Nigerian communities. Participants at the training programmes are usually selected from the two sides of a conflict environment. The training given to them is geared towards equipping them with the necessary skills for solving their problems themselves. The training programmes and workshops are directed at enabling the trainees understand theories of conflict and conflict management; acquire knowledge on how to analyse and map conflicts and acquire the skills for needs-based approach for dealing with conflicts.

Parties in conflict are usually represented at workshops on equal basis. During the first day of the training the two sides usually find it difficult to trust each other. The good intentions of the trainers are also doubted. The programmes therefore usually start on a dull note as the groups sit separately and try as much as possible to avoid each other. But as the programmes unfold and members of the two groups are made to work together during role plays and simulation and discussion groups, they learn to interact with each other and the tolerance gradually builds up to readiness to co-operate at finding solutions to the problems in their communities.

The trainings are interactive and thus permit the trainees to acquire skills (facilitation, negotiation and mediation skills) and theory for dealing with the conflicts and disputes around them in constructive manners. The participants are assisted to engage in analytic problem-solving designed towards generating mutually satisfactory solutions to conflict situations. What is taught is later tested through role plays and simulation exercises. At the beginning of each training programme, participants are paired up to exchange information about one another: name, place of work, life experiences, the happiest and saddest days in their lives. This exercise often serves the triple purposes of acquainting the participants with one another, (a form of trust-building exercise), stimulating thoughts about the nature of conflict and helping the participants to realise that others could have the same human feelings as themselves. Many usually identify as their saddest day a situation of bereavement, civil disorder etc. After listening to the feelings of one another, the participants often end up seeing each other as having the same concern about the sanctity of human life and the need for men to live in peace and harmony with one another. After this essential aspect of the training, participants from the two sides of the conflict become more relaxed and more willing to interact with one another.

The participants are later challenged to identify their expectations from the workshop. Many would want to acquire new skills for dealing with the local conflicts. All these "expectations" are therefore carefully worked into the training modules. Each day's work usually closes with an "open window" - a forum that enables the participants to ask questions and raise issues not accommodated by the programmes slated for the day.

At the end of the workshop, usually between three and five days, usually participants feel very happy that their peculiar needs have been met at the workshop. At the same time,they feel happy for acquiring new skills on how to deal with the conflicts in their community. At the end of each training programme, the participants usually discuss perspectives for local peace action and constitute themselves into peace committees and networks. As a result of this, AAPW has peacebuilding groups and committees (popularly referred to as "change agents") in all towns where it had organised peace workshops, namely, all the towns mentioned in this book and a few others such as Lagos, Ibadan, Kaduna, Port Harcourt, Maiduguri etc.

(National) Corps of Mediators

One of the greatest achievements of AAPW in building peace in Nigeria is its ability to revive, in 1997, the civil society "Corps of Mediators" (COM) which it had earlier established in 1994 during the visit of Richard Salem to Nigeria. COM is a body of senior Nigerian citizens, retired ambassadors, ministers, deputy state governors, civil servants, lawyers, school teachers, community leaders, influential academics and traditional rulers, specially trained on how to respond to community conflicts at national level. The first training for these new members of the COM was organised from 26-30 May 1997 at Ogere Conference Centre, Ogere in Ogun State. It was funded by the British High Commission and attended by participants from conflict-prone zones such as Zango Kataf, Tafawa Balewa, Jos, Kaduna, Maiduguri, Kafanchan,

Igbo-Ora, Makurdi, Takum, Kano, Owerri, Lagos and Port Harcourt. Those invited to the workshop were carefully hand-picked, having distinguished themselves in their chosen careers as leaders with credibility and respect. The selection process however took into consideration ethnic, religious and gender factors.

The objectives of the workshop for these mediators were to develop mediation and conflict management skills; create a network of credible Nigerians for mediation work in the country; develop with the participants a workable conflict management mechanism/structure for communities, local government and state levels; and to, as a follow-up, test the mechanism/structure in real life situations after case studies and analysis.

The guest facilitator of the workshop was Paul Clifford of Responding to Conflict in Birmingham, United Kingdom. He was supported by Major-General Ishola Williams, Dr. Judith Asuni and three other scholars, Professor Thomas Imobighe, Dr. Sabo Bako and Dr. Ishola Olomola who delivered working papers on land, religious and chieftaincy conflicts respectively. As usual, the workshop was designed to be highly interactive and included several role-play and simulation exercises.

At the end of the workshop, the participants met and decided to organise themselves into a peace committee and this was how the Corps of Mediators was relaunched as an independent non-governmental organisation. AAPW was asked to co-ordinate the activities of the group until COM was considered to be strong enough to have its own permanent administrative structures, officers and office accommodation. The Corps immediately established three conflict monitoring centres in parts of Nigeria considered prone to violent conflicts: the far North with the headquarters in Kano, the Middle Belt in Jos and the oil producing areas in Port Harcourt . Members from each zone were challenged to closely monitor the conflicts in their zones and call upon members from other parts of the country if there was the need for any large-scale national intervention.

The activities of each zone were placed under a mediator who was expected to be in close touch with AAPW in case of any need to contact the other groups for any peace-making or peacebuilding project. An advisory committee was also established for co-ordinating the activities of the organisation at national level. Conflicts occurring from different parts of the country were to be brought to the notice of the co-ordinating members for prompt attention (Asuni 1997).

The second workshop for the Corps of Mediators was organised at Hotel Presidential in Port Harcourt in April 1998. Paul Clifford of Responding to Conflict again assisted with this training. The basic aim was to train new members of the Corps as well as upgrading the knowledge of the old members on how to deal constructively with conflicts. The new members were therefore at the training venue for a few days before the old members joined them. The Port Harcourt training included a tour of some of the areas devastated by the oil producing companies in Bayelsa state. Members of the Corps interacted with some of the youth leaders championing resistance movements against the oil companies in this part of Nigeria. The training programme also enabled the older members of the corps to share with the other members their practical experiences in community peace-making and peacebuilding since the 1997 training at Ogere. The trainees jointly analysed three potential future interventions most especially in the Warri and Ife-Modakeke crises. Suggestions were made on the best way to intervene in these conflicts.

At the end of the training in Port Harcourt, Ambassador B.A. Clark a retired Nigerian diplomat was elected as the president of COM, and Chief Ason Bur - a retired federal permanent secretary and former Deputy Governor, Benue state - as the vice president. The advisory committee constituted at Ogere in 1997 to manage the affairs of the corps was thus dissolved.

Practical interventions in Community Conflicts

AAPW does not only teach people how to make or build peace. It also intervenes in community conflicts and has successfully done this in a number of places in Nigeria. Against the background of the fact that accurate and comprehensive information plays a crucial role in conflict management, AAPW never intervenes in any conflict until it has commissioned a researcher to carefully study the conflict in question. The researcher, usually drawn from a

Nigerian university, goes into the conflict society, speaks to the two sides in the conflict, goes to the archives to study the records on the conflict and then writes his report. A typical case study developed by an AAPW researcher usually has some essential components: parties to the conflict; causes and courses of the conflict; positions, interests, needs and fear of the parties; past methods of management and possible ways of de-escalating the conflict. All the nine papers in this volume were produced within this framework. They were originally produced for those seeking to do mediation work in the affected communities.

The research report is carefully studied and criticised at an analysis meeting of the organisation. Should there be any gaps to be filled, the researcher is asked to return to the field to complete the work. Since the formation of the Corps of Mediators, it has been active in planning intervention in community conflicts. Once the necessary resources for intervening in a conflict have therefore been procured, AAPW staff work closely with key COM on choice of mediators and methods. At least one AAPW staff member is also assigned to each intervention.

Issues taken into consideration before appointing a particular mediator in a conflict include:

1. Place of origin - will the parties in the dispute see the person as an unbiased mediator?
2. Past or present status in the society;
3. Willingness to serve.

Once the mediators are chosen, a date is fixed for a brainstorming session on the conflict. The researcher who worked on the case study will carefully explain all essential issues and facts in the conflict to the mediators and staff, and these are debated and sometimes reassessed. This is followed by a brainstorming session on the approaches to use in de-escalating the conflict. Issues arising from the brainstorming session are carefully and thoroughly debated and agreement reached on the *modus operandi* for the intervention. Such meetings usually last two days. All the interventions in which this kind of approach has been carried out to date have turned out to be successful. Conflict management training or problem solving workshops for youths and adults, and peace education training-of-trainers are part of any intervention. Socio-cultural activities have also been included in the Takum and Ife/Modakeke interventions. Conciliation activities by the member of the COM are key to helping would-be peacemakers achieve their goal.

Since its inception, AAPW has successfully intervened in several conflicts. These include Tafawa Balewa, Zango Kataf, Igbo-Ora, Tiv-Jukun crisis in Wukari, Ugep and Mangu/Bokkos. Current interventions in 1999 include Takum, Ife/Modakeke and Warri. In the following discussion, three of these interventions: that of Igbo-Ora for southern Nigeria; Tiv-Jukun for the Middle-Belt and Tafawa Balewa for the North are examined more closely.

The Igbo-Ora Intervention

The are six quarters in Igbo-Ora in Oyo state, namely, Igbole, Pako, Iberekodo, Idofin, Sagan-un and Igbo-Ora. Each quarter consists of a people that migrated to the settlement at a specific time. Each quarter has its own *Baale* (ruler) with traditional powers of government independent of the other. The ancestors of the six, according to existing oral traditions, agreed that the six quarters, despite their different historical antecedents, should form and remain as one community. To this end, there is an informal Igbo-Ora Council of Traditional Rulers under the leadership of the Olu of Igbo-Ora. The Igbo-Ora conflict started in the 1980s when some of the Baales (especially of Igbole, Pako, Iberekodo and Idofin) asked that the chairmanship position of the Igbo-Ora Traditional Council be rotated. Some of the *Baales* also wanted the collective name of the town to change from Igbo-Ora to Ilupeju since Igbo-Ora only reflects the name of one of the quarters. Until 1993, there was also one single development union for the settlements known as Igbo-Ora Progress Union (IPU). Between 1993 and 1994, a faction of IPU broke away to form Ilupeju Progressive Union (ILPU) with membership from Igbole, Pako, Iberekodo and Idofin. IPU therefore retains only members from Igbo-Ora and Sagan-un. This worked negatively against the development of the settlements. The Council of Patrons, an advisory body of IPU, could no longer meet. The *Baales* of the quarters also became sworn enemies.

The opportunity to de-escalate this conflict came on December 24, 1996 when General Ishola Williams and Dr. Judith Asuni were invited by Stimulus Wits - an Ibarapa youth organisation based in Igbo-Ora- to deliver some lectures on "Sub-ethnic conflicts and their effects on development". This opened the doors for other peace activities in the town by AAPW. Alhaji Abbas, a former Chairman of Ifeloju Local Government Council, who seemed neutral at the December 1996 lectures was invited to participate in the training programme organised for members of the Corps of Mediators at Ogere in May 1997. This enabled AAPW return to the town to organise a peace education training in August 1997. The training was so successful that elders from all sides of the conflict decided to attend its closing session.

This was followed up with a problem-solving workshop for the elders of the town which took place between 5th and 7th January 1998. The workshop was organised for thirty-four participants drawn from members of the Council of Patrons, IPU, ILPU, youth and religious leaders from all the quarters in Igbo-Ora town. The general objectives of the workshop were as follows:

- To facilitate a forum where all sides in the dispute would analyse the conflict in their society and generate options for sustainable conflict transformation;
- To assist the community in enhancing their skills in peace-making and peacebuilding on a sustainable basis;
- To use skills in improving the relationship between the local government chief executive and the community;
- To assist the community in building the necessary machinery and mechanisms for preventing and managing future disputes/conflicts.

The workshop was declared open by the Olu of Igbo-Ora in the presence of the Baales of the five other quarters. The workshop enabled AAPW to work differently and jointly with the factions. Each group was asked to determine the issues in the conflict, analyse the actors and their relationships, and finally find solutions to the conflict. There were similarities in all the reports that were received and this enabled the groups to have a clearer vision of the way forward. At the end of the workshop the participants, having realised that they could solve the problem themselves, resolved as follows:

1. That Ilupeju Progress Union should reunite with the Igbo-Ora Progress Union;
2. That the Council of Patrons should be reactivated for the town;

3. That a Peace Monitoring Group be set up;
4. That the issue of the paramount ruler should be referred to the Traditional Council.
5. That a new executive council should be formed for IPU

The Igbo-Ora Peace Monitoring Group held its inaugural meeting on 30 January 1998 and has been very active since then at building peace in Igbo-Ora. For the first time in several years, the popular " Igbo-Ora Day" was marked by all the groups on August 15 1998. The Igbo-Ora intervention is a good example of preventive action, where conciliation and facilitation were sufficient to lead to a transfromation of the conflict.

Intervention in the Tiv-Jukun Crisis in Wukari

The Tiv-Jukun crisis in Wukari is a deep-rooted crisis revolving around the questions of access to land, respect for traditional structures and political enfranchisement. Five to six years into this conflict, the Tiv people, many of whom had lived in Wukari for decades, were forced out of the town. Their schools and health centres were forced to close down and the people were denied access to farmland and political positions. Between July and August 1997, AAPW commissioned three researchers to critically study the conflict. By this time, communication had completely broken down between parties to the conflict to the extent that only few Tiv men and women felt safe to spend a night in Wukari.

During the Corps of Mediators steering committee meeting that was held in Lagos in September 1997, the conflict was thoroughly discussed and plans of action were mapped out. Chief Ason Bur, a Tiv man and former deputy governor of Benue State, and Honourable George Maiangwa, a Chamba, a group closely related to the Jukun, retired school headmaster and a former law maker, were appointed to work on the conflict, each with his own ethnic group. With the help of the case study team, they identified youth leaders in Wukari who had been very active in the conflict. These youth leaders were invited to a conflict-management training which took place at Jos - a neutral ground. At the end of the training the youth leaders agreed to be united and resolved to work together at de-escalating the disagreement between their people. They set up a Youth Forum for advancing peace works in Wukari. Immediately after the training, the youth leaders and the two mediators went straight to visit the Jukun king (the **Aku Uka**), who expressed enthusiasm about the peace effort.

A workshop was to have been held for the community leaders and elders in December 1997, but it had to be postponed due to the reluctance of the Jukun people. Further conciliation and information sharing, as well as pressure by the youths for positive action, eventually led to willingness on all sides. The workshop was held on 27 and 28 January 1998 at Wukari with all major players on both the Tiv and Jukun sides in attendance. The presence of General Williams and Dr. Judith Asuni as facilitators, with the support of the two senior mediators, as well as preliminary visits to the Aku Uka and the Chairman of the Local Government Council struck a high note for the workshop. Again the participants spent much time in working groups and at the end came up with their own plan of action for the future. This included allaying the Jukun fears of disrespect for their king and traditional structures, and providing for Tiv needs for farmland, schools and other social services. One decision was that the Tiv should also be included in the traditional all-Jukun Council of Elders.

Although this plan of action was agreed upon by all participants at the January problem-solving workshop and a peace committee was set up, little happened for several months thereafter. During his frequent visits to Wukari, Chief Ason Bur soon discovered that one thorn in the flesh of the Jukun was a lawsuit against the Jukun king (Aku Uka) by a Tiv elder, over a disputed piece of farmland. An AAPW team and the two mediators had to visit Wukari in June 1998. The team had an extensive meeting with the Peace Committee and visited the king. In subsequent months, two members of the Peace Committee, the senior Jukun chairman and a Tiv youth leader became extremely active in visiting both parties to the conflict. They obtained a promise that the Tiv would drop the lawsuit. It was hoped that in appreciation of this demonstration of willingness on the part of the Tiv, that the king would open their schools. It appeared then that the deadlock was finally broken, after a year of conciliation, mediation and facilitation. Mediators, Chief Ason Bur and Honourable George Maiangwa were key in the whole Wukari peace process.

The Tafawa Balewa Intervention

The conflict in Tafawa Balewa is covered in Chapter Eight in this volume. It was between the Muslim Fulani population and the Christian-dominated Sayawa. The conflict culminated in several thousands deaths, destruction of community social trust and threatened developmental efforts generally in the local government area as members of the communities were dagger-drawn against one another. To reverse this ugly trend, AAPW decided to intervene in the conflict. As a way of building local capacities for responding positively to the conflict, AAPW started to conduct conflict management training for the community leaders, youth and religious leaders as well as local government officials and secondary school teachers in the area in 1997. The first group to be trained was the secondary school teachers, from 21-24 May 1997.

A few months later, three members of the Corps of Mediators, Hajiya Fatima Muazu, now on the Independent National Electoral Commission; Alhaji Maikano Gori and Mr. Kaka Sara assisted AAPW to organise a conflict management workshop for the community leaders and local government officials of Tafawa Balewa and Bogoro Local Government Council Areas. This was the first time any member of the Corps of Mediators was taking up the challenge of experimenting with what they were taught at Ogere. They thus set a very positive precedent and became role models for other members of the COM. The work of these three mediators were supported by some peace education teachers that AAPW had trained in the area in May 1997. These young teachers produced plays at the local government council headquarters, telling community leaders about the programme and, under the banner of "peace singers", moved around Bogoro and Tafawa Balewa entertaining former warring parties in the area and preaching to them the need for peace. At the end of the workshop conducted by Hajiya Muazu and her group, the officials of Tafawa Balewa and Bogoro Local Government Councils vowed that there would be no further conflict in their domain. There has been peace in the area since then.

These different peace groups from the workshops have been promoting peace objectives in their communities. Both Tafawa Balewa and Bogoro Local Governments have appointed senior personnel department staff to co-ordinate conflict management affairs in their areas. The conflict management manual usually given to trainees during AAPW's workshops has been translated by officials of the Tafawa Balewa Local Government Council into Hausa language as a way of bringing the peace messages of AAPW closer to the people. There was also the plan of using trained secondary school teachers to promote peace campaigns in the rural area.

The three intervention programmes mentioned above are just a few of the many community peace initiatives of Academic Associates PeaceWorks. Full reports of other interventions can be obtained form AAPW library located at 9, Esomo Close, Ikeja Lagos.

Learning from the success of the Igbo-Ora and Wukari interventions, AAPW has started interventions in the conflicts in Warri, Takum and Ife-Modakeke. Both conflicts are entrenched, currently violent conflicts. Government efforts to date have failed. The plan of AAPW is to try middle range and grassroots approaches of building peace in the communities. The conflict management training already conducted in Ile-Ife in 1998 had already prepared some ground for the work to be done there. In addition to its traditional focus on training, research and intervention, AAPW has established a third sector on enlightenment. This sector is aimed at increasing awareness and appreciation of peace, through the media, music, the arts and theatre. The organisation also plans to increase activities in the Niger Delta and among the pastoralists in the far North.

An External Evaluator's Report on AAPW

As earlier noted, a substantial percentage of the resources used by AAPW came from the British High Commission Good Governance Programme which is managed by the British Council. In March 1998, the British High Commission commissioned Mr. Robert Dodd, a retired staff of ActionAid, London to evaluate the work of AAPW in Nigeria. The main term of reference was whether the Commission and the British Council were really getting "value for money" from the activities of AAPW which they funded in the area of conflict management in Nigeria. In his report, Mr. Dodd had this to say about the activities of AAPW, having toured all parts of Nigeria where the organisation has been quietly working towards building peace:

> Over the years AA has built up considerable expertise in peace and conflict analysis and has augmented its skills by drawing on the experience of specialist institutions and individuals within Nigeria and through international contact. Among the latter are the Centre for Conflict Resolution in South Africa, the Community Board Programme in San Francisco, Conflict Management Initiatives in Illinois, USA, and Responding to Conflict, at Birmingham in the UK... The main thrust of AA's approach has been to provide training through workshops which are tailor-made to the requirements of the participants being targeted at any one time. The AA Handbook for workshop trainings, for example, is an eclectic collection of ideas drawn from a number of sources and adapted to the needs and the context of conflict situations in Nigeria.

> During 1996-97 AA carried out over 30 workshops throughout the country and provided training in conflict management to around 1,500 individuals. This was an impressive achievement by any standard... The workshops are much appreciated. Several people, some of whom described themselves as former fanatics, told the evaluator that they had been surprised that techniques for conflict resolution existed. What they had learned during the workshops was that it was possible for antagonists on both sides of a conflict to hold legitimate grievances and that these differences could, with care, be reconciled without recourse to violence. Conflict management was of overriding importance, they said, and peace was preferable to conflict. Informants in different parts of the country consistently told the evaluator that they had felt inspired by the workshop training.

> It was clear, therefore, that the combined content, form and presentation of the workshops had been highly successful and that they had had an impact on the way that people thought about conflict and peace. In particular was the diffusion and dissemination of values which would lead to conflict avoidance and to peace-building. In terms of "value for money" ...such work must be seen beyond price (Dodd 1998: 4-5)

The success of AAPW's works derives largely from the absolute commitment and managerial acumen of its Executive Director, Dr. Judith Burdin Asuni. She ensures that the organisation is democratically managed with a high degree of financial transparency which several Nigerian NGOs lack. Money meant for any project is completely spent on the project and should there be any left-over from any particular programme, it is ploughed back into new projects. The organisation has therefore been able to maximise the use of the little resources at its disposal.

Decisions concerning project management are collectively

taken. The minutest details about the NGO are regularly shared with all members of the Management Board and everybody is free to come in with whatever project that pleases him or her as long as this has to do with peacebuilding. Everybody is therefore easily carried along as different projects are executed. Advisers and consultants to the organisation are carefully chosen. For example, Major-General Ishola Williams who usually chairs the strategic planning meetings and the brainstorming sessions preceding every intervention programme of the organisation, is one of the best experts ever to have been produced in the field of strategic studies in Nigeria. The success of every intervention programme mentioned above can be partially credited to his planning abilities and positive thinking that every conflict can be de-escalated no matter how intractable it might appear from the outer surface. The consultants and staff of the organisation are products of, or have working partnership with leading Peace Studies institutions and agencies around the world: Peace Studies programmes of Bradford University, University of Ulster (both in UK) and Eastern Mennonite University in the US; INCORE, Northern Ireland; Centre for Conflict Resolution, University of Cape Town in South Africa; Responding to Conflict in Birmingham, United Kingdom; Nairobi Peace Initiative; World Bank's Urban Management Programme, Africa Regional Office, Abidjan etc.

To keep pace with the increasing appreciation and demand for conflict management activities in Nigeria and West Africa, AAPW is gradually developing structures and programmes that will enable it to become an international NGO. It has twelve members of staff, a large office space and efficient computing and communication facilities. It holds regular strategic planning meetings with its staff and sends them on regular trainings. It has therefore not been too difficult for the organisation to reach some other African countries with its peace programmes. It developed a peace education for northern Ghana in partnership with ActionAid Ghana in 1997 and 1998; officially participated in the "Africa Project" of the Centre for Conflict Resolution, University of Cape Town in South Africa by developing for the latter four case studies for conducting conflict management training in Africa; it sent five delegates to the peacebuilding course jointly organised by the Nairobi Peace Initiative and Eastern Mennonite University (USA) in Ghana in October and November 1998. AAPW has written five case studies on Nigeria for a project on conflicts in Africa for the European Centre for Conflict Prevention in the Netherlands. The organisation is also working towards collaborating with other African NGOs at placing conflict management training in Africa on similar platform with what obtains in Europe and America.

A major problem faced by AAPW is how to sustain its activities among the grassroots population and develop new programmes through internally generated revenue as it cannot depend on the British High Commission or USAID for ever. The organisation has trained thousands of "change agents" across different parts which it can no longer support in terms of local peace activities. Many of the local peace committees find it difficult to generate local funding for their peacebuilding projects. This issue was noted in Mr. Dodd's report:

> While the quality of the workshops was excellent in providing skills and generating a high level of motivation, some people felt that after the AA team had departed from where a training was conducted, they had been left to their own devices and were not quite sure of the next step to take.

In an effort to address this problem. AAPW staff have begun periodic visits to areas of previous training. Also in February 1999, AAPW formed a Peace Support Network including representatives from the seven towns where AAPW has been working and some degree of peace has been established. These representatives shared their experiences at a workshop and each town drew up its own action plan, which AAPW is helping to implement.

Travelling back to co-ordinate the activities of these past trainees or give them further training will cost a lot of money which AAPW can not afford. A number of suggestions had been made on how AAPW's financial problems could be solved. During a management board meeting of the organisation, it was suggested that AAPW should establish a subsidiary organisation that would conduct conflict management training programmes for industrial establishments on commercial basis. The money derived from such projects would be used for supporting community peace works. The Board of Trustees of AAPW, on its own, is of the view that the organisation should launch an endowment fund for its works. Only time will tell which of these two suggestions will be used by the organisation. What is clear to everybody for now is that AAPW has the human and intellectual resources for dealing with community conflicts in Nigeria and is seeking support from within and outside the country for sustaining what it has started and what it plans to do in the area of peacebuilding and peacemaking in Nigeria.

The enthusiasm with which people, even initial skeptics, participate in AAPW's workshops, and then put their new skills into test and practice is amazing and extremely gratifying to any assessor. It is exciting to see former antagonists, be they Muslims and Christians, Tiv or Jukun, Fulani and Sayawa, Hausa and Kataf, Ife and Modakeke working together to improve their communities. When asked how they will apply their new knowledge and understanding, participants in the training programmes often say, "It starts with me, in my heart." From there, the peace message spreads to the family, to social or religious groups and then to the community. One hopes that when this ripple of peace spreads to thousands or millions, it will make Nigeria a better country and Africa a better continent.

References

Agbola, Tunde [1994]." NGOs and community development in urban areas", *Cities*, 11[1] pp. 59-67.

Asuni, J. [1997]. "Report on the workshop for the Corps of Mediators", Academic Associates, July.

Asuni, J. [1998]," Academic Associates PeaceWorks Summary of Activities, April 1997- September 1998"

Ball, C. and Dunn, L. [1996]. *Non-governmental Organisations: Guidelines for Good Policy and Practice,* London: The Commonwealth Foundation.

Banks, M.H. and Mitchell, C.R. [1991]. *A Handbook of the Analytical Problem-solving Approach,* Institute for Conflict Analysis And Resolution, Fairfax, Virginia.

Boekestijn, C. [1984]. " Intercultural migration and the development of personal identity: The dilemma between identity maintenance and cultural adaptation", Paper given at the seventh international congress of cross-cultural psychology, Acapulco cited in Adrian Furnman and Stephen Bochner, *Culture Shock: Psychological Reactions to Unfamiliar Environments,* London and New York: Methuen p.230.

Broome, B.J. [1993]. "Management differences in conflict resolution: The role of relational emphathy", in Dennis J.D. Sandole and Hugo van der Merwe [eds], *Conflict Resolution Theory and Practice: Integration and Application,* Manchester and New York: Manchester University Press.

Burton, J.W. [1969]. *Conflict and Communication: The Use of Controlled Communication in International Relation,* London: Macmillan.

Burton, J.W [1987]. *Resolving Deep Rooted Conflict: A Handbook,* Lanham, Maryland: University Press of America.

Casmir, F.L. and Asuncion-Lande, N.C. [1989]. "Intercultural communication revisited: Conceptualization, paradigm building, and methodological approaches", in J.A. Anderson [ed.], *Communication Yearbook,* 12, Newbury Park, California: Sage.

de Reuck, A. [1990]. "A theory of conflict resolution by problem-solving", in John Burton and F. Dukes [eds], *Conflict: Readings in Management and Resolution,* Houndmills, Basingstoke, Hampshire: Macmillan.

Dodd, R. [1998]. "Evaluation of the British High Commission Conflict Management Programme in Nigeria".

Fisher, R.J. [1983]. "Third party consultation as a method of conflict resolution: A review of studies", *Journal of Conflict Resolution,* 27 pp. 301-334.

Foltz, W.J. [1977]. "Two forms of unofficial conflict intervention: The problem-solving and process promoting workshops", in M.R. Berman and J.E. Johnson [eds], *Unofficial Diplomats,* New York: Columbia University Press.

Kelman, H.C. [1986]. "Interactive problem-solving: A social-psychological approach to conflict resolution", in W. Klassen [ed], *Dialogue Toward Inter-faith Understanding,* Jerusalem: Tantur Ecumenical Institute for Theological Research.

Kelman, H.C. [1993]. "Foreword", in Dennis J.D. Sandole and Hugo van der Merwe [eds], *Conflict Resolution Theory and Practice: Integration and Application,* Manchester and New York: Manchester University Press.

Lederach, J.P. [1997]. *Building Peace: Sustainable Reconciliation in Divided Societies, Washington, DC.*

Mitchell, C.R. [1993]. "Problem-solving exercises and theories of conflict resolution", in Dennis J.D. Sandole and Hugo van der Merwe [eds], *Conflict Resolution theory and Practice: Integration and Application,* Manchester and New York: Manchester University Press.

Montville, J.V. [1993]. " The healing function in political conflict resolution', in Dennis J.D. Sandole and Hugo van der Merwe [eds],

Conflict Resolution Theory and Practice: Integration and Application, Manchester and New York: Manchester University Press.

SINA [1986]. "IYSH NGO Plan of Action", Mazingira Institute, Nairobi.

Triandis, H.C. and Brislin, R.W. [1984]. " Cross-cultural psychology", *American Psychologist,* 39 pp. 1006-16.

UNCHS [Habitat 1987]. *Shelter for the Homeless: The Role of Non-Governmental Organizations,* Nairobi, Kenya.

Wilmot, W.W. and J.L.Hocker [1998]. *Interpersonal Conflict,* Boston, Massachussetts: McGraw Hill.

Chapter 3

Oka Martin Obono

The Ethnodemography of Yakurr Conflict: A Case Study of the Ugep-Idomi War of 1992.

Introduction

The idea of synthesizing demographic and ethnographic perspectives in the analysis of social phenomena is a very recent one; it is even more novel in conflict studies. In this paper, we examine the ethnodemographic contexts of conflict among the double-unilineal Yakurr of southeastern Nigeria, and show how conflict is associated with the human social condition and population factors.

The double-unilineal Yakurr are a cluster of seven closely-knit agrarian communities whose historical and social biological connections paradoxically provide the account of their propensity for war. By and large, they are a warring people and their strong ties to the land in the face of rapid population increase help explain the short tempers which periodically flare up in both overt and covert conflicts. The present paper examines the ethnographic and demographic contexts of the Ugep-Idomi war of 1992, arguing that the event was not an isolated incident but one that must be seen in relation to fundamental cultural and population factors. An account of conflict among the Yakurr must draw attention to antecedents that could be found useful for the analysis of conflict among similar peoples whose economy is basically governed by the scarce resource of farmland and the cultural beliefs and attitudes regarding scarcity.

Ugep and Idomi are the largest and smallest Yakurr settlements, respectively, and the 1992 war between them is a good example of painful internecine conflict. War broke out between them in the past (in 1929) and the present report, based on empirical research sponsored by Academic Associates Peace Works, identifies the immediate and remote causes of the 1992 conflict. Careful attention is paid to the implications of double-unilineal descent principles for the war mobilisation effort and the difficulty which the conflict introduces in the relationship among people who are otherwise related by blood. The ethnographic setting is important to an appreciation of the interplay of political, geographical, psychological,demographic and economic factors that combine to make wars inevitable.

Historical Background

Ugep and Idomi present important social dichotomies in terms of their geographical and population size. The former is the largest of the Yakurr settlements while the latter is the smallest, from a spatial and socio-economic point of view. Ugep is one of the most populous villages in West Africa while Idomi is the least populous Yakurr settlement. Both occupy the south-eastern part of Yakurr Local Government Area (LGA) and share a common land boundary, a fact that sets the stage for our perception of this territory as an arena of perennial conflict.

The mono-lingual Yakurr of the Middle Cross River have a common tradition that their forebears migrated from the east together with the people of Okuni, a settlement some fifty-eight kilometres up the Cross River (Forde, 1964). Harris (1965) argues that the Yakurr lived first in the hilly country to the south of the Cross River (possibly in the region of the Oban Hills and the Awai Hills), together with the peoples of Ikom and Okuni. Other neighbours included the Ekoma and the Aban-Yongo. Most anecdotal accounts seem to support the idea that these peoples had enjoyed a deep and harmonious relationship that encouraged both political and ritual co-operation, especially as it pertained to the burial of the dead.

Serious feuding and high tension resulted in a series of out-migrations that dispersed these peoples, with the Yakurr forming one party and migrating due north to the present settlement in the course of several years. Ukpawen (in Ugep) was their first main settlement and, of the smaller Yakurr settlements, Idomi and Mkpani were established by migrations from Ugep. The early nature of Idomi settlement accounts for its current geo-demographic size. In an interview with HRH, Obol Lopon of Ugep, Obol Ubi Ujong Inah, I gathered that a pregnant woman had fallen behind in the course of the migration. Alone with her husband, she gave birth to her baby, opting to remain there while the main Yakurr party moved on to settle first at Ukpawen in Ugep, as noted above.

In time, relatives of this couple went back in search of them and, as the area was not far from the main settlement, a few chose to remain there, forming the nucleus of what is today called Idomi. In other words, Idomi was formed by a detachment of the main body of Yakurr migrants and the story of the town's origin is significant from the viewpoint of explaining its momentum for population growth. Forde (1964: 169) reports that initially, there were just Ijiman and Mkpani, noting that "separate wards were subsequently established from Ijiman to form Idjum and Ukpakabi and, two generations ago, a new ward, Biko-biko, was established mainly by migrants from Ukpakabi".

According to the historian, Ubi:

> At the foundation of Ugep c. 1653-1688... there were three wards: Ijiman, Ibe and Umor Otutu. Following a disagreement between Ibe and Ijiman, the former migrated to found a "fresh" settlement called Mkpani. Later lured by the attraction of vacant lands to their Northwest, the Otutu ward migrated to found Ekori (1981: 147).

There are several elements in the above accounts that help explain the proclivity of Yakurr settlements to war.

1.   The element of low birth and growth rates, which at the time of Forde's *Yakurr Studies* (1935 and 1939) had not led to any "deleterious pressure on land" (Forde, 1964: 4). This pattern of low growth rate attendant upon fertility and mortality rates is consistent with stage one of the classic three-stage demographic transition theory. Population growth rate was slow at the earliest stage of Ugep settlement as a result of profound stress within the social system, decimation of the population by the Akpa war, and the difficulties associated with dislodging the first settlers in the new territory they were determined to make their home. In the latter context, it is important to observe that war drove the Yakurr people to their present settlement, and it was through war that they possessed it.

It is noteworthy also that fertility occupies an important place in the cosmology of the Yakurr people, responsible as it were for the destiny of some of the settlements. The notion of birth is further significant because the socio-political organisation of the people is unequivocally premised upon the beliefs surrounding the practices of an august council of priests who regularly make atonement to an impressive arrray of fertility spirits. However, while this feature of Yakurr society may appear functional from the viewpoint of social solidarity and the maintenance of peace and order, it may have become dysfunctional by being implicated in the region's current crisis of development, especially as it pertains to war. It is arguable that what Forde described as "the comparative stability of Yakurr settlement [in the 1930s]" was related to the corresponding fact that "the overall density of population had not so far risen high enough" to provide the required setting for war.

2. The element of tension. This particular element indicates that fission and accretion are central functions of Yakurr socio-political, socio-cultural structures. As indicated above, it is partly the product also of the history of the people themselves, as well as of their settlement and how they came by it. It is clear that these structures and the tranformations they have undergone over time, are results of the people's interactions with themselves and one another in the contexts of scarce resources.

3. The third element is a cosmological summary of the first two. The fact that internecine strife is not something alien to this people is an important background against which the current conflict among them must be understood. In other words, it would be erroneous to approach the Yakurr (Ugep-Idomi) war of 1992 as an isolated incident, or as something not related in any way, for instance, to the strained relations of 1929. A more useful perspective is one that sees the nature, scope, context and conduct of war among the Yakurr as products of its social history, as historical tinder which can be ignited by the explosive combination of demographic, cultural, historical, economic and political factors.

It emerges from the foregoing that the very ethnographic antecedents of conflict in the territory are viable means of arbitration and it is in this sense that Yakurr conflict can be so paradoxical. Negative trends in the economy at the macro level, intensified by strong population pressure, can make war inevitable. Nevertheless, the recognition of blood ties can so minimise the scope of hostilities that the outcome becomes a careful study in grief and anguish for both parties, without reference to who was the victor or vanquished. In a Yakurr war, those statuses always seem to be short-lived because, in the long run, everybody loses the war, a part of everybody's heritage is compromised or destroyed, as we shall see, by the principle of double descent.

Contemporary Social, Political and Economic Organisation

The Yakurr are a double-unilineal "semi-Bantu" people found in the northern part of the Cross River State of Nigeria. They share a high degree of linguistic and cultural homogeneity maintained by "a continual interchange of visitors, temporary residents, and permanent migrants" (Forde, 1950: 286). In contemporary times, this homogeneity has been reinforced by the local government status of the area - a departure from the traditional absence of centralised political organisation - as well as the implications of party politics for regional formation of social ties. Massive in-migration of workers and traders of non-Yakurr origin into the Ugep area has promoted the rise of an urbanistic culture that, for present purposes, is a good setting for commending dialogue as a means of safeguarding peace and security within the region.

The political organisation of the Yakurr de-emphasizes vertical control (Obono, 1995: 29). The double-unilineal principle of descent places authority in overlapping, concentric spheres that throw up internal checks to absolutism. Tyranny is effectively curtailed by the primary loyalty of all individuals to the corporate interests of their own matrilineages and patrilineages. In this way, the principle of agnatic descent forestalls the imposition of one man's will over the rest of the people as that might so readily be interpreted as constituting a clash of lineage interests. Political authority progresses in ascending order from the corporate patrilineage (*eponama*, pl. *yeponama*), the patriclan (*kepun*, pl. *yepun*) and matriclan (*lejimo*, pl. *yajimo*), the district (*kekpatu*, pl. *yekpatu*), to the town at large (*lopon*). Under this structure, the individual belongs to groups and collectivities which are in turn parts of larger configurations, each of which extracts obligations commensurate with its size and complexity of ties. The jurisdictions of these units overlap, complementing one another through either common descent or membership to common voluntary or obligatory associations (Obono, 1995: 29).

Within the patrilineage, "political loyalty was spoken of in the idiom of kinship and the political composition of the family was explained by reference to descent - matrilineal or patrilineal" (Ubi, 1981: 158). The patriclan is headed by the *Obol Kepun*, traditionally its oldest living male member and, by implication, leader of his own *eponama*. As may be expected, this gerontocratic criterion is no longer essential to the election of *Yabol Kepun*. In the first place, the average life expectancy in the region has been declining steadily in the decades since the civil war (1966 - 1970) and there is attrition in the elderly segment of Yakurr society that has expanded the scope of political competition to include much younger persons. This demographic effect (of declining life expectancy on the political process) depends on the collective orientation of the respective groups and may show significant inter-relationships with the nature of land tenure, if that factor is important to the determination of individual and group nutritional status and overall well-being. The *Obol Kepun* plays an important role in the ritual life of the Yakurr community by attending to the *epundet*, "a low mound of small boulders surmounted by some chalk-stained pots usually set in the shade of a tree" (Forde, 1964: 51) which symbolises the corporate and spiritual unity of the *Kepun*.

The districts make up the town and are composed of adjacent dwelling areas (*akomma;* sing. *lekoma*) of a dozen or more patriclans. Contiguity is thus central to understanding the nature of Yakurr boundaries and the underlying descent principles which grant affinal ties so much residential expression. The leaders of the *akomma* ensure the security of life and property within their respective settlements and refer internal disputes involving members of different *Yepun* to the *Ogbolia*, who is their head and could enlist the support of the *Eblabu* (Ghost-Dog) society in ward level administration and conflict resolution.

The Yakurr society is characterised by the following properties:

1. No single level or group has a monopoly on the exercise of violence.

2. At all levels, groups extract ritual and military loyalty from the individual.

3. When superordinate claims to these loyalties collide with subordinate ones in the concentric circle, the former are considered to acquire precedence. These features permit what Evans-Pritchard describes as "the fusion and fission of segments". This is better known as "segmentary opposition" and is to be taken as an important category for the analysis of background and fundamental factors that predispose certain settlements to conflict.

Being a dispersed settlement, the matriclan is more powerful in the realm of ritual, and provides an important key to war mobilisation. Because of the rule of exogamy and the co-residential status of the patriclan, the anguish associated with the killing of its member is by that fact localised. With respect to the matriclan, on the other hand, a similar murder is capable of affecting numerous families simultaneously and this makes the mobilisation of sentiments so much easier than in a thorough-going patrilineal society. The process of war mobilisation in the latter kind of society may be more tenuous as the relationships between the different groups that make up the entire settlement may not be firmly established and only few, if any, could trace them directly. The principle of matrilineal descent in a double-unilineal society therefore imbues war mobilisation with the required "natural sentiment" or passion that is necessary to make it swift. This was the scenario in which hostilities nearly broke between the two communities at the tail end of 1998.

The mainstay of both the Ugep and Idomi communities is agriculture. Every adult person is a subsistent farmer. A degree of petty trading is common, although it may not be a primary source of household income. Some men also engage in hunting of wildlife, and this accords each male the privilege of possessing firearms, usually a single-barrelled dane gun. Farm plots are held individually by men as household heads within the framework of the wider collective rights of kin groups. During each farming season, the farmland is fragmented into farming plots to all male members of the patrilineage. The process ensures that widows and divorcees, depending on where they reside, are catered for. It is highly interesting that divorce in Ugep follows a trend or pattern that is closely related to the annual allocation of farm plots, with women timing their divorce or separation to coincide with, or precede the period in which this is done. This is further evidence of a need to develop a framework for studying conflictual human behaviour in terms of the macro-level processes that induce that behaviour; otherwise the interpretation of it would not be comprehensive.

The Yakurr practice the traditional agricultural method of shifting cultivation. This practice requires that previously farmed land be allowed to fallow and leads to two implications. First, either farmland must be taken on lease from landlords, or second, unlawful encroachment into other people's farmlands would become inevitable. Rapid population growth rate affects everybody in the communities and significantly reduces the amount of food available to most families. Rapid increase in population also renders most landowners incapable of leasing out land as they too have come under the influence of a truncated fallow period. For this reason, the first approach to ameliorating the pressure brought on by population pressure is not generally feasible. This leaves the second option more likely, especially as the traditional boundaries between contiguous settlements are in constant dispute.

One cannot say for certain who was the guilty belligerent in the Ugep-Idomi War and perhaps one should not attempt to. It were probably better to adopt the proactive Khoi-Khoi jurisprudential idea of pointing out *what,* rather than *who,* was wrong. There are greater prospects for peace that way.

What is known, however, is that it was a land-related problem for which existing mechanisms for resolution proved temporarily ineffectual. It is arguable that these mechanisms could not have worked anyway, at least at the onset of hostilities, because they always depended on unequivocal goodwill among the neighbours for them to be applied. At the time in question, all such goodwill had completely disappeared.

The Conflict: Its Causes and Dynamics

Peace had reigned in Yakurr country since the late 1920s when

Ugep and Idomi fought a limited war. The theatre of conflict was re-opened on 21st January, 1987, when war broke out between Ugep and Mkpani. The composition and organisation of that war throw much light on the dynamics of the Ugep-Idomi war, which broke out on Thursday, 19th March, 1992. In the Mkpani war, fourteen-year old youngsters established themselves as the main warriors of Ugep society. The brutality of that war knew no bounds and I personally had wondered how peaceful co-existence could thereafter be re-established. But it was.

The Ugep-Idomi war had its immediate cause in a boundary dispute that later culminated in the kidnap and subsequent murder of some Ugep people, namely, *Obol* (Chief) Ebri Obla, Ete Onun Obeten, and Madam Ojekon Ejeng. Ugep respondents insist that the kidnap and murder of *Obol* Obla, more than anything else, was the most painful as he was a helpless old man who was at the same time an *Obol Kepun* and, by implication of our analysis, head of a military constituency. However, the matrilineal descent principle, as noted, implied also that grief over his death was felt town-wide. The anger was not concentrated or localised to Ijiman where he came from, but spread out among his matrikin everywhere in Ugep town. The same principle holds for each of the other murdered persons. It explains why war mobilisation among the double-unilineal Yakurr is not such a difficult matter, although the summed value of each person in relation to his or her position in the total concentric is a crucial factor to bear in mind in calculating the probability of war. Where such summed value is low, there may be retaliatory attacks, but these would more likely take a clandestine form, or there may be none at all.

Many factors, remote and immediate, are responsible for the incessant crisis common at the border between Idomi and Ugep. Quite often, the crisis takes the form of *Nyuduwo* (the "hidden fight"). This form of warfare involves clandestine murders between the warring parties long after formal hostilities have come to an end. The murders may pass unnoticed by government, and defy monitoring by investigators and other observers. *Nyuduwo* typifies the local understanding of war, and in this too Yakurr conflict is paradoxical. While trading and other economic aspects of co-operation may be restored, and while migration and temporary settlement back and forth may be resumed, there would yet prevail a siege mentality that admonishes everybody to be vigilant as the war may actually not be over.

The remote factors of the Ugep-Idomi war included:

1. The long standing issue of undefined borders between the communities;
2. Simmering thoughts of vengeance over the previous murder of a patrikin or matrikin that went unavenged;
3. Persistent pressure on land for agricultural purposes prompted by an increase in population;
4. A largely belligerent attitude by a section of the people whose faith in the power of black magic to make them invincible in war was unshakable.

The immediate factors for the war included:

1. Claims and counter-claims of kidnappings and killings of innocent indigenes (mostly farmers) in the area;
2. Violation of the terms of peace moves earlier initiated by the communities over the disputed area and the subsequent land encroachments, molestation of persons and uprooting of farm products.

The background factors included the central geographical position of Ugep in the region. Ugep is bounded in the North by Ekori, in the East by Mkpani, West by Bahumono communities of Abi Local Government Areas, South east by Idomi, South and South West by Abanyongo villages of Biase Local Government Area respectively. By its central position, Ugep is prone to incessant boundary conflicts with its surrounding neighbours. This perhaps explains why the town is a more frequent participant in the conflicts that occur.

The rapid population explosion in the region intensified the effects of land scarcity. The basic Yakurr response to pressure on residential space was for a segment of the patriclan to detach itself and migrate to "free-lands" belonging to the patriclan; but this has the corresponding effect of extending the area used for its farming activities. Where similar demographic pressures existed in neighbouring settlements and the response of building hamlets (*liwu*) on "free-lands" was the same, what prevailed was a recipe for crisis. From a demographic point of view, therefore, the tendency for expansion through the establishment of *liwu*, seen in the context of ill-defined boundaries between the Ugep and Idomi, was the most obvious scenario within which their war took place.

Psychological factors also contributed to the readiness to wage war as, historically, deaths of innocent farmers in the area usually generated so much animosity among the families of the victims towards the offenders that retaliation was merely a question of time. This is what may be referred to as "the historical tinder for war". The question was hardly ever whether a retaliatory attack would occur but how soon and in what form. Such families almost always appeared ready to fuel any crisis in a bid to seek "justifiable" revenge, managing or mismanaging information and propaganda to maximum effect.

This finding is important for intervention. A chronicle of heads of such families must be secured in order for peace workshops to be organised for them. They should be integrated into activities aimed at developing a culture of peace in the region. The nature of *Nyuduwo* leads to one implication: There is always a backlog of families seeking revenge at any given time. It is the mode of conflict among the Yakurr, an endless vendetta that acquires the character of a vicious circle of blood-letting whose original cause is now lost in history. It is important to chronicle the heads of households and families that lost members in this gruesome manner within the past few decades. If these can be trained to be peer motivators, especially family members who are already vocal and whose views are widely respected, there is a fair chance that the peace initiative might develop into a permanent feature of culture.

One group that played a prominent role in the conflict under review is a seething, frustrated, jobless and restless army of unemployed youth. Their existence is the result of decades of government neglect or failure to inspire or complement the community-level developmental efforts on the ground. The situation created a near complete absence of industrial development in the area with the consequent focus on the farm as the exclusive means of survival. It created a third paradox in our analysis such that industrial progress was kept at bay by the very broiling tensions that it could help eliminate.

In the absence of gainful employment, the youth took to

farming and by so doing exerted heavy pressure on the competition for land. In their unemployed or underemployed state, they became further sensitive to real and imagined threats to the land and, *ipso facto*, their own existence. This observation is notable because, if this restless army were engaged in other forms of economic activity, the competition would neither be so fierce nor the fallow period so short. The dependency on land would not be so total and exclusive, and they would recognise that their stake in peace ought to be higher than its current level since their livelihood could only best be secured thereby.

The strong belief of whole groups in the area in the invincible supernatural powers of protection offered by shrine worship and the exaltation of valour and war by groups such as Kojor, Eblembi, Obam, and Kikoko in Ugep Urban suggest the complicity of ideational culture in the perpetuation of war. These beliefs, fired up by intoxicating songs of past bravery, strengthened the desire in an otherwise bored populace to experiment with the new ideas learnt from old rituals and those that were recently diffused to them. A regular source of some of the war cults was Agwagune with whom the Ugep people enjoy close historical ritual ties that often mean the same thing as a military alliance.

The membership of the war groups found ready allies in retired veterans who, one suspects, were not adequately demobilised or deprogrammed by the Nigerian Armed Forces, despite the existence of a resettlement centre at Oshodi, Lagos. It was these veterans who, on both sides of the conflict, it was alleged, organised training in modern combat strategies and the use of weapon systems for their local hirers. Thus the war was fought on the basis of a bizarre co-operation between modern military methods and methods derived from the most ancient and occult traditions (see the subsection on "War Technology"). If scud missiles were available, they would probably have launched them. But they would also have clung to the belief that the naked virgin girl waving a broomstick in front of the advancing troops was offering them protection from enemy bullets.

The most disturbing aspect of the war was the institutional rise in both communities of what approximates a standing army. This development was hitherto completely alien to Yakurr institutional arrangements. The traditional war mobilisation effort was conducted on an *ad hoc* basis, on the spur of the moment, in heated times when sentiments seemed to act in outright defiance of seated reason. That there was a deliberate preparation for war taking place at a time of relative peace was a spin-off of a global illogic traceable to Karl Von Clausewitz's oft paraphrased dictum to the effect that *If you will have peace, you must prepare for war.* The illogic of this doctrine must be exposed and its danger demonstrated to the Yakurr communities. Peace can only result from a preparation for peace, and not war. By working close to such positive cultural structures, there is a greater promise of building a culture of peace based on a traditional pattern, which is therefore sustainable.

An Elder in the Apostolic Church at Idomi blamed the conflict on the *Yabol* and their council of chiefs in charge of affairs in both Ugep and Idomi. For him, the chiefs thought it prestigious for them to be accorded the dubious fame of having had a war fought and won during their time. For him, instead of the *Yabol Lopon* organising community development projects in their communities, they engaged in the yearly acquisition of firearms and dangerous weapons, which they stored in their armoury.

In this statement, we find an intersection among patriarchy, pro-natalism and a war-mongering worldview among the people. Nevertheless, although this was the report filed in from the Idomi field, it is on record that the *Obol Lopon* of Ugep, owing to his pacifist posture during the crisis, was personally threatened by youth who would have nothing but revenge for their murdered kin. A season of alienation in fact ensued during which it appeared the warriors of Ugep society were unwilling or unable to heed the pleas for peace made by the *Obol Lopon* and his council. The Elder's assertion may therefore not be wholly correct. The nature of democracy among this people poses a challenge to peace initiatives in the area.

The Yakurr War of 1992 claimed lives and property on a scale that was unprecedented in the entire history of conflict in Yakurr society. In comparative terms, the human loss was minimal and uncertain. For strategic reasons, there were conflicting records but the lives lost could not have been less than ten or more that twenty. More than ten houses were burnt. The secondary school at Idomi was burnt. Looters from both communities raided the school's laboratory and carted science equipment away. Other losses included the destruction of yam barns with tubers and seedlings meant for that year's planting season.

War Technology

The belief of the Yakurr people in the use of invocation and incantations to fight their wars was one of the prominent features of the Yakurr War of 1992. In the war, the Ugep invoked the aid of the war deity *Ojilikportor (a.k.a. Eyum)*. *Ojilikportor* is a society that has all its functions connected with incantations and the use of herbs and roots. The priests of this cult produce concoctions that are swallowed by warriors to provide them with immunity from gunshots and machete cuts.

The Ugep/Idomi War of 1992 involved in addition to this "Juju" the use of *Ekpondem* (a.k.a. *Akumakpa*) which was used to complement *Ojilikportor*. In interviews held with the *Okpebri* of Ugep (whose duty it is to declare war) and the Chief Priest of *Ekpondem*, a young man simply called "Cato", I surmised that the use of *Ekpondem* was further proof of a systematic build-up of military and pseudo-military alliances within the region. *Ekpondem* is a society imported from among the Agwanume, a people notorious for their powerful charms. The strong belief of many youngsters in the potency of *Ekpondem* made them eager to join it in order to display their prowess in war.

From FGDs it was gathered that the weapon systems used during the 1929 Ugep/Idomi war underwent a change in the recent war of 1992. While machetes, clubs and guns were used during the 1929 war, the two communities during this recent war used catridge rifles, machine guns and even locally produced explosives. As noted, however, the primitive weapons were not completely avoided.

Planning was carried out by the elders, ably assisted by the young men and war societies and social organisations some of which provided funds for munitions and food. Female initiates of *Ekpondem* took food to warriors at the war front.

Impact of the Ugep-Idomi War of 1992

The effects of the 1992 Idomi-Ugep conflict were multi-dimensional and cut across the social, political, economic and cultural spheres. Socially, this war caused an automatic stoppage of the construction of the Ugep-Idomi road project, and the Idomi electrification project, whose contracts were awarded in 1991 and 1992 respectively.

Politically, Idomi was cut off from her kith and kin and political friends. During electioneering campaigns, politicians from Ugep did not go to Idomi for their campaigns for fear of either being molested or killed. Politicians from other areas also were afraid to go down to Idomi for campaigns. This resulted in Idomi being politically alienated from other parts of the state in particular and country in general. But for the cancellation of the result the impact of that war in political terms could have been resonating even now.

From an economic point of view, the Idomi community saw the war as a blessing in disguise. According to one source, "never in the history of Idomi had we sold a basin of *garri* for ₦700.00 (seven hundred naira), except now that there is no link with Ugep people." According to the respondent, this was because "strangers now came through Adim directly into Idomi to buy from us, the producers, instead of the Ugep playing a middleman role in our business." Moreover, the war caused the re-opening of the Idomi-Adim road constructed by communal labour in 1974 which was abandoned by the Idomi people. Since the commercial link between Idomi and Ugep was cut off, the Idomi people had to take a circuitous route to Calabar (the state capital) for all their commercial ventures and the attendant economic strain and stress no doubt greatly minimised the benefits of the "blessings in disguise".

More latently, the disruption of the educational system through the involvement of students in the war retarded prospective progress. While their counterparts in other towns were intensifying their studies through extra-mural lessons, for example, the basic school programme was destabilised in both communities thus adversely affecting the chances of that generation of finalists to gain admission to the university. It would be interesting to empirically investigate the relative proportions gaining admission among those school children normally resident in the two communities and examine those figures in a trend analysis.

Perhaps the most salient effect of the Ugep-Idomi war was the least calculable but the most far-reaching. One refers here to the ruination of trust and its replacement with mutual suspicion and unalloyed hatred. Reciprocal feelings of distrust and anger were largely responsible for the great delay that attended the peace process, and that made it so tenuous in the first place. It was for this reason that a peaceful resolution of the conflict took five years (1992-1997) to complete.

Arbitration into the conflict started immediately the war ceased in 1992. Government swung into action and inaugurated a seven-person judicial panel of inquiry into the conflict. Traditional rulers from the Yakurr villages headed by the clan head of Assiga involved themselves in the arbitration process but these moves failed. Independent bodies such as the Yakurr Development Union (Lagos, Jos, Onitsha, Ikom and Benin branches) made attempts at arbitration to no avail. Even traditional rulers from the neighbouring Abi Local Government Area waded into the dispute, but failed in their mission. Various churches organised themselves into arbitration groups and attempted a peaceful settlement. Among them were the Assemblies of God Church, the Presbyterian Church, and the Apostolic Church. Women and cultural organisations also made frantic efforts at a resolution of the conflict, which finally yielded dividends on 22 February, 1997.

According to the secretary of the Apostolic Church arbitration committee that attempted peace settlement on 4 December, 1993, several reasons were adduced for the failure of these reconciliation attempts. First, government issued a white paper on this conflict whose recommendations were not implemented as a result of a high court litigation on it by the Ugep people. The Court ruled in favour of Ugep. No doubt, the acrimony surrounding the litigation itself further delayed peace-building. Perhaps more significantly, the arbitration mechanisms were not sensitive to the fact that by the time the war was underway, new patterns of leadership had emerged with new stakes in the conflict. The arbitration process did not seem to take cognizance of the possible cleavage between these leaders and the more traditional ones, hence they were not integrated in the peace parleys that were held. Furthermore, it did not appear as though the kin sources of the conflict were taken into account. The implication here was that while arbitration was taking place, those responsible for the war in the first place were sidelined and left correspondingly free to carry on their war by other means.

Conclusions

The background to the conflict as presented in this paper portrays Yakurr territory as a area where land-related conflicts are to be expected, especially as the worldview of the people remains ardently pro-natalist. The widespread belief in fertility spirits and their support for a large population, captured in the aphorism *"Lesou leta otoba"* (a large population is better than a machete), means that fertility can be expected to increase even more rapidly in the next decade. Arable and residential land will come under increasing pressure and, as tension builds, more wars may be expected.

A reasonable solution to the crisis is to explore the possibility of locating agro-allied industries and the establishment of tertiary educational institutions in the area. This recommendation is designed to break the total focus of the youth on farming as well as persuade them practically to appreciate other viable options in life. Once they perceive their livelihood to be more reasonably protected by a culture of peace it is less likely that they will readily go to war. It must be borne in mind that, as our analysis has shown, warfare among the Yakurr is deeply rooted in economic, demographic and cultural arrangements that are meant to enhance welfare. The pressure of population on land resources has resulted in the dysfunctionality of the traditional patterns and it is through war that the former interests may be preserved. It is either that these interests change or they must be secured by other means.

A careful study of the calendar of war displays the seasonality of conflict in the region. A panoramic view of the Ugep/Mkpani, (1987), Ugep/Idomi (1992), Ugep/Adim (1996), conflicts indicates that war has a greater likelihood to occur during planting seasons than at other times. This pattern suggests a need to establish Farmers' Peace Committees made up of influential pacifists from other groups so that they can pursue bilateral and multilateral prospects of development and co-operation among themselves. Such peace committees would monitor implications of political

affairs in the area and liaise with the grassroots population on the one hand and government and non-governmental organisations (NGOs), on the other.

Whatever strategies the committees adopt must be continuous and sustainable and made more pronounced at planting seasons. Nationally monitored peace games with appreciable rewards could be organised during the planting season in a bid to make the conduct of war less likely as any signs to that effect would be detected early. The two communities should be encouraged to examine the traditional system of acquiring land with a view to making it viable. The arbitration panel set up by government should work continuously to demarcate boundaries and to erect suitable pillars to make them less ambiguous. Toward this end, the state government should set up a land allocation and boundary demarcation committee comprising government officials and members of the warring communities.

Joint commercial ventures should be embarked upon whose industrial site should be on land jointly owned by the two communities as a means to diffusing tension there, and building co-operation instead. Similarly, workshops and symposia should be organised by the different cadres of participants in order to spread progressive awareness to the area, as well as impart non-violence and conflict management skills to the people.

References

Forde, Daryll 1950. "Double Descent Among the Yako". *African Systems of Kinship and Marriage*. (eds) A.R. Radcliffe-brown and Daryll Forde. London: Oxford University Press 284-332.

... 1964. *Yako Studies.s* London: Oxford University Press.

Harris, Rosemary. 1965. *The Political Organisation of the Mbembe, South Eastern Nigeria*. London: HMSO.

Obono, O.M. 1995. "The Cultural Process and Vital Registration: From the Demography of Africa to African Demography", *West African Journal of Archaeology* 25 (2): 19-45.

Ubi, O.A. 1981. "*The Yakurr: A Reconstruction of Pre-Colonial History*". Ph.D. Dissertation, University of Lagos, Lagos.

Chapter 4

Shedrack Gaya Best. Alamveabee Efhiraim Idyorough. Zainab Bayero Shehu

Communal Conflicts and the Possibilities of Conflicts Resolution in Nigeria: A Case Study of the Tiv-Jukun Conflicts in Wukari Local Government Area, Taraba State

Introduction

> You see, these Jukun people are people who loved trouble since from the day that God created them. They will never live in peace with anybody. How can you make peace with a Jukun man?
>
> *A Tiv interviewee at Wukari, 6.08.97.*

> A Tiv man, what will make him happy? Nothing, except that which he chooses. They are a very stubborn people and you can't satisfy them permanently.
>
> *A Fulani interviewee at Wukari, 28.07. 97.*

> The Tiv people have a unique problem, different from others. They don't consider anybody of fame, except criminals who cause trouble. They prefer such people to lead them to prison. The Tiv have no structure of authority. If for example, you bring their elders to talk about peace, they may agree but the youths will reject it, and it stands. The elders will remain helpless.
>
> *A Jukun interviewee at Wukari, 28.07.97.*

The above citations typically demonstrate the types of stereotypes that were found among conflict-prone communities in Nigeria. People on each side of the conflict divide believed that the problem was with the opponent, but never with themselves. They initially created the impression that the conflict was not manageable because the actors on the other side would not co-operate. This was one of the challenges that each conflict manager was confronted with. In Wukari where this conflict occurred, these stereotypes had to be demolished in the process of conflict management.

During the past three decades, dysfunctional conflicts occurred between major ethnic and religious communities in Nigeria. These conflicts were not confined to any specific geo-political region of the country. Recent examples include the seemingly unceasing religious and communal conflicts in Nigeria, the Tiv-Jukun conflicts, the Owerri massacres, the communal conflicts on the Jos Plateau, the Takum conflicts, the Warri conflicts, the Ife-Modakeke conflicts, etc. The repeatedness of these conflicts meant that explanations and solutions should be found for them. In addition, common denominators should be identified. The understanding of the conflicts was a necessary pre-condition for sorting out the issues for possible resolution. This was especially important in view of the fact that for a long time, conflict resolution and peacebuilding were grossly underdeveloped in Nigeria. While some of the conflicts represented evidence of changing times, they also suggested that the traditional institutions and mechanisms for conflict management were becoming increasingly weaker.

This case study was made mainly in Wukari Local Government Area of Taraba State. It sought to identify the main issues and underlying causes of the conflict between the Jukun and Tiv communities. We classify this conflict, along Edward Azar's classifications (Azar 1990) as a local social conflict. This is because the conflict was characterised by large scale human suffering and atrocity, prolonged threats to human rights, and to stability, etc. Furthermore, the conflict had structural, economic, political and resource dimensions.

The Conflict

The conflict being analysed here was the prolonged dispute that the Junkun and Tiv communities in Taraba State had over land, traditional rulership, political authority and differences, and fears of domination and marginalisation. This conflict burst out in 1990, and lasted for almost two years. It left an exceptionally high death toll and destruction of property. The carnage associated with the conflict was also probably unprecedented in the history of communal conflicts in Nigeria. The conflict completely changed the look and social profile of Wukari Local Government, and this may take a long time before it is rebuilt.

Toward a Theoretical Explanation of the Conflict

There are competing theoretical paradigms in conflict analysis; few of these are generic. This conflict can, however, be perhaps better explained in terms of Robert Ardrey's "territorial imperative" (Ardrey, 1967). In his study, Ardrey traced the animal origins of property, nations and territoriality. A territory is defined as an area of space which an animal or group of animals defends as an exclusive preserve. It is within such territory that the basic needs and interests of such animals are gratified. These needs include security of space and food, identity, prestige, etc. (ibid:5). They therefore defend such an area at all costs, and strive to keep out those who undermine their interests and needs.

All animals, including humans, have a sense of territoriality, and would patrol, secure and defend their own environment (land mainly). This applies to physical territory, girl friends, wives, families etc., as it does to nations, states and ethnic communities. These animal traits apply to man by evolutionary inheritance. To Ardrey, "If we defend the title to our land or the sovereignty of our country, we do it for reasons no different, no less innate, no less ineradicable, than do lower animals" (ibid). Conflict erupts when the claims of one party to land and territory become incompatible with the desire of others to satisfy their own basic interests and needs within the same physical territory. This, to a large extent, fits the case in Wukari where the Jukun have tried to keep a defined space as their preserve. A Tiv informant likened the Wukari conflict to the case in the time of the Pharaohs in Egypt, when the Egyptians were recorded in the Bible to have felt increasingly threatened by the growth in the population of the Israelites. They had to curb it to assert their sense of control and ownership in Egypt.

Objectives and Scope of the Study

As stated earlier, the main objective of this study was to unveil the underlying causes of the conflict with a view to identifying the possible issues for resolution. To facilitate this, we summarised the principal identity groups in the conflict as well as other stake holders. These same actors were capable of playing constructive roles in peacebuilding and the resolution of the conflict.

The study was mainly preoccupied with the most recent clashes from 1990 to 1992. However, to achieve a proper understanding of the conflicts within this period, we did a historical overview of events and issues in the relationship between the two communities which, in the final analysis, found a vent in the 1990-1992 imbroglio.

Data Sources

The main source of data for this study was oral interviews and discussions conducted in Wukari Local Government Area of Taraba State. We chose this method because of the opportunity it gave us to probe our interviewees with an enormous amount of detail. This enabled us to get the perspectives of the conflicting communities in the conflict, their understanding of the issues, their perceptions of their colleagues on the other side of the conflict, and what they believed to be the issues for negotiation, or which issues were non-negotiable.

We talked to key Jukun and Tiv leaders, in Wukari. We were also privileged to interview the Aku Uka (King) of Wukari. We could not do the same for the Tor Tiv in Gboko due mainly to logistic and time constraints. As the interviews progressed, we discovered that boundary issues were only marginal in the conflict, and that the theatre of the conflict was Wukari.

In addition to the Tiv and the Jukun, we also interviewed leaders of other communities living in Wukari, such as the Igbo, Hausa, Kanuri, Nupe, and Igala. Some of these people had lived in Wukari for over fifty years. We believed that as third-party observers, they had their own accounts of the conflict which could further our understanding. We also talked to youth leaders and women activists.

Further to these sources, we examined the main publications that were rolled out by Jukun and Tiv authors on these conflicts. They were quite informative. We also obtained some data from archival sources. We deliberately used fictitious names for our interviewees.

Limitation

The research on the Jukun side was quite smooth and relatively easy and straight forward. However, that of the Tiv was an uphill task. This was mainly because the Tiv lived in nearly impossible terrain. Their villages were mostly inaccessible during the rainy season. The only easy means of getting there were on motorcycles, pick-ups and tractors. We chose to use motorcycles, riding through long distances of rough, sandy and murky roads.

Secondly, the egalitarian nature of Tiv society sometimes had its advantages, but was often a liability. With the exception of one case, it was difficult to interview individuals. Once visitors (researchers) were sighted, it became a community affair. There was no secrecy about the interviews. Passers-by could also stop to listen to what was being discussed, and would join the discussion and make contributions. What we ended up having on the Tiv side were group discussions (perhaps unintended focus groups) rather than private interviews.

The Barbarity of the Conflicts

The Tiv-Jukun conflicts were characterised by barbarity and atrocities of unimaginable proportions. The methods by which the two sides killed each other were at best heartless. Road blocks were mounted by each side, and "the enemy" was identified and slaughtered or shot in the nearby bush. Often, victims were set ablaze. Beheading was a common method of killing. There were also reports of pregnant women who had their wombs cut open with knives, and the babies were removed and put on their dead mothers' breasts. Residential houses, business premises, schools, and other public places were set ablaze and pulled down by the warriors. Looting of property and foodstuff by opportunists was a mark of the conflict. Signs of the devastation of Wukari Local Government Area were still visible at the time of fieldwork (1997) given that the Government failed to assist the victims to rebuild their property.

Although it was known that the Tiv-Jukun conflicts were perhaps the most violent and well organised ever witnessed outside the Nigerian civil war, no data existed about the exact figure of casualties in this imbroglio. The Tiv and the Jukun both agreed that it was impossible to peg a figure of the casualties. Some people who went missing can only be assumed dead since their bodies were not sighted anywhere.

It was shameful that government at all levels did not give this conflict the amount of attention it deserved especially at the end of the hostilities. In the typical government manner, once fighting was crushed by use of superior military force, the assumption was that peace had been achieved. No effort was made at peacebuilding. Rather, units of the Nigerian Army deployed to the area remained in the place up to the time of fieldwork. Often, they were engaged in extortion at the road blocks they mounted.

The role of the Police in quelling the conflicts was very controversial. They left a tale of woes behind. It was alleged by some of our interviewees that the police did more destruction than the conflicting parties did to each other. One District Head was sure that the police looted foodstuff and carted them away in trucks, and thereafter, shot dead any persons in sight, and finally set the town ablaze. It was outside our scope to verify these claims, but the mere fact that some of our interviewees believed that the police did not help de-escalate the conflict, but did just the opposite, deserves a mention here. The allegation was that the police had been paid to fight on the side of one of the parties in the conflict.

Jukun Perspective of the Conflict

The Jukun contended that the Tiv arrived the Benue valley in the late 18th century and met the Jukun at their present locations which they dominated for centuries in the ancient Kwararafa Empire. The Tiv were also said to have sought their permission before establishing their earliest settlements, including Gboko. The Jukun added that they taught the Tiv how to wear clothes, as well as the concept of rulership. A section of the Tiv were once placed under the Aku Uka, thanks to the colonialists, and were then said to be very loyal people. They were initially used as messengers and help hands for the Jukun. Finally, that they migrated into Jukunland based on their hunger for farmlands.

The perspective of the Jukun on this conflict was thus shaped by one philosophy: that the Tiv were in-comers and settlers in Wukari, that the Jukun were the indigenes of Wukari, and therefore, landlords. The Jukun were believed to own the land, but they gave portions of it to the earliest Tiv immigrants when they first arrived. As settlers, therefore, the Jukun expected that the Tiv had no claim to lands which, in the first instance, were given to them by their 'hosts', the Jukun.

Secondly, they viewed with suspicion the ambitious orientation of the Tiv expressed by their desire to lead Wukari politically on the one hand (by daring to be interested in the Chairmanship of the Local Government Council especially), and to get involved in its traditional affairs on the other. The Jukun found it embarrassing when the Tiv referred to Wukari, which they regarded as their ancestral, political and spiritual headquarters, as a land belonging to the Tiv people at most, and at least, to both Tiv and Jukun.

Tiv Perspective of the Conflict

The Tiv understanding of the conflict was based on a number of grounds. First, they rejected in its entirety, the suggestion by the Jukun that they were strangers, squatters, or rural farmers attracted to Wukari by the fertility of the land. The Tiv believed that they were not squatters but co-landlords for a number of reasons. First, they were there before the Jukun. Secondly, even those who came at a later date than the Jukun lived in Wukari for too long to be seen as squatters and in-comers any longer. Thirdly, the Constitution of the Federal Republic of Nigeria allowed people who settled in a place to have full rights, to live in any part of the country.

According to Tiv account, the name 'Wukari was a corrupted form of a Tiv word called *Waka*, the name of the Tiv man who first settled there. "Waka" was believed by the Tiv to be the centre of a Tiv ritual and traditional religious practice called "Aseta". They contended that in pre-colonial times, the Tiv settled down far beyond the boundaries of present Wukari Local Government Area, and that when the Tiv first settled at Wukari, the Jukun were still at the location of the ancient Kwararafa Kingdom, some eighty-three kilometres north of Wukari.[2] The climax of this argument was that both the Jukun and the white men met the Tiv at Wukari, and that it was the Tiv who invited the Jukun to Wukari. Many young Tiv people believe this story.

The earliest Jukun immigrants in "Waka" (the Mbakpa-Riga, and much later, the Wakpai), according to Tiv account, passed on to Akwana. This source added that the Jukun later migrated from Akwana to "Waka" when the white man came and created new political boundaries. In this process, the name was changed from "Waka" to Wukari.[3] The Tiv were said to have left Wukari en masse because with colonialism, it was becoming urbanised and the Tiv naturally hated living in towns. They preferred rural areas for farming. The Tiv opined that once the Jukun settled at "Waka" and named it Wukari, they turned the place into their own, and would not accept even the Tiv who first settled there to share it with them! This position was at best an outrage to the Jukun.

Another Tiv source contended that while the Jukun began to move southward in the 19th century as a result of pressure from the Fulani to the north, the Tiv were moving north-eastward and in other directions. In the process of these movements, both the Jukun and the Tiv allegedly met at Wukari. Using this argument, the opinion was that Wukari belonged to both the Tiv and the Jukun. That by the time the colonialists came, the two communities were interwoven. Thus, the claim of the Jukun was unacceptable to the Tiv.

These conflicting claims were the tonic that sustained this conflict. The other issues raised by the conflict, such as land, territoriality, boundaries, politics of participation or exclusion in the local government, employment, denial of indigenisation letters to the Tiv, the siting of government projects, involvement of the Tiv in the traditional council of Wukari, etc., derived from the claim of settlership or non-indigeneship. If, for instance, the Tiv agreed that they were settlers in Wukari, and gave up all the claims that indigenes made on farmlands and the local political processes, this conflict would possibly have been over long time ago

Historical Perspective of the Conflict

The most remarkable political factor within the area in question up to the 17th century, and into the late 19th century, was the ancient Kwararafa Kingdom. The location of the Kingdom headquarters, according to the Aku Uka of Wukari, was eighty-three kilometres north of present Wukari, between Dan Anacha and Sabon Gida in Gassol Local Government Area of Taraba State. Incidentally, there was a large population of Tiv rural farmers in this area.

The Tiv migrated into the Benue valley form Cameroon in the 18th century, by which time the Kwararafa Kingdom had been a dominant political kingdom in the region for centuries, albeit with diminished political significance. Its fame was highest in the 17th century when Kano was fought and defeated. An attempt was also made at Katsina. If the Jukun were good warriors at this time, they were poor political administrators. Unlike the Dan Fodio forces, for instance, they failed to consolidate their gains.

Be that as it may, until the Tiv migration in the 18th century, according to the Aku Uka, the Jukun had no boundaries with any ethnic group except the Kanuri to the north east, the Hausa to the north west, the Igbo and the Atlantic ocean to the south. The Jukun identified nearly every other ethnic group in the Middle Belt, such as Idoma, Igala, Igbira, Gwari, Nupe, Alago, Eggon, Mada, Goemai, Angas, Jarawa, Taroh, etc., as Jukun descendants,[4] with whom the Jukun had no history of conflicts. Some of them were said to be tributary states of ancient Kwararafa. They regarded the Tiv as strangers who came into their midst in the 18th century, and messed up the hither-to peaceful relationship between them and their 'brothers'. The Jukun recalled that they related with the Hausa, Kanuri, and Fulani, but more with the Kanuri with whom they had earlier migrated from Yemen. The account added that while the Kanuri settled in the Chad Basin, the Jukun moved southward and established the Kwararafa Kingdom.[5]

Interestingly, there were no records of wars fought between the Tiv and the Jukun in pre-colonial times. Rather both groups, being neighbours, often fought on the same side, as was the case when the notorious slave raider (Dankaro) raided both the Tiv and the Jukun for slaves.

Another isolated example was the 1874 episode when the Fulani Emir of Muri, Mohammed Nya, succeeded in imposing tributes on the Jukun, payable in foodstuff and slaves (30-40 requested at any one time). The Jukun often raided their Tiv neighbours in turn for these slaves (Hogben and Krik-Greene, 1966: 450). The Fulani did not, however, succeed in establishing any permanent political control over either the Tiv or the Jukun. However, Muri once went as far as Katsina Ala, sacking its population, burning villages and catching slaves, but no lasting political administration could be established (*ibid*).

This was the situation between the Tiv and the Jukun until the arrival of the British, which was the next significant milestone in the history of the two communities. By 1900, the Tiv and the Jukun had both taken positions within the Benue valley. However, that of the Tiv was comparatively more fluid than any other ethnic nationality based on their growing population and ever increasing demand for, and reliance on, land. Relations between the two groups at this time was cordial due to a number of reasons. First, the Aku Uka was the only paramount ruler, since the Tiv lacked a centralised political authority. Secondly, land was not yet an issue that anybody would fight over. Thirdly, the Tiv worked as rural farmers and had no cause to interfere with the administration of the Jukun. Fourthly, party politics was absent.

Table 1: Population of Wukari Division by Ethnic Groups(1946)

Tribe	Total	Percentage of Total
Tiv	40,400	37
Kuteb	20,284	19
Junkun	10,867	10
Ichen	6.775	6
Hausa	5,287	5
Chamba	4,500	4
Others	20,229	12

Source: *National Archives, Kaduna (NAK/MAK/PROF/4377)*

However, the Tiv continued to occupy more farmlands during this period, and their numbers continued to increase. By the 1991 census, through 1946 (as evident in Table 1), the Tiv officially out-numbered the Jukun in Wukari Division. This was the same for the 1952 census. Curiously, the Jukun were not even listed as one of the ethnic groups in Wukari Division in 1952! However, the Tiv remained the single largest ethnic group in Wukari Division at this time. The Jukun were more urban-based, and took to schooling, fishing, and other urban occupations. More significantly, the Tiv were the largest ethnic group in the Nigerian Middle Belt. It was no surprise that their culture dominated their immediate neighbours, just like the Igbo did in Eastern Nigeria, the Yoruba in Western Nigeria, and the Hausa/Fulani in Northern Nigeria.

Indirect Rule

Under this policy introduced by the British, and based on its reliance on existing political institutions, the Tiv in Wukari and Muri were placed under the Emirate of Muri from 1901 until 1926, when they were placed under Wukari, mainly because the Tiv had no traditional monarch. By implication, those Tiv under Wukari came under the Aku Uka's jurisdiction.[6] The British were perhaps overwhelmed by the glorious political history and rich culture of the Jukun, an element that was relatively lacking among their Tiv neighbours. This administrative development further integrated the Tiv and the Jukun, and it was advantageous to the Akus at this time because of the implications for tax, territory and prestige. There was no record to suggest that during the early era of Tiv migrations into Wukari Division, the Jukun saw any danger. Thus, the stiffest of the conflict between the Tiv and the Jukun could be found within this historico-geo-political radius created by the colonialists from 1926 to 1933.

The southern part of the Tiv was ruled from Obudu and Ogoja, a people the Jukun also believed to be their descendants. A Tiv Division was created in 1933, an exercise that brought together the Tiv people, including those in Katsina Ala, under one administration. The Tiv in Wukari were still seen as settlers, and nothing about their administration was considered.

The migration of Tiv farmers into Wukari Division during the early years of colonialism became a subject of concern to the colonialists, and they deliberately tried to keep out the Tiv from what they believed to be Jukun territory. This was based on the conclusion of anthropological studies which suggested that the Jukun had a strong culture capable of being corrupted by the Tiv once they migrated in large numbers into Wukari. This, in itself, was another element of the colonialists' general policy of non-interference practised all over northern Nigeria. The policy in Wukari was led by J.M. Fremantle from 1918. The policy, however, could not be sustained because the Tiv could not be bothered with the concept of ethnic and territorial boundaries, especially when there were fertile, uncultivated lands that stretched for miles.

The colonial regime also created the Wukari Federation Local Council with the Aku Uka as Chairman. Membership was drawn from Wukari, Takum and Donga districts. As such, the main ethnic groups (namely Jukun, Kuteb, Chamba) were represented in the council. The Tiv, based on the philosophy of their being settlers and immigrants, were not represented. The fact that other ethnic groups were represented did not necessarily demonstrate that the Tiv were discriminated against. Rather, as stated earlier, it was on the understanding by both the 'indigenous' ethnic groups and the colonialists, that Wukari was not a Tiv sphere of influence, and that they belonged to Tiv Division. This notion was passed down to subsequent generations.

The Tiv protested their non-inclusion in the Wukari Federation Council, but this did not significantly alter the way they were perceived in Wukari Division (simply settlers). A section of the colonial regime represented by Richard Palmer, the Lt. Governor, reasoned along with the Jukun that the Tiv were immigrants in Wukari and had no grounds to feel that, as immigrants, they qualified for representation (NAK/SNP/17/K.2441 vol. 1) . The agitation for inclusion by the Tiv, which began in 1947, materialised ten years later when in 1957, the Tiv were given representation within the Wukari General Purpose Council (WGPC) of the Federation Native Authority. In 1960 when the British left, the Tiv were displaced from the council. Their place was taken over by the Jukun.

The Historical Role of Party Politics in the Conflict

The origins of the conflict between the Tiv and the Jukun were traced by a section of the Jukun, and nearly all Tiv interviewees, back to the introduction of party politics in Nigeria. The contest for electoral victory between the Tiv and Jukun, based on numerical superiority, became pronounced, especially from 1959. In 1945 and 1949, Mallam Ibrahim Sangari, a Jukun candidate, was elected to represent the Wukari Federal Constituency in the Federal House of Representatives. This was the beginning of representative party politics in northern Nigeria. The Jukun had a natural sense of security with this election. However, the Tiv increasingly became aware of their number in Wukari Division, and that this number could be translated into a political weapon. The political mobilisation and conscientisation of the Tiv, including those in Wukari Division, was enhanced with the formation of the United Middle Belt Congress under the leadership of Joseph Tarka.

To the embarrassment of the Jukun, the Tiv presented a candidate (Charles Ta..gur Gaza) under the platform of the UMBC for the 1956 federal elections, on the eve of independence. Tangur Gaza conveniently defeated Mallam Ibrahim Sangari of the NPC. The Tiv thus graduated from mere rural settler-farmers into a significant political factor that threatened the Jukun within an area they had previously considered to be their sphere of jurisdiction. In effect, peace was to elude the communities on this matter for a long time

By 1954, the relationship between the Tiv and the Jukun had taken a more hostile turn. The Jukun and the Tiv belonged to two different political parties. The Tiv in Wukari Division, like their brothers in Benue Province, were strong supporters of the Joseph Tarka-led UMBC. They were mobilised into the UMBC partly on the account that they should not, even in Wukari, sacrifice their Tiv identity for land. The Jukun on the other hand, were largely supporters of the ruling Northern Peoples' Congress (NPC). They enjoyed the support of the northern regional government. The mere fact that Charles Tangur Gaza won the elections on the platform of the UMBC, a party perceived to be Tiv, and that he defeated the NPC candidate, raised so much dust in Wukari.

Thus, when the so-called Tiv riots began in 1959-1960, it capitalised on these existing divisions. The clashes started mainly between the supporters of the NPC and the UMBC.[7] The riots were motivated by perceived marginalisation and insecurity on the part of the Tiv, and their feeling that the members of the NPC were responsible for their condition. The Tiv were especially suspicious of the authoritarian Native Administration system and its attempt to forcefully penetrate the hither-to egalitarian Tiv society. They saw the Native Authorities as an embodiment of the NPC. This campaign was tagged *nande-ior,* meaning "arson or burning down houses" in Tiv. It brought many Jukun and Tiv people on a collision path. It was marked by large scale killings and burning of houses of people the Tiv believed to be NPC supporters. Because of the large Tiv population in Wukari, and because majority of the Jukun supported the NPC, the conflicts wrecked havoc on the Jukun.

In 1964, another round of violence broke out again tagged *atem tyo, and kura cha cha* meaning " head breaking" and "clear them all" respectively. Again, the targets were supporters of the NPC, most of whom were Hausa/Fulani and Jukun people. The First Republic was thus marked by enormous political hostilities between the Tiv and the Jukun.

The Military coup of 1966 brought about a natural end to these hostilities because of the ban on party activities. The Tiv people were contented that General Gowon, who came to power in July 1966 incorporated the leader of the UMBC. In addition, Chief Obafemi Awolowo whose Action Group forged an alliance with the UMBC was given a key position in the government of General Yakubu Gowon. They thus had a great sense of security. Thus, during the period of military rule, all was calm between the Tiv and the Jukun. Moreover, when Benue-Plateau State was created in 1967, both the Tiv and the Jukun were incorporated in the State.

When party politics resumed during the Second Republic, the Tiv and the Jukun were coincidentally in the same party (the National Party of Nigeria). Some Jukun and Tiv were in the Nigeria Peoples' Party (NPP). The leader of the UMBC in the First republic, Joseph Tarka, had led the NPN into Tivland,[8] and it became acceptable for the Tiv in Gongola State (now Taraba) to embrace the party. As such, the Tiv and the Jukun shared out the elective offices for Wukari. Mallam Ibrahim Sangari (Jukun) was running mate for the governorship candidate.

Sadly for the Jukun, the NPN did not form the government in Gongola State. The Great Nigeria Peoples' Party (GNPP) candidate who won the elections, Alhaji Abubakar Barde, decided to punch the Jukun where it hurt the most, by appointing a Tiv, Iyotyer Tor Musa, as the Chairman of Wukari Local Government.[9] The Jukun did all they could to avoid a repeat performance of this 'mishap'. Even though the NPN won the elections in Benue State, the NPN at the level of Gongola State was an opposition party. Thus, the Republic brought mixed feelings to the Jukun.

Embarrassingly enough, when Alhaji Bamanga Tukur won the governorship elections for Gongola State in 1983, he attributed his victory in Wukari, Takum, Bali and Sardauna Local Government councils to the numerical superiority of the Tiv, and accordingly appointed a Tiv, Dr. Samuel Tor Agbidye as Commissioner. This was yet another blow to the Jukun, who saw the Tiv gaining increased recognition in a state not considered to be theirs. After the 1983 coup that brought the General Muhammadu Buhari regime to power, all was calm between the Jukun and the Tiv. Moreover, the outrage created by the appointment of a Tiv commissioner had died a natural death with the coup.

When partisan politics returned under General Babangida,

with the local government elections of 1987, trouble resurfaced in the relationship between the two groups. Six candidates contested the elections (five Jukuns and one Hausa man). The Tiv formed an alliance with the Hausa Community, and a Tiv man was appointed as Deputy Chairman of Wukari Local Government. The Tiv also had four councillors in the Local Government Council. Since the Jukun were divided and had their votes split, the Hausa candidate, Alhaji Danladi Shehu, won the elections comfortably with the support of the Tiv. At the Taraba State level, the Tiv also recorded a major victory with the appointment of Hon. David Orbee Uchiv by Governor Jolly Nyame as Special Adviser. Indeed, Hon. Uchiv was appointed in the heat of the war between the two communities. The Jukun were enraged. They accused the Governor of showing open preference for the Tiv and indifference to the conflict.[10] The period witnessed the worst yet in violent confrontations between the Tiv and the Jukun.

In May 1993, the elected Chairman of Wukari Local Government, Mr. Samuel Adda (Jukun) was removed from office, and the entire Local Government Council was dissolved by the Taraba State Governor on behalf of the president. A sole administrator was appointed. This was another political setback for the Jukun. Before the year ended, General Sani Abacha sacked the Third Republic and assumed leadership of Nigeria. This again rested the case of party politics.

By the time elections were conducted on non-party basis in 1996, Wukari had not yet recovered from the 1990-1992 fracas. Many Tivs had been displaced and had not returned to their homes and farms. Some of those who returned could not be registered for elections. The situation, being far from normal, militated against any attempt to judge whether or not this wave of politics brought renewed confrontation. What was certain, though, was that the Tiv had been weakened, and the Jukun and other groups conducted these elections quietly and peacefully. This was the same for elections on party basis conducted in March 1997. No hostilities broke out. This was one of the outcomes of the fight of the Jukun: to keep the Tiv out of their political processes and therefore, enjoy 'peace' or at least weaken them to a point where they did not use their numbers to dictate political events in Wukari.

What was evident from this historical review was the fact that political issues and the fight for political control of Wukari, as well as participation and representation of Wukari at the state level, always caused tension and conflict between the Tiv and the Jukun. There were deep fears of political marginalisation. It was these fears, in the main, that translated into the conflicts that bedevilled the area.

The Theory of Previously Peaceful Co-existence

A basic assumption about the relationship between the Tiv and the Jukun was that they always co-existed peacefully. Opinion was however divided about this. A section of the Jukun opined that the relationship between the two groups was a marriage of convenience which was characterised by repeated episodes of conflict. The theory of peaceful co-existence was presented as a fallacy.

According to this source, from 1922 to date, the Tiv and the Jukun never lived in peace. The Jukun blamed the Tiv for causing all the trouble, not only with their non-Tiv neighbours, but also among themselves. A document was prepared by the Jukun titled *Historical Dates of Tiv Uprising in Nigeria Starting From 1960.* The document which contained twenty-three episodes of conflict, most of them violent, aimed at portraying the Tiv as an inherently aggressive society that would never live in peace with anybody, not even themselves. Discussions with the Tiv also showed that they had the same image of the Jukun: as a people inherently aggressive.

States Creation: The Jukun and the Tiv Disagree

When states were created by the Gowon regime in 1967, the Jukun and the Tiv came together in Benue-Plateau State. There were no records of large-scale violent clashes during this time. However, petitions were written by the Tiv against the Joseph Gomwalk government in the state, alleging in part that the Jukun were favoured to the detriment of the Tiv (Atoshi, 1992:13). Intra-Tiv affidavits, such as Godwin Dabo against Joseph Tarka, also became a subject of public interest.

When more states were to be created by the General Murtala Mohammed regime in 1976, the Tiv wished that the former Benue

Province (comprising Lafia, Nassarawa, Tiv, Otukpo and Wukari Divisions) should be put together to form Benue State. The case of Wukari, the Tiv expected, would not raise trouble given the so-called history of mutual co-existence between the Tiv and the Jukun, and the large number of Tiv in the area. The Jukun rejected this move based on fears of domination. They opted to be merged with the former Plateau province to form Plateau State. In an advertisement put up in the *New Nigerian* of 18.12.74, the Jukun explained that they would no longer welcome a situation where the Tiv who migrated into their lands in large numbers, would be allowed to dominate their politics and occupy their lands. They hoped to have their own lands, like any other ethnic group, over which they would exercise sovereignty. The Jukun ended up neither in Benue nor Plateau, but in Gongola State.

The Tiv in Wukari Division requested to be merged with Benue State, based on alleged discrimination, non-representation in the local authority councils, denials of social amenities, etc. The question of merging the Tiv in Wukari was a physical and logistic impossibility, unless the Jukun and other ethnic groups were also merged with Benue. The Justice Mamman Nasir's Boundary Commission, in 1976, rejected the demands of the Wukari Tiv, and defined them as immigrant settlers in Wukari. They, too, remained in Gongola State with the Jukun.

In 1992, Gongola State was split into two, and Taraba State was created, with the Mumuye, Jukun, Kuteb, Tiv and other groups as key ethnic groups. During the 1996 states creation exercise, the Tiv proposed that the problem between them and the Jukun could be solved once they were in the same state. They moved for the creation of Katsina Ala State which, it was hoped, would bring together the Tiv and Jukun mainly, as well as other ethnic groups.

On their part, the Jukun suspected that such a move was an attempt by the Tiv to dominate and further antagonise them. They argued that if they could not live in the same local government area with the Tiv, living in the same state was out of the question. The Jukun demanded, instead, for the creation of Kwararafa State, Neither of these two requests was granted. The Jukun and the Tiv have therefore remained in Taraba State as two strange bedfellows.

Manu Uva Vaase and Traditional Rulership in Wukari

The Tiv upon discovering the potential power in their numbers, also made attempts on the Aku Uka's stool in 1954. A 'peaceful' procession was led by a Tiv leader in Wukari called Manu Uva Vaase into Wukari town, the traditional and ancestral headquarters of the Jukun. He was accompanied by his fellow Tiv in a symbolic event that suggested to the Jukun that the Aku's throne was about to be taken over by the Tiv. Uva Vaase was carried shoulder high amidst dances and the glamorous events of a Tiv Aku. This was not taken kindly by the Aku Uka, Atoshi Ugbumanu, and his fellow Jukuns .

This episode threatened the Jukun people wherever they were. They reasoned that the Tiv "immigrants" had become too gutsy and had to be put in their correct place. The import of this episode as a factor in the conflict between the two communities was to be seen in the importance the Jukun attached to their tradition generally, and to the Aku's office in particular. We asked an Igbo man what anybody in Wukari ought to do in order in live in peace with the Jukun. He opined that the Jukun frown at anyone, however highly placed, interfering with their tradition and culture. In Jukun tradition, the Aku was a divine being. An offence against the Aku was an offence against the gods, a sacrilege.

Interestingly, a Tiv informant revealed that Uva Vaase's "triumphant entry" into Wukari was a Tiv way of having fun, a joke, and that it did not mean that the Tiv wanted the Aku Uka's stool. The Tiv simply wanted to announce their presence. If this was the case, it was indeed an expensive way of having fun.

Causes of the Conflict

The discussions in the previous sections demonstrate that the background for conflict had already been laid for both parties. We shall now consider some of the other factors that deepened the crisis of insecurity in Wukari.

Political Dimensions of the Conflict

The political issues in the conflict were in two parts: traditional and modern. The first had to do with the political participation in, and control of, Wukari Local Government Council as well as political appointments and other resources. The second was about membership of the Wukari Traditional Council, precisely the desire by the Tiv to be a part of this council, given that they consider themselves to be not only residents of the local government area but the majority numerically. As noted, past censuses where ethnic categories were identified had consistently given the Tiv numerical superiority in the defunct Wukari Division. The Jukun, however, explain that these figures were of migrant Tiv from Benue State.

Political Control of Wukari Local Government

This was perhaps the most vexed of all the issues. Wukari, like any other local government council in the federation, had a wide combination of ethnic groups. Among them were the Jukun, Tiv, Hausa, Fulani, Kanuri, Nupe, Igala, etc. Of these groups, the contest for power was stiffest between the Jukun and the Tiv. Often, the Hausa/Fulani would find it convenient to forge political alliances with especially the Tiv because of their number (any group in power would probably do the same). This was unacceptable to the Jukun. The Jukun desired that the Tiv, whom they regarded as settlers, should not meddle in the politics of the council.

Party politics, as earlier discussed, always caused distress time for group relations in Wukari, particularly between the Tiv and the Jukun. It was at such times that the attempt by each of the main ethnic groups to prove that they were the majority resulted in conflict, often bloody.

Since the local government reforms of 1976, Wukari Local Government produced only one Tiv Chairman in the person of Hon. Iyotyer Tor Musa. He was appointed by the GNPP government of Abubakar Barde to spite the Jukun who were supporters of the National Party of Nigeria in the Second Republic. His appointment was unacceptable to the Jukun. Hon. Iyotyer Tor Musa confirmed to us that for a long time, the Aku Uka would not talk to him. Relations between them later improved, however. Since that development, the Jukun ensured that no Tiv emerged as local government chairman in Wukari. According to one of the leaders of the other 'natural' ethnic groups in Wukari, one of the strategies adopted by the Jukun was to stir trouble during elections in order to drive Tiv voters out of Wukari. The Jukun would then hold their elections without the numerical terror of the Tiv, and a Jukun chairman would emerge. The Jukun however dismissed this theory.

On their part, the Tiv were sometimes pushed into forging alliances with the Hausa-Fulani-Kanuri group in Wukari. An example of this occurred during the tenure of Alhaji Danladi Shehu, who appointed a Tiv man as his deputy, notwithstanding the Jukun who believed that there was a plot and conspiracy against them by settler elements to deprive them of participation in the political affairs of their land. As Jukun leaders confirmed to us in Wukari, that the Jukun had already lost the land to the Tiv was bad enough. That they could be schemed out of the administration of Wukari was totally unacceptable. Thus, violent clashes like those of 1990-1992 provided a vent for such tensions to be let out.

Finally, the control of the local government council was only an instrument which both groups sought to use to achieve other broader goals. For instance, employment in the council generated trouble. The Tiv told us that their people were not given employment. They argued that there was not a single Tiv employee in Wukari Local Government Council, not even a messenger. Hon. Iyotyer Tor Musa told us that he hired two Tiv who were immediately sacked when he left office, but the two Jukuns he hired were retained. Following the war of 1990-1992, many of the Tiv teachers were made redundant as a result of the inability of the Local Government Council to re-open the schools. Thus, the Local Government Council remained an arena for this conflict.

Tiv Representation in Wukari Traditional Council

This was another heated issue in the conflict between the two groups. The Tiv insisted that they must be appointed into the Wukari Traditional Council, since they were residents of the Local Government Area who paid tax. Moreover, they reasoned that they were in the majority. We asked why the Tiv would want to be in a council that was chaired by the Aku Uka. Their explanation was that they wanted to be there for security reasons. Certain decisions were taken within the council which were detrimental to the interest of the Tiv people in Wukari, but there was no one to represent them.

The Jukun, however, totally rejected the idea of Tiv people being granted representation within a traditional council that was essentially Jukun. They asked why the Tiv traditional council in Gboko did not have other ethnic groups. More importantly, the ambition of the Tiv was believed to be sourced from a gross misunderstanding of the very strong Jukun culture and tradition. To be a member of the Jukun traditional council, a person had to be a title holder. These tiles were hereditary and guided by centuries of Jukun history and culture. They are not just given on a representative basis.

The Jukun explained that their culture was very different from that of the Tiv which was a colonial innovation to bring the people under one traditional administration. The conclusion of the matter was that the Jukun thought that to have the Tiv represented in the Wukari Traditional Council was a dream that would not be realised, because it conflicted with Jukun tradition. Meanwhile, a section of the Tiv described Wukari as an apartheid state based on their exclusion from the Traditional Council.

Political Appointments in Taraba State: The Tiv Quota

The Tiv contended that because they were indigenes of Wukari and other local government areas like Takum, Ibi, Gassol, Bali, Donga, Ardo Kola, etc., they were eligible for top political appointments in Taraba State along with the Jukun, Kuteb, Chamba, Mumuye, etc. Among such offices were commissioners, directors-general, chairmen and managers of government boards and parastatals, etc. On the other hand, the Jukun regarded the Tiv as settlers in Taraba State. They defined Benue State as the traditional sphere of the Tiv, and so all appointment of Tiv people should be in Benue State. This again raised the issue about the guiding philosophy of this conflict: the Tiv were settlers and should not demand equal rights with the indigenes. As such, the appointment of Tiv people into positions of responsibility in Taraba State was often an embarrassment to the Jukun, except for the few times when elective offices were shared by both groups, as was the case in the Second Republic when both were in the National Party of Nigeria (NPN).

The Siting of Government Projects

The Tiv accused the Jukun of using the machinery of Wukari Local Government and other levels of government to deny them access to modern government facilities in areas where Tiv populations were concentrated. This was one of the many reasons why the Tiv felt that they had to be in government.

Land as a Factor in the Conflicts

So much was said about land as the cause of this conflict that a casual observer would attribute these conflicts to land. Land meant farmlands from which rural agricultural communities made their living. This was related to, but also separate from, territory. In a wider sense, the land question also touched on territoriality. Each group sought to lay claim to jurisdictional authority as stated in our discussion on the ownership of Wukari as claimed by both identity groups in the conflict.

Opinion was divided among the Tiv and the Jukun about land as the underlying cause of the conflict. A large section of the Tiv people did not agree that land was the cause of the conflict. This view was also shared by a section of the Jukun, as well as most of the other ethnic groups interviewed in Wukari. The argument was that land served only as a vent for political and other forms of conflict. It was suggested that all forms of disagreement among the Tiv and Jukun found expression in farmlands. Most Jukuns insisted that the conflict was about land, and that other factors were secondary.

The position was that the Tiv occupied farmlands illegally, and refused to follow traditional laws of land administration which require them to first seek and obtain the permission of village heads, ward-heads, district heads, and paramount rulers. Furthermore, it was said that the Tiv upon arrival in Wukari were given lands either on loan or on lease, but later resisted (using even violent methods) releasing such lands back to their rightful Jukun owners on demand. This was the cause of the 1990 fight that started at Uban Igyaba compound. Moreover, the Tiv were said to invite other Tiv brothers of theirs from Benue State (the so-called third party) to settle on, and possess lands nearer to them without permission. This was believed by the Jukun to be a vicious circle that left the Jukun with a raw deal. The conflict of

1990-1992 was regarded as a way of defending and repossessing these lands from the migrant Tiv population.

Paradoxically, there was so much fallow land in Wukari that it made little sense for land to be a subject of conflict in the area.[11] Both the Tiv and Jukun agreed that land was not in short supply. However, the rate at which the Tiv occupied and exploited these lands threatened the Jukun. And the Tiv were not modest about their methodology either.

While it was expedient to admit that land could be a victim of the political dimensions of this conflict, it was also necessary to point out that land was capable of being a cause of this conflict in its own independent right. The problem could only be delayed for some time. A time would come, if events continued as they were, when land would become a leading question. The delay at the moment was caused by the fact that the Jukun, compared with the Tiv, were not great farmers. Their demand for land was, therefore, less than that of the Tiv. A journey round Wukari and many parts of Taraba State showed that the Tiv occupied an estimated 75% of the rural farms. Such a disproportionate share of lands in an area considered to be outside the Tiv sphere of influence was itself a time bomb. Worse still, the Tiv did not accept that they were settlers, and would not surrender the lands when the Jukun asked for them in future, because their very existence was tied to the land. They would be even reluctant to share. Thus, land was not just a secondary factor in these conflicts.

Land as a Symbol of Prestige

Land has become a symbol of prestige for the Jukun. Like the Kataf versus the Hausa/Fulani communities, like the Birom against the Hausa irrigation farmers in Jos, or the Tsayawa against the Hausa/Fulani in Tafawa Balewa, the supposedly aboriginal communities, often found themselves materially worse off than the so-called settler populations. Land was used as an instrument of political control and prestige. It was used to remind the settlers that they were only immigrants who lived at the pleasure of the indigenes. Traditionally, it did not matter how long these so-called settlers had settled in these lands. In conflict situation, land was an important factor. The Wukari conflict was an example of this.

The Theory of Tiv Long Plan to Colonise Jukun Lands

Another issue in the conflict between the Tiv and the Jukun was the belief by the Jukun that for a long time, the Tiv hatched and secretly executed plans of colonising plenty of farmlands round about the Benue valley, without the knowledge of their Jukun neighbours. Evidence of this was to be found in a Tiv document titled *A Short History of the Tiv*, part of which was read at the funeral service of the late Tor Tiv. It states in part:

> The main economic pursuits of the people, for example farming, seems to have dictated the political decision to acquire more lands. The people are basically farmers. They normally require plenty of land to till and grow different crops.... There was apparently no group capable of threatening their existence as a group or halting their colonisation of more lands. Colonisation for instance, was carefully and systematically planned and brilliantly executed.

Such citations from a Tiv document, which were widely quoted by the Jukun to buttress their point about Tiv expansionist intentions, raised much anxiety and caused the Jukun to believe that the Tiv had for a long time a sustained agenda of occupying farmlands round them. Jukunland was believed to be a victim of this plan, and the Jukun believed their lands had to be liberated through *Operation Patswen* (operation claim back your lands).

Interestingly, the Tiv also accused the Jukun of having a long-term plan of exterminating them in Wukari. A section of our interviewees were of the opinion that the Jukun planned and armed themselves for a long time, their objectives being the ejection of the Tiv. They added that the youths masterminded this campaign tagged *"Operation Patswen"*. Farmlands, according to the Tiv, were only used to trigger the violence. These accusations and counter-accusations were typical of this conflict, and indeed of any conflict situation. What was certain, however, was that both groups successfully found the manpower and the sophisticated skills and weapons needed to carry out the violence they unleashed on each other.

Shifting Cultivation and Land

Another factor that made land a subject of controversy was the practice of shifting cultivation by Tiv rural farmers especially, and often, by the Jukun farmers. This was a system where farms were left to fallow after being tilled for a given period. The farmers then moved to new lands. Such continuous movement brought them into conflict with other people, in this case, the Jukun. It also meant that the scope of Tiv participation on the lands increased tremendously. In principle, both the land left to fallow and the new bushes cleared belonged to the persons working on them. Anyone attempting to cultivate them faced resistance. Futhermore, the Tiv worldview saw land as God-given, and hardly understood why anyone would restrain another from freely using virgin lands.

Tiv Tradition of Visitors Having Right to Land

Discussions with the Tiv also revealed that by Tiv tradition, every visitor had a right to land on which to farm. This practice complicated the land question in the conflict. Already, the Jukun complained that they hated a situation where the Tiv who came from Benue State were given lands by their fellow Tiv brothers in Wukari, and the produce from such lands was moved to Benue at the end of the harvest. This freedom which the Tiv had to give lands to their brothers was covered by Tiv culture, and this needed to be appreciated. But it deepened the conflict with the Jukun who regarded it as part of a vicious circle.

Rapidly Growing Tiv Population

The Tiv had perhaps one of the fastest population growth rates in Nigeria. This was demonstrated in the 1922, 1923, 1946, 1952, and 1963 population figures. The Jukun, on the other hand, had a comparatively sluggish rate of population growth. As noted earlier, the Jukun were not listed as an ethnic group in the population census of 1942 and 1956. The Tiv stood out as the numerical leaders in Wukari. These people who numbered about .75 million in the 1920s increased to an estimated four million. This made the Tiv the largest ethnic group in the Middle Belt, and probably among the first of the Nigerian ethnic minorities (after the Hausa-Fulani, Yoruba and Igbo). Added to their total dependence on land, such a rate of growth in population put pressure on land and threatened the neighbouring ethnic nationalities. This threat perception also accounts for the conflict between the Tiv and the Jukun. The growth in population led to increased demand for land. The rural inclination of the Tiv and their migrationist tendencies caused them to spread beyond Wukari, into nearly all the local government areas of Taraba State.

Naming Settlements in Tiv

As stated earlier, the Tiv were the largest ethnic group in the Middle Belt. They had, therefore, a pervasive culture that impacted on practically all the neighbouring communities. This was equivalent to the effects of Hausa and Fulani in northern Nigeria, Igbo in the East, and Yoruba in the west of Nigeria. Thus, Tiv language and culture permeated many other cultures, altering the sociology of most settlements. Moreover, the Tiv hardly spoke any language other than theirs. As a result, it was common to hear many Jukun people speaking Tiv, but not as many Tiv spoke the Jukun language.

As the Hausa and Fulani did in northern Nigeria, the Tiv successfully changed the names of places where they settled in Wukari, even where such places had been known to have Jukun names in the past. This was mainly because they tended to out-number any other ethnic group in the rural areas. Futhermore, the huts in which they lived were easy and cheap to construct, and so it did not take long for a major settlement to emerge. They then named such places in Tiv language. Examples included Tsukundi renamed as Ayu, Chanchanji changed to Peva, Rafin Kada to Genyi, Bako to Abako, Kente to Santyo, Wukari to Waka, among others. Perhaps, even more provocative to the Jukun was the fact that in the middle of Taraba State, the Tiv would name a settlement in Tiv and under it, put "Benue State".

The Jukun regarded it as embarrassing to have these Tiv place-names in Wukari. The phenomenon was seen as part of the general attempt by the Tiv to complete the take-over of their lands. They, therefore, embarked on a conscious "rejukunisation" process of these settlements. The Tiv did not take kindly to this.

Elite Farmers and the Conflict

There were also social and economic factors in this conflict. It was suggested by the Tiv interviewees that one of the causes of the land conflict was the decision by elite farmers to take large areas of land for mechanised agriculture and, in the process, displaced thousands of Tiv peasant farmers. The Tiv were so entrenched in practically every part of the rural lands that it became nearly impossible to acquire land for mechanised farming or forest and game reserves without first displacing them in large numbers. Indeed this position was appreciated; the conflict between capitalist farmers and peasant farmers was unlikely to cease.

Having said that, it would be far from addressing the conflict to even suggest that these elites should be denied access to land if they desired to farm, not by fellow Jukuns, but by the Tiv whom they saw as settlers and irritants. As a matter of fact, it would be unheard of in any part of the conservative North, that a ruler of the Aku's status would be contesting land with his subjects. If Jukun people were the ones on the land claimed by the Aku, for instance, chances were that they would have given it up voluntarily. But that was Jukun tradition. The Tiv saw rather differently.

Mechanisms for Conflict Management and Resolution

The steps so far taken by government to mange the conflict between the Tiv and the Jukun, which from its magnitude should have received priority attention, were quite inadequate. It was not out of place to even suggest that government did practically nothing in the area of conflict resolution. The only steps taken were in the traditional authoritarian model using state power/ force to thrash the violent aspects of the conflict. The underlying issues, however, remained untouched.

Steps Taken so Far

1.   The peace committee set up by the Wukari Local Government Council in 1990 had a total of fourteen members, made up of seven Jukun and seven Tiv. The composition of the committee made it clear that the government perceived the conflict as one between the Tiv and the Jukun. The members of the committee went round calming the people after first wave of hostilities. This success was later reversed after events leading to the 1991 elections. The committee died a natural death when the two communities resumed hostilities.

The Gongola State Government promised to set up a commission of inquiry, but nothing was done. It was shameful that government did not deem it fit to set up an inquiry into the conflict of such a magnitude.

2.   The Sultan of Sokoto and other top traditional rulers in northern Nigeria visited the area and appealed for calm. This went a long way in helping the cessation of hostilities, but did not touch the underlying causes of the conflict. This peace mission should have been used as a window to allow for negotiations to start between the two communities, but the opportunity was lost.

3.   The two civilian governors of the Third Republic in Benue and Taraba States, Moses Adasu and Jolly Nyame, reported the conflict to the presidency. The federal government, under the office of the then vice-president, Admiral Augustus Aikhomu, invited the leaders of the Tiv and the Jukun, including the Tor Tiv and the Aku Uka of Wukari, for a dialogue in Lagos. This was perhaps the first time issues in the conflict were raised and discussed. But the tempo was not sustained, and so it did not persist in addressing the causes of the conflict. It was a bureaucratic and administrative step, and it ended as such.

4.   An ad-hoc committee was set up by the Taraba State House of Assembly to look into the conflict. This was soon interrupted by the coup that terminated the life of the government.

5.   The armed forces were mobilised for action in Wukari. First, the quick intervention force of the police was used, followed by the Mobile Police when the former failed to solve the problem. The Mobile Police were later replaced by members of the Nigerian Army, who finally brougnt the fighting to a halt.

It was concluded that among the steps taken so far, nothing significant was done to resolve the issues in the conflict up to May 1997, early November 1997, and January 1998 when Academic Associates PeaceWorks intervened through a peace education and conflict management workshop for youths and elders respectively. Subsequent activities were held, with details contained in Chapter Two. The cessation of violence provided the needed window for negotiations.

Perceived Obstacles to Negotiation and Challenges for Conflict Transformation

The Jukun believed that they already achieved much in Wukari by ridding the area of most of the settler Tiv population, especially those they believed migrated from Benue State recently, and settled illegally. They did not want to imagine a situation where they would be brought back to square one, of facing the numerical terror of the Tiv on their land, especially in its political dimension. They already contended that the high Tiv population in Wukari was artificial, made up mostly of squatters from Benue State. The various intervention activities showed that the extremists believe strongly in this position. Luckily, they were a very small group.

Unfortunately, there were many Tivs who were displaced by the fighting of 1990-1992, who still did not have a place to go to. Some of them could not go back to Benue State because they left the place too many generations ago to call it home any longer. They also could not be admitted on some of the lands they used to live on before the conflicts. Indeed the Jukun resolved not to allow the Tiv to encircle them in Wukari as was the case in the pre-1990 era. This issue of resettlement was made more difficult by the demand on returnee Tiv farmers to first seek the consent of the village, ward and district heads before returning to their farms and homes. The Tiv were not receptive to this idea, because they believed it amounted to their consenting that they were settlers.

Sheer reluctance to negotiate which could plague any attempt to broker peace between the Tiv and the Jukun was initially anticipated. One of the top leaders of the Jukun (better classified here as an extremist) who lived true to this reputation throughout the peace process, told us that as a people, the Jukun were not interested in any form of help from anybody. They did not trust the government, as they accused them of betrayal in previous negotiations. They contended that any negotiations would be sabotaged by interference from top Tiv military officials who would prefer to manipulate government outcomes to their favour. While this was the position of a few individuals, it should not be dismissed either. It was interesting to note that the peace workshops and programmes all demonstrated that the two groups could talk about peace, and did work for peace.

There were also cultural and religious inhibitions to peace. One district head, for instance, told us that in Islam, a Muslim must make peace with his enemy no longer than twenty-four hours after a quarrel. He noted that religiously, they had made peace with those who hurt them during the fracas, and that it would be inappropriate to again raise the issues that had been resolved. The whole Western notion of conflict resolution was thus incompatible with some traditional practices and conflict management. However, it was evident that even though he was a Muslim, this respondent was quite bitter over losses encountered in the conflict. There were also few Muslim elders in Wukari. No Tiv elder was known to be a Muslim. All the same, such a perspective must be noted by conflict managers.

Poor knowledge of the doctrine and concept of peace was yet another obstacle. A number of the key actors in the conflict believed that there was no conflict, because of the cessation of hostilities. However, what Wukari had was simply a graveyard peace. The local actors were grateful to the government for sending in the Army and other forces of occupation, and these were believed to have restored the peace. They did not understand that the underlying issues remained untouched, and that force was only used to suppress the violent dimensions of conflict, and swept the issues under the carpet.

Over-reliance on government as the only authority that could resolve conflicts was yet another major difficulty. Most respondents had a limited understanding of any conflict management or resolution outside government. They believed that it was the government that could find solutions to the conflict. The suggestion of a third party non-governmental body sounded strange to many of them.

Mutual distrust existed between the two communities based on a long history of conflict, and especially the latest wave of conflicts. For instance, some of the Jukun elders agreed that negotiation would be desirable, but at the same time they were skeptical about its ability to achieve anything. They believed that the Tiv were such an impossible people to deal with, that to negotiate with them was a waste of time. Some suggested that Tiv society lacked a hierarchy of authority, and that anything agreed upon could be overturned by a section of the Tiv who might disagree. These were possible stereotypes.

On their part, the Tiv also thought that conflict resolution with the Jukun would be a waste of precious time. One of them particularly said that the Jukun people were born trouble makers in whom conflict resolution had no place. They believed that the Jukun loved trouble and would pursue it vigorously.

If the *raison d'etre* of the conflict was to eject the Tiv from Wukari, however, it could not be said to have been a success. The Tiv were so deeply entrenched that the majority of them returned to their former homes. It would only take time for them to return to the former dispensation.

Issues For Negotiation

This was a critical question because the Tiv seemed to have more complaints and issues they wanted discussed in the short run than the Jukun. The following matters were more likely to be raised for dialogue:

The most urgent of the issues would be the re-opening of schools closed down after the conflicts. Many of these schools were destroyed during the fracas, some by Tivs and others by Jukuns, some still by the Mobile Police. These schools remained shut for about seven years after the fighting. Most of them were in Tiv territory. The re-opening of these schools might be expensive, but still it is a necessary relief that would allow for frank negotiations. Closely related would be the jobs of teachers who were made redundant after the fracas. Most of them, again, were Tiv.

The politics of Wukari, particularly on the participation of the Tiv in the office of the chairman, would be an issue for discussion. There was a feeling of marginalisation by the Tiv. They would love to have a standing arrangement through which the chairman would be rotated. At the very least, the Tiv would want to be involved, in whatever capacity, in the administration of Wukari Local Government.

Generally, the employment of the Tivs in Wukari should feature. Although their contribution to the local economy, particularly in the agricultural sector and tax were quite evident, they were not employed in Wukari Local Government. If at all they existed on the pay roll of the local government, their number was insignificant. This was a very sensitive issue that needed to be tackled.

The right of Tivs to permanent ownership of land in Wukari was in contrast with that of the Jukun who wished to see them as squatters. This would have to be discussed. A large number of Jukuns believed that the conflict was all about land.

There was the question of who qualified to be indigenes, Tiv or Jukun. What were the implications of this? The Jukun might even feel that this issue was non-negotiable. The Tiv must think that it was provocative to even contemplate that they were not indigenes. A "win-win" outcome would be needed here. This should not be pursued based on historical facts, or on academic or legal considerations. It should be based on human integrity, mutual respect, peaceful co-existence and the benefits derivable from these.

The Traditional Council of Wukari, as stated earlier, would be an area of contention. However, not much would be achieved, if the objective was to get the Tiv into this Council. It would make more sense to find another channel for the Tiv within Wukari through which their culture would be expressed and preserved. This should, however, not compete with the stool of the Aku Uka. Although there were Tiv on the pay roll of the traditional council (village heads and tax collectors), they were not members of the traditional council, and they could not be elevated beyond their level.

There was the problem of the demarcation of boundaries in parts of Benue State that bordered Wukari, notably in Ukum and Katsina Ala Local Governments. Some of the boundaries have continued to be disregarded by the Tiv , and the Jukun felt they lost some settlements under Wukari in the process. They even felt that the government was inconsistent with regard to these boundaries. This problem could be tackled administratively, but also needs the understanding of the two parties in the conflict. The federal government decreed an adjustment of boundaries in these areas, but without comprehensive consultations. There were misgivings about this exercise, which might not help issues.

The method of land acquisition should also be addressed. The traditional laws governing the acquisition of farmlands in the villages were weakened or disregarded by some of those who needed land for farming. Traditionally, requests were channelled from the lowest traditional administrative head to the highest. The hunger for land by some of the actors in this conflict led to gross disregard for these principles. When bush farms were cleared indiscriminately with no form of control, it surely led to land conflicts in the event that competing interests are shown. The point is to get both groups, and especially the Tiv, to agree to some form of principle about land administration. Indeed both the Tiv and Jukun were all Nigerians, and the constitution allowed people to live in any part of the country. But it did not allow people living in other locations to disregard the laws.

Stake Holders in the Conflict

In the course of the discussions, certain names and groups were mentioned, regarded as stake holders in the conflict. It was easier to generate more Jukun names than Tiv names because the Tiv were a differently structured society. The key stake holders who were also capable of making positive contributions to peace-building and the resolution of the conflict were as follows:

1.   The Jukun ethnic nationality in Wukari on the one hand, and the Tiv community in Wukari on the other. While the possibility that these two groups received external support and sympathy from their kith-and-kin beyond might not be ruled out, they remained the primary groups in the conflict.

2.   The Jukun King and the traditional title holders. These were in the forefront on the side of the Jukun. They were the principal custodians of Jukun tradition, culture and identity. They were responsible for perpetuating the strong Jukun culture and defence. They also prevented any interference and possible contamination by the Tiv who wanted to be a part of the system. Since culture and identity were expressed within a territorial space, these title holders also become defenders of farmlands and territory in Wukari. Other Jukun elites only reinforced this position.

3.   Other Jukun elites who supported this tradition and culture. Most of them were retired public servants. They include a retired permanent secretary and large scale farmer; a retired federal commissioner of the Federal Civil Service Commission; and a former chairman of Wukari Local Government Council who was in office during the conflict, and was engaged in farming. Others were a veteran politician and elder resident in Wukari; a Jos-based legal practitioner and business tycoon said to have acquired several square kilometres of land for a fruit juice project; and another large scale farmer whose mechanised farm was close to one of the trigger spots of the 1990 fracas. These elites, among others, regarded themselves as the defenders of Jukun land for subsequent generations.

4.   Among the Tiv were the only Tiv that ever became a local government council chairman in Wukari, a former adviser to Governor Jolly Nyame, and others. These people made their names mostly in either politics or farming, and were advocates of the Tiv participating in the local political process and other rights that accrued to the indigenes.

5.   The Wukari Youth Organisation provides the militant support for the leadership of the elites and elders. The youths felt that they had a responsibility to defend the motherland, and would do it any time. They maintained a crucial interest in the conflict. Their role on settling the issues in the conflict would be a very significant one. They were, by Jukun tradition, in close contact with, and answerable to, their elders and especially to the Aku Uka.

Other stake holders could only be speculated. There were accusations and counter-accusations about the roles of senior military officers on both sides of the conflict. There is, however, no evidence to directly associate these people with the conflict as their stakes were unclear in Wukari. The mention of them by both sides, however, should be noted.

In conclusion, all the people and groups mentioned above could play constructive roles in resolving the conflict. The leaders of each group could form a starting point for any intervention. Even though religion was not a factor in these conflicts, the church could play a constructive role in peacebuilding. The Tiv-dominated N.K.S.T. Church, the Catholic Church, and the Christ Reformed Church of which most Jukuns were members, could be involved in peacebuilding. Challenging these bodies whose members were the key contestants would give them a stake in the peace process. They could be constituted into a single group. After all, the fighters returned to the church after completing what they believed to be their soldierly roles.

Footnotes

[1] See for instance, Edward Azaz, *The Management of Protracted Social Conflict: Theory and Cases* (Aldershot, Darmouth: Wheatsheaf Books and Azar and John Burton (1991), *International Conflict Resolution: Theory and Practice* (Sussex: Wheatsheaf Books), Edward Azar (1991), "Analysis and Management of Protracted Conflict", V. Volkan *et. al*, eds., *The Psychodynamics of International Relationships*, vol. 11.

[2] It is worth noting that even this place has a very large concentration of Tiv rural farmers.

There is practically no part of Taraba with agricultural lands where the Tiv cannot be found.

3. Interview with Tyoazer Nyajo at Uban Igyaba. This was also repeated in another interview at Ikyaor on the Wukari border with Benue State.

4. This claim was at best controversial as some of these communities mentioned did not accept that they were descendants of the Jukun. For instance, someone contended that they were of Bantu ancestry, which conflicted with the Aku's claim.

5. Interview with Aku Uka of Wukari, Dr. Shekarau Angyu Nasaibi Kuvyo II at Wukari, 16.06.97.

6. Under Indirect Rule, traditional monarchs like the Aku headed the Native Authorities in Northern Nigeria. This was reversed during the 1976 Local government reforms. These powers were taken over by local governments. As such, the contest in the local government has frequently become an object of conflict.

7. Martin Dent, a good friend of the Tiv, did a brilliant analysis of the Tivs riots. See M.J. Dent, "A Minority Party: The United Middle Belt Congress", in J.P. Mackintosh ed., *Nigerian Government and Politics* (London: Allen and Unwin, 1996). See also Tyu Abeghe's *The Tiv and Tiv.*

8. At the end of the coup that ousted the First Republic, the northern leaders brought themselves together in the name of northern interests and Tarka was also included on this forum. The fraternity was maintained. By the late seventies, Tarka felt that he and the Tiv had now been taken into confidence by the Northern oligarchy. He came into the NPN on the false hope that he saw himself as a Presidential hopeful. He did contest the primaries, but he performed poorly and lost to Alhaji Shehu Shagari, an outcome that anybody could have predicted correctly (See details in Takaya and Tyoden).

9. Hon. Tor Musa confirmed to us in an interview that his appointment infuriated the Jukun so much that initially, the Aku Uka would neither speak nor talk to him for a long time. However, the two later developed a good working relationship. Coincidentally, it was during the tenure of Tor Musa that Aku Uka was elevated to first class status, a status that had been denied the Jukun for close to a century.

10. This was documented in a book by the former Chairman of Wukari Local Government Council and a key actor, Mr. Samuel Adda. See his *For Posterity , The Roles of Governor Nyame, Others and Myself in the Tiv-Jukun Conflict,* Target Publicity, Jos, 1993. The book has been banned by the State Security Service (SSS).

11. Even though land was in abundance, the use of the term "virgin land" was frowned at by the Jukun. They contended that uncultivated lands were owned by communities, families and individuals, and should nor be mistaken for just bush lands. All they wanted was for the Tiv to follow the proper administrative channels for acquiring land.

References

Abeghe, Tyu (1964). *The Tiv and Tiv Riots,* Tyu Abeghe, Jos.

Adda, Samuel, (1993). *For Posterity: The Roles of Governor Nyame, Others and Myself in the Tiv-Jukun Conflict,* Jos: Target Publicity.

Adi, Atohinko (1993). *Jukun-Tiv Communal Clashes: A Reconsideration,* Adi Atohinko, Wukari.

Ahire, Philip Terdoo ed., (1993). *The Tiv in Contemporary Nigeria,* The Writer's Organisation, Zaria.

Akinwumi, Olayemi and Abereoran, Joseph (1996). *Shaped by Destiny: A Biography of Dr. Shekarau Angyu Musa Ibi Kuvyo II, The Aku Uka of Wukari.* Ilorin the University Press.

Ardrey, R. (1967). *The Territorial Imperative: A Personal Inquiry into the Animal Origins of Property and Nations,* London: Collins.

Atoshi, Grace (1992). *The Story of the Jukun-Tiv Crisis: Why and How They Happened,* Amune Printing Press.

Azar, E. (1991). *The Management of Protracted Social Conflict: Theory and Cases,* Aldershot, Darmouth: Wheatsheaf Books.

.... (1991). "The Analysis and Management of Protracted Conflict", V. Volkan et. al (eds), *The psychodynamics of International Relationship,* vol 11.

Azar, E. and Burton, J. (1991a). *International Conflict Resolution: Theory and Practice,* Sussex: Wheatsheaf Books.

Dent, M. (1966). "A Minority Party: The United Middle Belt Congress", in J.P. Mackintosh, (ed.), *Nigerian Government and Politics,* London: Allen and Unwin.

Hogben, S. J. and Kirk-Greene, A.H.M. (1966). *The Emirates of Nothern Nigeria,* London: Oxford University Press.

Takaya, Bala and Tyoden, Sonny, (eds)., (1987). *The Kaduna Mafia: The Rise and Consolidation of a Nigerian Power Elite,* Jos: Jos University Press.

Chapter 5

Akin Akinteye

Intra-Ethnic Conflicts Among the Yoruba, A Case of Igbo-Ora

Introduction

Intra-ethnic conflicts and wars are found throughout the early and contemporary development of the Yoruba of Western Nigeria. References can be made to Kurumi, Ogunmola, Owu wars (1817-1824), the Ijaye wars (1860-1865), Kiriji wars (1877-1893) (Omolewa, 1986). Another example is the Alaafin and Afonja crisis. Disputes involving indigenes and settlers are common in modern day Yoruba societies, for example the Ifes and the Modadekes, the Ijebus of Lagos State and those of Ogun State, and the Ijaws and the Ilajes in Ondo and Delta States. These conflicts seem to have defied solution. Government's efforts to constructively transform or manage them have not yielded any positive results.

The Yoruba people of western Nigeria had developed a monarchical structure of government. At the head was the Oba or Baale. He was usually selected after consultation with Ifa oracle for divine approval. "Once crowned, the Oba's person became sacred. He was considered as the representative of God on earth" and an associate of the Supreme Being, *Igbakeji Orisa* (Omolewa, 1986). Traditional positions represent power, status, influence, wealth and authority. Prior to colonial rule, the Oba or Emir occupied the highest status in his societies.

The Yoruba had evolved a palace culture where the Oba lived a ceremonial life. The Oba is the head of his society. He exercises legislative, executive and judicial powers over his subjects. "The attractions of the throne are immense; the traditional rulers received homage and enjoyed innumerable privileges" (Olomola, 1996). His word was law for his people. During the colonial era, the Oba was paid stipends and later salaries and allowances which practice has continued till today. The position of the Oba became attractive in the past decade when Nigerian administrations engaged in the distribution of cars and money to traditional rulers to seek their support in their corrupt practices.

Igbo-Ora is a micro example of multiple problems associated with traditional rulership in western Nigeria and in the Nigerian federation in general. Situated on the border of Ogun and Oyo States, it has a population of about 110,000. Agriculture is the major occupation of the populace while a small percentage of the people are petty traders. However, about 0.2% of the populace are retirees. This is significant in the analysis of the evolution of the 1994 crisis. Another 10% of the population belong to the elite circle. The elite are either employed in the town or in other parts of Nigeria. The elites' interest in the 1994 crisis escalated the conflicts tremendously.

Igbo-Ora is made up of six different communities: Igbole, Pako, Iberekodo, Sagan-un, Idofin and Igbo-Ora. It is not yet known which of these communities first settled in the present day Igbo-Ora land. It also remains obscure how the six communities became amalgamated and adopted the name Igbo-Ora as their common name. However, there are speculations and rationalisations adduced by the indigenes to assert the first settler among the six communities. In addition, common and individual ceremonies exist to prove the independent nature of each of these communities.

Origin of Igbo-Ora

Various accounts abound on the origin of Igbo-Ora. These accounts differ in some areas but they all agree that most of the original settlers migrated from Old Oyo in different waves at different times to this geographical part of Nigeria.

The advancement of the Jihadists from Ilorin which consequently led to the fall of Old Oyo Empire led to this historical exodus of people from the metropolitan Oyo in different directions. This event led to the emergence of many Yoruba towns and cities including Igbo-Ora. However, it has been discovered that people had been living in what is today called Igbo-Ora as far back as the 17th century AD. The most significant issue is that the different settlements that make up the town today were founded by hunters who, during their hunting expeditions, came from different directions to settle in Igbo-Ora.

There were five distinct settlements in the town before the

Dahomean invasion in the middle of the 19th century. They were Igbole, Pako, Sagan-un, Idofin and Igbo-Ora. However, after the invasion, the people who sought refuge in Abeokuta, especially from Igbole community, came back to settle in between Pako and Sagan-un, and are today called the Iberekodos. Therefore, Igbo-Ora now has six communities, which are also called quarters.This development, otherwise seen as an increase in the number of settlements can be interpreted as a replication of Igbole quarters which moved to Abeokuta in the wake of the Dahomean invasion and came back after the war to settle as Iberekodos.

The founder of *Igbole* is said to be a man known as *Oso.* He was popularly known as *Baba Aso* meaning the father of an only child. His only child, *Olupeeti,* was married to Lajorun the founder of Igbo-Ora. According to oral sources, this man Oso, or Baba Aso, came to Igbo-Ora in search of his only daughter Olupeeti who left home looking for Lajorun, her lover. Baba Aso was accompanied by an Oro priest called Ajade. On their way down to their present location, Ajade decided to stop and settle in a village along Abeokuta and the village is today known as Ijade village. Baba Aso continued his journey and finally settled at the present location of Igbole after establishing the presence of his daughter in a place known as Igbo-Ile near the preseent site of the General Hospital. However, another oral source states that Baba Aso left Ibara Orile due to dynastic dispute. That notwithstanding, he was the founder of Igbole quarter and he introduced Oro festival to the community through his friend, Ajade. Having settled in the area, Baba Aso married two women (an Iseyin and an Offa woman) and the two had two sons. The two sons *{Ojo Dudu (Lagbawaju) and Ojo Pupa (Lagbulu)}* formed the ruling houses in Igbole and Iberekodo till this day.

The Dahomean invasion had a devastating effect on Igbole settlement as it divided the community into three. During the war, some members of the community decided to stay and face the Dahomean army while some decided to seek refuge in Abeokuta. Those who moved to Abeokuta settled at a place known as Iberekodo which to date forms an area in Abeokuta. At the end of the war, the returnees moved a little inward and settled in-between Sagan-un and Pako and their settlement is today known as Iberekodo in Igbo-Ora.

Pako is another quarter in Igbo-Ora. A woman named Ogboja founded this quarter. She was a sister to Lasogba, the founder of Idofin. She rode on horseback from Ofin near Oyo Oro and settled at a place called Idi Ako where she tied her horse with *ako* (rafia plam leaves). She paid a visit to Baba Aso in Igbole where she met Awuje who later became her husband. It was Awuje who took Ogboja to Lasogba and Lagaye her brothers. The children of Awuje and his wife form the ruling houses in Pako till today.

Lasogba was undisputedly the founder of Idofin. He was a hunter from Ofin near Oyo Oro. Lasogba first settled at Igbo-Ile and later moved to Igbo-Idofin as a result of the incursion of Lajorun and his wife, and Lajomo his brother. History is silent on the name of Lasogba's wife. However, it was gathered that he married and had children and the children are the Aro families of Idofin. These families produce chief priests of *Oro* cult in the whole of Igbo-Ora today.

Sagan-un is another quarter founded by Lagaye who was a brother to Lasogba and Ladesu. Lagaye was sent out to look for his brother, Lasogba. On his way he first settled at a place near Lanlate in Ibarapa East Local Government Area. This place is still called Lagaye. He left the place and continued his journey until he got to Sagan-un hill where he saw a smoke and traced it to the forest where he met his brother, Lasogba. Lagaye did not go back to Ofin again; instead he went back to Sagan-un hill and settled. Lagaye introduced the Oro culture to the people living with him and the festival became an annual event.

The founder of Igbo-Ora quarter was Lajorun. He was a prince of the Elekole of Ikole-Ekiti. He was a hunter who after much hunting, accidentially found himself in Ibara Orile in Ogun State. At Ibara Orile, Lajorun showed signs of royal birth. This made the Olubara of that time to accord Lajorun a warm reception. He stayed in Ibara for some time during which he fell in love with Baba Aso's daughter, Olupeti.

Lajorun left his wife at Ibara-Orile with an undertaking to come back for her after finding a good place to settle. Lajorun crossed Rivers Oyan and Ofiki and settled temporarily at Fedegbo. He later moved eastward to a place known today as Asako, a few kilometres away from the present day Igbo-Ora. Having remained in suspense for several months, Olupeti decided to search for her husband. She moved towards the direction of her husband until she got to Igbo-Ile where she met Lasogba who hosted her until Lajorun accidentallly met her there. They lived together at Igbo-Ile where they had children who formed the ruling houses in Igbo-Ora then and till today.

Political, Economic and Social Organisation

Igbo-Ora was founded by hunters who came from different places and settled in distinct locations each with their own political independence (Babatunde, 1990). At the outset, no community could claim any form of superiority over the other, most especially during the pre-colonial era. The traditonal ruler of each community legislated over his subjects without interference from any other group or community. Power to distribute or allocate land to the people was the prerogative of, and was vested in, the traditional rulers of each community.

The end of the Dahomean invasion had a turning point in the history of the present day Igbo-Ora. The different communities decided to come closer to one another in anticipation that the Dahomeans could strike again. Thus, the Sagan-un people moved down the hill, the Idofin people who had earlier settled up the hill after the present location of Lasogba High School also moved down the hill and settled closer to other communities. The Igbo-Ile people moved a little out of the forest and settled at the present day Igbo-Ora quarter's location. The returnees from Abeokuta settled betwen Pako and Sagan-un and their settlement is today known as Iberekodo. There was a shift in location in Igbole as well. The Igbole people moved a little inward and settled at the present day location of the community bordering Pako in the north. However, it is significant to note that despite the shift in locations, each of the settlements still maintained its tradition, culture and identity.

It is of great significance to also know how these communities became clustered together and adopted the name 'Igbo-Ora', being the aboriginal name of one of the quarters, as their common name. It was a popular conception among the people of the town that Igbo-Ora had a rapid expansion due to its central location to all other towns in the district and the influx of people from various parts of Yoruba land to the area. This left a big question as to who the founder of Igbo-Ora is, after the amalgamation of the town and the adoption of the name Igbo-Ora as a common name.

The European and missionary accounts of the political history of the town favoured the traditional ruler of Igbo-Ora community. He was considered the traditional head over other communities' rulers. The factor(s) employed to determine this is yet to be established. However, some people are of the opinion that this was largely due to the population of Igbo-Ora settlement while some say that out of the five traditional rulers in the area at that time, the traditional ruler of Igbo-Ora was the most popular and powerful. He was highly respected among his peers for his wisdom and prowess. Whether or not the factors mentioned above were used in determining who controlled other traditional rulers, the fact still remains that the ruler of Igbo-Ora quarter had been exercising political control over others since 1895 during the reign of Baale Ajayi

However, the first recorded account of his superiority over other traditional rulers in Ibarapa division was in 1917 when the colonial administrators built a Native Authority Court in Igbo-Ora and made him chairman. The Baale of Igbo-Ora then adjudicated over all cases from Igangan to Igbole and this area was referred to then as Igbo-Ora Native Authority.

Another account was found in the salary structure of the traditional rulers of Ibarapa Division in the 1920s in which the Baale of Igbo-Ora was the highest paid. He received forty eight pounds per annum. The traditional rulers of Eruwa and Igangan were on thirty pounds while other Baales were regarded as minor chiefs . At the same period, the Baale of Igbo-Ora was also the chairman of traditional rulers in Ibarapa Division. In 1978, the Chiefs Law of Oyo State in Cap. 21 referred to the Baale of Igbo-Ora as the "Prescribed Authority" over the geographical area known as Igbo-Ora. Subsequently, he became a member of the Oyo State Council of Obas.

However, the fusion of the different settlements known today as Igbo-Ora and the adoption of Igbo-Ora as a common name was never based upon consensus or design. The colonial administration, as in other places where colonisation occurred, placed traditional Igbo-Ora settlement at an advantage over other five settlements that are now quarters under Igbo-Ora. The Olu of Igbo-Ora continues to exercise authority over other traditional rulers in Igbo-Ora till today. He is both the traditional and political leader of the entity known today as Igbo-Ora. He ratifies selection of candidates for *Baaleship* vacancies of other quarters and he presides over the Ibarapa Central Local Government Council of Obas and Chiefs meetings.

The people of Igbo-Ora experienced one major conflict in the 1890s. This was the period of war in the Old Oyo Kingdom. The Dahomean army was one of the most powerful armies of the time. They waged war across the Western part of Nigeria. They invaded Igbo-Ora in 1890. This marked the beginning of co-operation among the people. Some of the quarters came together under the leadership of Elegun of Igbo-Ora in association with Oyero and Olukotun-Ogun to win the war. Ever since, the pace of co-operation among the six communities was accelerated. As earlier mentioned, the six communities moved closer to each other after the war for security purpose. However, the rate of expansion and development picked up, demarcation lines disappeared and the communities became one.

A man known as Shitta from Abeokuta waged another war against the people after the Dahomean invasion. The name Igbo-Ora had been adopted at that time as a universal name for the groups that make up Igbo-Ora today. Elders confirmed that this was not a war of sword and gun but that of knowledge, a war of pen and paper. Shitta succeeded in causing animosity and discord among the people, especially the ruling class in Igbo-Ora and Iberekodo quarters. He was attacked and he moved out of the town when he could no longer contain the incursion of the people.

These were the noticeable conflicts in Igbo-Ora till the 1970s. The political imbroglio that ravaged the town then, which eventually led to the 1994 saga was a by-product of the European records mentioned earlier. Otherwise, the town remained in harmony for over a hundred years. Since it adopted Igbo-Ora as an umbrella name for all the communities, the people co-operated to bring about much development to the town. These included self-help projects for which they levied themselves and others which they jointly requested from Government. Among such projects were the construction of Igbo-Ora Post Office (1966-1978), Igbo-Ora High School (1963), Comprehensive Hospital (now

General Hospital), Igbo-Ora Town Hall (1951), the Technical College (1978), Igbo-Ora Grammar School (1978), Igbo-Ora Community Bank and a host of others.

The relationship that existed for decades between the six communities reached a greater height when in 1942 the elites came together to form Educated Young Elements (EYE), now Igbo-Ora Progress Union (IPU). This union was formed as an umbrella organisation for all sons and daughters of Igbo-Ora to come together and debate ways of lifting Igbo-Ora up. The union has been instrumental in several development initiatives in the town.

In 1986, the IPU formed an elders' council known as Council of Patrons. This was created as a therapeutic centre to offer "principles, perspectives and guidelines to widen the realm of choice for development and encourage the will for taking initiatives, which serve the spirit, the human being and the earth." COP also comes to the rescue when unsuccessful attempts are made to resolve conflicts in the town. The council consists of respected elders including businessmen from all the quarters. They direct the wheel of progress and development in the town.

The Igbo-Ora Progress Union is also instrumental in the initiation of Igbo-Ora Day Annual Celebrations. This was instituted as a means of raising funds to initiate and complete several developmental projects embarked upon by the union. The Igbo-Ora people, by the institution of Igbo-Ora Day celebrations, created a social arena of understanding, and willingness to do things required for the development of their community.

Another noticeable element of co-operation is seen in the formation of community-based organisations. There are numerous social clubs whose membership cuts across all the six quarters of Igbo-Ora. Some of these clubs have annual activities that usually draw people of the town together for dialogue and interaction. The Federation of Igbo-Ora Students' Union is perhaps one of the most powerful unifying social organisations in the town. This is an umbrella organisation of all Igbo-Ora indigenes in higher institutions of learning all over the world. They have well-articulated activities that bring people together for interactions and deliberations.

Politics seems to have played a more unifying role than a segregating role among the people of Igbo-Ora. From the first to the third republics, there were two major political parties in the town. The Action Group of 1951 was transformed into the Unity Party of Nigeria in 1978, and later to the Social Democratic Party in 1990. In the same way the members of the National Council of Nigeria and Cameroons of 1944 transformed into the National Party of Nigeria in 1978 and, in 1990, to the National Republican Convention. Although these processes of transformation might not be peculiar to Igbo-Ora alone, these parties usually had their membership across the six quarters of the town. It should be emphasized that under the name of Igbo-Ora, the people have maintained unity of purpose with the belief that whatever affects one part of the town affects other parts.

The Conflict

No heterogenous community in the world has lived without one form of crisis or the other. However, as a community, Igbo-Ora has lived for hundreds of years together in harmony. Its political structure reflects the different settlements created by several factors such as expansion, politics, security and socio-economic activities. It should be recalled that the name of one of the settlements was adopted as the common name, and that the lordship of the traditional ruler of that settlement over the others, though made, was never based upon any agreement, consensus or established law. Thus the Igbo-Ora situation could be likened to a landmine buried under the surface, capable of exploding at the slightest provocation.

John Galtung (1996), in his typology of direct and structural violence regarded violence as an avoidable insult to basic human needs, and more generally to life, lowering the real level of needs satisfaction below what is potentially possible. He mentioned survival needs, well-being needs, identity needs, and freedom needs as four important basic needs human beings seek to satisfy. He explained further that the non-satisfaction of these needs usually results into violence.

However, the case of Igbo-Ora can be classified as structural conflict with identity undertone. It is a conflict that is traceable to the origin and fusion of the town and the prevailing activities during the colonial administration. The arrival and administrative strategy of colonial masters favoured the Igbo-Ora traditional settlement. This was evident in the concentration of colonial seat of government in Igbo-Ora quarter. However, the leadership position of Igbo-Ora quarter was consolidated by Baales Ajayi and Adeoye, both of whom used their personalities and attitudes to completely win respect for this settlement.

It was the general opinion within four quarters in Igbo-Ora that there was threat to, or frustration over, such identity needs as dignity, safety and control. When people's essential identities, as expressed and maintained by their primary group affiliations, are threatened or frustrated, intransigent conflict almost always inevitably follows (Rothman, 1997). The manifestations of reactions to the non-fulfilment of these needs took long to come to the fore due to the fact that people from different cultural settings create meanings through shared and accumulated knowledge. These meanings were expressed and interpreted in different ways.

Alfred Schultz (1967) provides us with important perspectives and different lenses based on the construction of social meaning as a process upon which human conflicts are created. This offers a fundamental idea that social conflict emerges and develops as a result of the meaning and interpretation people attach to actions and events. Schultz further explains that people have their common "bank of knowledge" from where social meanings are obtained. From this starting point, conflict is connected to meaning, meaning to knowledge and knowledge is rooted in culture (Lederach, 1996). This further enhances our understanding of the intangible nature of Igbo-Ora conflict as rooted in history, psychology, culture and the belief systems of the people.

Education played an important role in the emergence of Igbo-Ora conflict. In the early days of the town, educated elites were very few. However in 1942 the number of educated elites increased. These elites began to question the status quo. Between 1980 and 1994 many of them retired from their various employments and returned to the town. Interestingly, most of them saw themselves as potential traditional rulers in their various quarters. The power of the Olu of Igbo-Ora was perceived as a detrimental factor to their ambitions. These ambitions and how to realise them were difficult to articulate before the people. Motivating factors were derived from the attitudes of the current

Olu of Igbo-Ora.

In 1980 the "prescribed authority" was withdrawn from the Olu by the Government of Oyo State for refusing to abide by a directive to install one of the important chiefs of the town (the Onilado). In the same sequence, the Olu also refused to approve the appointment of the successor to the throne of Baales of Igbole and Pako. He had argued that these people were not the right choices. Other chiefs, based on the directives of the Oyo State Government, installed these Baales. Since then, the authority of the Olu of Igbo-Ora came under serious contention. People were thus prompted by these attitudes to attempt to trace the root of the lordship of the Olu over other quarters. The consequence was the coming together of all the educated elites who saw themselves as potential traditional rulers, to avert the authority of the Olu over other quarters. The conflict was further compounded by the alignment on both sides of the elites and the traditional rulers to jointly pursue common goals in the conflict.

The creation of the Council of Patrons by the Igbo-Ora Progress Union with majority of its members from one section of the town, further compounded the problem. Some of the members of the council were potential traditional rulers. Feelers in Igbo-Ora quarter had it that these people sponsored the motion for a change of the name of the town and the rotation of succession to the position of Olu of Igbo-Ora.

In addition to the above, the IPU general election of December 26, 1993 in which all important offices of the union were occupied by people from Igbo-Ora quarter, aggravated the sub-conscious feelings among the people from other quarters against the lordship over them.

Traces of the current imbroglio were noticed on December 25 1974 during Igbo-Ora Literary Progressive Union (ILPU), now Igbo-Ora Progress Union (IPU), annual meeting when it was raised by some members that a "change of title of Igbo-Ora headship should be looked into before June 1975." No further discussion was held on this matter and it was not even discussed at the 1975 general meeting of the union. It was not until 1982 that similar issues came up again at the meetings of traditional rulers of Igbo-Ora. There were five of such meetings where issues about a central palace for the town and beaded crown for the ruler were given prominent attention. However, like the previous move, this move was not given further attention and the initiative was overtaken by other events.

About eleven years later (December 26, 1993), the conflict resurfaced, taking a different dimension. The Igbo-Ora Progress Union had elections into various executive offices of the union. However, key posts such as President, Secretary General and Treasurer were occupied by members from Igbo-Ora quarter. As a result of this, the other five quarters protested alleging that the election was stage-managed. A memo was jointly written by these five quarters on July 30, 1994 to Igbo-Ora Council of Patrons demanding the following:

1. That the town (Igbo-Ora) made up of six autonomous communities, namely Igbo-Ora, Idofin, Sagan-un, Iberekodo, Pako and Igbole, should continue to exist as one town under one name;

2. That the present name of the town, i.e. Igbo-Ora, be changed to Ilupeju;

3. That one crowned paramount sovereignty be instituted in Ilupeju with the title of Alaye of Ilupeju;

4. That succession to the throne should be rotated among the six quarters;

5. That the six communities build a befitting central palace for Alaye of Ilupeju;

6. That there be certain central chiefs subordinate to Alaye of Ilupeju whose authority would also cover the whole of Ilupeju;

7. That there be a body of eleven kingmakers made up of Baales excluding that of the ruling house whose turn it is to present a candidate and six central chiefs chosen equally from the six component communities.

The memo written in reply to the above demands by the Baale (Olu) of Igbo-Ora Ruling Families stated, among other things, that the proposal was "unacceptable". They hinged their rejection of the proposal on the ground that "it was under this generally acceptable structure of Igbo-Ora as a single indivisible town that the entire town has over several decades embarked upon self-help development projects." Interestingly, the Igbo-Ora people argued that the geographical entity known today as Igbo-Ora did not come about by design or arrangement; it was a legacy inherited from the founders of the town. It was therefore impossible for it to be changed by design or manipulation. They opined that a change in the inherited legacy was tantamount to derailing the tradition and might call for the wrath of the founders. They also stated that the town had always existed in law as well as in fact and no amount of historical manipulations would be able to alter the tradition. It was a general consensus by the Baale of Igbo-Ora ruling families that the office of the Olu of Igbo-Ora was created by law which clearly defined its status, authority, powers, functions and privileges and, as a result any argument for the rotation of the paramountcy was illegal.

The situation remained static for about two months while each group was busy preparing itself for further action. Meanwhile, new dimensions were introduced to the conflict. There were moves and counter-moves by the two parties. The first move made by the aggrieved party was the formation of Ilupeju Progress Union. This union drew members from four communities, namely, Igbole, Pako, Iberekodo and Idofin. The fifth party (Sagan-un) had earlier pulled out of the group demanding that the status quo be maintained and a campaign for the upgrading of other Baales be launched to the government. The people of Igbo-Ora quarter formed Lajorun Development Council as a counter move to the Ilupeju Progress Union. The leader of the group in the struggle headed this council. The council which drew members from Oke-Iserin, Isale-Oba and Oke-Odo, launched several development programmes. They even attempted to celebrate the 20th coronation anniversary of the Olu of Igbo-Ora.

At a stage, the conflict affected religious organisations and programmes. The Muslim community in Igbo-Ora became divided in the selection of their leaders. This nearly tore it apart. Churches were not left out of the sentiment. The selection of *Baba Ijo* generated controversy in one of the churches.

Embarrassingly, the conflict completely disorganised the Igbo-Ora Progress Union which was the mother union of all developmental projects of the town. Through 1995 to 1997, the warring factions held separate annual general meetings. The Igbo-Ora people, in association with people who perceived themselves as neutral in the conflict, met under the umbrella of Igbo-Ora Progress Union while the other four communities met under the umbrella of Ilupeju Progress Union. Interestingly, some of the neutral parties were from the aggrieved group. The conflict, before long, found its way into social clubs and co-operative societies. Mistrust and suspicion became menacing factors in the society and there were cautious discussions in social clubs and within peer groups.

The Federation of Igbo-Ora Students Union, which was supposed to be non-partisan and non-sectional, was also cut in the web of this impasse. The election into the executive council of the union in 1997 was a contest between the two divides. The students formed themselves into Ilupeju and Igbo-Ora groups and they mobilised for the election along those lines.

During the period of the conflict, there were about two elections into the local government council. The warring factions in the conflict viewed these elections as contests between them. It was the general belief that whoever won the election would definitely use the office to the advantage of his group. This belief was also held with regards to political appointments into public offices. Political appointees were constantly faced with threats of character-damaging petitions. There were attempts from both sides to make sure that political appointees were selected from their group.

The periods of the conflict were extremely difficult for the people and, to a certain extent, their neighbours. It was also noticed that the people experienced a great deal of uncertainty. How behaviours affected the conflict could not be explained. The situation became fragile. Actions and utterances were misinterpreted. No developmental activities were initiated and the ones already initiated could not be completed.

Attempts Made at Resolution

The situation was not left unattended to by some concerned individuals in the town. Many peace initiatives were made towards the prevention of the conflict from escalating into full-scale intra-ethnic war. The Christian Association of Nigeria (CAN) made the first major move. Its officials held several meetings with the representatives of the warring factions. The target of the meeting was the resolution of the crisis to bring about lasting peace in the town. They succeeded in bringing together the representatives of the two groups for dialogue. The initiative however failed because they confronted the aggrieved group with the fact that their demands would be impossible to achieve. They appealed to the aggrieved group to realise that Igbo-Ora had existed as an entity bearing that name for a long time. It was also an established fact that the Olu of Igbo-Ora enjoyed the leadership from the pre-colonial era. It would therefore be an herculean task to attempt to either change the name of the town or rotate the age-long paramountcy of the Olu. They appealed that the natural courses of human nature vis-a-vis the established tradition would not permit the Olu to negotiate any of the demands.

The Lanlate community, one of the towns in Ibarapa Division, made another attempt at the resolution of the conflict. The initiative led by Chief Jolaoso, one time commissioner in the old Oyo State in the Second Republic also held meetings with the conflicting parties. This initiative failed because the underlying issues in the conflict, that is group identity and value, proved difficult for a non-conflict transformation practitioner to handle.

The Stimulus Wits of Ibarapa, a youth club that cut across all the six communities in Igbo-Ora, took series of steps in finding a lasting solution to the conflict. The club, embittered about the cancellation of Igbo-Ora Day Celebrations decided to look into ways of resolving the conflict. At one of their meetings the club members decided to intervene and invite Academic Associates PeaceWorks, an NGO based in Lagos, to facilitate a process of conflict in the community.

The club was chosen to be an entry point in the intervention strategy. The first line of action embarked upon by both the NGO and the club was the establishment of an annual lecture by Stimulus Wits of Ibarapa. This lecture was inaugurated on the 24th of December 1996. The title of the lecture was "Sub-Ethnic Conflict and its Effect on Development." Stakeholders from both sides of the conflict were invited to the annual lecture. Two distinguished members of the NGO addressed the groups. This lecture marked the turning point in the history of the conflict.

The next action was the invitation of one of the neutral men in the conflict, Alhaji O. M. Abass, to a workshop in Ogere near

Lagos. It was organised by Academic Associates PeaceWorks for senior members of the society. This group, referred to as the Corps of Mediators, was drawn from all parts of Nigeria, particularly from conflict-prone areas. Members were trained as community mediators to intervene in conflicts as they occurred in their various locations. After the training, Alhaji Abass was charged with the responsibilities of conciliating in the conflict in conjunction with Akin Akinteye, a member of the club and the programme administrator of Academic Associates PeaceWorks.

Akin Akinteye and Alhaji Abass held several conciliatory meetings in Igbo-Ora after which most of the agitators began to shift from their hard positions. Most of these focused on creating awareness on the need for dialogue and possible resolution of the conflict. Leaders of these meetings always mentioned the consequences of violent conflicts, and they frequently cited examples from around the world. The people's value system of peace was also frequently appealed to.

The conciliatory meetings were followed by a Peace Education Workshop held in Igbo-Ora in August 1997 for teachers of secondary schools in the town and its environs. After the training, the teachers moved swiftly into action by initiating a Peace and Reconciliation Committee that assisted in further diffusing tension in the community. The teachers' committee mobilised the already fed up youths of Igbo-Ora into action. The committee specifically launched a house-to-house campaign for peace. They addressed all the traditional rulers in the town on the need to embrace initiates towards the peaceful co-existence of the town. The group also addressed community leaders on the same topic. Public meetings that included almost half of the town's population were also held at various stages of their initiative. Those who attended the public meetings agreed on the need for peace. After all the public meetings were over, the teachers met with the faction leaders and informed them that Igbo-Ora people gave the responsibilities for a lasting peace in the community to them.

At four different Corps of Mediators Steering Committee meetings, several analyses were made of the situation in Igbo-Ora and of conflicts in other areas. Intervention, conciliation and mediation strategies into the conflict were planned. These planning sessions led to the next action, which was a community leaders workshop.

The workshop was held in Igbo-Ora on the 5th and 6th of January, 1998. The turnout was very impressive, and the outcome was encouraging. Akin Akinteye and Alhaji Abass, the major planners of the workshop, invited to the workshop all stakeholders, hard-liners as well as the leaders and chiefs of each faction who had earlier taken strong public stands. Elders conversant with the history of the town were also invited. The forty-two people who attended reflected a good representation of all the quarters in the town. At the end of the workshop, the following options were suggested to be considered as solutions to the conflict:

+ The town's name should remain as Igbo-Ora;
+ The quarter known as Igbo-Ora should bear another name;
+ The two progress unions should merge to form a new Igbo-Ora Progress Union;
+ The new Igbo-Ora Progress Union should elect a new executive committee;
+ The new executive committee should review the constitution to reflect the confederal nature of the community;
+ The six traditional rulers should decide the issue of paramountcy and rotation because they are directly affected;
+ An Igbo-Ora Peace Monitoring Group should be formed to look into the suggested options and to implement options;
+ Igbo-Ora Day Celebrations should hold in 1998 as a sign to the world that the conflict is over;
+ The Igbo-Ora Peace Monitoring Group should look into any other issues and act on them;

The Igbo-Ora Peace Monitoring Group was formed. All the participants at the workshop and the teachers who were trained earlier were enrolled as members. The monitoring group also extended membership to the public. The group appointed a four-member committee to be temporary conveners of the next meeting. The committee was charged with the responsibility of organising and facilitating discussions at the next meeting on January 30th. It was expected that at the end of the January meeting, agreements would be reached on all the suggestions raised and an implementation committee would be put in place to implement and monitor the agreements.

At subsequent meetings, the following agreements were reached:

* The issue of paramountcy and rotation of chiefs should be dropped because the issues were too sensitive to be handled. Instead, for the time being, emphasis should be placed on joint programmes to rebuild trust and the deteriorated relationship among the communities;
* Two progress unions, Igbo-Ora Progress Union and Ilupeju Progress Union, should meet to form one executive body within the Igbo-Ora Progress Union;
* Igbo-Ora Day Celebrations should hold in 1998. The group was open to a number of different forms for the celebration;
* The name of the town should remain Igbo-Ora and proposals to change the name to Ilupeju should be dropped;
* The Council of Patrons should be reconstituted.

A two-man committee was put in charge of the implementation of the agreements, including assisting the Council of Patrons as they worked to rebuild the Council, and assisting the members of Igbo-Ora and Ilupeju Progress Union Executive Committees as they met to form one executive. The committee was also charged with the responsibility of making sure that awareness was created in Igbo-Ora that the conflicts had been resolved. The two-man committee was to report to the traditional rulers after every meeting of the monitoring group.

A mark of success was noticed as from August 15, 1998, when Igbo-Ora Day celebrations were held after four years. The celebrations signalled the intention of the Igbo-Ora people to begin to live together again as one community. The annual general meeting of Igbo-Ora Progress Union was also held on the 26th of December 1998. Members of the two warring factions attended the meeting. The two executives were dissolved and a caretaker committee that cut across all the six quarters was appointed. The new committee was charged with the responsibilities of reviewing the constitution of the union to reflect the confederal nature of its quarters, organise Igbo-Ora Day '99 and usher in a new IPU executive by December 1999.

Current Situation

It would be naive to conclude that the Igbo-Ora conflict was finally resolved. This was far from it, although there was peace and people seemed to be pursuing common goals since January 1998. Feelers among the elites presupposed that the underlying causes of the conflict were yet to be addressed. There were also noticeable feelings of lack of trust and confidence among the people. One could therefore deduce that the common goal was being pursued because the people were tired of the conflict and wanted development to continue in the community. However, lack of resolution of the underlying causes and the inability to bring about trust and confidence among the people might generate another conflict in a more violent way than had been experienced.

The December 5, 1998 local government elections and the IPU annual general meeting of 26th December 1998 created a new understanding of the level at which the conflict was resolved and what needed to be done. A survey through the town as well as a post-IPU annual general meeting interview conducted by the researcher with some community leaders and the Baales, revealed the need for more conflict transformation activities in the town. Most of these activities were of varying degrees.

It was the general belief among the Ilupeju agitators that the conflict was not completely resolved. Some of them were of the opinion that even if the rotation of succession was not possible, some important traditional titles that were currently limited to Igbo-Ora should be extended to other quarters. Once again, one could at least say that the conflict was transferred unto the on-coming generations without necessarily leaving a structure behind on how this could be dealt with in case of future re-occurrence.

Realising the delicacy of traditional issues in the conflict, the elites referred its settlement to the traditional rulers. Since the referral, the traditional rulers have not met once to discuss this issue. However, their inability to meet might be a blessing in disguise as they were not equipped with skills to handle this conflict on their own.

With the aforementioned issues looming, the local government elections brought another dimension that called for urgent attention to the conflict. There was a widely held suspicion among all the quarters of Igbo-Ora that lack of trust , and deep-rooted animosity still operated in Igbo-Ora quarter and this was to have been reinforced by one of the community leaders. This leader was quoted to have instructed his people to vote for the candidate from that quarter regardless of their political affiliation. The voting pattern of the quarter was sited as evidence to this claim. To some people in Igbo-Ora, this was tantamount to opening an almost healed wound and was capable of reversing all the peace efforts already put in place in the town.

Suggestion for further Conflict Transformation Activities and Policy Implication

Undoubtedly, there is the need for further intervention activities in the Igbo-Ora conflict. Such activities should focus on people who function in leadership positions and are highly respected in the community. Although some of these people have been identified and trained in the elders' category, it is imperative that youths of the same status be identified and trained as well. These can be situated in the middle range leadership proposed by Lederach (1996) in his conceptual framework to peace-building.

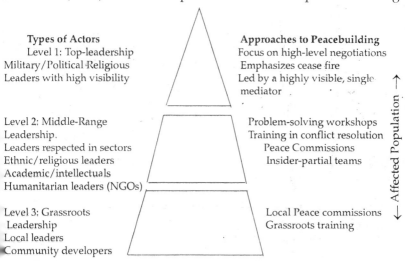

Types of Actors
Level 1: Top-leadership
Military/Political Religious
Leaders with high visibility

Approaches to Peacebuilding
Focus on high-level negotiations
Emphasizes cease fire
Led by a highly visible, single mediator

Level 2: Middle-Range Leadership.
Leaders respected in sectors
Ethnic/religious leaders
Academic/intellectuals
Humanitarian leaders (NGOs)

Problem-solving workshops
Training in conflict resolution
Peace Commissions
Insider-partial teams

Level 3: Grassroots Leadership
Local leaders
Community developers

Local Peace commissions
Grassroots training

← Affected Population →

Actors and Peacebuilding Foci

These people occupy strategic positions in that they are likely to know and be known by the top-level leadership and yet they have significant connections with the broad-based grassroots people. These people do not derive their influence from political or military might, but from their established ongoing relationships with the people. Among the people in this category are envisioners and historians as postulated by Lederach in his Integrated Framework to Peacebuilding.

An Integrated Framework for Peacebuilding

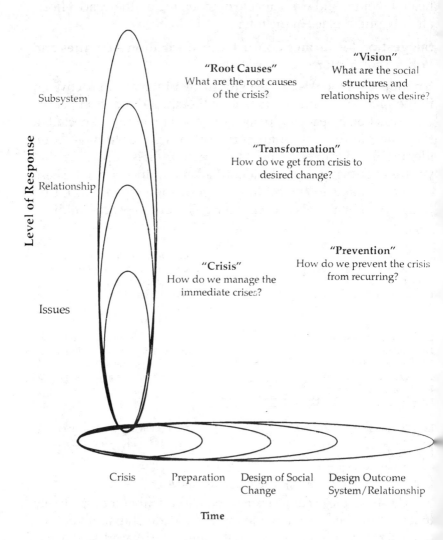

"Root Causes"
What are the root causes of the crisis?

"Vision"
What are the social structures and relationships we desire?

"Transformation"
How do we get from crisis to desired change?

"Prevention"
How do we prevent the crisis from recurring?

"Crisis"
How do we manage the immediate crises?

Source: Academic Associates PeaceWorks

These approaches to Igbo-Ora crisis were meant to promote a positive transformation of conflict, and, at the same time, help in establishing a structure that would enable the Igbo-Ora community to prevent the crisis from recurring. Apart from training identified groups in problem-solving and conflict resolution, attention should also be focused on building of trust and confidence among the peoples in conflict. This is not to say that the identification of social structure and relationships desired by the people is not of paramount importance in the training to be designed. These trainings should be directed at developing the capacity of the trainees to think about the design of social change in time-units of decades, in other to have a linkage between crisis management and long-term, future-oriented development. It is important that these trainings develop approaches that succintly anchor issues, within a set of relationships and sub-systems. Attempts should also be made to itemise the steps to be taken towards the achievement of any articulated desired future change in Igbo-Ora.

In addition to the suggested activities above, the need to train the Baales, Chiefs and the newly constituted Council of Patrons could not be over emphasised. The Igbo-Ora Peace Monitoring Group should study the values attached to traditional institutions in Yoruba land and the issue of rotation of the paramountcy, and saddle the traditional rulers with the responsibilities of handling this aspect of the conflict. Complicating the matter further was the fact that the other five traditional rulers in Igbo-Ora were minor chiefs, but the Olu of Igbo-Ora was a "Prescribed Authority" for Igbo-Ora and its environs. It might be difficult for a "prescribed authority" to agree to share power with minor chiefs.

The researcher gathered that most of the elites had vested interest in this issue and were waiting to see the way this aspect of the conflict would be handled. Above all, the traditional rulers attempted in the past to deal with this issue without any success.

Furthermore, the newly constituted Council of Patrons need to be trained to assume their rightful role of making peace and playing advisory role in the development initiatives of the town. It was the belief of several people that some members of the Council of Patrons started this conflict because of their interest in Baaleship positions. It was also a glaring fact that, no matter how long, the traditional rulers must deal with this issue. Therefore they should be equipped with conflict handling skills with which to handle this issue constructively.

It might also be necessary for the Igbo-Ora Progress Union to adopt, as a matter of policy, the need to always train their executive members in conflict handling skills. As the apex body in charge of development in the town, the union needs to develop sharp lenses to be able to identify warning signals of conflict resulting from development. It is my recommendation that the group of already trained people in the community be used to train the newly constituted IPU executive members under the supervision of a staff of Academic Associates PeaceWorks.

In conclusion, strategic and responsive monitoring tools should be created to see to the implementation of whatever outcome of conflict resolution is arrived at in the town. This is essential because conflict transformation and peace-building are meant to seek and sustain processes of social change. This monitoring should be designed such that the community can later control the process and its dynamism.

References

Adam, C. (1990). *Tools for Transformation, A Personal Study.* Oxfam: Hawthorn Press.

Akinteye, B.A. (1987). "Islam Christianity in Igbo-Ora: Areas of Conflict and Harmony." An NCE project submitted to the Religious Studies Department, Oyo State (Osun State) College of Education, Ilesha.

Babatunde, A.R. (1990). "History of Education In Igbo-Ora and its Implication for Local History Teaching." A degree theses submitted to the department of Curriculum Studies, University of Lagos.

Blumer, H. (1969). *Symbolic Interactionism: Perspective and Method.* New Jersey: Prentice Hall.

Folger, J.P., Poole, M.S. and Stutman, R.K. (1997). *Working Through Conflict Strategies for Relationships. Groups and Organisations.* New York: Addison Wesley Longman Inc.

Galtung, J. (1969). "Peace, Violence, and Peace Research" *Journal of Peace Research* 6. pp167-191.

Igbo-Ora Progress Union. (1990). Igbo-Ora Day 90 Programme. Igbo-Ora: Igbo-Ora Progress Union.

Lederach, J.P. (1996). *Preparing for Peace: Conflict Transformation Across Cultures.* New York: Syracuse University Press.

Lederach, J.P. (1997). *Building for Peace: Sustainable Reconciliation in Divided Societies.* Washington: United States Institute of Peace Press.

Max-Neef, M.A. (1991). *Human Scale Development: Conception, Application and Further Reflections.* New York: The Apex Press.

Montville, J.V. (1991). *Conflict and Peacemaking in Multiethnic Societies.* New York: Lexington Books.

Omolewa, M. (1986). *Certificate History of Nigeria.* Lagos: Academy Press.

Olomola, I. (1997). "Disputes in Succession to Traditional Rulership in Nigeria and the Impact on the Socio-political and Socio-economic", A paper delivered at the Workshop for the training of National Corps of Mediators in Ogere, Ogun State.

Rothman, J. (1997). *Resolving Identity Based Conflict in Nations, Organisations and Communities.* San Fransisco: Bass Publishers.

Schaefer, C. and Voors, T. (1985). *Vision in Action.* Oxfam: Hawthorn Press.

Schutz, A. (1967). *The Phenomenology of the Social World.* Northwestern University Press, Evanston, Illinois.

Weeks, D. (1994). *The Eight Essential Steps to Conflict Resolution. Preserving Relationships at Work, at Home, and in Community.* New York: G.P. Putnams's Sons.

Williams, I. (1996). "Sub-ethnic Conflict and its Effect on Development". A lecture presented at the maiden edition of the Stimulus Vits of Ibarapa Annual Lecture in Igbo-Ora, Oyo State.

Chapter 6

Isaac Olawale Albert

Ife-Modakeke Crisis

Introduction

The Ife-Modakeke crisis is one of the oldest intra-ethnic conflicts in Nigeria; it has been going on for more than a century and is still claiming lives. The inability of the successive regimes in Nigeria to find a long-lasting solution to the problem mirrors the extent of governance problems in the country. As issues connected with this sub-ethnic conflict are increasingly politicised, the problem is assuming more dangerous dimensions: the interests of the parties are becoming more complex, their unchanging positions more hardened and the response of the government more epileptic. The problem is a typical example of an "unchanneled and undirected conflict" which Augsburger said is usually self-perpetuating and viciously cyclical in character. The conflict, as it is, has been detached from its original causes to become its own self-energising cause. It is a typical example of a conflict that has "become its own *raison de etre*, its own self-empowered, self-fulfilling cycle". (Augsburger 1992: 53).

As at the time of fieldwork, in the warring communities, the positions of the disputing parties were common knowledge. The Ifes "resolved once-and-for-all" to send the Modakekes away from Ile-Ife. The government could resettle them elsewhere. The Modakekes, on the other hand, regarded Modakeke as their only home-land from which "nobody", including the government, could remove them. They were also prepared to spill the last drop of blood to resist the abuse of their rights "under whatever guise."

Though it looks like one, the Ife-Modakeke crisis was not an intractable conflict. It could be easily resolved especially if the government was truly determined to support such peace initiatives. This chapter serves as an invaluable resource material for those who might be making contributions towards resolving the problem in the future. It identifies the issues in the conflict; discusses its changing phases and assesses how it has been officially managed in the past and why these past approaches of

142

conflict management did not yield any long-lasting results. The chapter identifies a number of steps that have to be taken for restoring peace to Ile-Ife. In a nutshell, it is intended to inform policy-making and constructive interventions in the conflict by non-partisan third party peace-makers.

The grant for fieldwork that led to the production of this paper came from USAID, the British High Commission and British Council in Lagos respectively. I am grateful to the organisation for their support. I also wish to thank Major-General Ishola Williams [Rtd] of AFSTRAG, Drs. Judith Burdin Asuni of AAPW and Okechukwu Ibeanu of CASS, Port Harcourt, and Professor O. Otite of the University of Ibadan for reading the first draft of the paper and making useful suggestions on how its quality should be improved. I however take responsibility for all the views expressed in the work.

Contact Between the Ifes and Modakekes

The nineteenth century was a watershed in the history of Yorubaland. This was a period when several powerful Yoruba kingdoms collapsed leading to the founding of several new ones. These dramatic changes were set in motion first by the collapse of the Old Oyo Empire in the early part of the century following the revolt against the Alafin by Afonja, the *Are-Ona Kakanfo*, the head of the Oyo cavalry force and consequent invasion of Oyo by Fulani jihadists from Ilorin (Akinjogbin 1965,1966). In the attempt to fill the political leadership vacuum created by the fall of the Old Oyo empire, there were series of wars in different parts of Yorubaland between 1840 and 1894 (Ajayi and Smith 1964; Law 1970; Akintoye 1971). These two historical events, that is the collapse of the Old Oyo empire and the subsequent wars that occurred up till 1893, led to mass movement of Oyo refugees to different parts of Yorubaland.

Most of these refugees headed towards Ile-Ife. They must have been attracted to Ile-Ife by the historic image of the city as the aboriginal home of the Yoruba people [*Orisun Yoruba*]. Professor Akinjogbin suggests that a large section of the refugees could also have been relatives of the Oyos married to the Ifess (Akinjogbin 1992). The Fulani invasion of Oyo-speaking territories continued up till the 1840s. As the invasion intensified, more Oyo refugees fled to Ife and the surrounding communities. There were so many of these in Ipetumodu that the reigning *Apetumodu* had to consult the *Ifa* oracle on what to do with them. The *Ifa* described the refugees as *alejo ti ngbale lowo onile* [stranger that would soon displace their hosts in their homes]. To save himself and his kingdom from the impending dangers, the Apetumodu appealed to the reigning Ooni of Ife, Akinmoyero Odunlabiojo, to help him decongest his town by accommodating the refugees. The Ooni gladly welcomed the refugees as they relocated to Ile-Ife (Akinjogbin 1992).

The relationship between the Ifes and these Oyo refugees was very cordial at the initial stage. The Ooni and his Chiefs found them and their Oyo kinsmen, back home, to be good allies in moments of warfare and good hands in farm work. The Oyos provided military support to the Ifes during the Owu War of 1825 and various Ijesha invasions. This encouraged Ife chiefs to throw their doors open to more Oyo refugees as they came in greater numbers. Land was given to them and several of them worked for Ife farmers.

Origin of Ife-Modakeke Crisis

An Ife war chief, Okunade, the Maye, was the leader of the Yoruba warriors that settled in Ibadan in the early nineteenth century. Though a brave warrior, the Maye was an autocrat. He wielded so much influence in Ibadan politics that the Ifes started to see Ibadan as an extension of their town. In 1835, Okunade's autocracy was challenged by some Oyo citizens in Ibadan; he was consequently expelled from the town. He attempted to recapture the city during the Gbanamu battle. He was killed and the Oyos thus took over the political leadership of Ibadan to the utter exclusion of their Ife allies. The Ifes responded by venting their anger on the Oyo refugees in their town (Akintoye 1970; Ajayi and Akintoye 1980). The refugees therefore were getting ill-treated and were sold into slavery.

Around this same 1835 when the Ife hostility commenced against the Oyo refugees in their midst, rumours were circulating that the Fulani jihadists were preparing to invade some parts of Yorubaland from their Ilorin base. The surrounding Ife territories of Ikire, Iwata, Gbongan, Ipetumodu and Origbo became evacuated and the refugees came to settle in Ile-Ife. But the attitude of the Ifes to strangers had changed. Ooni Abeweila, who ascended the throne in 1839, had to send some of the refugees back to Ipetumodu, Gbongan and Ikire in 1847 following the defeat of the Fulani Invaders at Osogbo in 1840. By the same year, the Ooni created a separate settlement for those Oyo refugees who had no home to return to. The settlement was named Modakeke after the cry of a nest of storks on a large tree near the site. The leader of the Oyo refugees was given the title Ogunsua (Johnson 1973; Akinjogbin 1992)

The Pre-Colonial Phase of the Conflict

Shortly after the establishment of Modakeke, the Ife people started regretting the "mistake" of Ooni Abeweila. Now that the Oyo refugees had a segregated settlement, they started to see themselves as having a separate identity from the Ifes; they started to see Modakeke as an independent polity. This was more than a wishful thinking. The Ifes could no longer force the Oyo refugees to their farms. The political influence of the Ifes over the refugees also diminished. This incensed the Ifes against their king. As they plotted to kill him, the Ooni sought refuge under the Modakekes as palace guards. The Ooni was poisoned around 1849 and denied royal burial by the Ife people (Akinjogbin 1992).

In order to consolidate the gains of their victory over Ooni Abeweila, the Ifes attacked the Modakekes but they suffered a great defeat. As a mark of appreciation for the favours done them in a past, the Modakekes released all Ife prisoners caught during the battle and none of them was sold into slavery. This provided the Ifes with another opportunity to regroup. Under the leadership of Chief Ogunmakin who got reinforcement from Oke-Igbo, they launched another attack on Modakeke a month after the initial defeat. Once more, they lost the battle; those captured were sold into slavery and the town itself was burnt beyond recognition. Ife became desolate as all its principal Chiefs evacuated to Isoya. Ibadan, an Oyo-dominated refugee camp, seized this opportunity to extend its area of influence to [the vacant] Ile-Ife.

Between 1853 and 1854, Ibadan tried to reconcile the Ifes and Modakekes. By the time the two parties were finally reconciled, the Ifes had become the vassals of the Ibadans. Ile-Ife, like

Modakeke, Ipetumodu, Gbongan and Edunabon, was placed under the control of the viceroys [*ajele*] of the Bale of Ibadan (Awe 1964). Under this "colonial" system, Ife was thus up till 1882 obligated to pay tributes to Ibadan and also support Ibadan with food and soldiers in times of warfare. In line with the *Ajele* system, the Ifes were forced to contribute a contingent to the Ibadan army during the Ekitiparapo war of 1877-1893 despite the fact that this was a liberation war against Ibadan domination. The Modakekes, on the hand, were too pleased to participate in such a war which was aimed at consolidating the Ibadan ascendancy over the likes of the Ifes. This further created a gulf between the Ifes and Modakekes.

Meanwhile, the Ifes secretly addressed themselves to the need to throw off the Ibadans' yoke. The opportunity came in 1881 as the Ekitiparapo war [between the Ibadans and a coalition of the Ekiti, Ijesa, Akoko and Igbomina warriors] was raging. The Ekitiparapo army seemed to be gaining the upper hand against the Ibadan people because of their easy access to repeater rifles which they got from their kinsmen in Lagos (Akinjogbin 1992:158). The Ibadans had no access to Lagos; neither the Egba nor the Ijebu would allow them to pass through their territories. Therefore, the only available route to Lagos was through Ife, Oke-Igbo, Ondo, Ikale and Ilaja. The Ifes were determined to use their strategic geographical location to fullest advantage. They were determined to deny the Ibadans access to Lagos if they asked for such a privilege. The Ibadan warlords decided to test the water by asking the Ifes to give them free passage through their town to attack the Ijesas in the rear. This was bluntly refused. The Ibadan political authorities started to woo the Ifes with money and slaves to co-operate with them. Rather than supporting the Ibadans, the Ifes sent free arms to Ikire and Gbongan and encouraged them to rise against the Ibadan. They were however disappointed as the arms were turned over to the Ibadan by these towns.

The Ifes continued their hostility against the Ibadans by turning back those of them that tried to pass through their territories to Lagos. The Ekitiparapos were supportive of the Ifes in their intransigence against the Ibadan people and exploited the situation to their advantage. They promised to cede Osu, an Ijesa territory, to the Ifes if the latter agreed to join the Ekitiparapo war. And this was how the Ife declared for the Ekitiparapo in 1882. This was the strategic moment that the Ibadan people had been waiting for.

Now that peaceful overtures to the Ifes had failed, the Ibadans tried to used force, with the Ife alignment with the Ekitiparapos as an excuse. On one of such attacks on Ife in 1882, a prominent Ife Chief, the Obalaye, was killed. The Ifes reacted by asking all their citizens in the Ibadan army to change allegiance by joining the Ekitiparapo forces. The Ibadans too called on the Modakekes to fight on their side. The Modakekes, who stood to lose their independence should the Ifes win the battle against the Ibadans, gladly agreed to take arms against their Ife neighbours in December 1882. The defeat suffered by the Ifes at this particular encounter was legendary. Ife was totally destroyed despite the military support given to it by the Ekitiparapo and Ijebu forces (Johnson 1973:447; Akinjogbin 1992: 158-159). Several Ife art works were either burnt or looted and the city became deserted until 1894.

The Ifes were overburdened with grief by all these developments. Their frustration was graphically pictured by the lamentations of some of their chiefs at one of the several peace meetings that was summoned to settle the impasse in 1886:

> We need not say that our guests, the Modakekes, have become too mighty for us. They have rewarded us evil for good. They have thrice dispersed us and destroyed our town. We can no longer live together with them (see *Parliamentary Papers*: 27 April 1886).

Playing the role of an elder who should not be found to be pushing too hard a position, the Ooni elect, Aderin Ologbenla, noted a day later that the Modakekes could remain in Ife so long as they:

> ...remove with us to Ile-Ife and reside among us as they did originally. The Modakekes are our relatives, we want them to amalgamate with us and no more live as a separate people (Derin 1886).

Clause 5 of the " Treaty of peace, friendship and commerce" that was signed between the British and some Yoruba traditional authorities on 4th June 1886 touched on the Ife-Modakeke crisis:

> In order to preserve peace the town of Modakeke shall be reconstructed on the land lying between Osun and the Oba rivers to the north of its present situation, and such of the people of Modakeke as desire to live under the rule of the Bale and Balogun

of Ibadan shall withdraw from the present town to the land
mentioned, at such times and in such manner as the Governor, his
envoy or messenger shall direct after the conference with the
governments of the parties principally concerned and such of the
people as desired to live with the Ifes shall be permitted to do so but
shall not remain in the present Modakeke, which shall remain the
territory and under the rule of the king and chiefs of Ife, who may
deal with the same as they may think expedient. (Johnson 1973: 529)

The peace treaty was ratified on 23rd September 1886. The
first problem that was encountered after the signing of the treaty
concerned how to implement the aspect dealing with the
relocation of Modakeke to a new site. Opinion was divided on
this issue. The Ekitiparapo allies of the Ifes, like the Ifes
themselves, wanted the Modakekes to be driven to the bush; the
Ibadan people wanted them to be retained in Ife on humanitarian
grounds; the Alafin of Oyo was also opposed to the idea of
evacuating them, and the Awujale of Ijebu-Ode considered it more
rewarding to reconcile the two parties than to ask the Oyo refugees
to leave Ife. The Modakeke themselves could not imagine being
sent out of Ife. The leader was said to have gone into hiding when
invited to sign the peace treaty containing the expulsion clause.
He was virtually forced to sign the treaty (Akinjogbin 1992: 161 ;
Johnson 173: 54). It was however the case of forcing a horse to the
river; it could not be forced to drink water.

Therefore, when the Modakekes were invited to comply with
the terms of the 1886 treaty asking them to leave Ife, they started
to give one excuse after the other as to why they could not leave
immediately. On 7th October 1886, for example, they asked the
British peacemakers to give them a period of five months grace
within which to relocate to Ipetumodu. The Ifes objected to this
demand expressing the fear that once the British officials agreed
with them and left Ile-Ife, the Modakeke would once again become
intransigent. The British officials were therefore left with no other
option than to give the Modakekes and their Ibadan allies as well as
the allies of the Ifes ten days to move from Ife (Johnson 1973: 534).
They were simply ignored by the Modakekes.

On 28th November 1886, the Modakekes came up with some
key reasons why they were reluctant to leave Ife. First, they
claimed that most of them were born in Ife and married Ifes and
therefore had no alternative place they could refer to as their home

Secondly, they argued that the civil strife between them and Ifes was not as intractable as to warrant their complete expulsion: "We have often had civil wars and although we always have the advantage yet we always give up the captives voluntarily". Thirdly, the Modakekes argued that many Ife people did not want them to leave their town. They came to them at night, as opposed to what they say in the day time, asking them not to leave. Fourthly, they argued that they had some rights over the land on which they were settled as the land was bought by their forefathers: "To ask us to move... is as good as if our town was destroyed." They preferred to be killed on the graves of their forefathers than to leave Modakeke alive. (Akinjogbin 1992 :162)

The Ifes insisted on remaining in exile as long as the Modakekes refused to relocate elsewhere. By December 1886, the peace commissioners became fed up with the deadlock reached over the Ife-Modakeke crisis. They therefore left the two to their problems. By January 1887, the Ekitiparapo allies of Ife also withdrew from the peace process and Ife therefore remained unoccupied until 1894.

The Colonial Phase of the Conflict

British colonialism which could be said to have been established over Lagos since 1861 was extended to Yorubaland in 1893 following the British intervention in the Ekitiparapo war, leading to more British interest in the peace questions in Yorubaland. The British needed peace to be able to carry out their social, economic and political objectives. Ooni Aderin Ologbenla and some of his people were encouraged to return home in early 1894. Later in the year he died and was succeeded by Oba Adelekan Olubuse 1.

The opportunity to "resolve" the conflict started to gather storm in 1903 following the invitation of the Ooni to Lagos, in his capacity as the "titular spiritual head of all the Yoruba to testify as to whether or not the Elepe of Epe had the right to wear a beaded crown. (See *Government Gazette* February 21 1903 p. 153) The Ooni was excited about the invitation as he saw it as an opportunity to seek the support of the British administration against the overbearing Modakekes and Ibadans. The impressive performance of the Ooni on the Lagos assignment had great impression on Governor William MacGregor of Lagos Colony to the extent that he offered to help the king rebuild his burnt palace; the Ooni was also offered an annual stipend of two hundred pounds. Work was completed on the renovated palace of the Ooni in 1905. (Omosini 1992: 171-6)

During the Lagos trip, the governor assured the Ooni of helping him to recover all the Ife territories lost to Ibadan and of the expulsion of the Modakekes from Ife in line with the 1886 treaty. The Ooni now became freer to discuss the Modakeke problem with Captain Fuller, the Resident in Ibadan to whom that matter had been referred by the governor. An Arbitration Committee headed by Mr. J.B. Ross, the acting attorney-general was later set up by the government to look into the matter. The committee recommended that the Modakekes must regard the Ooni as their lord and the owner of the land on which they were settled. The Modakekes were also asked to pay royalties, in the form of half of their farm yields, to their Ife landowners. The Ooni and some of his radical subjects considered this recommendation to be too mild; what they expected was a total evacuation of the Modakekes. Due to continued pressures on the government, Modakeke was broken up in 1909 and its inhabitants were dispersed to Owu/Ipole, Edunabon, Ede and Odeomu (Omosini 1992: 177; Johnson 1973: 647).

The Modakekes who settled in Odeomu soon started to face the problem of land scarcity and social adjustment. Therefore, some of them started thinking of returning to Ile-Ife when Oba Adelekan Olubuse who drove them out of the ancient Yoruba city died in 1910 and was succeeded by Oba Ademiluyi Ajagun [1910-1930]. Starting from 1912, the Modakekes and the new king started exchanging ideas on the possibility of re-admitting the former into Ile-Ife. After surmounting the fierce opposition of his subjects on the matter, Ooni Ajagun allowed the Modakekes to return to Ile-Ife in 1922 but with the proviso that "the new Modakeke quarter is to be known as the Modakeke quarter of Ife, and is not to be regarded as a separate town. (See Resident memo to District Commissioner in Oyediran 1974: 67-77; Omosini 1992: 178).

To further reinforce his policy of reconciliation between the Ifes and Modakekes, Ooni Ajagun recommended in 1928 that the Ogunsua of Modakeke should be given an active role in the administration of Ife District. The Ogunsua and the Osa of Modakeke were subsequently granted salaries of seventy-two and twenty-four pounds respectively for their contributions to the native administration. The Ogunsua was also made a judge of the native administration court. The tenure of Ooni Ademiluyi Ajagun was therefore marked by peace and amity between the Ifes and Modakekes.

Ooni Adesoji Aderemi [1930 -1980] who succeeded Oba Ajagun in 1930 was as determined as the latter to promote peace among the Ifes and Modakekes. He was very disappointed when the Ife-Modakeke crisis resurfaced in 1946 following the commercialisation of cocoa and the huge revenues accruable to Modakeke farmers. Before this period, Ife landowners merely collected a token fee [*Ishakole*], usually some farm products, from Modakeke farmers. With the boom in cocoa trade, Ife landowners started asking the Modakekes to pay them *Ishakole* as much as 10% of the harvested cocoa. The Modakekes considered this exploitative and formally complained to the Ooni in November 1946 through the Lagos Branch of Modakeke Progressive Union. The Ogunsua also registered the protest of his subjects to Oba Aderemi. The Modakekes claimed that though they promised Oba Ajagun, who called them back to Ife in 1922, payment of Ishakole in the form of farm produce, it was not in the exploitative degree now demanded by the Ifes.

Oba Aderemi simply asked them to comply with the payment of what his Ife subjects demanded since it was [1] payment resulting from private negotiations; and [2] since there was nothing criminal about a tenant paying rent to his landlord. The Modakekes were not surprised by the position of the Ooni on the matter since he too was a landlord. They therefore dismissed him and his subjects as exploiters and resolved to settle the problem using whatever methods they considered appropriate.

When the conflict was getting to a violent level, Oba Aderemi had to call for the intervention of the colonial authorities. He was disappointed by the indifference of the government which regarded the conflict a private problem that could be settled in the court of law. [Akinrinade and Akinjogbin 1992: 192-216]. The Oba tried to resolve the conflict by bringing the two parties together but not much was achieved. At a stage in the conflict, the king offered a virgin land to the Modakekes which they rejected. The Ifes too were not supportive of the idea of giving a virgin land to the Modakekes. This would deny Ife landowners of their main source of earning their living. The Ifes favoured two radical options: either sending the Modakekes away completely or forcing them to pay whatever Ife landowners asked them to pay if they wanted to remain in Ile-Ife.

The matter was finally taken to the Native Authority Court of Ife on January 30, 1948. The court ruled that there was a contractual agreement between the Ife landlords and their Modakeke tenants. To this extent, what the Ifes were asking for were their legitimate entitlements. The Modakekes appealed against the judgement at the Supreme Court and the earlier verdict of the lower court was upheld on October 13, 1948 though the amount to be paid as *Ishakole* was reduced. The Modakekes further appealed to the West African Court of Appeal. Before the hearing of the case could come up, riots broke out in Modakeke on May 18,1949. By this time the Modakekes had broken into various factions. The Ogunsua who was probably no longer interested in the conflict blamed the riot on some "troublemakers" within his community. The Modakekes who were disappointed with the attitude of their king decided to prove to him that they were more peace-loving than him. They therefore started to make reconciliatory moves towards the Ifes. The two groups met on September 29, 1949 and pledged to abide by the settlement terms earlier suggested Egbe Omo Oduduwa [which later became Action Group] that the *Ishakole* should be collected based on the number of harvested cocoa trees.

Another series of riots soon broke out as the terms of the earlier agreement were not strictly adhered to. Because the Modakekes lost their appeal at the West African Court of Appeal, they returned to the Ooni asking him to give them the virgin land he promised at the wake of the 1947 crisis. They were told that the land had been acquired by the Native Authority. Up till 1954, fruitless efforts were made by the Minister for Land to find alternative land for the Modakekes. The latter continued to blame their problems on Oba Aderemi who refused to help their situation despite the fact that he had the power to do so. The Ifes on the other hand were disappointed with their king that he did not expel the Modakekes from Ife when they were resisting the payment of *Ishakole* demanded by their landlords. Writing on the Ooni's difficult situation, Akinrinade and Akinjogbin noted:

> Oba Aderemi chose to bear the accusations of both sides with tolerance and tact. He felt that the two parties to the dispute were his subjects and saw no reason to favour one against the other. He decided to keep mute on the subject because any statement issued would be interpreted [or, more appropriately, misinterpreted] by both parties to suit their moods (1992: 200).

The situation of the Ooni was aptly captured by a Nepalese proverb which says "When the first wife fights with the second, the husband gets his nose cut off." A Montenegrin proverb also says: "The peacemaker gets two-thirds of the blows." Beyond the negative perceptions of the colonial period, the Ifes and Modakekes were of the view [during our fieldwork] that Ooni Aderemi was very fair in handling the Ife-Modakeke crisis. This opinion, the two sides explained, was based on the fact that the king's mother hailed from Ipetumodu and one of his favourites wives came from Modakeke. This situation illustrates the positive role which mixed parentage and cross-cultural marriage can play in the mitigation of conflict.

The Post-Colonial Phase of the Conflict

The Modakekes saw the 1960 Nigerian independence as a challenge to change their modus operandi. They therefore focused their attention, starting from 1957, on having their own local government council instead of asking for rights that they might never be granted under Ife-dominated local politics. The leadership of the Action Group [A.G] that controlled government in this part of Nigeria was however not supportive of the aspirations of the Modakekes. It was therefore not surprising that in the April 17, 1958 edition of *Daily Times*, Chief Obafemi Awolowo, the Premier of Western Nigeria and leader of the A.G., told the Modakekes that he did not recognise them as having a separate town:

> Ife Town was one town and the request for a separate local Government council for Modakeke amounted to an attempt to divide a single town.

This statement and the role that Chief Awolowo played as the solicitor to the Ifes in the various cases between them and the Modakekes, made the latter to regard the former Premier as a permanent enemy.

The other issue that the Modakekes gave attention to in the post-colonial period was the *Ishakole* problem. They considered it as an uncivilised taxation in a nation that claimed to be independent of colonial forces. The Modakekes got a reprieve in 1978 when the federal government, led by General Olusegun Obasanjo, promulgated the Land Use Decree entrusting all land in the country to state governments on behalf of the federal government. While localising the implementation of the Decree in Western State, Governor David Jemibewon announced the cancellation of the *Ishakole* system. This was a big relieve to the Modakekes.

The Resumption of Hostility: The 1981 Riots

The disagreement between the two communities fully came alive with the commencement of party politics in 1979. The issues in the Ife-Modakeke conflict came handy for the politicians who needed the support of the people. The Unity Party of Nigeria [UPN] was obviously a Yoruba party and needed little or no effort to win the votes of the Ife people. The party could therefore do without making any "far-fetched" promises to the Modakeke people. But a political party like National Party of Nigeria which was generally seen to be an Hausa-Fulani party saw the Ife-Modakeke crisis as a means of gaining entry into Modakeke. The efforts of politicians in this direction gradually resuscitated the conflict.

One of the things that the rivals of the UPN in Oyo State, especially the NPN, promised the Modakeke people during this period was to give them a local government council of their own in which they would exercise all rights of an independent people and cease to be an appendage of the Ifes. Several Modakekes still joined the UPN believing that they could change things to their own advantage from within rather than from outside the party. Majority of them later withdrew from the party.

The relationship between the Modakekes and UPN began to turn sour starting from December 1980. It all started on December 27th, 1980 during a fund raising ceremony organised by the Modakekes. The money raised from the ceremony was to be used to complete the building of a town hall, offices, library complex, king's palace and a post office for the Modakeke community. The point that the Modakekes were simply trying to make by this function was that they did not need to wait for anybody or any government before developing their town.

The executive governor of Oyo State, Chief Bola Ige, was represented at the occasion by his special adviser, Alhaji Oladunni Ayandipo. As the latter was reading his address at the ceremony, two lorry load of policemen arrived on the scene and asked everybody to disperse.[2] In a petition sent to the governor of Oyo State, the Modakekes blamed the whole development on the Ooni of Ife:

> The Ifes have started to boast about that Ooni Sijuade has used police to disrupt our Launching Ceremony, and this is one of the reasons why we are still backing up our request for a separate Local Council.[3]

The Modakekes claimed to have met the Ooni on the 25th December 1980 to inform him about the forthcoming ceremony. Ooni Sijuade Olubuse was said to have told the Modakeke representatives that he did not recognise Modakeke as a town and by implication that the people had no right to raise any fund for developing their "town". The Modakekes considered the position of the Ooni to be a "perversion of history". "The history is there to back our argument. Our development programme started in 1977 and as such we are not doing anything new."

The Modakekes did not receive any response from the government on their petition. This made the people to start to suspect the intentions of Chief Bola Ige. From this point the Modakekes started to make political points out of their desire to have their separate local government council. Politicians from both the UPN and NPN exploited the conflict, from time to time, as found necessary. A few months later, the atmosphere in Ile-Ife had become fully charged with rumours of a possible violence between the Modakekes and Ifes.

Meanwhile, the representative of Modakeke/Akinlalu [Oranmiyan North 1 Constituency] in the Oyo State House of Assembly, Chief Odelola, took it upon himself to formally handle all matters relating to the creation of a separate local government council for the Modakeke people. On the 11th of February 1981, he caused the leaders of the UPN in Akinlalu [Oranmiyan

Constituency 1] to write a petition stating that they, with the people of Modakeke and the Oyere group of villages [Oranmiyan Constituency 111], would want to merge into a separate local government council of their own. A similar petition was sent to the Chairman, Oyo State wing of the UPN through Chief Odelola by the people of Oyere villages. The two petitions were well received by the leaders of the UPN in Oyo State. It was against this background that a bill was formally tabled before the Oyo State House of Assembly by Chief Odelola asking for a separate local government council for the Modakekes. The bill was popularly supported by the House but was later vetoed by the leader of the UPN, Late Chief Obafemi Awolowo through the Speaker of the House (Oladiran Ajayi n.d: 30a). In defending his role in the entire set-up, Chief Awolowo said he was told that some legislators wanted to reverse his party's decision on the matter and he had to write to the Speaker of the Oyo House of Assembly reminding him of the supremacy of the party (*Daily Times,* April 8 1981).

Matters got to a crisis level starting from April 2, 1981 when Chief Bola Ige announced the creation of some new local government councils. The Modakekes were disappointed that they were once again placed under the Oranmiyan Central Local Government Council while smaller communities were allowed to have their own separate Councils. In his speech, the governor made the ambiguous statement that he would see that justice was done to the Ifes and Modakekes; he was not clear about how and when such justice would be done. This was seen by the Modakekes as diversionary tactics.

The NPN immediately cashed on this new development to improve its political image in Modakeke. The party which had always assured the Modakekes of a separate local government council of theirs sent some of its stalwarts, namely, Chief Richard Akinjide, Chief M.K.O. Abiola and Chief Fani-Kayode to Modakeke to address a political rally on the issue. The April 11, 1981 rally was used by the trio to make inflammatory statements about the Ife-Modakeke crisis. They blamed the whole problem on Chief Obafemi Awolowo, the leader of the UPN and Chief Bola Ige, the UPN governor of Oyo State. The two were alleged to have sworn not to give the Modakeke people a separate council of their own.[4]

Chief Richard Akinjide, who was at this time the federal minister of justice, was particularly reported to have said: "The Federal Government stands firmly behind the people of Modakeke in their struggle for a local government of their own and they should continue this struggle" (Adelugba 1981). The Modakekes were encouraged not to see the UPN as a friendly political association; if the Modakekes wanted to be independent they were requested to declare enmass for the NPN.

The political atmosphere in Ife and Modakeke became charged after the April 11, 1981 rally of the NPN. The Ifes, who severally belonged to the UPN, were alleged to have started harassing the Modakekes both physically and verbally. The Modakekes were allegedly referred to by the Ifes as *Omo Isale-Ife* [the people of lower Ife] and *eru* [slaves]. In a petition sent to the federal government by the president and secretary of the Modakeke Progressive Union on 13th April 1981, the Ifes were said to have mounted road blocks between Ife and Modakeke "for the purpose of attacking the Modakekes who may be passing by, thereby restricting the free movement of the Modakekes and all other Oyo-speaking people of this area.[5] The Modakekes accused the police in Ife of being indifferent to their plight and asked for the direct intervention of the federal government.

> There are strong rumours that the Ifes will continue to attack the Modakekes and other Oyo-speaking people both in Modakeke and Ife from now on. Since we are a peace-loving people, it would be highly appreciated if the President would see to it that we, the people of Modakeke, are given our Police Station with sufficient number of Policemen to maintain law and order in Modakeke, and on Akinlalu, Famia, Oku-Omoni, Oyere and other villages around Modakeke. In the interim, it would be highly appreciated if the President would send some non-partisan Police Officers to Modakeke for the safety of life and property of the inhabitants. If the Ifes continue their rampage, the people of Modakeke may be forced to react in the ....ne way.

Copies of this petition were sent to the governor of Oyo State, minister of police affairs and security chiefs in Ibadan and Lagos.

On the 14th April 1981, the Ife-Modakeke feud escalated into a full blown violence. Several people were killed on both sides and several houses were burnt. Within a few days of its commencement the riot spread to the neighbouring Modakeke villages.

The government drafted several hundreds of policemen to the warring communities. In a statewide broadcast on April 15, 1981, Governor Bola Ige slammed a dusk-to-dawn curfew on Oranmiyan Central Local Government Council area; banned all public meetings in the area for the next fourteen days and instituted a judicial inquiry into the crisis. Members of the judicial panel were Justice O. Ibidapo Obe [the chairman], Mr. M.S. Adigun and Dr. Tunde Adeniran. Mr. L.O. Dada was asked to serve as the secretary to the panel. In concluding his speech, Chief Ige warned:

> I must, however, make it clear that our Government will not tolerate any attempt by any one, either to blackmail this Government into rushing reforms or to stampede us in doing injustice to any group or individuals... I wish to assure everyone that the security of Oyo State will be further tightened so that all those who play with fire will have their fingers burnt (Ige 1981)

The Ibidapo Obe judicial panel held all its sittings at Ilesa. This neutral ground enabled all parties freedom of expression and movement. As usual the Ifes noted that they recognised Modakeke as no more than a mere ward in Ife. A memorandum sent to the panel by Ife Action Council, represented by its chairman, Chief Orayemi Orafidiya, recommended that the Modakekes should be returned to their kith and kin in Ode-Omu beyond Shasha river; "There they belong." He maintained that until the Modakekes were resettled elsewhere the restoration of peace in Ile-Ife would be impossible (Falade 1981). Professor J.F.A Ade Ajayi, who was invited from the University of Ibadan to shed more historical light on the origin of the Modakekes maintained that the people were migrants from Oyo and that they always occupied a ward in Ile-Ife and did not have a separate town of theirs.

The Ibidapo Obe panel, among other things, recommended the creation of a separate local government council for the Modakeke as a way of permanently appeasing them.

The 1983 Crisis

Following the inability of the Modakekes to get a local government council of their own in April 1981, they massively decamped from the UPN to NPN, led by Chief Olaniyan Alawode. This further charged the political climate in Ile-Ife. The battle line was thus better drawn: the Ifes for the UPN and the Modakekes for the NPN . The Modakekes were resolute in their determination to change the fortunes of the UPN in the State as this was seen as the only way by which their yearnings for a separate local government council could be achieved.

The opportunity to deal the first blow on the UPN came in July 1983. The campaign team of the UPN which was asking for the re-election of Chief Bola Ige as the executive governor of Oyo State got to Modakeke on July 7, 1983. To demonstrate their opposition to the campaign team, the Modakekes chose the same date for the outing of their masquerades. Trouble started at about 3.15 p.m. when an advance party of the UPN gubernatorial campaign team left Trans Motel, near the then University of Ife, now Obafemi Awolowo University, in four vehicles for the Itamerin Square, Modakeke which was the venue of the campaign rally. The campaign team, driving at top speed, ran into the masqueraders who had converged at the Square. In the process, one Edward Adesiyan of Modakeke was knocked down and injured. The Modakeke people reacted by throwing stones and missiles at the UPN team. Following this attack, a UPN driver lost control of his car and crashed into an electric pole. The driver and other occupants of the car were attacked and burnt to death.

In the stampede that followed, several cars crashed into one another and were set ablaze by the irate Modakeke crowd. Those burnt in one of the vehicles included Chief Wale Odelola, the representative of the Modakekes in the Oyo State House of Assembly. The death of Odetola was not accidental. Though an illustrious son, who is still remembered as having worked very hard towards getting a local government council for the Modakekes, the people were against him for failing to quit the UPN when other Modakekes were doing the same. In his mimeograph on the Modakeke people, Chief Oladiran Ajayi, the Otun Asiwaju of Modakeke, for example, described Chief Odelola as a "tactless politician who knew how and when to fight but did not know when to run away." He wrote further:

> In Modakeke, Chief [Honourable] Olarewaju fought well, ran away from the UPN when it was totally negative to Modakeke and today he fights on. Like the Biblical Moses, Late Odelola played his part; but did not reach the promised land (Oladiran Ajayi n. d. p. 30a).

The others who died along with Odelola were Ganiyu Deji Odetayo from Ile-Ife, Jide Awodapo, an Engineer in Ife, Ayoola Joshua Odeyemi, from Ife and Alli Otun, an Ife contractor. Other people who died in the free-for-all fight that followed included Chief Fatoki and Chief E. Oluomo from Ilesha. Twenty one other people were injured: 11 UPN members, 9 Modakekes and a policeman (Obideyi E 1983 : Aweni B. 1983). The police reacted by banning public processions, political campaigns and rallies in Ife and Modakeke.

The Oranmiyan West Local Government Council that never was

On October 1, 1983 Chief [Dr.] Omololu Olunloyo of the NPN became the governor of Oyo State at the end of a gubernatorial election. The new government was favourably disposed towards the cause of the Modakekes. Therefore Oyeladun Oyemade, a Modakeke man became the Speaker of Oyo State House of Assembly; Chief T.O. Oloyede, another Modakeke man, was made the Commissioner for Agriculture, and several other Modakeke citizens got board appointments. The stage was now set for the creation of a Modakeke Local Government Council.

On 13th December 1983, two months after becoming the governor of Oyo State, Dr. Olunloyo sent a bill, entitled "A Law to Amend the Local Government Law Cap 66 of December 1983", to the Oyo State House of Assembly calling for the creation of Oranmiyan West Local Government Council with its headquarters at Modakeke. The bill was signed by the commissioner for local government, Mr. S. A. Abidoye. In the official letter that accompanied the bill, Governor Olunloyo noted that the proposed Oranmiyan Local Government Council will incorporate the area associated with Oranmiyan North 1 and 111 State Constituencies. He appealed to members of the House to put aside partisan interest in considering the bill:

> May 1 point out... that the matter is of a very delicate and urgent nature, and as such, requires a thorough and exhaustive treatment. It is a matter which appeared to have defied lasting solution since the past one hundred and fifty years, with its attendant human tragedy laden with loss of lives and property of immense proportions. Whilst we, by the exercise of our constitutional powers, are hereby concretizing the yearnings and aspirations of Modakeke people, we would not be seen to be doing justice to all concerned if we do not simultaneously take

adequate steps towards allaying the fears that Ifes seem to have. We have therefore to entrench in the instrument creating the new Local Government Council safeguards and guarantees designed to ensure permanent and lasting peace between the two communities. In addition, it is considered necessary to give recognition at all times to the paramountcy of the Ooni of Ife over the entire Oranmiyan area including the new Local Government Council. These measures and other safety valves that can be usefully employed to restore confidence, respect, honour and dignity in the minds of the people of the entire area generally have to be employed as the existing climate affords a singular chance to solve the problems once and for all (Olunloyo 1989).

The bill sailed through the House and the local government council was thus created. Work on the legal instruments establishing the local government council had hardly been completed when the NPN government of Alhaji Shehu Shaghari at the federal level was overthrown by the military. That was the last of the new local government council as the Generals Buhari and Idiagbon regime threatened to deal ruthlessly with all "subversive elements" that tried to intimate the new administration with "irresponsible demands". The Ife-Modakeke crisis therefore went to sleep.

The iron hands with which the Buhari/Idiagbon administration ruled Nigeria was one of the excuses cited by the General Ibrahim Badamosi Babangida for seizing power in 1985. In his maiden and other addresses, General Babangida presented his administration as a listening one. Agitators for states and local government councils therefore came out from their hidings to continue their struggles. The Modakekes were not left out.

On May 27 1989, General Babangida created additional 149 local government councils. The former Oranmiyan Local Government Council with its headquarters at Ile-Ife was broken into three local government councils. One of them was Ife North local government council incorporating Modakeke Wards 1 to 14, Origbo and Oyere. The headquarters of the new Local Government Council was located at Ipetumodu along Ife-Ibadan road. The other local government councils in Ife territory were Ife Central Local Government Council for Ile-Ife and Ife South Local Government Council for Ifetedo, Olode and the surrounding villages.

The memorandum leading to the creation of these three local government councils was prepared by Professor Wale Adeniran of the Department of Linguistics, University of Ibadan who was representing Ife North Federal Constituency in the Constituent Assembly, Abuja, 1988/89. Professor Adeniran also served on the Committee on Local Government and Concurrent Legislative List of the Assembly and must have been motivated to prepare the Ife memorandum as a result of insights from the activities of this Committee. The memorandum was supported by the Ooni of Ife, Oba Okunade Sijuwade. In the memorandum, all the Obas, chiefs, elders and community leaders in the former Oranmiyan Local Government [but those in Modakeke] were said to have agreed on the following:

i. the demand for three local government council areas;

ii the delineation of the boundaries of each proposed local government council area, and

iii the location of Modakeke, as part of Ife township, within the proposed Ife Central Local Government Area (Adeniran 1997).

The Modakekes dissented to this arrangement but would rather want to be grouped with Origbo/Oyere in Ife North "against the wishes, demand and aspirations of the people of that area." In the course of Constituent Assembly's sittings, a Modakeke delegation led by Chief Adedoyin visited Abuja to lobby for the creation of Ife North Local Government that would include Modakeke. The delegation was however not supported in their demands at Abuja by Professor Adeniran because:

> The case against Modakeke being in Ife North was very strong, convincing and persuasive. Modakeke quarter, by its location in the heart of Ile-Ife, has no boundaries with Origbo. And in the creation of a local government, one of the crucial prerequisite is geographical contiguity: it is a *sine qua non*. It follows logically therefore that there is no way in which Modakeke could be lifted from then Ife Central to Ife North. Apart from the fact that the people of Ife North did not want Modakeke in the proposed local government, it is important to note that the two communities have no *common* boundaries. (Adeniran 1997)

The Ife North Local Government was created on May 27, 1989 and contrary to expectation of the people of Origbo/Oyere, Modakeke was incorporated into the new local government councils. The Origbo and Oyere communities petitioned the government but the latter stood its ground that Modakeke must be part of the new local government council. The government saw this as a simple way of stemming further Ife-Modakeke crisis but the Professor saw it as "a gross demonstration of insensitivity" to the yearnings of another group. It was like robbing Peter to pay Paul.

The Modakekes were however highly pleased with this arrangement that removed them from Ife domination. Chief Oladiran Ajayi, the Otun Asiwaju of Modakeke, summed up the feelings of his people on this in the following terms:

....it is sure that WE ARE IN THE PROMISED LAND. Agitation, oppression and unhealthy rivalry between Modakeke and Ifes have been solved after 150 years [1839-1989] of wars and near apartheid situation in an independent Nigeria. What an uneasy journey of 150 years TOWARDS THE PROMISED LAND. (Ajayi n.d. 31)

On May 24th 1989 Barrister A.A. Odetunde, a Modakeke man, was elected as the acting chairman of Ife North Local Government Council at an electoral college of councillors at Enuwa, Ile-Ife. Five days later the acting chairman and seventeen other councillors were sworn in by the governor of Oyo State, Colonel Sasaenia Adedeji Oresanya, to manage the new Council.

For some years thereafter, peace reigned in Ile-Ife, but political violence characterised the inclusion of Modakeke in Ife North Local Government Council Area between 1989 and 1996. Every election in the area was characterised by electoral frauds and violence, perpetrated by either the Modakekes or the people of Origbo in the desperate efforts to control the new local government council.

Killing the Dreams of a Promised Land: The 1997 Crisis

The Modakekes did not sojourn in their promised land for too long. In 1996, the federal government created 143 new local government councils. One of them was Ife East Local Government Council. This new council included Modakeke with headquarters located at Enuwa in Ife. On March 3, 1997 the government further announced the creation of new local government councils and new local government headquarters. The headquarters of Ife East Local Government was consequently changed from Enuwa to Modakeke. This new arrangement was strongly opposed by the Ifes. Due to intense pressure from the Ifes, the military administrator of Osun State, a new state incorporating Ife, Col. Anthony Obi, announced on August 14, 1997 the decision of the government to shift the headquarters once again from Modakeke to Oke-Ogbo in Ilode area of Ile-Ife. By taking the headquarters away from both Enuwa and Modakeke, the government thought the Ife-Modakeke feud would be laid to rest (Akanbi 1997). He was proved wrong. The Modakekes saw Oke-Ogbo as part of the same Ile-Ife to which Enuwa belonged. They therefore used all the channels at their disposal to protest this "injustice".

On August 16, 1997 the protest escalated into full-blown violence with the Ifes and Modakekes attacking one another. It took the police several days to put the crisis under control. A peace committee, headed by Oba Ashiru Olatunbosun Tadese, the Oluwo of Iwo had to be set up by the Osun Council of Traditional Rulers to look into the issues in the conflict and make appropriate recommendations to the government. Officials of the National Reconciliation Committee [NARECOM] also visited the warring communities and promised to recommend a long-lasting solution to the government.

The reports of the traditional rulers and NARECOM had hardly been made public when the second stage of the conflict started to gather steam on September 15, 1997. The military administrator of Osun State, Lt. Col. Anthony Uzoma Obi, who had gone to visit his Ekiti State counterpart, Lt. Col. Mohammed Bawa, for surviving a bomb attack, was reported to have told media men on that day in Ado Ekiti that the decision of the government to relocate the headquarters of the Ife East Local Government to Oke-Ogbo, rather than Modakeke, was irrevocable. The Modakekes saw this as act of aggression from a military administrator who had once promised them a non-partisan handling of the conflict. The Modakeke Progressive Union immediately petitioned the military administrator on the matter and copied the presidency. The Modakeke Youth Solidarity Group [MYSG][6] also issued a strongly-worded press statement accussing Lt. Col. Obi of attempting to prejudice the recommendations of both the National Reconciliation Committee [NARECOM] and the seven-man peace-committee set up by the State Council Of Traditional Rulers on the matter (Balogun 1997; Sayo 1997). As the Modakeke charged: "Obi was already teleguiding the Obas' peace committee and NARECOM in coming out with reports favourable to the Ifes." Obi's statement, the

Modakekes argued, was "another way of causing fresh war between the Ife and Modakeke people" (Sayo 1997). Five days later, the "war" which Mr. Sunday Aghedo, the commissioner of police for Osun State later described in a press report as "ferocious" resumed.

Trouble started on the night of September 22, 1997 as a result of the abduction of a Modakeke man around 9.30 pm by some people suspected to be from Ife. The reaction of the Modakekes to set the man free was violent. Between the night of September 22 and 23, 1997, the two sides fought fiercely using petrol bombs, double-barrel guns, locally made revolvers and dane guns. The Ogunsua's palace and the Ife City Hall served as the military headquarters of the combatants. Food and ammunition were served in these places. Matters relating to tactical counselling and transportation to the "war fronts" [i.e. commonly shared areas like Odo-Okun, Ita-Agbon, Surulere, Iyekere, Akarabata, Oke-Eso] were handled in the two places. The sites also provided first aid services to the wounded.

The police took effective charge of the situation in the afternoon of the second day of the conflict. But by that time not less than twelve people had been killed. The injured were officially put at eighty-six, and the houses burnt were not less than two hundred. The burnt houses included the Lagere home of Chief Orayemi Orafidiya, the Asiwaju of Ife and the spokesman of the Ifes in the 1997 and 1998 crises. Also burnt by the rioters was the popular Oranmiyan Shopping Complex belonging to Ife Central Local Government Council.

The state of the conflict was epileptic between September 1997 and December 1998. It would die down for a few days, re-escalate and die down. Until August 1998 when Colonel Theophilus Bamigboye took over the leadership of Osun State[7], the response of the government to the crisis was equally feeble and ill-organised to the extent that it appeared that the warring parties had been left to themselves. The two sides killed each other freely. It was during the widespread carnage of the late 1997 that the popular Sijuwade Estate in Modakeke, belonging to the Ooni Sijuwade Olubuse 11, was burnt. Between January and December 1998, the killings continued but largely restricted to the rural areas. Farmers were brutally attacked and killed in their farms. The worst hit were the Modakekes farming on land considered to belong to the Ife people.

Impact of the Conflict

The impact of the conflict has been very devastating for both the Ifes and Modakekes. Since the pre-colonial period up to the end of field work, the conflict claimed several lives. As things are, more people are likely to die as a result of the conflict. The conflict led to complete evacuation of Ile-Ife, the cradle of Yoruba people several times especially in the pre-colonial period. The later dimensions of the conflict were as devastating as the pre-colonial and colonial phases. In 1981 and 1983, several houses, vehicles and persons were burnt in both Ife and Modakeke. Some of the families that were affected by these 1981 and 1983 crises had hardly regained their losses when the 1997 riot started. As usual, several hundreds of people were shot, slaughtered or lynched; housing estates, fuel stations and shops, especially the popular Oranmiyan Shopping Complex and Sijuwade Estate, were set ablaze by irate youths.

A drive round both Ife and Modakeke during the 1997 violence showed quite clearly that what the Ifes and Modakeke burnt in the two communities were the few modern buildings that gave Ile-Ife its modern look. As a result of the crisis, Ile-Ife, like Kano and Lagos known for religious fundamentalism and street violence respectively, was increasingly becoming known on the social map of Nigeria as a violent city that might find it difficult in future to attract external support for its development efforts. A worried lecturer at the Obafemi Awolowo University (OAU) observed that:

> ...Ife might not be able to grow beyond its present state. No sane person would want to invest anything [money, time or talent] in this kind of environment where, even as a stranger, you are not sure of the safety of your life in a market place. The Ifes and Modakekes seem to have sworn before one of their gods to destroy what was once known as the cradle of man.

An implication of the above statement, which several lecturers at OAU expressed in different words was that the University in Ile-Ife in a near future, might not be able to attract the best calibre of staff and students for security reasons. Each time the crisis occurred, movement of staff and students of the University was usually restricted to the campus areas for fear of being attacked.

In almost the same fashion, primary and secondary schools in Ife and Modakeke were usually closed down. During the 1997 crisis, the schools were closed for more than three months. Some parents had to change the schools of their children to the neighbouring towns of Ilesha, Odeomu, Ipetumodu etc.

The 1997 crisis created very serious refugee problem in Ile-Ife. Thousands of people, most especially the non-indigenes in the warring communities were rendered homeless. Most of these stranger elements, for example those from Oyo, Ekiti, Kwara and Kogi States, fled to the refugee camp established by the Seventh Day Adventists Development and Relief Agency [ADRA]. The organisation provided the refugees with food and other basic needs. The students of OAU living off campus inside Ile-Ife and Modakeke had to flee back to the campus to squat with their colleagues for several days. Some Modakeke people also fled to their relatives at Ode Omu and Gbongan, and as far as the remotest . parts of Ondo and Ekiti States, to escape being killed.

As a result of the 1997 crisis, several mixed marriages involving the Ifes and Modakekes broke up. Ife men married to Modakeke women were pressurised to divorce such women on the grounds that women could later become "agents of death". The same thing happened to Ife women married to Modakeke men. Several Modakeke civil servants serving in other parts of Osun State considered to be dangerous fled back home and refused to return to their stations. The most affected were local government officials. The 5th December 1998 House of Assembly elections could not hold at both Ife Central and East Government Council due to the crisis.

Efforts at Managing the Crisis

As we have seen in the foregoing explosion, there were no conflicts in Yoruba history, whether in the pre-colonial , colonial and post-colonial times, which were as dangerous and destructive as that of Ife-Modakeke peoples. One is surprised that no sustainable solution has been found to this crisis which started since the 1830s. As a first step to rethinking solutions to the problem, we need to re-examine all past strategies for resolving the conflict.

In our discussion of the various phases of conflict, we touched on various conflict managements styles that were tried by various governments. One important thing that is worthy of note is that the Ife-Modakeke crisis did not start from within Ile-Ife. The hostile disposition of the Ifes to the Oyo refugees resulted from the problem that Okunade, the Maye of Ibadan, faced with the Oyo people in Ibadan. The hostility against the Oyo refugees in Ile-Ife in the 1830s was simply a digressed hostility. Until this period, the Modakekes had a cordial relationship with their Ife hosts.

The first attempt to "resolve" the Ife-Modakeke feud was made by Ooni Abeweila who decided to create a separate settlement [Modakeke] for the Oyo refugees in 1847. This later became a problem and not a solution to the feud; rather than solving the problem the measure compounded it. As in the case of the Sabon Gari settlement for southern Nigerian immigrants in Kano (Albert 1993 and 1995) and the residential segregation system practised in Northern Ireland cities (Poole and Doherty 1996), segregation hardly solves the problem of a plural society; it rather compounds it. For example, since the Modakekes were segregated they always saw themselves as a separate people from the Ifes. They thus clamoured for a separate social and political identity of their own. That identity became the bone of contention between the two groups: the Modakekes claimed that their town was not part of Ife and the Ifes said that Modakeke was merely a quarter in Ile-Ife.

Had the Modakekes been allowed to integrate into the Ife society rather than be segregated in a particular settlement, they would have by now mixed so much with the Ife population that it would be difficult for them to lay claims to any separatist identity. The ownership of buildings in the city would have been mixed in the area that now constitutes "Ife" or Modakeke"; more Ifes and Modakekes would have been inter-married and no part of Ife would have been "underdeveloped" as the Modakekes now claim. Ibadan is a typical example of a Yoruba city in which all migrant groups, including those from Ife and Oyo, have now integrated. The physical development of the city as well as its traditional political system left no room for any group to allege discrimination against it.

The 1886 treaty, which was implemented during the first decade of the twentieth century, was another effort at settling the dispute. The treaty asked for the expulsion of the Modakekes from Ile-Ife. Ooni Adelekan Olubuse who implemented the treaty in

1909 was remembered by the Modakekes as their number one enemy. Part of the problem that the Ooni, Oba Okunade Sijuade Olubuse faced in managing the Ife-Modakeke crisis resulted from the fact that the Modakekes did not trust him as a son of Ooni Adelekan Olubuse. They saw him more as a problem than a solution to the crisis. Many Modakekes believed that the major objective of Oba Sijuade was to complete what his father started: "to permanently expel the Modakekes from Ile-Ife". They regarded those Ifes who fought them as being sent by the Ooni and that each time the king travelled abroad, all he did was to buy weapons for his subjects to fight the Modakekes. The Modakekes also believed that the local government headquarters controversy would not have arisen but for the close connections that the Ooni had with Abacha administration "who cannot call him to order."

The futility of the 1909 expulsion order was made manifest in 1922 when most of the expelled Modakekes returned to Ile-Ife. The king who received them back, Oba Ademiluyi Ajagun [1910-1930], decided to try his hands on a policy of reconciliation. He treated the Modakekes like his Ife subjects and incorporated their leaders into the native administrative system. The Ogunsua of Modakeke thus became a N.A. court judge; he and some of his chiefs started receiving salaries from the government. All these made the reign of Oba Ajagun to be very peaceful. No riots whatsoever occurred during his tenure.

Oba Adesoji Aderemi who succeeded Ajagun as the Ooni in 1930 tried to build on the peace initiatives of his predecessor. His administration was however bedevilled by the *Ishakole* controversy. As a way of resolving the problem, he offered a virgin land to the Modakekes on which they could farm and pay no land rent to anybody. The Modakekes however preferred to take their case against the Ife land owners to court. When they lost in the court they returned to the Ooni for the promised land but by then the land had been occupied by the native administration. All efforts to get another vacant land for Modakeke farmers proved abortive throughout the colonial period. In handling the crisis, the Ooni treated both the Ifes and Modakekes alike and was, as much as possible, fair to the two sides.

Since independence, two major issues characterised the Ife-Modakeke crisis. The first was how to solve the *Ishakole* problem

and the second was whether the Modakekes had the right to exist
as a separate town from Ile-Ife and consequently have their own
local government council. The first issue was formally laid to rest
in 1978 with the promulgation of the Land Use Decree by the
federal government. The Decree entrusted all land in different
parts of Nigeria to the government. The Modakekes thus became
less subservient to Ife land owners. Until 1989 when the Ife North
Local Government Council was created, efforts at resolving the
local government problem had always been in favour of the Ifes.
With the headquarters of the Ife North Local Government Council
located at Ipetumodu, the 1989 local governments reform removed
the Modakekes from the control of the Ifes. By 1997 however, they
were merged with the Ifes. The Modakekes would not have been
very worried had the government kept its first decision of locating
the local government headquarters at Modakeke. Trouble started
when the headquarters was taken to Oke-Ogbo in Ile-Ife.

Various panels of inquiry were set up to look into the Ife-
Modakeke crisis. The most popular were those set up to look into
the 1981 and 1997 incidents. None of the panels came out with a
permanent solution to the problem. With the publicity given to,
and resources pumped into, the Ibidapo Obe panel of Inquiry in
1981, the peace initiatives of the traditional rulers in Osun State
in 1997 and the NARECOM visits to Ile-Ife in 1997, one would
have expected some concrete policies to have been formulated to
end the crisis. The impact of any of these panels was yet to be felt
at the end of the study period.

The report of the Royal Peace Committee, headed by Oba
Ashiru Olatunbosun Tadese, the Oluwo of Iwo, was submitted to
the government in 1997. Although the Report was not made public
by the government it was probably obtained unofficially. The
content of the report and the refusal of the government to release
a white paper on it therefore became another issue in the conflict,
rather than a solution. The Ifes saw the report as a vindication of
their position in the conflict, that the best way to resolve the
differences between them and the Modakekes was to relocate the
latter to a new settlement where they could fulfil all their
aspirations. The Ifes were therefore in a total agreement with the
content of the report, especially the aspects describing "the present
abode of Modakekes" as being "within Ile-Ife"; the Modakekes

"are tenants on the lands presently used as their farmland, and the landlords need to be compensated by way of rent or royalty"; and that the "position of Ooni is too sacred to all Yorubas and can therefore not be allowed to be toyed with".[9]

The Modakeke, on the other hand, regarded the report as a betrayal of the trust reposed in the traditional rulers. According to many Modakeke informants, "The Obas know the truth but are unwilling to say it for reasons best known to them." The basis on which the Obas reached their various conclusions and made their suggestions seemed very clear and incontrovertible to a neutral assessor of the report. Of course, in a conflict situation characterised by a win-lose struggle, a group that considers itself not favoured by a position would always complain. This was probably why the Ifes and Modakekes differed in their assessment of the report. Had the report favoured the Modakekes, the Ifes too would most probably have found reasons to blame those who wrote it.

The aspect of the report stating that Ife landlords had the right to collect rents and royalties on their farmlands further boosted the conflict. Several Ife landlords were said to have increased the rent collectable from their land, probably as a way of forcing the Modakekes to vacate the land. This issue led to more problems in some "Modakeke villages". Between late 1997 and 1998, several Modakeke farmers were kidnapped and brutally murdered in their farms by some unknown assailants whom the Modakekes believed to be Ife people. As a way of reducing the rural guerilla attacks, the Osun State government had to force the leaders of the two communities to sign a peace agreement at a ceremony held in Osogbo on 9th December 1997. The government thereafter threatened to hold the traditional rulers in the two communities responsible for any subsequent outbreak of hostility in the area. The crisis consequently abated for a short period: it started later and the killing in the villages continued up till November 1998.

By the time Lt. Col. Obi left Osun State and was replaced by Colonel Theophilus Bamgboye in August 1998, it was clear that he [Obi] was not in any way equal to the task of dealing decisively with the Ife-Modakeke crisis. The Modakeke people never trusted him and merely saw him as a willing tool in the hands of the Ooni. Realising that the task before him was not an easy one, the new military administrator, Col. Bamgboye, employed a "multi-track" approach to deal with the crisis: posting of "peace-keeping" policemen to the two communities, appeals to the federal government for the necessary policy action, appeal to religious sentiments of the people, visit to villages where killings were still taking place to appeal for calm, issuing of stern warnings to those behind the killings in the villages, and refusal to have any private dealing with any of the traditional elites in Ife and Modakeke lest he was accused of taking sides like his predecessor. By December 1998 when the second phase of our interviews were conducted in Ife and Modakeke, Colonel Bamigboye had warmed himself into the hearts of the warring parties. Members of the two communities saw him as a "great man of God". Despite all these, people continued to be killed on the two sides of the conflict up to November 1998 when calm once again was restored to the communities.

Suggested Interventions and Policy Implications

The historical trend suggests, quite clearly, that the Modakekes would always resist being absorbed into the Ife socio-political system. They will continue to promote a separatist identity and ask for a local government council of their own. So long as things remain like this, the crisis would continue.

Giving the Modakekes a local government council of their own would be a necessity. It would however not be the last step towards restoring peace to Ile-Ife. Just as the Modakekes are presently not pleased that the past dispensations in Ile-Ife favoured the Ifes, the Ifes too would feel "defeated" should an independent local government council be granted to the Modakekes. Even if the Ifes raise no further objection to the creation of the Modakeke local government council, peace might still elude Ile-Ife. There would likely occur between the two groups, in the nearest future, local government boundary disputes and conflicts related to the collection of taxes. Each of these problems could be as fatal as the present sub-ethnic violence.

The most reasonable thing to do in the circumstances should be the reconciliation of the Modakekes and Ifes. After this, all other things would fall in place. A non-partisan third party, supported by Osun and federal governments, should convene series of peace meetings between leaders of the warring communities. The emphasis of the meetings should be on problem-solving rather than the determination of who is right or wrong in the conflict. The mediators in the conflict must therefore be able to encourage the disputing parties to drop their hard positions and be ready to address the problem realistically. These peace meetings should be held outside the two communities, at a neutral location. The issues in the conflict must not be lumped together. Each should be given deep and carcful consideration. Such issues should include the possibility of establishing a Modakeke Local Government Council; the citizenship of the Modakekes in Ile-Ife; political relationship between the Ooni of Ife and the Ogunsua of Modakeke etc. If such meetings were creatively handled by the mediators, some "natural" solutions to some of the problems in the conflict would come out through concessions on both sides. This would enable permanent peace to be restored to the communities.

A careful look at the history of the contemporary Ife-Modakeke crisis shows that most of the problems were caused by the youths of the two communities. These youths also fought most of the battles on behalf of their parents. The startling discovery during my fieldwork in Ile-Ife was that some of these youths had a very poor knowledge of the history of the conflict. Why were they fighting? Several Modakeke youths argued that they were fighting so that more jobs could be available in their community once they had a local government council of their own. Some were fighting because the Ifes killed some of their relatives in 1981, 1983 and 1997. The pattern of answers obtained from Ife youths was almost similar. They felt that a lot of their problems [joblessness most especially] would be solved once the Modakekes were eliminated. Each party in the conflict saw the other as "the problem".

As a way of sustaining whatever peace agreement was reached between the Ifes and Modakekes, the government should address, very urgently, the problem of mass youth unemployment in the warring communities. There were too many unemployed young men and women in the two communities. These youths formed the bulk of the arsonists. Some of them were not afraid of being killed. Until these young men are gainfully employed, problems would continue in Ile-Ife.

It is recommended that series of conflict management training workshops be organised for the various youth movements. Secondary school students in the two communities witnessed so much of violence that some of them could develop into a generation of avengers if not quickly "debriefed". Series of conflict management training programmes should also be organised for them, from time to time.

There were also various community-based organisations [CBOs] in Ile-Ife that consisted of both Modakeke and Ife members. Such organisations included those dealing with market situations, religious matters, access to credit facilities, professional ethics etc. Members of these CBOs should also be given specialised training on how to positively transform conflict situations to peace. At the end of each training programmes, the trainees should be enlisted as members of Nigeria Peace Network.

Although the training programmes could cost several millions of Naira, the results therefrom would justify the means. Dr. Omololu Olunloyo recently described the Ife-Modakeke crisis as a problem of the Yoruba people, not merely an Ife-Modakeke affair. He saw it as one of those problems that could "destroy the Yoruba completely", given the place of Ile-Ife as the Yoruba holy city. "If modern day Ife is destroyed, and remember the place is small, compact and full of treasures, then the Yoruba is finished" (Olunloyo 1997). Dr. Olunloyo was merely referring to the cultural consequences of the conflict, but we can also talk of its educational and political consequences.

The Ife-Modakeke crisis, since the post-colonial period, has been a veritable weapon in the hands of those interested in creating political tensions in Yorubaland. Its permanent solution would reduce the opportunities for such trouble-makers to operate. The Obafemi Awolowo University which is located in the ancient city would enjoy the much-needed peace for fulfilling its educational mandates. The efforts of the government towards promoting peace and democratic governance in Nigeria would also be better enhanced.

One last important point is that the crisis is a crisis of confidence between the present Ooni, Oba Sijuwade Olubuse II, and the Modakeke people. The father of the Ooni, Oba Adelekan Olubuse I, as earlier noted, was responsible for the evacuation of the Modakekes from Ife in 1909 and their subsequent dispersal to Owu/Ipole, Edunabon, Ede and Odeomu. They were resettled in Ife in 1922 after the death of the king. Since Olubuse II became the Ooni, he seemed not to have been trusted by the Modakekes. The last Ooni, i.e. Oba Adesoji Aderemi, never had any major problems relating with the Modakeke people though his own administration was also involved in the management of the crisis. Several Modakeke informants held the opinion, rightly or wrongly, that it was the primary mission of the Ooni to drive the Modakekes away from any Ife territory as his father did. It would therefore not be enough to reconcile the Ife and Modakeke peoples. Any sustainable peace effort must also reflect strategies for building trust and sustain cordial relations between Ooni Olubuse II and the Modakeke people.

Community Conflicts in Nigeria

Appendix 1
The Royal Committee on Ife Modakeke Crisis

1. After a close and detailed appraisal of the documents submitted by the leaders of both the Ife and Modakeke and our interrogation of the people, the following facts emerged;

    a.   That there are many juridical evidences to show that the Modakekes migrated at one point in time or the other to Ile-Ife. It was also alleged that they moved away between 1909 and 1922, but some of them returned to Ile-Ife in 1922.

    b.   The Ifes never contested the claim of Modakeke to the place where they now settle as their homestead. But the land which they use as their farmland belonged to some families, and the Modakekes used to pay royalties as tenants to these land owners. The Landlords to the farmland are not prepared to part with the family land to the tenants, without the continued payment of royalties. The Modakekes were in effect customary tenants to the land owning families.

    c.   The Modakeke's spokesmen claimed that they only re-occupied the farms which their forefathers used before they were evacuated in 1909. That claim did not in our view disprove the existence of original ownership, even before 1909. The law does not recognise prescriptive title. You do not become an owner of land by long possession. The Ijesatedo experience in Lagos where the supreme court ruled in favour of Onitire is an example in view.

    d.   The Modakekes saw themselves as a separate settlement from Ile-Ife and therefore entitled to all the rights and privileges as a district community including a separate administrative set-up and the choice and installation of their Baale as an Oba.

    e.   The Ifes believed that there was no basis to concede any separate existence to Modakeke, which is only a quarter, like the Hausas at Sabo within Ife. Other similar settlements or groups of people are the Offas, the Egbas, etc., who live in Ife without claiming any autonomy from Ife. The agreement signed by the Modakekes in 1922 also support the Ife's claim.

f. Even though the immediate cause of the recent confrontation was the creation and the siting of the headquarters of the Ife East Local Government, it was obvious that there were more fundamental reasons for the crisis, which has to do with the vexed question of identity.

g. The past interventions on the matter, particularly during the colonial era, were based entirely on juridical evidences, which can only be enforced by governmental power, but these did not eliminate the underlying deep-rooted sentiments of the warring factions, which keep coming up again and again.

2. Our committee decided to seek a solution that will address the realities of present day polity and remove, or at least minimise, the areas of confrontation and fears. In that direction, we are faced with the following realities that will inform our conclusions and recommendations.

a. That the present abode of the Modakekes is within Ile-Ife and completely encircled by the Ifes.

b. That the Modakekes are a group of very aggressive and progressive people, who have not seen themselves as Ifes, but will like to be identified as Oyo.

c. That the Modakekes are tenants on the land presently used as their farmland, and the landlords need to be compensated by way of rent or royalty.

3. We have given serious thoughts to the claims and counter claims, to the juridical evidences available to us and to the above realities and come up with the following options in addressing the immediate and remote causes of the crisis.

a. To accede to the claims of the Modakekes for a separate identity will involve their complete relocation as they are presently encircled by the Ifes. But to achieve that would necessitate the provision of land and massive investments in property to accommodate the dislodged people.

The following questions would therefore need to be answered: Are the Modakekes ready for this option ? Will the Ooni-in-Council be prepared to provide the land on which to build the new settlement ? Will the state government and/or the federal government be prepared to provide initial financial and logistic support for the new settlement ?

Even if all the above questions are answered positively, we should still ascertain the terms and conditions that will be attached to the new autonomy; i.e., the status of the new settlement [town, village or clan, etc], and the status that will be given to the leadership of that new community [Baale, Oba or what] and of course determine who confers that status, that is, from whom will he derive his authority.

The above are potent areas of solution that should be explored through questions, diplomacy and negotiation with each of the relevant entities, i.e. Modakekes, Ooni-in-Council, the state government.

    b.   Another option is to confirm the claims of Ife that Modakeke is only a quarter in Ife and therefore should not be granted an independent identity in Ile-Ife. This would entail a process of complete integration of the Modakekes into the Ife polity. That process will involve the preparedness of the Modakekes to renounce that claim to separate identity as Ifes. It will also affect the status of the Baale as a traditional ruler because he will only be a quarter head, even though that status can be elevated by the Ooni-in Council in future.

    c.   One more option is to maintain the status quo, but with the imposition of some realities and conditions that will promote peaceful co-existence. Such realities and conditions will include the following amongst others:

[i]   As sons of Oduduwa, the Modakekes cannot and should not be denied existence in Ile-Ife, which is the ancestral home of all Yorubas. Even if any Yoruba is driven away from anywhere in the world, he or she should have a first claim to being re-settled in Ile-Ife. The Ifes should be proud to be in that unique position to play that role.

[ii]   The Modakekes should however be made to recognise the hospitality of their host and therefore make deliberate efforts to sink their claims to independent identity, and be fused into the Ife social, cultural and economic life.

[iii]   The position of Ooni is too sacred to all Yorubas and can

therefore not be allowed to be toyed with. The complete allegiance of the Modakeke leadership and their Baale to the Ooni should be total and unconditional.

[iv]   The status of the Baale of Modakeke should be handled very carefully because of its implications to other chieftaincy positions in Ile-Ife, such as the Obalufe and Obalaaye. Elevation of the status of the Baale would appear only possible if Modakeke is relocated to a place where they can assume the status of a separate settlement.

[v]   The issue of the farmland should be addressed by the Ooni-in-Council with a view to negotiating with the current land owners to give some concessions to the farmers. Even here, members of this committee should be actively involved in the negotiations.

[vi]   Ife and Modakeke elites should make conscious efforts to build the bridge of confidence which has reached its all time low judging by the publications from both sides since the beginning of this confrontation. It is suggested that the elites of the two communities should take positive steps to create a conducive environment for peace and social integration.

Appendix 2

The Peace Building Activities of AAPW in Ife and Modakeke

Shortly after the foregoing case study was completed, Academic Associates PeaceWorks set about the implementation of some of the recommendations therein. The first task that the organisation set for itself was that of training women and youth in Ife and Modakeke on how to respond constructively to conflict situations.

Between the last week of April and first week of May 1998, AAPW organised two conflict resolution training workshops for some women and secondary school teachers drawn from Ife and Modakeke. The assumption underlying these training programmes is that men and youth who engage in violence in the two communities can easily be reached with peace messages through women. The training for teachers is towards equipping them to preach messages to their students, who sometimes participate in the communal violence.

In all, thirty women took part in the training programme which lasted three days. Thirty secondary school teachers were also trained for another three days. At the end of the training programmes, each group constituted themselves into peace committees and have since been working among the grassroots population towards promoting peace objectives in the two communities. The two groups [i.e, the women and the teachers] merged and constituted themselves into a community based organisation known as Peace Alliance [hereafter referred to as "the Alliance"] under the leadership of Dr. [Mrs.] Funmi Soetan of the Department of Economics, Obafemi Awolowo University, Ile-Ife.

Each school which was represented at the April/May 1998 conflict resolution training programmes now has a Peace Club for promoting peace objectives. All these schools were formally visited by the officers of the Peace Alliance in September 1998 as a way of giving further impetus to the work of the Peace Clubs. The Peace Alliance also visited the training camp of Man-O-War in Ile -Ife as a way of encouraging them to giving more attention to peace objectives in their activities.

On the 22nd and 29th October 1998, members of the Peace Alliance paid a courtesy call on both the Ooni of Ife and the Ogunsua of Modakeke respectively to brief them about their peace objectives. They were warmly received and the two traditional rulers offered to assist the group in achieving their goals. This was an important landmark in the history of peace-building in Ile-Ife. The group is now formally known to the two royal fathers. The steps they have taken shows that peace could be built in Ile-Ife using a bottom-up approach and anybody having an elaborate peace programme for the two warring communities can now boast of a local partner [well trained in conflict resolution strategies] to work with.

From November 30 to December 1, 1998 the Alliance organised a conflict management workshop for the religious leaders [Christians and Muslims] in the warring communities. After acquiring the necessary skills for conflict transformation, the pastors and Imams that attended the meeting openly pledged to inject peace ideals into what they preach to their congregations. The Modakeke group of the Alliance incorporated conflict resolution training into their 1998 Youth Anniversary of the Gospel Faith Mission International. With a grant from the British Council, AAPW will be organising problem-solving workshops for youths and community leaders drawn from both Ile-Ife and Modakeke. The training shall take place at a neutral location [i.e. outside Osun state].

Notes

1. The treaty was actually not signed by the Modakekes. The three signatories to the agreement – one as "representing" the Ogunsua and two others tagged "acting" officials of the town were Ibadan people. Whether these Ibadan citizens had the authority of the Modakeke people to sign the document is another issue entirely.

2. Petition sent to the Executive Governor of Oyo State by Dr. A. Oyewole [Chairman Modakeke Development Committee] and Mr. I.O. Ajayi [Secretary M.D.C.], 27th Dec. 1980 cited in Chief Oladiran Ajayi, *Modakeke: Towards the Promised Land*, n.d. p. 4 : While testifying before the Ibidapo Obe's panel that probed the riots which broke out in Ile-Ife a few days later, the Divisional Police Officer of Ife Mr. S.O. Ogundare claimed that the Modakeke people did not obtain Police permission before holding the fund-raising ceremony. They were advised to delete certain offensive words from their invitation cards before Police permission could be given. This the Modakeke people refused to do. The D.P.O. noted that he ordered the anti-riot Mobile Police to terminate the ceremony because he felt there might be a breach of public peace if it was allowed to be held. See *Nigerian Tribune* 26th May 1981.

3. *Ibid.*

4. "How Abiola, Akinjide caused riot", *Nigerian Tribune*, May 7, 1981; "Modakeke riot: Abiola, Akinjide blamed" *Nigerian Tribune*, April 17, 1981; "...Akiinjide accused", *Nigerian Tribune*, April 18, 1981.

5. "Insecurity of life and property in Modakeke, Oyo State", Petition sent by Drs A. Oyewole and Ayo Isawumi on behalf of the Modakekes to the President, Federal Republic of Nigeria, 13th April 1981.

6. This is a coalition of Modakeke Youth Movement, Modakeke United Front, Modakeke Liberation Council and Peace Keepers Club ot Modakeke.

7. He is believed to have been specially posted to the state to deal with the Ife-Modakeke crisis having dealt with a similar situation [i.e. the Tafawa Balewa crisis] while serving as the Military Administrator of Bauchi State.

8. See Isaac Olawale Albeert, "Ethnic and religious conflicts in Kano" in this volume.

9. See the appendix for the full text of the Obas' report.

References

Adelugba, S. (1981). "Modakeke riot a Shode-Ooni", *Nigerian Tribune*, April 22.

Adeniran, W. (1997). "Ife-Modakeke, Yoruba problem; some untold truths" *Nigerian Tribune*, 15 December.

Adisa, J. "Lagos: Street Culture and Families in the Street", in G. Herault and P. Adesanmi (eds), *Youth, Street Culture and Urban Violence in Africa*. Ibadan: IFRA.

Ajayi, J.F.A. and R. Smith (1964). *Yoruba Warfare in the Nineteenth Century.* Cambridge.

Ajayi, J.F.A. and S.A. Akintoye. "Yorubaland in the Nineteenth Century" in Ajayi, O. n.d., *Modakeke: Towards the Promised Land.*

Akanbi, O. (1997). "Ife/Modakeke Local Government Rift: Government Shifts Headquarters", *Daily Sketch* August 15.

Akinjogbin, I.A. (1965). "Prelude to the Yoruba Civil Wars of the 19th Century", *Odu University of Ife Journal of African Studies* 2.

Akinjogbin, I.A. (1966). "The Oyo Empire in the 19th Century. A Reassessment", *Journal of the Historical Society of Nigeria*, 111, 3.

Akinjogbin, I.A. (1992). "Ife: The years of Travail 1793-1893" in I.A. Akinjogbin (ed). *The Cradle of Race: Ife from the Beginning to 1980,* Port Harcourt: Sunray Publications.

Akinjogbin, I.A. (ed). *The Cradle of a Race.* pp 192-216. Port Harcourt: Sunray Publications.

Akinrinade, O. and I.A. Akinjogbin (1992). "The Aderemi Era, 1930-1980", in Akintoye, S.A. (1970). *Ife's sad century: The Nineteenth Century in the History of Ife,* Nigeria, No. 104.

Akintoye, S.A. (1971). "*Revolution and Power Politics in Yorubaland,* 1840-1893. Longman.

Albert, O. "Kano: Religious Fundamentalism and Violence" in G. Herault and P. Adesanmi (eds). *Youth Street Culture and Urban Violence in Africa,* Ibadan: IFRA.

Albert, O. (1993). *Inter-ethnic Relations in a Nigerian City: A historic perspective of the Hausa-Igbo Conflicts in Kano 1953-1991.* Ibadan: IFRA.

Albert, O. (1995). "Ethnic Residential Segregation in Kano, Nigeria and its Antecedents", *African Study Monographs*, vol. 17, No. 2. pp 27-42.

Augsburger, D.W. (1992). *Conflict Mediation Across Culture: Pathway and Pattern,* Louisville. Kentucky: Wesminister/John Knox Press.

Awani, B. (1983). "Modakeke Now Calm", *Daily Times*, Aug. 4, 1983.

Awe, B. (1964). "The Ajele System: A Study of Ibadan Imperialism in the Nineteenth Century", *Journal of the Historical Society of Nigeria,* 111, 1.

Balogun, S. (1997). "Crossing the Battleline", *Sunday Punch,* October 4, 1997.

Daily Sketch, August 18, 1997.

Daily Times, April 8, 1981. July 21, 1983, August 4, 1983.

Devin (Ooni-Elect) (1886). Statement of 28 April, 1886 in *Accounts and Papers.*

Falade, T. (1981). "No Rooms for Modakeke - Ifes Told Probe", *Nigerian Tribune,* May 21, 1881.

Ikume. O. (ed). *Groundwork of Nigerian History.*

Johnson, S. (1973). *The History of the Yorubas,* C.M.S..

Law, R.C.C. (1970). "Chronology of the Yoruba Wars of the Early Nineteenth Century,"*Journal of the Historical Society of Nigeria. Nigerian Tribune,* April 7, 16, 17, 18, 21, 1981, May 26, 1981.

Obideyi, E. "Police Accounts of Modakeke Killings", *Daily Times,* July 21, 1997.

Olunloyo, O. (1989). "Letter to the Hon. Speaker, Oyo State House of Assembly December 13 and 18, "Modakeke Riot", *Nigerian Tribune,* April 16.

Olunloyo, O. (1997). "Ife-Modakeke, Yoruba Problem: Insights. *Nigerian Tribune,* 29 Sept. 1997.

Omosini, O. "Ife. The Years of Recovery, 1893-1930 in I.A. Akinjogbin (ed), *op. cit.*

Oyediran, O. (1974). "Modakeke in Ife: Historical Background to an aspect of Contemporary Ife Politics", *Odu,* 10 July, pp 67-77.

Parliamentary Papers: Accounts and Paper 12 vol. LX of February 1887. See "Statement of the Chiefs", 27th April, 1886.

Poole, M.A. & P. Doherty, (1996). *Ethnic Residential Segregation in Nothern Ireland.* Coleraine: Centre for the Study of Conflict.

Sayo, I. (1997). "Again Ife-Modakeke on the Boil", *The Guardian,* Sept. 29, 1997.

Chapter 7

I. Williams, F. Muazu, U. Kaoje and R. Ekeh

Conflicts Between Pastoralists and Agriculturalists in North-Eastern Nigeria

Introduction

The following preliminary points should be noted.

This study was carried out in the Hadejia-Jama'are-Chad Basin which consists of wetlands and arid zones. The prominent areas of the Basin are:

(a)   Hadejia-Nguru Wetlands which are seasonally flooded riverine plain. They are only one of their kind in the north eastern part of Nigeria. Wetlands are productive natural systems which are of great economic importance and many communities are heavily dependent on their resources for their livelihood. These wetlands support livestock and food and other crops that are required locally and nationwide.

(b)   The arid zone which has a flat and very gentle slope towards Lake Chad basin. This area is covered by sandy soil in part, while the rest is above the Komadugu-Yobe, Komadugu and Gana rivers. The North East Arid Zone Development Programme (NEAZDP) management report of 1990-95 did show that this area was less productive than the wetlands and the tuduland. Therefore, there was a lot of pressure on the flood plains because the land was much more fertile and therefore could produce high value crops of rice and vegetables. However, lower and variable flows of the rivers on the basin have increasingly become a serious problem over the last twenty-five years.

We visited the markets to confirm what we were told about the economic importance of the wetlands to the rest of the country and to Nigeria's neighbours, i.e. Chad and Niger.

The north east fed Nigeria with cowpeas, wheat, rice and other grains from the fadama. This was recognised by the Federal Government when it introduced the National Fadama

Development Project especially for growing rice, vegetable and pepper.

The introduction of *Guna* (cow melon crop) increased the economic importance of the area which needed to be conflict-free if food production must be maintained.

The Chad basin was well known for its smoked fish which was sold as far as Lagos. The production was decreasing because of disputes amongst the fishermen, and between the fishermen and farmers. The real causes of these disputes were still to be studied in depth. It was estimated in 1992 that the Hadejia-Jamare flood plain produced 6% of the national inland fish, (Amans *et. al.* 1992). At the time of our visit, both Hadejia-Nguru Wetlands and Conservation Project (HNWCP) and NEAZDP staff confirmed that the quantity and sizes of catches were declining while fishery project areas were neglected. In spite of this unfortunate neglect, fishing was still an important economic activity and a lot of smoked fish was still sold to various traders from different parts of the country.

According to the programme manager of NEAZDP, the basin had the largest number of livestock in Nigeria. More than 90% of the livestock was owned by the Fulani pastoralists. (Amans et. al. 1992) The population of cattle for example varied from about 200,000 in the wet season to over 500,000 in the dry season (Shalangwa 1995). The number of other animals such as goats, sheep, donkeys, camels etc. probably exceeded 1.5 million. However, with the decreasing rainfall and area of grazing land, pastoralists' mobility became restricted and the number of livestock was reduced over time, thus creating a new wave of sedenterisation. To support this view, we spoke to a few young Fulanis who told us that they were looking for non-herding jobs because of the increasing difficulty in earning enough as herders and therefore, the remote possibility of purchasing their own animals. However, some of the pastoralists were migrating southwards where they came across hostile farmers with resulting conflict which led to deaths and destruction.

In the latter part of 1996, there was a Radio Nigeria report that one district head and twenty-three others were killed in Katsina State when farmers and pastoralists clashed. These conflicts occurred as long as pastoralists continued to depend mostly on open range lands, crop residues, and adopting browsing instead of fodder for feeding their animals.

In a chart we obtained from HNWCP in March 1997, the estimated livestock population in the wetland in 1992 varied between 200,000 in the wet season and about 500,000 in the dry season. In his paper on the importance of adequate river flows to the economy of the NEAZDP area, P.B. Shalangwa (1995) produced a graph of total value of livestock sold weekly in four livestock markets from May '94 to September '95, to show the importance of that area to Nigeria's economy and food security.

There was no doubt that constant re-examination of the actual and potential causes of the conflictual relationship within and between the fishermen and especially between the agriculturalists is necessary. The recent phenomenon of forcing Fulani pastoralists to move after decades of settlement in a location could lead to violent conflicts. The Fulanis told us that in places where they were allowed to settle, they were made to understand that they had no rights to land. In short, they were living on borrowed land for a borrowed period of time. It was expected that as pressures on land increased, the Fulani Agro-pastoralists and their landlords had to fight till death to resolve the land issue. This new wave of conflict could be avoided if there were initiatives from the traditional and state institutions on the ground, and taking note of the land use decree of 1978 that allowed customary rights over land, including grazing reserves.

There was "graveyard peace" during the period of field work because conflicts which would appear resolved have a habit of continuing (Roger Blench, 1997) and that was why we spoke about conflict accommodation instead of conflict resolution. Secondly, new conflicts tended to surface as old ones were being accommodated. The new conflicts was between the semi-sedentary Fulani Agro-pastoralists and their host communities in the north eastern part of Nigeria.

There was no doubt that the governmental agencies like NEAZDP, a quasi-governmental organisation like HNWCP, and traditional agencies, played separate and collective roles in developing strategies for managing old conflicts and could do the same in avoiding and preventing new ones. Their roles, strategies and initiatives shall be discussed later while new strategies and initiatives will be developed.

It is enough here to say that the federal government with resources and support from the World Bank and the European Community encouraged the state government to use ADPs and EU-funded NEAZDP (up to 1995) in carrying out development programmes that unexpectedly increased the likelihood of disputes and conflicts within and between the different economic actors in northeastern Nigeria. These agencies found themselves being forced to display skills they did not have to settle disputes that could lead to violence.

Unlike the southern part of the country, and like many other countries in Africa, there was no NGO working in the Basin. The quasi-NGO, HNWCP that existed had its management team, a director , and a deputy director seconded from the Federal Environmental Protection Agency (FEPA) and Bauchi State Agricultural Development Project respectively. However, it was funded by foreign organisations involved in conversion activities. Its expatriate staff were European volunteers who carried out action-oriented studies for policy formulation apart from working on hands-on projects. HNWCP carried out a lot of useful and relevant studies and we were sincerely grateful to them for their invaluable assistance and encouragement.

Other development agencies were Hadejia-Jama're River Basin Development Authority and Lake Chad Basin Authority. Both organisations were starved of funds and were no longer playing any prominent role. NEAZDP, and especially HNWCP had the structure and resource funding of an NGO but the autonomy was limited because of its ties to government. With its expatriates, it played a conflict-avoidance role in the past and it could still continue to do that separately and collectively with NEAZDP, ADPS, federal and state ministries with respect to water resources.

NEAZDP was already on a pilot programme for the grazing reserves. It was in a position to work with the ADPS to expand the pilot programmes. There was also room for NGOs to work with the pastoralists in the management and development of the

5,000 hectares of grazing land that could be acquired through the traditional institution as part of a permanent conflict-avoidance strategy.

The conflicts in north eastern Nigeria provided an opportunity to design and implement new conflict resolution strategies. We shall attempt to do this in our recommendations in chapter six.

Objectives

The objectives of the study were to:-

— Assess Cousin's five variables as they relate to the conflict situation in the area.
— Develop an assessment of underlying causes of the conflict in the area.
— Develop a preliminary outline of conflict management mechanism for the area, including an assessment of the potential role of established NGOs, community groups, local government structures and the two structures. We were also to develop an outline for follow-up activities, including a workshop and training activities.

Background to the Study Area

Physical Environment

The Hadejia-Nguru wetlands, an area of 22,860km, is in the north eastern sahel zone of Nigeria between latitude 12-13N and longitude 10-11N. The wetlands form an extensive area of flood plain where the Rivers Hadejia and Jama're flow through a fossil dune field. The area consisted of several local government councils from four states, namely, Yobe, Borno, Bauchi and Jigawa.

The local government councils were:

From Yobe State:	From Borno State:
Geidam	Mobbar
Bade	Kukawa
Nguru	Munguno
Bursari	Ngunza
Karasuwa	Abadam
Jakusko	Sundam Kali
Machina	

From Bauchi State:	From Jigawa State:
Ningi	Birninwa

Warje   Kirikasama
Jama're   Nguri
Zaki   Hadejia

Most of the areas were subjected to annual floods which made it economically very productive. Large quantities of rice, vegetable and wheat were produced annually through rainfed irrigation. The area also provides large quantities of fish, fuel wood and fodder. It was widely acknowledged to be of national importance in the quantities of rice, fish and livestock produced. Thus, it provided subsistence means of livelihood to its estimated 1 million inhabitants and made a significant contribution to the regional and national economy.

The climatic condition of the area varied in cycles over the years. Rainfall was notably seasonal, concentrated in the three months of July, August and September. Since the early 1970s, the climate tended to be drier. The current annual rainfall (400mm in the south west, 250 in the north east) fell to 15 and 20mm over the last 29 years.

Population

Kinmmage and Adams (1990) estimated the population of the study area at about one million people. The major ethnic groups were Fulani, Hausa and Bade who were also the main users of the natural resources, land and water. The first group was mainly nomadic or semi nomadic cattle herdsmen and an increasing number of them were becoming sedentary farmers. The other groups were mainly farmers but often owned few cattle for family upkeep.

Typology of Producers

The economic actors in north eastern Nigeria were of five main types, namely:- pastoralists, agro-pastoralists, farmers, fishermen, and wood-cutters. The farmers were more in number while the number of agro-pastoralists was increasing. It was also observed that an increasing number of the nomads were becoming farmers or agro-pastoralists because of the increasing difficulties in grazing and getting water for their increasing herd size.

These main types were sub-divided, especially the pastoralists who settled as farmers, or as agro-pastoralists or semi-sedentary pastoralists, i.e. they had a permanent location which they returned to during the wet season. Lastly, there were pastoralists who moved seasonally or when it was necessary. There were also fishermen and cultivators who were marginalised out of economic importance.

The farmers and the agro-pastoralists were settled but some were migrating from within and outside the area especially to the wetlands during the dry season.

A look at the statistics from NEAZDP and all the economic indicators showed that the people had an informal market economy in the zone. The farmers performed better because they had access to, and control of, the flood plain which was fertile and produced high value crops of rice and vegetables. Rainfed farming on upland produced millet and sorghum but it was observed that there was decreasing fertility and less rainfall.

M. Kalachiwi (1995) confirmed the well-being of the farmers, that the market value (1994 prices) of flood rice was in order of N6,000/ha or a total of 672 million naira annually while irrigated vegetable production value was N200,000 in 1994. The dry level farming on the sandy soils (tudu) was however decreasing in importance because of the increasing spread of sand dunes. From the gloomy report of NEAZDP and from what we saw during our short stay, the present and potential economy was likely to worsen if there was no improvement in the management efficiency of land and its uses. It was important that livestock production which appeared to command the same economic value with farming product be a key consideration.

This consideration required the protection of the grazing reserves, forest reserves, cattle routes and access to water for the pastoralists. Neglect of these key inputs could lead to decrease in livestock and its attendant consequences on meeting the national need for meat. Furthermore, the pastoralists should resist if these lapses occurred. Livestock must not suffer the same as fishing which was neglected in the area.

Crop Production

Three main cropping systems were practised in this part of the country : fadama: rainfed, upland and irrigated.

Fadama means seasonally flooded. It is used for wet season rice cultivation and for dry season culture with residual soil moisture. Under this condition, a problem for rice cultivation, always, is the non-predictability of the intensity and timing of floods. Early flooding submerges young rice plants and exposes them to damage from herbivorous fish. Late flooding results in desiccation. We found out that land with a high water table on the fadama edge supported the growth of some mango and guava trees and annual crops such as cassava and cotton. Rainfed cultivation in upland or tudu was widespread in the area. This was mainly for domestic food production of mainly millet and sorghum. Low rainfall and its uncertain timing was a major source of risk for farmers.

Irrigation cropping expanded in recent years following the introduction of motorized pumps. High value crops such as wheat, tomato, pepper and onion were grown in the dry season. The use of inorganic fertilizer was highest for irrigated crops. The cultivation of wet season maize using supplementary irrigation was recently adopted in some parts of the study area.

Labour shortage was a problem for all cropping systems, particularly for rainfed farming. Pest, particularly aphids and blister beetles, were a constraint on crop production. Soil fertility was also a great problem to rainfed and irrigated farming.

Livestock Production

Livestock was brought to the area in the dry season to benefit from available fodder on the fadama land. The population of cattle fluctuated around 200,000 in the wet season. Estimates suggested that sheep and goats exceeded one million in the dry season. More than 90% of the livestock was owned by Fulani pastoralists. Increasing population pressure on natural resources greatly reduced the availability of grazing and fodder for livestock. The major sources of concern of pastoralists in the study area were: inadequate grazing area for increasing animal population, lack of dependable sources of supplementary feed and poor veterinary services. The constant clash with cultivators because of inadequate grazing land was a result of inefficient management of land and water resources.

Cousin's Variables

Introduction

Natural resource conflicts cannot be discussed without addressing the particular resources, the right of the users and the recognition of the rights of each user by the other users, the traditional authorities and the various levels of government. In this particular study, the livelihood system involves the utilisation of both arid and wetland zones. These zones were used for cropping by farmers, grazing by pastoralists and fishing by fishermen mainly. Disputes and conflicts were found to be common in this situation in the zones. The conflicts, including that of our particular interest between the pastoralists and the farmers, were studied in greater depth in eastern and southern Africa. The studies led to a better understanding of the underlying causes of these conflicts and their management in those sub-regions. Using these studies, Ben Cousins of the University of Western Cape School of Government made a proposal (1996) to accommodate, manage and even resolve these conflicts once and for all. In developing the process, he identified five under-mentioned variables which we adopted for discussing the conflict situation with respect to the resources, the rights and their recognition. These discussions were useful in developing our own mechanisms for conflict resolution.

Different Categories of Users

Multiple resource use is a predominant feature of agriculture, pastoralism and agro-pastoralism. It is also common with cultivators. In fact most of the resource users in the study area were either organised on kinship or household production relations. We found that cultivators were organised on household system, and production relation was based on family labour. The family cultivated the lands which in most cases were inherited from their parents. In this type of production relation there was no intra-group competition over the resource use. The product from land belonged to all the family members, and most of the products were consumed collectively.

In the case of pastoralists, another category of resource users, the production was organised mainly on the kinship system. Perhaps the reason for pastoralists' preference for kinship system was to ensure that they moved in groups so that they could defend themselves from external attack. This kind of collectivism was common in all places where there was keen competition, especially between pastoralists and cultivators, over the use of natural resources. This system was therefore practised here by the pastoralists because they were the most underpowered group in the area.

The fishermen were another group that competed over natural resources in the study area. This group demanded for water mainly. Fishermen were resented by both cultivators and pastoralists because of their application of chemicals to kill fish. The chemicals also killed the animals and in most cases young plants as well. This prevented pastoralists and irrigation farmers from using the water and it led to disputes among the users.

Firewood cutters were also resource users in this area. Firewood was the only source of energy for cooking in most of the villages. For this reason, they also competed over the resources. There were also those who cut firewood for commercial purpose. These groups usually came from Kano. It was estimated that about 14,000 tonnes of wood was cut from this area annually. The wood-cutting, especially in grazing reserves, was a source of disputes between firewood cutters and pastoralists who were legally allowed the use of the resources. These people also cut the grasses in the grazing reserves to re-sell to the pastoralists.

Users of Different Status

With the loss of thousands of hectares of arable land to desertification in the north-eastern part of the country, the pressure on the highly fertile farmlands of the Hadejia-Nguru Wetlands increased the consequent movement of land cultivators and pastoralists towards the basin (here the availability of water and access to pasture were guaranteed).

The land tenure law of northern Nigeria (1963) which vested the administration of land in the traditional rulers on behalf of the community, turned some of these traditional rulers into big time absentee farmers. They leased out farmlands to migrants where they worked as primary, secondary or tertiary farmers, depending on the number of persons involved in the allocation/sales chain. In certain cases, the traditional rulers gave out farms on permanent basis whereby the beneficiaries became owners of their farms. With the promulgation of the land use decree of 1978, when the management of land was transferred to the state governments, some traditional rulers still continue to give out and illegally. Such illegal allocations were particularly serious where traditional authorities in coalition with the staff of the local and state governments gave out hundreds of hectares to farmers in the grazing reserves. This encouraged the unrecognised and the illegal use of these lands. Thus, majority of the big time farmers operating in these unofficial de-reserved forests, were illegal holders.

Majority of the indigenous small and big holder-farmers (i.e. the Hausa, Ngizim and Manga of Hadejia, Ngizim and Barde and the few settled Fulanis of the Ngure and Gashua axis; and the Kanuri, Mobbar and Badawi of the Chad Basin) acquired some of the farms through purchase but others did largely through inheritance. Some farms were co-owned when such ownership was either through inheritance or communal holding. Even though the wetland area was originally not put to agricultural use due to permanent flooding, the settled peoples around the area continuously extended their ownership as more land became vacant with the decrease in the water flow. Consequently, the nomadic pastoralists were never given the chance to acquire land for pasture in this area.

There were cases where land transactions were supposed to have been concluded but no papers were signed to legalise such actions. This practice was particularly rampant in the Lake Chad area where a Hausa farmer who confirmed buying a farmland some twenty years ago was not issued with any written evidence to that effect.

While the status of the farmer as regards ownership of his land could be identified and classified, the status of the pastoralists (especially the Fulani) was vague. Though some of the semi-settled Fulani pastoralists stayed in their locations for a long time, they were usually regarded as non-settlers and their rights to land ownership as a result of long usage was hardly recognised. The case of a village(near Guri in Jigawa State) where the Fulani inhabitants were eventually requested to vacate their village (even though they had been resident there for over 100 years) was a case in point. The Fulani communities living along the Yobe river on the outskirts of Gashua were in the same situation because they were slowly eased out of their ancestral base by farmers who continuously turned the flood plain into all season.

Judging from the farming activities going on in the flood plain, there seemed to be very little land left to be shared. For the pastoralists to have reasonable holding in the flood plain, nothing short of a government intervention by way of legislation and enforcement could make that possible. The holding on the flood plain had to be redefined and farming in the encroached forest and grazing reserves must be brought to the barest minimum.

The North East Arid Zone Development Program (NEAZDP) identified the land problem facing the pastoralists. It was looking into the possibilities of convincing the Yobe State Government to give pastoralists rights over some grazing reserves with the hope of minimizing their hardships. As an interim measure, NEAZDP provided facilities (including water, basic medical scheme). The success of the Jakusko-Nasari reserve was expected to determine the future of the scheme.

It was obvious that given the limited land available, nomadic pastoralists evolved a means of finding a place they could call their own . Driven by circumstances, for example, the pastoral Fulani of Faurau were fully involved in all-season crop cultivation including the growth of irrigated vegetable. The pastoralists of Kuka Maiwa of Jakusko-Nasari reserve and those of Bune-Garel in Jigawa State took to crop farming for years. It must be noted that such efforts on the part of the pastoralists was usually accompanied by conflicts. Government must therefore intervene to help enhance the status of the pastoralists with regards to land ownership

Different Uses

Multiple resource use is a central feature of many production (Ben Cousins 1995). It typically involves complex combination of users. The socio-economic activities in the area of study were complex and diverse reflecting the complexity and diversity of the natural system that were exploited. The main resources used in the basin included water and land for food, grazing and other domestic use.

Agriculturists or crop cultivators were the main users of natural resources in the basin. Crop production supported large number of people than other sectors of the economy. Three main cropping systems were practised in the basin.

(a)　Fadama' seasonally flooded land used for wet season rice cultivation.

(b)   Irrigation cropping expanded in recent years and high value crops such as wheat, tomatoes, pepper, onions were grown in the dry season.

(c)   Rainfed cultivation in the upland or "tudu" land was widespread for domestic food production of mainly millet or sorghum and recently Guna.

Grazing also constituted one of the major uses of natural resources in the basin. All livestock in the study area depended almost entirely on grazing from natural pastures and browsing of trees for their nutritional needs. Almost all animals were raised under the conventional open access grazing system with many of them adapting traditional to the seasonal pattern of water and fodder availability through migration.

Fishing was the main resource use of the basin. The Hadejia-Jama're flood plain was an important area for the production of fish, estimated at 6% of the natural inland fish production. The rivers were the major source of fishing while the wetlands were seasonally fished especially when water was released from the dams.

Wooded land provided a resource use for domestic fuel wood. This was also one of the major non-agricultural resource use of the basin. It was the only source of energy for cooking in rural areas. It was also an important source of dry season employment, particularly for communities without access to the dry season irrigation water.

Hunting also constituted another non-agricultural resource use of the basin. Due to the vast area of wooded land, bush meat abound, thus providing subsistence for the rural dwellers.

The wooded land also provided a resource use for mat-makers and timber extractors. Their products were sold for subsistence.

Finally, food and grass gathering also constituted an economic use of the basin. These gatherers were people who depended on gathering of food and grasses for subsistence. Food gatherers for instance obtained dadawa which were sold. Also grass gatherers sold their grasses to the pastoralists during the dry season.

Resource or Differential Productivity Economic Value Ease of Control

It was obvious to us that land had high economic value especially when rich and fertile. It was also obvious that farmers had easier access to land and its control. However, it was not all the land in the zone that could be cultivated except the fadama land with its fertile, high-yielding soil and other areas of wetland that could be used for all-year-round farming with irrigation.

The Fadama was also a grazing area for the animals of the pastoralists and the agro-pastoralists who were settled within the fadama land. The rest of the arid zone of the area had sandy soils (tudu) which was rainfed and used for upland farming during the wet season. These areas suffered from low or no rainfall and the soil was of low fertility and thus of less economic value to both the farmers and the pastoralists who migrated to the fadama during the dry season. It was not surprising that all grazing reserves and cattle routes within the fadama land suffered encroachment by cultivators with decreasing area for grazing by the pastoralists.

The open access grazing and browsing system with crop residues as supplements continued as the main provider of food for the animals. There was little attempt to develop other modern methods of alternative food system for the animals. There was need to develop a new integrated system in which settled farmers and agro-pastoralists could grow fodder crops all year round and sell to pastoralists at affordable amounts. The fodder development programme by NEAZDP and ADPs was still at its pilot stage. This condition increased the cost of cattle in the market as foods for animals became difficult to get apart from being expensive. In spite of this, the farmers believed that the pastoralists were better off. They forgot that the cost of cattle varied with the season and climate as it was with farm products. It was a situation in which farmers, agro-pastoralists and pastoralists benefited economically but with the cultivators in an advantageous position with respect to land and water. All that the users needed to know was how food-chain operated. This would enable them to understand each other's importance.

Water and land are important for both crops and animals. In the study area, there could be no farming without rainfall, especially upland, while the fadama land depended on the releases of water from the two dams into the flood plain.

Apart from the problem of low rainfall, water resource management was inefficient. However, the situation on the ground was not too serious with respect to water for the animals. Therefore, water for irrigation and upland farming could be inadequate during the dry season but not in the fadama for the animals. Water did not add to the market value of the animals even though they paid maintenance fees for some of the water points using generator-operated pumps. Most of them were replaced by solar operated pumps like the newly installed ones, especially by NEAZDP.

It appeared to us that while the economic value of the animals might equal the crops, the land tenure and rights did not adequately protect the rights of the pastoralists. However, the pastoralists in turn understood their increasing economic influence in the market place by organising: "Dogor Pulako" which meant refusing to do business in any market of any town or village that did not allow them easy access to grazing land and water. There were two confirmed cases. One was a threat to Muguram district but was not carried out. The other was carried out against Girgir market.

The fishermen had traditional priority rights over rivers but had difficulties with inland fishing in the fadama land because of the bunds built by farmers for all-year-round cultivation and the claims of ownership of all resources within and around the bunds. The conflicts between the fishermen and the farmers resulted in reduced fishing activities especially in the fadama land. This probably led to increase in the costs of fish in the local market. In fact, fishing activities in the area were on the decline. Neither NEAZDP nor HNWCP had fishery development plans in the immediate future.

An economic activity that affected the environment and the pastoralists was cutting of trees and grass in the grazing reserves for sale by cultivators granted licence by the local government council for generating revenue. The grass was later sold as fodder to the pastoralists instead of being left in the reserves in its natural state for the animals. While the state and local government stood to benefit from licence fees, the woodcutters and gatherers made profit while the animals and environment suffered.

At the end of the day, the basin (wetland and upland) faced the danger of decreasing economic activity leading to increasing poverty and emigration by the people.

Different Sets of Rights

The rights to different uses of land in Hadejia-Nguru-Jama're and Chad Basin were not only determined by the different land laws but also largely by their seasonal utilities and the social status of the various ethnic groups residing in the area. The numerous forests grazing reserves were established to preserve the fauna and flora of the area, provide adequate grazing land for livestock and resources for domestic use (i.e. the making of mat) and also eat from the fruits of the wild trees therein. Government also demarcated cattle routes for the easy movement of livestock and safety of farm produce from animals.

Farmers and pastoralists had an unwritten but well adhered-to symbiotic existence where the farmer allowed the animal to consume the residues from his crops while in return the animals' droppings fertilised the farm for the next farming season. In the areas around Lake Chad Basin and most parts of Bornu, the nomadic and semi-settled pastoralists jointly kept their herds under the care of the pastoralists. However, with the influx of farmers and pastoralists (from other neighbouring countries and from other parts of Nigeria) into the basin and the introduction of all-year-round farming, most of the land was converted into farmlands and the pastoralists' access to the farm residues was greatly jeopardised as the farmers burnt down the residues immediately in readiness for dry season fadama farming. The presence of farms around the water bodies, the insufficient passage provided for livestock as access to drinking points, with the resultant straying of animals into the nearby farms and the consequent legal harassment and psychological trauma, all made it impossible for the pastoralists to take their animals to either the rivers or the lake. The additional illegal conversion of most cattle routes into farmlands grossly limited the pastoralists access to fodder and water.

Contrary to what existed in some other parts of the country where ownership of land by women was a problem, in the Hadejia-Jama're and the Lake Chad Basins, women acquired land either through direct purchase or inheritance. Effective enforcement of the methods of land reforms spelt out above could determine the success or failure of the reform. Of particular significance was the government's ability to reclaim and re-define the forest and grazing reserves.

Underlying and Immediate Causes of Disputes/Conflicts

The underlying and immediate causes of conflicts between the pastoralists and agriculturists were not complex yet, they were diversified. The causes of these conflicts were both natural and man-induced. The immediate cause however was the behaviour and action of the core parties in precipitating these conflicts.

Underlying Causes

Drought

Incidence of drought and erratic rainfall pattern affected crop production and fodder growth resulting in food shortages for both human and livestock, particularly in the uplands. Therefore, people in the study area relied more on water supplied by streams and rivers of the lowlands than on rainfall for the sustenance of both crop and livestock production. Drought reduced flooding not only along the Hadejia river which was dammed, but also along the Jama're river which was not dammed (Adams and Holls 1987).

Management of Water Resources

There was clear ineffectiveness and inefficiency in the management of water resources. With the construction of dams and irrigation projects, the wetland was badly affected. The productivity of many of the flood plain resources was directly related to the extent of the floods. Any reduction of flood led to the reduction of the area under rice cultivation. It also translated into recession in the areas available for water resources.

This inefficiency was demonstrated by the inadequate monitoring and releasing of water from the dams without consideration for the needs of the pastoralists and agriculturists. This altered the traditional rotation of usage of the wetlands by the two groups and subsequently led to clashes between them. The rapid changes in irrigation techniques and subsequent expansion of dry season cultivation areas were not accompanied by any form of integrated management planning and development in the basin. These planning lapses were a source of conflict in the basin.

Land Management and Policy

The management of land resources based on the land tenure system became a source of conflict because of deliberate incompetence of the empowered authorities. Under the Land Use Decree of 1978 the control of the rights of occupancy of certain lands were vested on the local/state government. The 1978 Decree did not specify clear land-use rights for pastoralists nor did it guarantee their access to land resources. However, the Decree allowed traditional authority over customary lands, by empowering customary right of occupancy over 500 hectares for farmland and 5,000 hectares for grazing land. The state and local governments however never enforced any law to guarantee free access to, and control of, land for livestock production in the basin. Rather, rights over land for farming were sometimes acquired by giving the village head or local government authorities "Goro", i.e. bribe and, most times, the 5,000 hectares of grazing land were given out through this kind of corrupt means. This view was substantiated by many farmers and agro-pastoralists, especially those that were non-indigenes.

Also, lack of balance in policies by governmental agencies constituted a source of conflict in the basin. For instance, while NEAZP encouraged farmers to leave their crop residues on the farm, ADP advised against this practice preferring, instead, the burning of these crop residues as a means of traditional pest control. This did not go well with the pastoralists who depended on the residues to feed their animals during the dry season.

Preferential Treatment

The federal government in a bid to promote crop production, initiated programmes and policies which tended to favour the crop production sector to the detriment of the livestock sector. Also in the case of disputes between them the pastoralists always got blamed instead of the offenders. It was also discovered that encroachment on grazing reserves was with the consent of the government officials.

Loss of Traditional Relationship

According to some village heads and Lamidos interviewed, there used to be a symbiotic relationship between the pastoralists and agriculturists; both had co-existed in a mutual state of interdependence for a long period of time. The pastoralists recognised this and usually stayed clear of cropped fields during the rainy seasons. After the crop harvest, the herds returned to graze not only on the natural vegetation but also on crop residues. These residues became an important source of dry season feed for livestock while in return the crop fields benefited from the animals manure.

The director of Hadejia-Nguru Wetlands Project was however of a different opinion. To him, there was nothing symbiotic about their relationship. This was because the nomads were migratory and did not spend enough time in farmlands as to manure them. Rather it was the semi-sedentary or agro-pastoralists who enjoyed symbiotic relationship with the farmers.

Interest Groups

Due to the change from the traditional conflict resolution mechanism to that of police and courts, organisations were formed claiming to represent the pastoralists and farmers. In the course of our research, we discovered organisations like the Myatti Allah and Kautalfore representing the interests of the Fulanis, Alhayal representing the Shuwa Arabs and the Farmer's Council representing the farmers. We found that these organisations took advantage of the pastoralists' and farmers' ignorance and in many cases instigated conflicts between the groups to satisfy their selfish political or economic needs.

Bush Burning

Another underlying cause of pastoralists/cultivators clashes was the issues of bush burning. This practice was widely used by cultivators but the pastoralists did not like it. Interviews with both groups revealed that bush burning served several purposes. From the point of view of NEAZDP programme manger, the head of livestock department and most of the cultivators, bush burning served the following purposes:

a. It facilitated fast clearing of the remains of previous season's crop residues on the fields.

b. To the Director of HNWCP and the ADP zonal manager in Hadejia, Jigawa State and in Nguru respectively, bush burning destroyed the hideouts of the rodents that damaged farm crops.

From the point of view of the pastoralists, bush burning was an intentional act to prevent animals from eating crop residue. Apart from bush burning, the pastoralists complained that wood and grass cutters colluded with the cultivators to carry out extensive wood and grass cutting for commercial purposes and that the practice greatly reduced browsing and fodder available for the pastoralists. The most annoying thing to the pastoralists was that the grass cutting from grazing reserves were resold to them at very exorbitant prices. Investigations revealed that wood cutting was not limited to agro-pastoralists but was extended to businessmen from areas like Kano and Jigawa States.

Population Increase

Oral sources indicated that increase in population of both settled cultivators and pastoralists, as well as that of the animals, meant an increasing pressure on the limited available natural resources - land and water. This pressure led to keen competition among the producers over the resources. The competition sometimes culminated into open clashes. This factor operated under both underlying and immediate causes of violent clashes between the pastoralists and the cultivators in the study area.

To eradiate these causes of friction between the two groups and restore cordial relationship, the Kaska model should be encouraged. In Kaska, both Fulanis and non-Fulanis were agro-pastoralists. For this reason, the community set aside a separate grazing land and water for the pastoralists and their animals. No member of the community could cultivate the land or use the water set aside for animals for irrigation. The pastoralists in turn looked after the community animals.

Planting of Guna

Planting of guna was becoming the cause of friction among the pastoralists and settled cultivators. All the pastoralists interviewed expressed concern over the planting of guna. Because it needed little or no water, it was planted almost everywhere in the study area and that meant reduced grazing area for animals. In actual fact, guna planting could also be a solution to the conflict between the two groups. If planted in large quantity, guna could serve as fodder for animals and at the same time serve the commercial interest of the farmers. On the part of the farmers, guna crops, when planted all the year round, gave them the opportunity to make money all the year round. At the same time, the pastoralists could use the crop residues to feed their animals as substitute for grazing land lost.

Immediate Causes

Crop Damage

From information gathered from both pastoralists and cultivators, it was evident that one of the immediate causes of conflict between the two producers was crop damage by the animals of the Fulanis. The damage attracted quick reactions from the cultivators either in form of litigation or open clashes. Most of the clashes took place only during the dry season farming period. At this time, the fadama pastures were the only viable grazing resource.

Most of the traditional cattle routes with water were already encroached upon, making it impossible for the pastoralists to have access to water. For example, Ismaila Abdullahi (1993) indicated that the land area that was supposed to be reserved for grazing purposes in the north east was four hundred and thirty thousand acres but only one hundred and thirty-eight thousand, two hundred and sixty-three acres was actually devoted to grazing. He further explained that out of that total, 30% was already being cultivated. Out of the remaining 70%, 33% was also partially encroached upon by the farmers.

Futhermore, as a result of commercialisation of production, even the traditional areas for grazing by pastoralists was eventually taken over by the crop cultivators. Thus one of the reasons why the pastoralists inevitably damaged crops was the inefficient management of the limited resources, especially land, by the local government and traditional institutions. They appeared not to sanction farmers who worked on grazing areas knowing full well that violent conflict between the cultivators and the pastoralists was the result of their conspiracy with the farmers. Sometimes, the traditional rulers were helpless when it concerned government officials.

Bigol

The conflict between cultivators and pastoralists could also be based on the volent activities of a group of young Fulani boys known in Hausa as Dabalde, and in Fulfulde as Bigol (rearing cattle without being accompanied by older people or women). This group of young armed herders damaged crops intentionally, usually at night, and attacked any farmer who tried to prevent them. These immature young pastoralists beat and at times killed cultivators in the process.

The problem usually arose as to how to identify them since they moved away as soon as they committed this atrocity and the older innocent cattle pastoralists became the unfortunate victims of retaliation by the cultivators The district head of Muguram in Jakusko Local Government area of Yobe State said that the major problem his district faced was the irresponsible activities of this group. The security committee (formed by the Fulani pastoralists and cultivators in the area) met and agreed to outlaw the group. As such, no pastoralist was supposed to move or migrate without their families.

Law Enforcement Agencies and the Legal System

The use of police and courts to settle disputes between these groups led to the promotion of adversarial relationship between the pastoralists and agriculturists and therefore constituted a source of conflict.

According to the village head of Dagona, the police and court officials extorted money from the groups, but especially the pastoralists. Hence, a simple case that could be settled traditionally and jointly was prolonged and sometimes resulted in sanction and extortion by the police.

According to the Lamido at Munguno, one Fulani was still lying critically ill after being shot by the police. Most people who complained of this type of activities by the police were the Fulani pastoralists. They complained bitterly about the joint patrol team of the army and police who victimized the Fulanis for "no just cause". The Fulani pastoralists believed that it was the farmers who arranged these security personnel activities on them. The pastoralists also suffered from juridical discrimination owning to the fact they did not have any land title or land rights, and thus the courts acted in favour of the farmers when cases of damage to crops were referred to them.

Outline of a Conflict Avoidance and Management Mechanism

Methods

Conflict management experts have three basic methods of managing conflicts. These are:

a. Violence and coercion in physical or psychological form according to the Fulanis.

b. Various forms of bargaining and negotiations which could be multi-track with special emphasis on track 1 (governmental organisations especially for land disputes), track 2 (non-governmental organisations acceptable to all the parties) and track 3 (opinion leaders). This could be a conflict avoidance or prevention strategy.

c. The involvement of a third party-binding (legal system), non-binding (traditional rulers) and NGOs if (b) above does not work. This is a conflict avoidance strategy if core parties have confidence and trust in the third party.

Outline Mechanism

Therefore, in developing an outline mechanism, we must consider (a) and (b) above with more emphasis on the combination of tracks 1 and 2 working in symbiosis. A situation of chronic endemic conflict is a central feature of non-equilibrium settings. Mediation and arbitration are required to settle conflicts between individuals and groups. There should be emphasis on procedures which could specify the framework within which interested parties could legitimately put forward claims to resources, the criteria for choosing between opposing claims and enforcement procedures (Behnke 1994: 95).

Medium Term Strategy

The medium term strategy therefore is to develop procedural laws that will use the binding outcomes within an institutional framework that will not only legitimise the mechanism above but will also be used by both the traditional and the legal authorities as an alternative dispute resolution system. This must be the objective in order to complete the process of de-escalation and settle the political grounds for conflicts.

Existing Mechanism and Structure

HNWCP & NEAZDP

The assessment and brief analysis of the facts and information gathered over a 12-day period demonstrated that the causes of the conflicts were not as we were made to believe at the beginning of our study. This is not to say that the crises and conflicts were over but unlike the past, there was a gradual de-escalation in the last two years. The de-escalation was as a result of series of consultations, dialogues and meetings between various concerned governmental and quasi-governmental institutions, and the interested parties in the basin.

In the wetlands, the Hedejia-Nguru Wet and Conservation Project played a prominent role in settling disputes and sometimes preventing violent conflicts between the multiple users of land and water as resources in its project areas of the wetland. However, the projects which were more concerned with water management dealt with agriculturists, fishermen, pastoralists and wood cutters making the socio-economic activities diverse and complex. This was an integrated system that worked well in the past with the co-operation of all the multiple users. The rapid expansion of cultivated land, year-round cultivation and construction of bunds created conflicts not only among cultivators themselves but also between them and the pastoralists as well as the fisher folks.

With respect to the pastoralists, they found their grazing land and pastures encroached upon by expansion and year-round cropping while the barriers formed by the bunds also led to loss of grazing land in the fadama area.

Since 1990, the HNWCP has been involved in series of consultations for avoiding conflicts. It held series of meetings with the pastoralists and the fishermen. The need for this conflict avoidance strategy was demonstrated when in the Gorgoram area of the wetlands, violent conflicts erupted apart from the serious environmental consequences. In fact, the Director of HNWCP saw the need for development project planners to equip project staff with mediation skills. The HNWCP thus realised that it had to play the role of a mediator if its development plans were to be actualised within the budget and within the planned period. Conscious of this role, HNWCP did:

a. start an annual series of workshops that brought together all governmental agencies and institutions involved in the management of water in the basin. The next workshop was planned for May 1997. Earlier ones were held in 1993 and 1995 at the National Institute of Policy and Strategic Studies in Kuru, near Jos.

b. form, with five state ministries of agriculture, joint consultative stakeholders' forum that included government, traditional and multiple users' representatives. The HNWCP was the secretariat with the director as the secretary. A director-general from Borno State Civil Service was the chairman as the organisation brought together all the north eastern states of Nigeria and the organisations representing the various ethnic and economic groups in the area.

This Consultative Forum succeeded in bridging the communication gap between the affected parties, in opening a strong channel for communication with the federal government and its concerned agencies and above all, in preventing potential violent conflicts within the multiple users (Mkalachiwi 1995). In short, HNWCP working with these agencies contributed to the successful management of the conflicts in the project areas within the last two years. The HNWCP also conducted many studies to improve the management efficiency of the wetland resources, especially water, while developing conflict management strategies as the situation arose. Unfortunately, these strategies were not passed on from one project officer to another either in writing or orally. None of the present staff was involved in any mediation exercise in the past. Therefore, there was need to develop a method for not only codifying these practices but also having conflict management models in the project plan with a period for equipping some key semi-permanent personnel and field staff with conflict management skills.

One of the key government agencies that worked closely with HNWCP was the North East Arid Zone Development Programme (NEAZDP) within the HNWCP area. The two bodies according to NEAZDP management report summary, 1990-95, used existing facts and figures to defend, on technical, environmental and socio-economic grounds, the water requirements of the programme area and the urgent need for timely releases from the upstream dams. Therefore, NEAZDP played a prominent role in the consultative council of stakeholders.

Their joint efforts led to the promulgation of Federal Government Decree 101 of 1994 which provided for the harmonisation of national and sub-national water policies in the country. There was continuous improvement in the efficient and effective management of water resources to satisfy the minimum requirements of all multiple users in the five states. This was important to NEAZDP because the greater part of its project area included both the rainfed and irrigated upland with low rainfall and decreasing soil fertility, thus making dry land farming increasingly marginal.

During the wet season, the upland supported the livestock population. It was therefore the home of the pastoralists during this season when flooding and intensive farming in the flood plains obliged the pastoralists to move up. During this period, the pastoralists sometimes had to trek long distances to graze and water their animals with the adverse effects on the nutrition and growth of herds. The situation would grow worse if desertification continued unabated as 80% of NEAZDP area was already covered by sand dunes. This problem forced the pastoralists to move southwards and eastwards or across the national boundaries. Some even became agro-pastoralists. The future economic consequences caused anxiety apart from becoming a source of conflict. NEAZDP therefore took some initiatives in the last three years. These initiatives included:

a. Introduction of farm forestry for sand dune stabilisation in Kaka and Karasuwa in 1992. The same exercise was replicated in six other locations. However, the animals of the pastoralists turned these areas into grazing land, a situation which might not help the stability of the dunes in the long run. Considerable financial, technical and manpower resources were required to continue with this project on a large scale. NGOs could also work with NEAZDP on this project with less bureaucracy and more efficiency.

b. Encouraging fodder production by settled farmers using species of leblab, elephant grass and sorghum almun and testing a development model for large grazing reserves as a contribution towards resolving the complex problems of range management. The model was already in place at Jakusko-Nasari grazing reserve since 1990. We met the Lamido of the pastoralists in the reserve where there were already farms with guna and fodder crops that needed little moisture to grow by settled farmers and Fulani agro-pastoralists. However, the reserve served more as a water point than a grazing land. There was no doubt that if the exercise succeeded, the pastoralists might not need to move to the flood plains during the dry season. It might also be a model for the management of grazing reserves, reducing encroachment and encouraging cultivation of fodder crops by agro-pastoralists to meet the needs of their roving kin. However, it was hoped that if water was shared equitably, the tuduland could produce more fodder as a long term preventive action against conflict over crop residues.

To a great extent, the NEAZDP left the resolution of conflicts to superior government agencies because it was a governmental organisation whereas HNWCP was a quasi-NGO.

Interest Groups

The Nigerian farmers council has existed for many decades but it was unknown to many except those who were in the organisation for their own benefits. Their leaders in the states, local government and communities were recognised by government, and like those from the Emirate council they were part of all mediation exercises. The leaders of Myatti Allah and Farmers' Council also met on regular basis. However, the new breakaway group known as Practising Farmers did not establish themselves in those states of the northern eastern part of Nigeria at the time of fieldwork.

Government Agencies

The federal and state ministries of agriculture and their agencies, the Agriculture Development Project, carried out agricultural development activities before the HNWCP and NEAZDP were formed. The staff were therefore more familiar with the underlying and immediate causes of disputes and conflicts in the basin. On the other hand, the ADPs introduced new seeds and farming techniques including irrigation services to increase crop yield. New crops needing little moisture, e.g fodder crops and Guna, were also introduced for dry season farming in the flood plain and tuduland without any alternative for the Fulani pastoralists who came to fadama to find standing and sometimes harvested crops instead of crop residues, especially during the dry season. These new fodder crops and techniques did not reduce the conflicts because the crops were good for the upland soil.

In addition, the ADP in Jigawa State was, like NEAZDP in Yobe State, introducing fodder crop farming. They had realised that year-round cropping and expansion of farmland were reducing the number of cattle routes and grazing reserves available to the pastoralists. This exercise appeared to be a curative measure rather than a preventive one. Unfortunately, these measures were not helpful because of the series of clashes and deaths that were recorded in the past in Jigawa State, for example in Guri district of the State (Ismaila Hadejia 1993). The same thing occurred in other states of the north east. The federal government in its own way was getting World Bank assistance through funds and expertise to support the ADPs for the development of grazing reserves so as to increase livestock and stabilise pastoralists land rights. Part of the programme was for the states to enforce in line with the Land Use Decree of 1978, the customary allocation rights of 5,000 hectares per person or group and then preserve 10% of the total land areas in each state as gazette reserves. It was difficult to apply these directives in the flood plains or elsewhere.

The Ministries of Agriculture in Jigawa and Yobe States set up consultative fora at the state, local government and emirate levels as far back as 1989, but the ADP manager in Hadejia confirmed Ismaila Hadejia's written and oral submissions that these committees were not as active as expected, and neither played any significant role since 1994. This showed that the conflicts were not as frequent and not as destructive as they were in the late 80s and early 90s. Therefore, according to Ismaila Hadejia, these consultative fora did help. He gave the example of the Kirikasama Local Government Council setting up a committee, made up of its chairman, the council secretary, district head, the divisional police officer, and customary court judges which went in February 1990 to Kadira village to mediate between the core and interested parties.

Even though none of the committees was active, they existed to be activated when the need arose. It was necessary that these committees were activated to meet with the parties regularly, and pressurise federal, state and agencies to do what was necessary to avoid conflicts. These committees could be ADP-driven instead of the ministry in order to reduce bureaucracy. In short, ADPs with their reasonable autonomy could act as the secretariat of these committees similar to what HNWCP did for the consultative forum for water resources. For land resources, NEAZDP worked out models for development and managing grazing reserves in consultation and cooperation with district heads and pastoralists, as in the Jakusko Nasari Grazing Reserve. (NEAZDP Summary Report, 1990-95).

Security Agencies

The Nigeria Police Force and, to a minimal extent, the Nigerian Army, were involved in restoring law and order whenever they were called by the state, local government, traditional rulers or sometimes by the core parties and the farmers. According to the Divisional Police Officer in Gashua, the Nigerian Police Force not only always remained impartial but also encouraged the core parties to settle their disputes through the traditional system or outside the customary or western-type courts. His oral submission did not agree with the statements made by Lamidos and ordinary Fulani pastoralists in all the places we visited.

The Fulanis' view was confirmed by the Myatti Allah's representative in Gashua in the presence of the local leader of he farmers' council who accepted the fact that farmers had a greater influence than the Fulani agro-pastoralists and pastoralists. He confirmed that the fadama was always an area of conflict unless the farmers, not even the Fulani agro-pastoralists, had an upper hand. According to him, the farmers believed that the Fulani pastoralists had greater financial strength than the farmers, and therefore could afford to buy fodder at any cost instead of relying on free crop residues.

At the end of the day, the two gentlemen agreed that they settled cases themselves or through the village or district heads. On the other hand, the Nigerian Police Force and the Army were useful in fighting off the Toubous who carried out raids from Niger into Chad basin killing even Fulani pastoralists and stealing their animals. Unfortunately, many farmers took Toubou raiders to be Fulani pastoralists. In fact, the ADP manager was so convinced that the Fulanis from Niger and other parts of western and central Africa were responsible for most of the conflicts. One of the farming villages like Kaska experienced Toubou raids annually. They always called in joint army/police task forces to hoot raiders back across the border. The Police contributed to conflict management in the basin within and outside the various committees. However, it was important that they be less visible in these disputes while concentrating on anti-robbery patrols, and win the hearts and minds of the Fulani pastoralists.

Procedural Law

Earlier in this chapter, we discussed the "new thinking" and shifting from substantive law to procedural law. With the support of the traditional rulers and the concerned organisations law could be applied to prevent serious disputes at the beginning. NGOs with legal and land experts would be required to develop and test such laws and educate the core concerned and interested parties. This law when in place should be applied side by side with the traditional methods of intervention. However, it would replace the present substantive sharia/western laws. Procedural law was acceptable to all irrespective of ethnic or religious affinity.

NGO's Role

There was no real NGO in this zone. The HNWCP, federal and state governments seconded-staff, along with concerned public officials of NEAZDP who are trusted and acceptable to the interested parties could play the NGO role. They could get the core and interested parties to compromise since the conflict between the Fulanis and agriculturists were not structural even though endemic. It was also obvious to us that the Fulanis were not prone to violence neither were they a violent ethnic group. This also applied to the Fulani pastoralists from other West African Countries. The so-called violent pastoralists were not Fulanis but Toubous who came from Niger Republic to raid rather than to graze their cattle. In fact, they formed a group that was opposed to the Nigerian government. In conflict prevention, mediators must seek for "joint gain outcome" to make all sides believe that they got what they wanted.

Conflict Avoidance

Conflict avoidance strategy was used in the early 90s by the staff of the HNWCP when, according to Thomas (1991), they consulted the multiple users, took careful notes of their interests and concerns and designed the projects to resolve these concerns. He gave an example of Garbi where there was a meeting with the leaders of the pastoralists and the fishermen who competed for claims in the fadama. This strategy was concretised in the setting up of the consultative forum with HNWCP, NEAZDP and ADP field staff, and, given the resources, it could avoid further conflicts between the multiple users by early identification of early warning signals of potential disputes or conflicts. The forum could work better if it got its resources form outside the government, with HNWCP managing the resources. The consultative forum should continue to concentrate on management of water resources, acquire the necessary confidence, and obtain the trust of all parties in the avoidance of conflicts.

In addition to the above, the NEAZDP and the ADPs in all the states set up a consultative forum to deal with the land issues as in Decree 101. The forum should get the federal government to make amendments to the land use decree of 1978 to meet the pastoralists demands. In the meantime, the same decree could allow an individual to own up to 500 hectares of farmland and up to 5,000 hectares of grazing land through acquisition of customary rights of occupancy. Thus, traditional rulers could be empowered to allocate grazing land for the pastoralists as they did for cultivators, to prevent encroachment of the allocated grazing land by cultivators.

A conflict avoidance strategy was to use the World Bank/ Federal Government assisted livestock development programme for the priority development of cultivated pasture and fodder. The strategy was also to encourage quantitative and qualitative production of concentrates of cotton seeds, groundnut cakes, palm kernel cake and molasses (Hadejia 1993).

Myatti Allah, the religious-turned socio-politico-economic ethnic pressure organisation of the Fulanis was also included in every committee and consultative forum. The organisation mediated in many conflicts and it was looked upon by many Fulanis as a body that could pressurise the federal and state governments to grant legal rights over grazing land and wherever they were settled. The body on its own could pressurise the traditional councils to grant them customary rights of occupancy over 5,000 hectares of land in each community in line with the land use decree of 1978. The organisation could hold the land in trust for the pastoralists.

To achieve the above, Myatti Allah joining forces with Kautalfore, had three options that could be separately or jointly implemented.

These options were:

a. Working with a human rights NGO like Network for Justice in Kaduna to seek judicial interpretation of customary aspects of the land use decree of 1978 as it affected grazing land in particular and the Fulanis in general, whether settled or nomadic.

b. On its own and using highly influential Fulanis in the concerned states it could get state and local governments to direct the district heads to give customary rights of occupancy for grazing land for settled, semi-sedentary pastoralists and nomadic pastoralists only.

c. On a medium term, the organisation could work with the above human rights NGOs formulate procedural laws in line with the "new thinking" (Ben Cousins et al 1996).

In summary, there was an immediate mechanism of using NEAZDP and HNWCP staff as impartial mediators acceptable to the government and that could always set the core and interested parties to agree on binding outcomes that were fair and just to all. This would prevent recurring old conflicts and avoid new ones. As soon as possible, new NGOs could then work with the pastoralists not only in improving livestock quality production but also in assisting the pastoralists to ascertain their rights and benefits over their entitlements in terms of access to land and water. These NGOs must work towards building an integrated but manageable economic system of all users of these finite resources.

Conclusions and Recommendations

The following are our conclusions with respect to the underlying and immediate causes of the conflict.

a. Inefficient management of land and water resources even though the appropriate laws existed side by side with traditional powers to allocate land to, and protect the rights of both pastoralists and cultivators.

b. Corrupt practices of the local government council staff and traditional rulers compounded the problem by allowing encroachment in reserves and cattle routes by cultivators.

c. The pastoralists' leaders or Lamidos had no similar powers and were therefore not able to challenge the illegal act.

d. The pastoralists lacked trust in the non-Fulani traditional rulers (who were usually farmers) in settling disputes fairly and justly.

e. The belief by farmers that the pastoralists were rich and therefore colluded with some traditional rulers and law enforcement agencies to extort money or collect monetary claims for unfairly assessed crop damages.

f. The confused and unfair misrepresentation of the Fulanis as a violent ethnic group including those who came from neighbouring countries. Reliable information revealed that the Toubous from Niger, not the Fulanis were the culprits. The Toubous from Niger Republic were raiders and part of a guerrilla group opposed to the Nigerian government.

g. Lack of communication between the core parties on the benefits of Guna to man and animals. In addition, there was no enlightenment campaign by ADPs and NEAZDP that the grazing reserves could be beneficially used by both parties for growing fodder crops only.

h. The slow adaptation by the Fulanis to the changes in the agricultural methods and systems in the north eastern parts of Nigeria. The trend in the long term was for most of them to become agro-pastoralists or semi-sedentary instead of roving pastoralists in the future. As grazing land decreased and reliance on cultivated fodder pasture increased the number of agro-pastoralists was expected to grow and of nomads to decrease over time. There was economic opportunity also in making alternative animal feed from groundnut, palm kernel and cotton seed by marginalised agropastoralists farmers from outside the area under study.

i. There was the urgent need to educate the people on the maintenance of balance between the grazing area available and the number of animals (the herd size) that the area could support. This was a challenge to NGOs working with the pastoralists.

All the information made available to us showed that disputes/conflicts were common in these situations since terms of access and control over these resources differed and therefore one party was more empowered than the other. On the other hand, it was also necessary for the pastoralists to start adapting to these inevitable changes over time in order to become empowered.

Recommendations

It was obvious that any attempt at settling the disputes/conflicts in northern eastern Nigeria required the support of the two levels of government. This was because the orientation of the inhabitants was that only government through the traditional rulers or the local government council could make things happen. Therefore, our immediate recommendations are:

a. That NEAZDP, a government development agency, as the exclusive grazing reserve management agency, and HNWCP, a quasi non-governmental organisation be empowered by the state and local governments to mediate in all disputes dealing with land (NEAZDP) and water and environment (HNWCP).

b. That NEAZDP becomes the exclusive management agency for developing the grazing reserve to meet the needs of pastoralists and agro-pastoralists now and in future.

c. NGOs should be encouraged to work with the pastoralists and other economic actors in areas where NEAZDP and HNWCP cannot cover.

d. For these two organisations to assume the above responsibilities, conflict management workshops and training programmes have to be organised. The first workshop should be used to sensitise the staff of the two organisations, the core parties, the concerned parties and other influential parties. This can be followed by special programmes for selected NEAZDP, HNWCP, state, local government and some emirate council members.

e. On the medium term, there is the need to develop procedural laws as explained above. These procedural laws will legitimise procedures for assessing costs of damages, fix claims, eject illegal or non-cultivators of fodder corps in the reserves or occupiers of cattle routes and pastoralists settlements and make agreements reached with traditional rulers or mediators binding on both partes.

f. Except for very serious incidents, the law enforcement agents and legal system can be excluded. If the operators of these laws are fair and just, there will be joint benefits and outcomes for both parties. The impact shall be both conflict avoidance and conflict prevention.

g. Judging form the activities going on in the flood plain, there seems to be very little left to be shared. For the pastoralists to have reasonable holding in the flood plain, nothing short of a government intervention by way of new edicts can make that possible, so that the holding on the flood plain can be fairly redemarcated with farming in the encroached forests, and grazing reserves must be brought to the barest minimum. If not done properly, it may lead to destructive conflicts.

h. NEAZDP has identified the land problem facing the pastoralists and it is looking into the possibilities of convincing the Yobe State Government to give pastoralists rights over some grazing reserves with the hope of minimizing their hardships. As an interim measure, NEAZDP has provided facilities (including water and basic medical services) in the Jakusko-Nasari Reserve as a pilot fodder cultivation scheme. It is obvious that given the limited land available, nomadic pastoralists have to evolve a means of finding land available, nomadic pastoralists have to evolve a means of finding a place they could call their own.

Driven by circumstances, for example, the "pastoral Fulani of Farau are fully involved in all-season crop cultivation including the growing or irrigated vegetables" (Hadejia, 1993). The pastoralists of Kukamaiwa of Jukusko Local Government Area and those of Bunegarel in Jigawa State have taken to crop farming for years. It must be noted that such efforts on the part of the pastoralists is usually accompanied by conflicts. Therefore, the traditional institutional powers backed by procedural laws can be the instrument for preventing old conflicts and avoiding new ones between the agriculturists and pastoralists.

References

Adams, W.M. and Hollis (1987). Hydrology Sustainable Resource Development of a Sahelian Floodplain wetland. Hadejia-Nguru Wetland Project.

Aminu, Kano. (ed.) (1995). *The Critical Water Resources of the Komadugu Yobe Basin* 1995).

NEAZDP: *Management Summary Report 1990-1995.*

Hadejia, Ismaila. (1993). Socio-economic Basis of Farmer-Pastoralists Conflict in Jigawa State - 1993.

Thomas, D. (1991). Water Management and Rural Development in the Hadejia-Nguru Wetland North East Nigeria.

Cousins, Ben (1996). "Conflict Management for Multiple Resources Users in Pastoralists and Agro-pastoralists Contexts", *IDS Bulletin*, vol. 27, No 3. 1996.

International Centre for Development Oriented Research in Agriculture & CRA Institute of Agric Research, Lake Chad Reaearch Institute.: *Analysis of Farming System in the Hadejia-Jama're flood plain of Nigeria*. Working Paper Series 2, Nigeria 1992.

P.B. Shalangwa (1995). "The Importance of Adequate River Flows to the Economy of NEAZDP Area". Proceedings of the 1995 NIPPS/HNWCP workshop in Jos.

Mkalachiwi P.B. (1995). "The Dilemma of Sustainable Water Resources Management in Komadugu Yobe Basin: The Yobe View"- 1995 Proceeding of NIPPS/HNWCP workshops.

Appendix

GLOSSARY

Disputes

In the context of the study, disputes arise when multiple users of a resource e.g. water and land can no longer agree on the methods and the practices for sharing the diminishing resources because of human/natural causes. It stops shorts of complete breakdown of trust amongst the users. In this case identity, interest and positions not clearly defined but negotiable.

Conflicts

Arise when there is a complete breakdown of trust and the resultant action is violence which may be destructive or non destructive. Depending on the nature of the conflict, source and causes, it may be protracted or deep rooted or perennial as it was described by one of the local government chairmen in the study area. In this case, the identities, positions and interests of the users appear to be non-negotiable. The issue of the winner or loser is the key problem.

Conflict Management

Encompass all strategies employed to prevent, accommodate or settle conflicts. As it will be seen in the study, states, local governments and communities have employed various strategies to prevent or de-escalate conflicts in their areas of jurisdiction by creating dialogue committees from the village to the state level.

Conflict Accommodation

The South African school of thought led by Dr. Van Merve believe from observations and experience that no conflict has ever been completely resolved. It has to be settled and accommodated. In addition, resolution of a permanent conflict required too much time, resources and permanent changes in positions and interest of core parties. In development, time and resources are diminishing and are required elsewhere if they cannot be utilised where it is meant because of violent conflicts in the development area. Finally it is not easy to rebuild trust quickly.

Conflict Avoidance

Encompasses all strategies that can be employed to sustain trust between core parties by recognising early warning signals and responding appropriately in good time to the satisfaction of all parties.

Conflict Settlement

Has as its ultimate objective, to diffuse violence and promote compromise with its focus on the causes of the conflicts. The settlement exercises must move towards rebuilding trust amongst all parties.

Core Parties

Are the actual disputants of parties directly in conflicts, e.g. the pastoralists and the agriculturists.

Concerned Parties

Are those parties with an interest in the disputes/conflicts on a gradient of actively influential down to peripheral or marginal parties.

Uninvolved Parties

Do not have active interest in the disputes/conflicts. However, they may intervene thereby indicating a shift from uninvolvement to marginal involvement and may be active influence.

Embedded Parties

As found in many disputes/conflicts, are individuals and groups who emerge from within the situation (i.e from the core parties) to adopt the role of a concerned party, e.g. a village head who is usually a farmer.

Chapter 8

Akin Akinteye, James M. Wuye and Muhammad N. Ashafa

Zangon Kataf Crisis: A Case Study

Introduction

The methodology used in the course of this research was oral interview. The society studied was stratified, hence we divided our interviewees into three important classes - the upper, the middle and lower classes. We also conducted interviews across these classes.

At the end of our research, we found that the 1992 conflict in Zangon Kataf was ethno-political, caused by socio-economic and cultural factors, due to lack of governmental and non-governmental conflict prevention/management organs. The historical background of both communities in Zangon Kataf was important in understanding the 1992 crisis. The crisis only served as an outlet to several idiosyncrasies that had long been buried in the minds of the communities against one another.

A noticeable culture among the youths of both communities was that of violence. This could be likened in part to what they inherited from their parents, and to what they witnessed during the crisis. In some cases some youths knew who did what to either a neighbour, their parents or relations, their brothers and sisters during the crisis. Some youths were still full of vengeful spirit awaiting another opportunity. We have therefore recommended that conflict prevention structures be put in place in the local government area with immediate effect. There should be conflict resolution and management workshops for the youths and local government staff, community mediator training for the adults as well as establishment of a conflict prevention centre to be managed by the people themselves.

Background to the Study

In 1992, a riot occurred in Zangon Kataf area of Kaduna State. The riot which was believed to be religious spread to Kaduna city and some other parts of the state with losses of many lives and much property. It was gathered that the riots broke out as a result of an order to relocate the market in the area.

In 1988, the then Kachia Local Government Council of Kaduna State passed a resolution on the relocation of the Zangon Kataf district market from its old site to a new and more spacious site. Reasons adduced for this decision were that the old site was encroached upon by residential houses which made it difficult for any form of expansion. In addition, there was the lack of public conveniences in the old site. It was also inaccessible. The LGA Council felt that the relocation of the market would further enhance revenue generation.

However, the decision could not be executed till the local government was divided and Zangon Kataf created out of it in 1989. The creation of this local government area put a temporary stoppage to the execution of the relocation decision. The creation of Zangon Kataf Local Government Council ushered in a Kataf (Atyap) man as the executive chairman in December, 1990. As one of the programmes of the local government, the new chairman ordered on the 30th of January, 1992 the clearing of the new market site and announced February 6th as the official take-off date of the new market. This announcement did not go down well with the Hausa community in Zango town where the market was originally located. On the 4th of February, there was a purported interview on Federal Radio Corporation of Nigeria (FRCN) Kaduna Jakar Mogori programme where one Mr. J. K. Apple was reported to have threatened that "there will be blood-bath if the market is ever moved" to the new site. In furtherance of this, the same man got a court injunction, on the eve of the take-off day, restraining the chairman of the local government council from implementing the relocation decision.

In compliance with the local government directives, some Kataf women went to the new market site for business transactions on the 6th of February, 1992. To their utter dismay, they were welcomed to the market with assaults and harassments by the Hausa community in Zango town. This action infuriated the already embittered Kataf men; hence the outbreak of the crisis that claimed many lives and property. Consequent upon this, the Kaduna State Government constituted a panel of enquiry known as the Zangon Kataf Market Riots Judicial Commission of Enquiry on 10th February, 1992. Unfortunately, before the commission could submit its report, another riot broke out on 15th May and this time, spilled over to Zaria and Kaduna metropolis, Ikara, Makarfi, Igabi, Zaria and Chikun Local Government areas.

This second riot was said to have been caused by some Hausa men who invaded the farms of some Kataf men and removed their yam and seedlings. These Hausa men afterwards sent messages to these Kataf men and damned the consequences by waiting for the Kataf men on the damaged farms. The report was taken by school children to their Kataf fathers at home and the second riot started. This riot spilled out of Zangon Kataf Local Government in the night of 17th May 1992. On the 18th of May the Nigerian Army was invited to help control the situation and a dusk-to-dawn curfew was imposed. Eventually, normalcy gradually returned and the curfew was lifted about four days later.

Prior to the outbreak of the second riot, government claimed to have made efforts to restore normalcy in Zangon Kataf Local Government Area by dispatching mobile police to the area. However, this effort could not prevent the second riot from escalating.

Analysis of Fundamental Causes

Ethnic Factors

In discussing the ethnic cause of the crisis, it is pertinent to briefly examine the history of Zangon Kataf as a community in Zangon Kataf Local Government Area of Kaduna State.

Zangon Kataf was a community in the south eastern part of Kaduna State, about two hundred and thirty kilometres away from the state capital - Kaduna. The community is situated between Lat. 9^0 N and Long. $8^0 3'$, and made up of about fifty autonomous villages. These were, in the north: Tagwayen Rimi, Anguwan Zaki Sako, Bakin Kogin Gidan Zaki, Sabon Kaura, Zarkwai, Anguwar Ruhogo and Anguwar Rimi Katab; in the east: Kitori, Achi-sa, Kurmin Masara, Zamman Dabo and Unguwan Yayo; in the west: Unguwan Wakili, Unguwan Kaya, Unguwan Tabo, Mashan, Mabuhu, Matal, Kwuaku, Anguwan Abet, Warkan, Yagbak, Anguwan Gawayi I & II, Anguwan Mofa, Goran Gida, Sagwaza, Dan Ayada, Boran Agba, Kakon Bilu, Rafin Salwa and Bafal Gora I & II; and in the south: Kurfi, Anguwan Itace, Gidan mando,

Magamiya I &II, Taligan, Gidan wuke, Anguwan Madaki, Anguwan Gaiya, Nungu, Anguwan Juju, Tagama, Samaru, Anguwan Jana, Bada Isohuwa, Mabushi I & II, Gidan Karo, Kan Zankan and Jankasa I & II.

The Zangon Kataf urban town was situated in the centre of the above mentioned Atyap (Kataf) communities. It was predominantly inhabited by Hausa Muslims. Zango, an Hausa word meaning "a temporary resting place" came into existence in 1650 as a result of the North/South Atlantic Trade. The first settler, Mallam Melle, a Baribari man, hailed from Borno. History has it that this Kanuri salt merchant, after using the place for several years, later asked the Atyaps to settle in the place and they obliged. Shortly thereafter, Melle was joined in this place by the highly enterprising Hausas, trading along this route. The temporary resting place soon assumed the status of an important economic centre where buying and selling and other social interactions took place. Trade transactions at this time were a mixture of trade by barter and the use of currency. The more civilised Hausas exchanged Atyaps farm produce for trinkets, clothings, swords, gun powders etc.

The trading system mentioned above was necessitated by the social condition in which the Hausas met the Atyaps whose ancestors originated from the Bauchi Plateau in a village known as Karje. They first migrated through Kano and later settled in Kargi in the present Ikara Local Government Area of Kaduna State. They were forced to move further southward to the present Atyap kingdom as a result of constant invasion of their settlement by the slave traders. The legendary ancestral father of the Atyap people, Agwatyp, had three children, namely: Miyam, Agbaad and Akhu. The first two were great hunters while the third was a farmer.

The Atyap communities co-habited alongside with the nomadic Fulanis. The Fulanis' operation and existence in the community resulted from the availability of red earth in Jankasa village which they claimed was good for their cattle's health. However, the Fulanis were not exclusive in their settlement. They built their temporary huts within the Atyaps and co-habited with them.

It is evident from the foregoing that the inhabitants of Zango town and the inhabitants of the surrounding Atyap communities were of different ethnic origins. They co-habited with each other having brought their peculiar differences with them from their different points of origin to their present location. It is also important to note that while the inhabitants of Zangon urban town were the Hausas, the inhabitants of the surrounding villages were Atyaps.

Political/Traditional/Chieftaincy

In 1902 and 1904, the British colonialists conquered Zaria and Jema'a emirate councils and established their authority over the two emirates. However, their authority could not be exerted over southern Kaduna provinces among which were the Atyaps because they were violently resisted in the province. In 1915, the colonialists conquered the province through the aid of their superior weapons and forced the people to submit to imperial rule. They were then subjected to indirect rule through the already conquered Zaria emirate. (SNP 17/8 K. 4046, "Pagan Subjects under Mohammedan Rulers" NAK).

To further consolidate their authority over the subdued southern Kaduna people, and having been empowered by the colonial masters, the Zaria Emirate Council imposed district heads from among its royal family members to administer the indigenous southern Kaduna people. With this development, Zangon Kataf town became the headquarters of the district where authorities of the emirate were exercised.

The introduction of indirect rule in the northern Region by the colonial masters forced the Atyap land under the authority and rulership of Zaria Emirate Council. This empowered the Emir to send a district head (Hakimi) to rule over Atyap land. In Zangon Kataf, Zango town was used as the district headquarters because of its commercial nature and easy accessibility as the centre of Atyap land. The emirate council also found it easier to operate from amongst the Hausas who were their brothers than the Atyaps who could not speak their language and whose orientation and culture were entirely different.

The only role of the emirate council as directed by the colonial masters was to enrich their treasury. This was carried out through indiscriminate taxation, seizure of animals and farm produce etc.

of their subjects - the Katafs. To further compound the situation, the Hausa tax collectors, on their own, increased the tax from the official rate of two shillings to four shillings. In addition to these the indigenes were subjected to inhuman treatment such as carrying grass roofing materials and their farm produces to the Emir annually. Kataf women were also forced to sweep the market square and in some cases were beaten before they were allowed to sell their wares. The tax collectors extended their inhuman attitude by forcing the tax payers to give their grains as free horses' food during tax collection.

In furtherance to realising their goals, the colonialists established Native Authority Schools. Admission to these schools was restricted to the children of the emirate council. On rare occasions when admissions were offered to the indigenes, they were mainly offered to females. These schools taught only the 3Rs i.e. Reading, Writing and Arithmetic. The purpose was to create a continuous pool of graduates for tax collection. With the growth in population, there was the need to train these graduates to assist in tax collection. As a result, admissions to Native Authority Schools were extended to the male indigenes so that they could assist in enumerating their kith and kin for taxation. With this development, sending indigenes' children to school attracted increase in the tax paid to the emirate council in Zaria.

The arrival of missionaries in the 1940s brought about the establishment of missionary schools. The Atyaps' enrolment in these schools was overwhelming. The indigenes were attracted to them by the gentle and humane nature with which Christianity was introduced to the people. Perhaps this was evident in the high conversion of the Atyaps to Christianity as an alternative way of escaping the oppressive Hausa/Fulani exploitation and religion. They perceived the missionaries as friendly people who would neither go after them if they tried to run away nor force them to accept this new religion or ask them to kill their domestic animals to feed the missionaries. The missionaries talked about something they did not know and taught them how to read and write, unlike the Hausa whom they considered aggressive in their approach to almost everything. The Katafs also directly linked Hausa with the Islamic religion.

The Hausa/Fulani, having settled in the community for

several years, never made any attempt to propagate the Islamic Religion which they brought with them. This explained why no single Atyap man was converted to Islam. All that was done by the Hausa/Fulani muslims was to condemn the traditional religion of the people.

There therefore existed two educational systems with different ideologies. Whereas the native authority schools were interested in training administrators, the mission schools were interested in training clergies and teachers. While the Hausas were concentrated in the native authority schools, the Atyaps were concentrated in mission schools. This explains the high number of Hausas in the administrative sector and the Atyaps in the military, engineering and technical sectors. We observed that the products of these schools were suspicious of one another. Perhaps this was a grand design by the colonial masters and the missionaries to achieve their specific objectives. However, these antecedents still persisted and manifested in the 1992 riots long after the departure of the colonialists.

Consequent upon the acquisition of education and the gradual introduction of reforms, the Atyaps recognised and resisted exploitation by the Hausa/Fulani emirate administrative system. This marked the beginning of the struggle for traditional autonomy and rulership.

However, the struggle was resisted by the emirate council which resulted in various crises. Even before the introduction of education by the colonialists and missionaries, there had been instances of clashes between the Hausas and the Atyaps. In 1844, there was a clash over the refusal of the Atyaps to pay tribute to the Hausas and the expansion of their original settlement without the consent of their Atyap hosts. (NAK 1844). This act was vehemently opposed by the Atyaps but it was later resolved.

There was another major conflict between 1915 and 1922 under the district headship of Mallam Jafaaru Isiyaku, who later became the Emir of Zazzau. On his assumption of headship of Zangon Kataf district, Jafaaru expanded the Hausa/Fulani settlement and farmland by four miles radius (6.4km) beyond the original settlement. This acquisition encroached on the Barado or Mabarado of the Atyap, the original ancient meeting place of the Atyap traditional council. All attempts to claim this land back proved abortive, but the Atyaps still had access to that portion where their traditional council met. However, in 1984, this land dispute re-echoed when an attempt was made by one Dr. O.O. Mango of Zango town to take over Barado from the Atyaps on the claim that it was an idol-worshipping place.

The 15th of May, 1946 marked a turning point in the history of Atyap/Hausa conflict in Zangon Kataf. This was during the reign of Mallam Jafaaru Isiyaku as the Emir of Zazzau, and of Katukan Zazzau, Mallam Suleiman as the district head of Zangon Kataf District. This crisis concerned tax. It was directed that two shillings be collected from the people as tax. However, the collectors forced people to pay four shillings. The Atyaps refused to pay the tax. This injustice among other factors made the Atyaps to demand for an indigenous chiefdom. The Emir of Zazzau identified and arrested the rebellious leader - Tatun of Jankasa village. His mode of arrest was said to have been highly inhuman and degrading. This provoked spontaneous revolt against the Emir and the District Officer. Against this background, about twenty-eight Atyaps were later arrested and detained in Zaria. Three of the accused were convicted and sentenced to one year imprisonment each. The remaining twenty-five were detained for three months without any charge against them. This crisis led to the death of their two sons in prison. Several others were injured.

Due to the incessant demand for self-determination by the Kataf, and to forestall future conflicts, the Atyap were granted a seat of Wakili (a representative) in the Emirate Council. The emirate council system of appointing non-indigenes as district heads continued till the advent of the first military regime in Nigeria in 1966. Under this new regime, the Atyap pushed their demand to the new government of the northern region under the governorship of late Major-General Hassan Usman Katsina, then a Colonel. Fortunately, their prayer was granted and in 1967, the first indigenous district head, Mallam Bala Ade Dauke Gora, was appointed as the district head of Zangon Kataf. The appointment of an indigenous district head put a tentative rest to all other communal clashes. There was a state of relative peace up till 1984. Mallam Dauke was the first and only indigene to live in Zango town with his deputies. Before then, previous district heads were appointed from Zaria.

Before the introduction of indirect rule, the Atyap had a way of governing themselves. There was the well established leaders forum where conflicts were resolved and other issues were discussed. The three most prominent clans - Miyam, Agbaad and the Akhu - had a process of meeting to resolve conflicts among themselves.

The feudal system of administration aggravated the already fragile relationship between the Hausa and the Atyap. The autocratic nature of the district heads in dispensing their duties as the representatives of the Emir was terribly exploitative and dehumanising. The Atyap were subjected to over-taxation. In some instances, some Hausa merchants impersonated and presented themselves as tax collectors. These people usually forced the Atyap to slaughter the best of their domestic animals and cook for them. If there was anything the Kataf valued most, it was their pride. It was a taboo for a woman to look into the reservoir (rumbu) of the family. Kataf custom demanded that foods were left in the reservoir to feed the family throughout the dry season. The district head's Hausa tax collectors went to the extent of breaking the rumbu in the presence of the women and the grains given to their horses to feed on.

These negative behaviours of the ruling class bred enmity and hatred between the two communities. The Atyap saw the Hausa in Zango town as part of the hated emirate council. It was therefore automatically believed that the Hausa of Zango did not suffer similar humiliation as the Atyap did. There was the general belief that all Hausa were wicked hence the name Ntyok-pat (meaning wicked man) was given the Hausa by the Atyap. An average Atyap man grew up to regard the Hausa as visitors and enemies on their land.

All these, put together, inspired the rebellious spirit in the Atyap hence the quest for freedom. The outbreak of the 1992 riots was seen as an opportunity by Kataf men to avenge the wrongs of the emirate council on the Hausa of Zango town who the Atyap perceived to be thwarting their efforts for self determination. On the other hand, the Hausa of Zango town claimed ignorance of any move by the Atyap to obtain their chiefdom. They claimed that if such moves were made known to them, they would have joined in the struggle because freedom for the Atyap meant freedom for them as well.

Socio-Economic/Cultural Disparity

The Hausa of Zango town controlled the economic well-being of the Atyap. The Hausa, through the North/South trade, started the Zango Urban Market. They determined the prices of farm produce to their (Hausa) advantage. These farm produce were then bought and sold at higher prices in international markets. This, to a large extent, improved the standard of living of the Hausa in Zango town while the Atyap languished in abject poverty. This disparity in socio-economic status of the two communities was reflected in the types of houses the Hausa lived in as against mud/thatched houses of the Kataf. It was said that the Hausa having made enough money, diversified into transportation business which they monopolised. To worsen the situation, the only hospital in the district was located in Zango town. The Atyap were compelled to pay for medical services before they were attended to, unlike their Hausa counterparts who were treated free. As a result of the foregoing, envy and jealousy developed against the economically prosperous Hausa community. The Atyap saw the Hausa as using Atyap sweat to develop themselves.

The upbringing of the Atyap and Hausa were very different. Ordinarily, the Hausa man was brought up under the influence of religion to know that it was forbidden to eat pork and drink alcohol while his Atyap counterparts ate pork and drank as a way of socialising. The situation was further compounded by the style of administration adopted by the colonial masters. The seeds of discord, deep-rooted animosity, mutual suspicion, intolerance and contempt were aided by the colonial masters in the creation of Pagan Courts with its president as Magaji Mugu (460 363 *Native Court (Pagan) Warrant*. NAK), as against Islamic Shariah Courts, Pagan Schools (later substituted for Mission Schools) as against Native Authority Schools. They did not interact except in the market place. The Hausas regarded Atyaps as dirty people, uncultured and non-religious , hence the appellation *Arna*, meaning infidels or unbelievers.

With the advent of education of Atyap women and their awareness of the socio-economic advantage of the Hausas, they became attracted to the young but rich Hausa men who in most cases impregnated them without seeking the consent of their parents to marry them. In most cases, these Hausa men later abandoned these women to suffer their fate alone. In some rare cases of marriage, these women were married away and never returned to the family. Their children were not allowed to visit their Atyap grandparents. "The superior attitude generally adopted by the Hausas toward the pagan and Christians alike undoubtedly arouses resentment in the Christians as well as many pagans." (C. 8/1946, *Zangon Kataf District Unrest, 1946-1951*, NAK). These, among other reasons, fuelled the Zangon Kataf riots of 1992.

The Atyap community regarded the area court as Islamic and Hausa/Fulani-oriented. They had long lost trust in the system because it failed to give them justice in cases involving them and the Hausa. Ironically, the Hausa also regarded the area court in the same way as Kataf. They complained that they also suffered injustice like the Atyap. This viewpoint about the area court added another dimension to the escalation of the 1992 crisis.

The pattern of settlement of Zango town rendered the community unique in relation to the surrounding villages. Since the inhabitation of Zango Kataf urban town, it remained an exclusive reserve of the Hausa for over 300 years. The Hausa did not interact with the indigenes other than in the market place. Hence the absence of communal integration. While the Hausa were into commerce, the Atyap were hunters and farmers. Their religions also differed. About 99% of the Atyap were Christians while the entire Hausa community was Muslim. Perhaps these' formed the basis why the two communities could not develop the spirit of living together.

Since 1920, the issue of the ownership of Zango town and its surrounding farmlands kept generating rancour between the two communities. In 1920, the then district head of Zangon Kataf land-Mallam Jafaaru Isiyaku confiscated about $2^1/_2$ miles (4km) of land as (*hurumi*) being under his protection and control. This generated disaffection among the communities. The Atyap regarded all the land being occupied by Zango Urban Town as Atyap land. They felt that expansion of the town or their (Hausa) farmland should be referred to them. However, the Hausa did not agree with this view. They claimed the ownership of the land through inheritance for more than three hundred years. Section 34(2) of the Land Use Act of 1978 was cited as an instrument to support this claim.

It is pertinent to say that the Atyaps regarded farming as their only means of survival, hence the high value attached to land. Coupled with this, a significant portion of the land in question was "fadama" land, i.e. a land that could be cultivated all year round. The Atyap perceived the Hausa as business entrepreneurs who exploited them through the purchase of their farm produce at fixed prices. On the other hand, the Hausa felt that they were the custodians of power, having total control over lands within the Zaria emirate jurisdiction. This probably informed Mallam Jafaaru's action in 1920.

Moreover, the Hausa were migrating in large numbers to Zango. This migration brought about an increase in the population of the town. Consequent upon this, there was need for diversification of the means of livelihood from commerce. Some percentage of Hausa took to farming instead of their traditional business or commerce. From the foregoing, it could be adduced that the Atyap were not contending the ownership of Zango town but the land that was extended by Mallam Jafaaru in 1920.

Religious Disparity

Since the introduction of Islamic religion in Nigeria, the Hausa/Fulani were regarded as its custodian. This was the belief in other parts of Nigeria so much so that the Hausa/Fulani are immediately taken to be Muslims. The Atyap also held this view. The Hausa of Zangon Urban town were Muslims. They regarded the Atyaps as unbelievers or "arna", meaning infields. The Atyap on the other hand were Christians, as a result of the advent of mission schools and the subsequent establishment of churches.

However, when the riot broke out in 1992, it took a religious dimension in Kaduna city and its environs. The Muslims in the city took it to mean the killing of the Muslims while their Christian counterparts took it to mean the killing of the Christians by the Muslims. It was reported that some Hausa corpses were brought to the city from the site of the incident and this action incited the Muslims in the city, especially in Tudun Wada where no single Christian was spared. On the other hand, in Sabon Tasha, the Christians made sure that no single Muslim was spared too.

Some Actors in the Cause, Prevention, Management and Resolution of the Crisis

The Elites

The elites of these communities, to a large extent, contributed to the deterioration of the already fragile relationships existing among the people. These elites, most of whom were retired officers from the army or civil service, exercised great influence over their people. They also questioned the administrative procedures/imbalances in their areas. Most of them lacked tolerance and patience. They incited and manipulated their communities for selfish gains. Such was the action of Mr. J.K. Apple on a radio broadcast.

Incidentally, these elites lived in the cities. They formed themselves into external pressure groups initiating acts of discord, contempt, animosity, prejudice and malice in their communities from time to time. They succeeded in confusing the ordinary man in the village with these complex issues which often made them react negatively at the slightest provocation.

The Youths

A known fact that brought about the May 1992 riots was the role of the youths. The uncontrollable action of the Atyap and Hausa youths after the February 1992 riots unleashed terror in May 1992. The youths became agents for the precipitation of the riots. This was considered to be a result of idleness due to unemployment.

Reactions of Individuals, Communities and their Allies

The activities and pronouncements of individuals, organisations, interest groups, and especially the print and electronics media, went a long way in escalating the already tense atmosphere in Zangon Kataf area and all over Kaduna State in May 1992. Some utterances by individuals, communities, interest groups, religious bodies and organisations, severally or collectively after the February 1992 riots, were inciteful, provocative and aggravative. Prominent among these groups were the National Council of Muslim Youth Organisation, The Christian Association of Nigeria, *The New Nigerian*, and Radio Nigeria, Kaduna.

For instance, the Muslim Brothers in Zangon Kataf called for Jihad in one of their letters to the Sultan of Sokoto while at the same time some Imams in Kaduna called for total destruction of the Christians. Their Christian counterparts did the same. The print and electronic media were observed to be taking side, either by their publications or by their broadcasts. *The New Nigerian* of Friday, June 5, 1992, in its editorial was quoted as follows:

> An Hausa man can choose to live in Ibadan; a Yoruba man in Zangon Kataf or Daura and they should be entitled to pursue their private endeavours without let or hindrance, and according to the law. Which is why the attempt at burning the Hausas in Zangon Kataf out of their homes because some people think they do not belong. This must be seen for what it is, a callous and cowardly act that must be punished with all the force of the law.

The Reporter of Saturday May 1992 was quoted as saying that

> The Kataf using their superior fire power moved into the Hausa/ Fulani settlement and demanded for the latter to drop all their arms. This was done. As soon as the Hausa/Fulani became thus defenceless, the Kataf started to gun and hack them to death.

There were also claims and counter-claims alleged by individuals, in Zangon Kataf after the February riots of crops being damaged on both sides of the farms. In addition some individuals took the law into their hands and served as police as well as court attendants to realise their goals. These collective and individual actions coupled with the fact that government was slow in taking action to prevent the riot, gave birth to the May 1992 riots.

The State Government

The roles the State Government played after the February 1992 riots added to the outbreak of the May riots. When the executive governor, Alhaji Dabo Lere, visited Zango Kataf after the February riots, he neither visited the local government chairman or the Atyap victims. He only visited the Hausa community and paid a visit to the Magaji of the Hausa instead of the District Head. The relief materials that were brought were distributed only to the Hausa community. All these pointed to the fact that they took side with one party.

Following the governor's visit, the Atyap were further offended by the way the deputy governor conducted the peace dialogue after the February 1992 riots. This led to the arrest of some Atyap leaders who were vocal at the dialogue. There was also a letter from the local government chairman informing the governor that the situation was still tense after the February riots and that there was need to beef up security in the area. The Governor did nothing about the letter.

The Atyap had to condemn the Justice Cudjoe panel of enquiry because it comprised five Hausa, one Yoruba and one easterner as its members. All calls from the Atyap and other concerned citizens to rectify this situation were ignored. In addition to the nonchalant attitude of the government, there was the sacking of the Zangon Kataf Local Government Council whose chairman and a large number of the councillors were Atyap. It was also observed that the government did not send security agents to the scene of the riots until the afternoon of the second day. The state government attitude left so much to be desired.

The Local Government Council

It was gathered that the local government did not consider the threats of Mr. J.K. Apple as serious. He was allowed to carry on a campaign on Radio Nigeria and to also get a court injunction to stop the relocation of the market place. In addition to this, the local government, despite the glaring fact that some people felt aggrieved about the relocation of the market, did not put any security in place on the take-off day. They were also reluctant in calling the police to the scene when the riots broke out. However, after the first riot was quelled, the local government did well by sending various security reports to the state government on the situation of things.

Zaria Emirate Council

To further raise the level of suspicion against the ruling class, the Emir of Zazzau, on his condolence visit, boycotted all forms of protocol. He did not visit the local government chairman or his representative – the district head of Zangon Kataf. The Emir, against all expectations, sent his relief materials to the Magaji to distribute in the Hausa community.

The Various Initiatives, Commissions/Committees

Immediately after the outbreak of the first riot, government made some moves to bring about peace in the area. Committees and commissions were set up to reconcile the warring parties and investigate the crisis. The following were committees and

commissions set up:
1. James Bawa Magaji Peace Committee;
2. Justice Rahila Cudjoe Commission of Inquiry;
3. Justice Benedict Okadigbo Special Tribunal;
4. Relief and Reconciliation Committee;
5. AVM Usman Muazu Reconciliation and the Search for Lasting Peace Committee;
6. Resettlement and Rehabilitation Committee.

Among all these, we will discuss the James Bawa Magaji Peace Committee, Justice Rahila Cudjoe Commission of Inquiry and AVM Usman Muazu Reconciliation and the Search for Lasting Peace Committee.

James Bawa Magaji Peace Committee

This committee was made up of five members hand-picked by the governor to broker peace in Zangon Kataf. The committee, under the chairmanship of James Bawa Magaji, the then deputy governor and a Bajju man - neighbours of the Atyaps, swung into action a few days after the first crisis. The committee sent invitations to the two parties for a peace dialogue in the local government area. Fortunately, the people responded and turned out in large numbers.

Unfortunately, the committee, instead of resolving the problems at hand, succeeded in creating more. The dialogue ended up in pandemonium, thereby setting the stage for the unknown which later manifested in another brutal crisis on 15th May, 1992.

A careful assessment of the dialogue revealed that the chairman of the committee, an engineer, lacked the patience expected of a peace broker. He neither had the experience nor the skills required to serve as a mediator. Above all these was the fact that the dialogue was wrongly timed. His role as the chairman dictated that he should be impartial. However, it was gathered that there was an age-long political animosity between the Atyap and the Bajju which, from all indications, stood as a barrier to the success of his assignment.

Justice Rahila Cudjoe Commission of Enquiry

This commission was set up on the 10th of February, 1992. It was made up of seven members – five Hausas, one Yoruba and one Easterner. The committee had the following as its terms of reference, to:

1. inquire into, or investigate, ascertain and identify the immediate and remote causes of the riot and or disturbance;
2. assess the extent of damage caused during the riots and or disturbance;
3. ascertain and identify the roles played by individuals and groups in causing tension and outbreak in the violence;
4. determine the extent of loss of lives and properties;
5. examine any other matter incidental to the foregoing.
6. In the light of its findings, recommend appropriate actions to be taken against those responsible for the riots and or disturbances and also recommend measures to be taken to prevent future occurrence.

The commission held several public sittings where people testified for or against several charges levelled against individuals and communities. However, after the conclusion of its public sittings and during the deliberations, the second riot broke out in Zangon Kataf. As a result, the commission's terms of reference were expanded to look into the riots of May, 1992 and subsequent riots in Kaduna and its environs, Zaria, Chickun and other local government areas in the state.

Unfortunately, the commission was seriously criticized from all angles for its composition. Therefore, the white paper of its report was still being held by the government at the time of fieldwork.

AVM Usman Reconciliation and Search for Lasting Peace Committee

This committee was set up on the 15th of December, 1994 by Col. Lawal Ja'afaru Isa, then military administrator of Kaduna State. The committee consisted of seven Hausa/Fulani and seven Atyap. The committee was given free hand to select its own chairman and they unanimously selected AVM Usman Muazu, one-time military governor of Kaduna State and a Muslim from southern Zaria.

The committee had the following as its terms of reference, to:

1. explore the possibility of addressing both remote and immediate causes of the disturbances in Zangon Kataf in February and May 1992;
2. determine the ingredients for lasting peace in Zangon Kataf;

3.   determine and suggest strategies on how this desirable
      lasting peace can be achieved;
4.   submit findings and recommendations within three weeks
      of inauguration.

Among all the committees/commissions set up to look into
Zangon Kataf riots of 1992, this committee appeared to be the
best in its terms of reference, the composition of members, fact-
finding methodologies adopted, the freedom given to the
members in selecting their own chairman and in the presentation
of their findings.

The success of this committee, to a large extent, was a result
of good timing, and free hand given to them by the state
administrator. The recommendations of this committee formed
the bedrock for the resolution of the conflict which was the Peace
Parley of Friday, 11th August, 1995.

The Peace Parley

The peace parley which was organised on Friday, 11th of August,
1995 by the state administrator, Col. Lawal Ja'afaru Isa, was well
attended by both disputants and their allies. The parley was
attended by all the members of Kaduna State Executive Council,
traditional rulers, religious leaders, opinion leaders, NGOs and
people from all walks of life.

The venue was the disputed market site. The parley lasted
more than thirteen hours. It was praised for its informal nature,
freedom of expression given to all that attended, the manner in
which it was handled by the administrator, and above all the
perfect timing.

At the introductory stage of the parley, the disputants were
sensitised by the administrator, the religious leaders of both parties
and opinion leaders present at the parley. The administrator used
active communication skills to make his points and the disputants'
points clear to the audience. He systematically elicited the bones
of contention from the disputants and assisted them in finding
not only useful and lasting, but mutually beneficial solutions to
the problems. He did this by tactically restraining the elites who
participated in various committees and commissions connected
with the riots from making any statement. Rather, he requested
people to select speakers from amongst residents of Zangon Kataf

to table their grievances.

The people identified the following as their problems:

Hausa: That the Kataf should release the (confiscated) land back
to them;

That the Government should appoint a District Head from
amongst the Hausa;

That the Government should pay compensations for
damages they suffered during the crisis;

That the Government should release the reports of Justice
Rahila Cudjoe's Commission of Enquiry.

Atyap: That the Government should give them their own
chiefdom;

That the Government should make Zangon Kataf
homogeneous;

That the Government should not release the reports of
Justice Rahila Cudjoes's commission of Enquiry.

The Resolution

At the end, the administrator assured them that the Atyap would
be given their chiefdom and the Hausa their district head. The
Atyap also agreed that the confiscated land would be given back
to the Hausa.

The agreement reached were sworn to by three elders selected
from each group by the people themselves. Religious leaders were
called upon once again to remind the people of the importance of
oaths and agreement and the need to abide by them.

From the foregoing, it could be observed that the issue of the
market did not even surface at all during the parley. To this end
we could safely conclude that the market issue only served as a
trip wire that exploded the hidden issue that had long been buried
in the minds of the people.

However, it was agreed that some issues be looked into by
the government. The administrator promised to look into the
proposed layout of the Zangon Urban Town to accommodate
people from all parts of the country and the completion of
buildings under construction in Zango town. He was however
silent on the release of the Justice Rahila Cudjoe's Commission of
Enquiry.

The Hausa community still felt the houses constructed for

them were below standard. They were without toilet facilities. They were however pleased that peace returned to the land. Both communities called on the government to put in place structures and other conveniences in the new market site and make sure that stalls were equitably distributed among the communities.

Further Analysis of the Crisis

The unfriendly relationship that existed among the Atyap and the Hausa of Zango town was enough signal that there would be a crisis. Various security reports from the colonial days revealed this fact. As was extensively discussed in the historical background and the statement of various conflicts, it was glaring that the Hausa and the Atyap lived in different worlds, yet in the same community. There were no structures in place where elders of both communities could meet and discuss their problems.

It is imperative to add that the Atyap were even skeptical of the indigenous district head. Their complaints were that the district head had worked for a long period in Zaria and had become an instrument in the hands of the Emirate Council. They claimed that his selection as the district head was informed by his long stay in Zaria. They observed that he could neither adjudicate in the Islamic way because he lacked the knowledge of the Holy Quran nor adjudicate to suit the Atyap because he referred most of their cases to Zaria.

Another known signal was the series of letters from the two communities of which copies were made available to the security agents and government. The Atyap elders vowed in one of their letters addressed to the chairman of Zango Kataf Local Government Council to reclaim their land by any means from the Hausa of Zango town. The Hausa also in their letter to the Sultan of Sokoto and the governor of Kaduna State stated that they were prepared to wage a Jihad in Zangon Kataf. They claimed that the land under question belonged to them by inheritance; therefore their ownership of the land was covered by law. There was also an interview on the 4th of February, 1992 about two days to the outbreak of the crisis when Mr. J.K. Apple was reported to have called for a bloodbath if the market was ever moved from the old site. The programme was said to have been repeated several times.

After the outbreak of the first riots, there were various security reports from the chairman of Zangon Kataf Local Government Council that there were indications that the situation was not yet calm. Three such reports were sent to the state government. There was also a radio message sent by the chairman to the State House reporting that the situation was tense and demanded more security personnel. Another indicator of the second crisis was the recorded movement of arms, which were said to be stored in a place in the local government area.

In addition to the above was the total rejection of Justice Rahila Cudjoe's Panel of Enquiry by the Atyap. They claimed that the composition of the panel was one-sided with two Hausa members and no Kataf representative at all. They therefore resolved that they would not be bound by the recommendations of the commission. This served as a pointer to the fact that the report of the commission might bring about another crisis.

From the foregoing, it could be deduced that the government was nonchalant in its attitudes to bring about peace in Zangon Kataf. If it were sincere and serious, it had ample opportunity to avert the crises before they escalated first on the 6th of February and again on the 15th of May, 1992.

Strategies for Preventing and Managing The Conflicts

The Zangon Kataf crises had with them several role actors ranging from the state government through the local government to religious bodies, youth leaders, elites and the community and district leaders. These role actors either overtly had direct or indirect impact on the Zangon Kataf crisis of 1992.

It was observed that some people still felt aggrieved about the issue of land. Some Atyaps were of the opinion that too much was conceded to the Hausa community by the Atyaps. Land from the community and compensation from the government were specifically referred to.

It was also noted that the elders of both communities including some youth leaders were of the opinion that the youths were still very volatile and should therefore be educated on the values of peaceful co-existence. The elders recommended that there should be a conflict prevention and management structure to always identify and nip crises before they escalated. To this end we found that there was an urgent need for several peace structures to be instituted in Zangon Kataf Local Government Area.

In considering strategies for preventing and managing conflicts in the local government area all the role players must be introduced to methods for making these structures work. In part, some of these role players were introduced to the skills of conflict management. For instance, the state government supported various initiatives of conflict management in the sphere of religion. Some youth leaders in Kaduna were also taught conflict management skills, and they became facilitators at various conflict management workshops. The military administrator's peace parley in one way or the other served as nerve soothing ingredient in achieving lasting peace in the area.

The first and most pressing of those structures was a workshop on conflict resolution and management where the youths would be taught skills of resolving conflict other than by violence and managing crisis before they get out of hands. This workshop could also give the youths the basic skills for identifying early warning signals of conflict and consequently prevent them from escalating.

We also deemed it important that the local government officials should be equipped with these skills, as we found that they lacked necessary skills to prevent or manage conflicts any time they arose. These officials were the closest to the people and were therefore bound to be faced with one conflict or the other in discharging their duties.

We also suggested that community mediators be trained from among the elders, to further assist in bridging the existing gaps between the two communities. The community mediator would then put in place a peace centre to which cases of noticeable impending crisis could be referred. In the peace centre, there should be a peace committee made up of all the role players earlier mentioned.

References

Atyap Development Association (1994). *Memorandum to the Military Administrator of Kaduna State on the Quest for Peace, Tranquility, Unity and Progress in Zangon Kataf and Kaduna State*. Kaduna.

Christian Association of Nigeria. (1992). "Letter by the leaders of the Christian Association of Nigeria (CAN), from eight Local Government Areas of Southern Kaduna State Concerning the Recent Religious Disturbances in Kaduna State." Kaduna: Christian Association of Nigeria, June 4, 1992.

Christian Association of Nigeria (1992). *Memorandum to the Judicial Commission of Inquiry on the Zangon Kataf (Market) Riots and Subsequent riots in Kaduna State.* Kaduna: Christian Association of Nigeria.

Christian Association of Nigeria (1992). "The fact the world must know: being a world press conference at NUJ Light House, Lagos", Kaduna.

Christopher, S & Tijno, V. (1985). *Vision in Action.* New York: Hausthon Press.

Concerned citizens of Southern Kaduna, (1994). " The Guarantee of the right of minority nationalities in the Nigerian Constitution and their enforcement in political practice: The case of the Southern Kaduna peoples". A memorandum submitted to the National Constitutional Conference.

Federal Government of Nigeria (1976). *Boundary Adjustment Revisited.* Lagos: Federal Government Press.

Federal Government of Nigeria (1959). *Willins Commission Report on Minority in the North.* Kaduna: National Archives.

Federal Government of Nigeria (1978). *Irikefe Report on State Creation.* Lagos.

Federal Government of Nigeria (1976) *Federal Military Government's View on the Report of the Boundary Adjustment Commission.* Lagos: Federal Government Press.

Human Rights Monitor (June 1996). *Legal Rights Monitor,* Vol. 1 No. 2. Kaduna.

Jafaaru I.K. (1931). *Report of Katuka Jafaaru Isiyaku as District Head Zangon Kataf, 1918-1931.* Kaduna: National Archives. N.A.K 91 C. 5.

Kataf Youth Development Association, (1992). "Memorandum Submitted to the Judicial Commission of Inquiry into the Zangon Kataf Market Riot of 6th February 1992".

Kaduna State Government. (1995). *AVM Usman Muazu Committee for reconciliation and search for lasting peace for Zangon Kataf report*. Kaduna.

Kaduna State Government. (1995). "A video record of The Peace Parley of Friday 11 August 1995 at Zangon Urban Town. Kaduna.

Magaji, S.S.& Canny, M.Y. (1992). *Investigative Report of findings on the Zangon Kataf Riot on the 19th & 20th February, 1992*. Kaduna: Being a report submitted to the government of Kaduna State.

Muhammed L.S., Re:"Peace Negotiation with Kataf: A memorandum submitted to peace and Reconciliation Committee.

National Archives (1987). *Kafanchan Crises 1987*, Kaduna: National Archives.

National Archives (n.d.) *Kasuwan Magani Report*. Kaduna: National Archives.

National Archives (n.d.) Gune Kahutu Report. Kaduna: National Archives.

National Archives (1946). *Report of Zangon Kataf District Unrest, 1946*. Kaduna: National Archieves, N.A.K. C. 8/1946. 54.

National Archives (1949). *Report of the S.I.M. Church Site at Magamiya, Zangon Katab, 1948-49*. Nak 2667 4546. Kaduna: National Archives

National Archives (1954). *Application to open 1st school by Roman Catholic Church* - 1946-54. NAK 2654-4524.

Kaduna National Archives.

National Archives. (n.d). *Proposed Elementary (Moslem) School establishment report*. NAK 2651-4520. Kaduna: National Archives.

National Archives (1929). *Proposed Pagan School Establishment Report*. NAK 162/1929/1. Kaduna: National Archives.

National Archives (1924). *The Pagans Court Report 10th May 1924*. NAK 460 363. Kaduna: National Archives.

National Archives (1942). Report on Sudan Interior Mission Schools and Religion Schools in Zangon Kataf District 1931 - 1942. NAK 427 309. Kaduna: National Archives.

The New Nigerian (1992). Editorial "Zangon Kafat Riot I". Kaduna: June 4, 1992.

The New Nigerian (1992). Editorial; "Zangon Kafat Riot II". Kaduna: June 5, 1992.

The New Nigerian (1992). " Nigerian- Israeli Association". Kaduna: August 8, 1992.

The Reporter (1992). "Zangon Kataf Crisis-The True Story". Kaduna: *The Reporter* May 23, 1992.

Zangon Kataf Development Association, (1996). *Re-union of Zangon Kataf Community:* "A Paper Submitted to the Peace and Reconciliation Committee. Kaduna: Author ZKDA/03/01.

Zangon Kataf Youth Development Association. (1996). "A Press Briefing of 20th March, 1996".

Chapter 9

Shedrack Gaya Best and Imran Abdulrahman.

The Mangu-Bokkos Conflicts on the Jos Plateau.

Introduction

Plateau State of Nigeria has, for a long time, enjoyed the reputation of being known as "The home of Peace and Tourism". This reputation is better appreciated in view of the cultural, ethnic and religious diversity of the state. Perhaps few states have such a wide combination of relatively small ethnic groups scattered across the state. Most of the ethnic nationalities on the Plateau had found its hills as safe havens from the insecurities of the pre-colonial era, as they tried to escape from invading forces and tendencies such as those of the Dan Fodio jihad and from previous inter-ethnic and inter-communal wars. Thus, most of these groups had enjoyed a state of relative peace up to the inception of British colonialism.

In recent times, however, the reputation of Plateau State as "Home of Peace and Tourism" has been greatly questioned following violent conflicts between different communities that had hitherto lived in peace and harmony with one another. Examples of these conflicts include the Mangu-Fier border conflicts in 1984, the conflicts in Jos and Bukuru between the indigenous communities and the so-called settlers, which culminated in the explosions of April 1994, the Mangu-Bokkos conflicts of 1992 and 1995, the Bukuru Gyero Road conflicts of 1997 between the Birom and Hausa communities, the Mangu-Changal conflicts of 1997, the conflicts between the Bassa and Igbirra communities in Toto Local Government (now in Nassarawa State), and the conflicts between the Tiv and Plateau communities in Doma, Awe and Keana (now in Nassarawa State), to mention but a few.

These episodes indicated that the times were changing, and that conflict was taking a more destructive and dysfunctional profile. This case study is, therefore, a modest attempt to understand the causes of the conflict between the Mwaghavul and Ron communities in Mangu and Bokkos Local Government Areas respectively. Both areas used to be under the same local government (Mangu) until Bokkos became a separate local government council in 1993. The identity groups in the conflict were the Mwaghavul and Ron ethnic nationalities. However, the conflict was confined to the areas where the two communities shared boundaries, notably Mushu/Kwahasnat, Manja/Rubwoi, Timnanle/Bandungang, Murish/Marish,[1] Kombun-Nting, Dankargung, etc. The involvement of the two relevant development associations (Ron-Kulere Chiefdom Development Association and the Mwaghavul Development Association) was not necessarily and directly at the level of violent conflict. Although both were involved in the pre-violence stage of the conflict, they became most active in the post-violence stage. It was at this point that elites probably became most involved.

The Conflict

This conflict in its violent expression first occurred in 1992, and then in 1995 for the second time. It involved two ethnic groups called the Mwaghavul and the Ron, both on the Jos Plateau. The conflict which had very shallow historical roots, was mainly about land and territory. The two farming communities depended so much on land, and wanted to exercise control over farmlands. Although the conflict resulted in loss of lives and property, it was not on a comparable scale with those of Wukari, Takum, Tafawa Balewa, etc. Property worth millions of naira was destroyed. Several communities were displaced on both occasions. It was not certain what casualty rates were in terms of human life. The conflict deeply affected the relationship between the Mwaghavul and Ron ethnic nationalities far and wide.

Objectives

The principal objective of the research was to unveil the causes of the violent conflict between the two communities in Bokkos and Mangu Local Government Areas of Plateau State, with a view to understanding the possible means of intervention and the issues for resolution.

The research attempted to identify the stakeholders in this conflict, and the various interests and positions of groups and individuals, if any. It was hoped too that those groups and persons who played constructive roles would be identified, and past efforts in managing the conflicts noted. Particular attention was paid to gender dimensions, identifying women groups across the conflict divide, for possible empowerment in leadership, organisation and conflict management.

Data Sources

The principal source of data for this research was oral interviews and formal as well as informal discussions with those identified as the most knowledgeable on both sides in the conflict.

We also used submissions made by both communities and their representatives to government inquiries: The submissions of the Mwaghavul Development Association and that of the Ron-Kulere Chiefdom Development Association[2] were widely referred to. Others were those from districts and individuals directly or indirectly affected by the conflict. Indeed the memoranda summarised the positions of the conflicting communities such that most of the interviews became repetitions of what was contained in the memos.

Government documents were another source of data for this work. We made use of the Plateau State government's white paper on the 1992 crisis following the Justice Jummai Sankey inquest. In the typical government fashion, the report of the 1995 inquest is yet to see the light of the day. Other government documents include minutes of local government meetings and memos from the local governments related to the conflict.

Finally, archival material was used for the earliest part of the conflict, especially in setting the tone for the pre-colonial and early colonial periods.

Conflicting Perspectives and the Philosophies of the Conflict

The Mwaghavul and Ron communities, within the disputed settlements, maintained mutually incompatible views about the status of the lands and areas in conflict. These were based on who they perceived to be the original inhabitants of these areas, and therefore, the owners of the lands. The conflict was fuelled by the perceptions of who was an indigene and who was a squatter.

a) The Mwaghavul Perspective

The Mwaghavul people resident within the border towns between

Mangu and Bokkos Local Governments, being the primary areas in dispute, believed they were the earliest to settle in these lands. As the supposed earliest settlers, therefore, they saw themselves as the owners of the land. They further contended that the Ron hitherto lived in very rocky terrain, but in recent times found it expedient to migrate into the plains for the purpose of agriculture. Such migrations were believed to have been caused by an increase in population, which in turn created a pressure on, and for land. This often led to conflict. They also contested the suggestion by the Ron that they were given farmlands by the Ron people when they first migrated from areas believed to be the original Mwaghavul districts into Ron land. Even though this contest was not strictly about territory but more about farmlands, there remained a sharp disagreement about where exactly the boundaries between the Mwaghavul and the Ron ethnic groups were. The areas claimed by the Ron were contested by the Mwaghavul people.

b) The Ron Perspective

The Ron, on the other hand, opined that the Mwaghavul people were expansionists who increasingly colonised more lands in order to meet their ever-growing demand, more so that their population, like that of the Ron, was on the increase and farmlands were becoming narrower. It was argued that the Mwaghavul migrated into Ron territory and occupied large areas of farmland, most of which were given to them free as an act of hospitality and goodwill by the Ron people. However, with the Ron needing more land and also perceiving a possible conflict in the future, they stopped this perceived expansionist tendency of the Mwaghavul by every means.

Thus, both communities were sharply disagreed over who owned the lands in dispute, and the precise locations of the boundaries between the two communities. In the absence of restraint, tolerance and positive management by the relevant authorities, major upheavals often occurred. It was appropriate therefore to summarise this conflict as one about land and territory between the two active farming ethnic nationalities.

The Historical Evolution of Conflict Issues Between the Ron and Mwaghavul Communities

Historically, there had been a close relationship between the Mwaghavul, Ron and Pyem ethnic nationalities. These three were the leading ethnic groups in Mangu Local Government before the creation of Bokkos Local Government in 1991. They were perhaps the closest knit communities within this particular region of the Plateau in pre-colonial times. It was suggested by one of the earliest colonial reports to the Resident of Bauchi in 1908 (Report No. 35), that the Ron (then called Baron), were a part of the Sura (Mwaghavul) ethnic group, and had joined forces in raids against the Kibyen (Birom).[3]

It was also suggested by the same colonial report that by the middle of the 18th century (over 250 years ago), the Birom owned and occupied all the lands on which the Mwaghavul lived.[4] The Birom had themselves displaced the Pyem tribe (whom they possibly met there) from parts of their lands, and pushed them to the foot of a hill called Pyem-Giji. The Pyem were said to have appealed to the Mwaghavul, who lived at Lankan, for assistance. The Pyem and the Mwaghavul were further said to have joined forces to eject the Birom from these locations backward into the present locations neighbouring the Mwaghavul and the Ron.

Emir Yakubu of Bauchi raided and defeated the Pyem.[5] In this account, the Pyem ceased to be a fighting power in the post-Dan Fodio jihad era. The Mwaghavul, however, resisted the Bauchi emirate invasions and maintained their independence. They continued to fight the Birom and drove them further into the hills at Fan, Ropp and Foron. These raids were, in many instances, believed to have been organised and conducted jointly with the Ron people.

Another instance of collaboration between the Ron and Mwaghavul was recorded by Hogben and Kirk-Greene (1966),[6] in which the Mwaghavul were said to have led the Ron and others to take on the forces of Emir Yakubu of Bauchi during the 1830s, in the bid by the emirate forces to invade Mwaghavul land and have access to the high Plateau.

It was also recorded by one of the colonial officers, Captain Faulkes, that when the colonial patrol force arrived Mwaghavul land in 1907, they were threatened by a military alliance of the Ron and Mwaghavul. The strategy worked out by the two ethnic nationalities, putting together an estimated force of some 30,000 to 40,000 people, was so comprehensive that, as the British patrol officer reckoned in his report, the people were capable of succeeding in annihilating the colonial force. Thus, the relationship between the Mwaghavul and the Ron predated the colonial era. There had been various levels of military, social and political collaboration between the two communities.

Having said that, it must be stated that as typical of political relations of neighbours of the time, there were often conflicts between the two communities. Some of these were over women and prestige. Often, the elders from either side would choose to test their powers and strength by taking on the neighbours, leading to occasional big fights for show of military prowess.[7] These were mostly settled almost immediately. Farmlands and territory were not subjects of conflict in the pre-colonial era, and indeed up to the 1980s.

Christianity as Cementing Factor

Following the introduction of the Christian gospel in the early part of the 20th century by British missionaries, Christianity became a key agent of social change in both Mwaghavul and Ron lands. Its modernising effects transformed traditional structures and aspects of culture. Unlike the Mwaghavul who experienced conversion from European missionaries directly, the Christian gospel was taken to Ron land by Mwaghavul evangelists. This process established a very close relationship between the top echelon of the Ron elite and the families of Mwaghavul Christian ministers especially in Panyam. Being the principal centre of learning in the colonial era, Panyam attracted many sons of Ron to her schools.

According to the president of the Ron-Kulere Development Association, the parent socio-cultural association of the Ron nation, Daniel Nji, himself a product of the Panyam-Ron evangelism-cum-educational alliance, "the Ron received every structure of Christianity from Panyam, and saw the people as symbols of Christ. They believed the church was a solution in the event of conflict, and Panyam was its centre." Other products of this close missionary collaboration include Mallam Dauda Shambor, Haruna Nji, Yohanna Mashilim, Retired Navy Commodore Samuel Atukum, Mr. Litta Shindai, etc., all leading sons of the Ron/Kulere ethnic group. This development was peculiar to only the Mwaghavul and the Ron, as no other ethnic group neighbouring the Mwaghavul enjoyed such healthy exchange. Rather than breed conflict, therefore, religious processes further cemented the relationship between the Ron and the Mwaghavul. The two communities enjoyed relatively healthy relations for a long time, at least up to the 1980s.

Church and Schools in the Conflict Zone

At Mushu where the conflict was stiffest, the first church there was established by the Sudan United Mission (SUM) in 1952. It was named SUM Church Mushu. The SUM has now metamorphosed into the Church of Christ in Nigeria (COCIN). The early church was attended, and continued to be attended up to the 1992 conflict, by both Mwaghavul and Ron worshippers. The symbiotic relationship between the groups led to aspire for common infrastructure such as a primary school which was established for the first time, as late as 1971.

The primary school was located at the old church at Mushu (pronounced Nshu by the Mwaghavul). The location of the school was the beginning of bad blood between the Ron and the Mwaghavul communities, as both groups had reservations about its exact location. A second church was later built on a hill which the Mwaghavul people referred to as Kwahasnat. The Ron were not happy with the name given to the church, and so changed it to COCIN Church, Mushu II. This name prevailed, but tension continued to mount between the two communities.

Notwithstanding this development, the two communities together established Tangur Community Secondary School through communal effort. They also jointly established a health centre through the same collaborative process. All these structures still stand.[8]

The consciousness about territoriality and land as issues in conflict between the Mwaghavul and the Ron was thus a recent development. However conflicts were generated later through the growth of the capitalist mode of production and the tendency for land to be privatised, as opposed to the former collective communal mode of land ownership. The privatisation of land was also marked by the acquisition of certificates of occupancy to legalise such individualistic claims. These features did not exist in the past.

Similarly, the increasing importance of traditional rulership, marked by its material attraction, enhanced tension between the two communities. Added to this was the growing significance of ethnic sentiments, as opposed to the Christian community spirit that was developed in the past.

The Background to, and Outbreak of, Violent Conflict (1992-1995)

The background to violent clashes between the Mwaghavul and Ron dates back to the mid-1980s. The conflict occurred in different areas and at different times. The first began as a legal dispute over land between a Ron man and a Mwaghavul man. These two went to court for the first time in 1985. The Mwaghavul man won the case. However, a brother of the Ron man who lost the case sued the Mwaghavul man who had earlier won, over the same piece of land in a different court of law. This case was again lost by the Ron man. In frustration, a different Ron man mobilised Ron people to go and cultivate the land in question in defiance of the court verdict.

The underlying current for this action was based on the philosophy of the conflict earlier mentioned, that irrespective of what the courts said and did, the Ron had a deep-seated feeling that the land belonged to them. The Mwaghavul people were seen as settlers and squatters. A legal victory for the Mwaghavul man over land in the disputed areas was at best an outrage, since the Mwaghavul had no business talking about land in a place where they were squatters. At this time, the conflict was still at the infant stage, and a few Mwaghavul and Ron people were involved. However, people were mobilised and conscientised on the need to defend their heritage. As such, more people from both ethnic groups who probably had little to do with the land in question got mobilised into taking part in the conflict. As it expanded and spread, the conflict became inter-ethnic.

During the 1988-1989 period, there were some disputes over

government forest reserves along the Mangu-Kombun junction, involving a Ron man from Tangur, Mallam Solomon, and a Mwaghavul family. This case went to court, leading to the victory of the Mwaghavul men. This spill-over effect of this case was later felt at Mushu-Kwahasnat in December 1990, when the Ron embarked on the planting of eucalyptus seedlings for large farmlands previously cultivated by Mwaghavul people. The Mwaghavul people protested against the planned take-over of their farmlands for this purpose. As a way of ensuring the security of their farms, some of them began to apply for certificates of occupancy from Mangu Local Government. These applications brewed a new dimension of conflict based on the understanding by the Ron that as squatters, the Mwaghavul should not even have attempted to apply for certificates of occupancy. Further, they suspected that the local government authorities would indiscriminately award such certificates to their own ethnic kin.

As part of a general effort to restate their authority as landlords, the Ron notified Mwaghavul farmers that, from April 1991, they should give up their farmlands to the Ron. In some instances, they were requested to share their farms with the Ron. The Ron made good their threat when in the planting season of 1991, they came out in large numbers to cultivate farms previously farmed by the Mwaghavul, through communal effort (*gaiya*). They planted corn on all the farms, often without fertiliser.

The then chairman of Mangu Local Government, Samson Mashat, attempted to intervene by setting up a committee under the district head of Langai, Mallam Iliya Yaktor. The committee succeeded in persuading the Ron people to allow the Mwaghavul people to take over their lands, subject to compensation for labour. This was, however, in the month of July, by which time it was too late to redeem some crops that had been destroyed by weed. The Mwaghavul people decided to wait till the following year.

In August 1991, the Ron again occupied these valleys and began to cultivate lands previously farmed by Mwaghavul 'squatters'. In response, affected peasant farmers staged a mass demonstration at the local government headquarters in Mangu, to protest to the local government authorities. They revealed that they had been denied farming opportunities in the rainy season, and that the Ron by farming their *fadamas* (valleys used for dry season irrigation) were going to make it impossible again for them to have a means of livelihood in the dry season.[9]

The chairman of the Local Government Council, a Ron, swiftly visited the conflict arena together with the divisional police officer and security officials. Meanwhile, the local government council had been ordered by the Plateau State Governor to resolve the looming crisis within a period of time and report to the government. After inquiries, the Ron farmers were instructed to vacate the farms for the Mwaghavul people. Mr. Samson Mashat requested both the Ron and Mwaghavul to agree and sign a peace agreement. Each side came up with six representatives. Although there was much politicking around this peace committee, they came up with some conditions for peace, including the following:

a) Each farmer should be allowed to cultivate his farmlands as was previously the case;

b) If conflicts over land and litigation ever came up, elders should intervene;

c) For court cases, the two parties should be left alone. There should be no involvement of ethnic communities on any side, in order to stop the conflict from degenerating to ethnic rancour;

d) Third parties should be kept out of conflicts.

It would appear that very little was achieved from the outcome of this peace committee and the Samson Mashat initiative, given the turmoil that followed in the months ahead. The Ron people proceeded to farm the valleys and irrigated lands of the Mwaghavul in defiance of the earlier directive of the local government chairman and the security officials. The Ron felt justified in their action based on what they thought to be the provocative and arrogant attitude of their Mwaghavul neighbours in laying claim to the ownership of the land in dispute. The Ron thought that unless they dealt with the situation, it could portend danger for them in the future.

The creation of Bokkos Local Government Council in 1991 was perhaps the straw that broke the camel's back with respect to the conflicts. The Mwaghavul in the disputed areas came under the jurisdiction of the newly-created Bokkos Local Government Area. As such, the taking over of their farmlands and other forms of harassment continued to increase. Their status as tenants had become even more sharply defined. The arena of the conflict had moved from Mangu Local Government Area. Furthermore, the conflict was extended to other border settlements where the Ron and Mwaghavul had peacefully co-existed.

The repeated harassment of people and seizure of lands led to several petitions (most of which received no response at all), and the arrest of some Ron people by the police. Two such incidents in June and October 1992 (often involving the C.I.D. Headquarters in Jos) were not taken kindly by the Ron who believed that they had accommodated their Mwaghavul neighbours, only to be paid back with such arrests.[10]

In response to these events, the Ron resorted to physical attacks on the Mwaghavul people. The first attack was launched on the night of Monday 19th October 1992, where food barns, domestic animals, buildings, fertiliser, vehicles, and any form of wealth was destroyed by the Ron. Property was also freely looted by the local ethnic soldiers. It was appropriate to describe this stage of the conflict as an attack on the Mwaghavul settlements at Mushu rather than a clash involving two sides, since there was no immediate response.

The immediate action that followed the 1992 imbroglio was the setting up of the Justice Sankey Panel of Inquiry. The government failed to act on the report for a long time. As such, the tension dragged on and brewed itself into more dangerous dimensions. The Ron continued to feel a sense of accomplishment with the 1992 attacks, while the Mwaghavul felt a sense of great loss. This probably encouraged Ron people from other locations to emulate the steps of those at Mushu by sabotaging, destroying and either taking or threatening to take farmlands.[11]

At this time, the Ron demanded that the boundaries between Mangu and Bokkos Local Government Areas be demarcated. They stated their willingness to abide by these demarcations once they were done.[12] This was to be dependent on the colonial maps of 1917, 1925 and 1935.

By 1994, most of the Mwaghavul who had been victims of the 1992 attacks went back to their homes. Tension however continued to rise in the conflict zone and the boundary investigations continued. The Boundaries Committee of Mangu and Bokkos Local Government Areas continued to do their work amidst disagreement between the affected communities. The Plateau State Boundaries Commission was drawn into the process of boundary demarcations. The 15th of May 1995 was fixed by the Plateau State Boundaries Commissioner for the demarcation of boundaries between Mangu and Bokkos Local Government Areas on the condition that the people maintained peace.

One week to this date, on the 8th of May 1995, a local farmer from the Ron community went to Bokkos to raise an alarm, alleging that his house had been destroyed, and all his family murdered, by Mwaghavul people. The chairmen of Mangu and Bokkos Local Governments Councils arranged to follow up this report and discovered it to be false. That farmer was arrested. His arrest displeased his fellow Ron people who responded by rounding up the car and threatening the police. However, the damage had already been done, as news of the alleged attack on the local farmer's house and family had spread far, with dangerous consequences.

The following day, one Galadima (Mwaghavul) was attacked on his farm by Ron people in the presence of the chairman and deputy chairman of Mangu Local Government Council. His motorcycle was destroyed by the attackers. The conflict then spread to other neighbouring settlements where homes, mostly belonging to Mwaghavul people, were set ablaze and property as well as food stuff and domestic animals were destroyed and carted away. The conflict blew into a full scale war between the two communities as they mobilised themselves to execute it. The May 1995 fracas came with fuller force and covered a wider scope than the 1992 conflicts.

The Role of the Church in the Cessation of Fighting

The church, especially the Church of Christ in Nigeria COCIN) denomination, came under heavy criticism as a result of these conflicts because over 50% of the Christian population in Plateau State was estimated to be COCIN. In the conflict area, about 95% of the population were Christian and COCIN members. It was, therefore, thought by many, and indeed by the COCIN administration itself, that they had to be relevant to the resolution of these hostilities.

It was worthy to note that what eventually brought about the cessation of the fighting between the Ron and Mwaghavul in 1995 was the intervention of the clergy from COCIN. The ministers went to the battle front and appealed for calm. The conflicting parties respected this call. As a matter of fact, throughout the conflict, both sides respected ecclesiastical structures and personnel. The churches were left standing, together with the houses of ministers and evangelists. They also similarly did not attack clergymen.

A Note on the Conduct of The Nigeria Police Force

Perhaps the most embarrassing role, as were the cases in other conflicts like Tafawa Balewa, Zangon Kataf, Tiv-Jukun, e.t.c., was the role of the police. Stories of atrocities perpetrated by men of the police force were reportedly quite irritating. These ranged from alleged rape, robbery, theft, to open partiality in the conflict. It was strongly believed that sections of the police did not want peace because they allegedly had a tendency to become richer in situations of conflict. Some of them were said to have removed and carted away roofing sheets from houses of displaced persons. It was also reported that they stopped a passenger car, tear-gassed the passengers, and removed all the money and jewellery in their possession. They lived on the domestic animals of the refugees from the conflict.

The Gender Question: Women and the Conflict

From the foregoing discussion, and from the evidence gathered during this research, women were a marginal factor in the conflicts either as activists and warriors, or as pacifists in the process of conflict resolution.[13] Yet, we found out that in Mangu Local Government Area, there were well over four hundred registered women community-based organisations (CBOs). In Bokkos Local Government Area, there were over two hundred registered women CBOs. Few of them, however, cut across the conflict divide, except for the COCIN Women Fellowship. What this suggested was that given the necessary empowerment and capacity building, the women's energy could be channelled into playing positive roles in conflict avoidance, conflict management and peacebuilding. The women appeared nearly totally uninformed about their capacities to contribute to peace.

Causes of the Conflict

Unlike most northern Nigerian conflicts which had roots dating back to the pre-colonial era and, or, the beginning of the 20th century, the historical roots of the Mangu-Bokkos conflict were not deep. The people had lived in relative peace as good neighbours, even though with differing political inclinations, as was natural in the relationship between majority and minority ethnic groups inhabiting the same state, local government area or any other geo-political area. In the following sections, we identify some of the key causes of, and issues in, the conflict between the Mwaghavul and Ron communities.

a)　Farmlands and Certificates of Occupancy

As explained earlier, conflicts emanated from the notions of landlords and settlers. Their livelihood depended on land. Those in the areas in conflict were largely rural farmers. They therefore depended on land to make their living over the years. Unfortunately, the population on both sides was on the increase, and land was a non-renewable resource. As such, the Ron people who believed that the Mwaghavul settled on their lands, felt insecure concerning their future and the fate of their children if they did not stop the Mwaghavul from asserting ownership over lands in question. In their submission to the Administrative Committee on the Bokkos-Mangu Disturbances set up in 1995, the Ron-Kulere community[14] argued as follows:

> ...One of the remotest causes of this dispute is the aggressive search for farmlands on the part of the Mwaghavul people who have acquired the notoriety of being a migratory and adventurous people. Being predominantly farmers like us, but with very little land to till, our Mwaghavul neighbours have, over the years, exerted great pressure on our communities in their search for farmlands to earn a living.[15]

The conflict initially resulted in litigation on the disputed lands between individual Mwaghavul and Ron farmers.[16] The Mwaghavul farmers won some of the cases. This was sometimes unacceptable to the Ron people who thought they were losing their lands through legal procedures deemed to be dubious.[17] Other methods of re-asserting their ownership were then considered.

A section of the Mwaghavul, on their part, also attempted to obtain certificates of occupancy on some of the lands. The case was made, for instance, of Alex Wetkos and Timothawus Yawu, both Mwaghavul , who applied for certificates of occupancy to cover their farmlands due to increasing threats and alleged trespass by Ron farmers.[18] The Ron people thought it was provocative for such farmers to even contemplate obtaining certificates of occupancy on farms which, in the first place, were not seen as theirs. In their submission to the government, the Ron pointed to this attempt to obtain certificates of occupancy as one of the causes of the conflict between the two communities. Moreover, the fact that the issuing authority was from the Mangu Local Government Area, which was largely inhabited by the Mwaghavul, as opposed to Bokkos Local Government Area which was largely inhabited by the Ron, has contributed to the conflict. As such, the Ron accused Mangu LGA of abetting the conflict by entertaining requests for the issuing of certificates of occupancy to Mwaghavul people living in the disputed areas.

In pursuance of this position, and against a background of perceived provocation from the Mwaghavul, the Ron in Mushu village forcefully took over farmlands from the Mwaghavul.

b)   Territoriality

Closely related to the land question was that of territoriality. Farmlands were a narrower dimension of territory. There was disagreement between the Ron and the Mwaghavul over the boundaries of the two ethnic communities. Both claimed lands far into what each side believed to be the boundaries. There was a deep feeling by the Ron that large areas of land on which the Mwaghavul from other settlements like Manja, Kombun-Nting, Fomulan, etc., farm, were part of Ron territory. This was an arena of conflict.

c)   Chieftaincy

Chieftaincy was another dimension of the conflict. The Mwaghavul in Mushu/Kwahasnat, for instance, had for a long time, paid their tax to the district head of Bokkos (Ron). This, by tradition, implied that they were under the jurisdiction of the district head. In recent times, a section of them developed the sentiment that such taxes should be diverted to the district head of Kerang (Mwaghavul).[19] This led to a feeling of treachery, threat, and betrayal by the Ron.

Taxes in Mushu, for instance, were collected by the village head of Tangur with the assistance of ward heads, for onward transmission to the district head of Bokkos. The Ron arranged their tax collection along the two existing clans of Ngelteng and Nyau. The Mwaghavul felt they did not belong, and asked for a Mwaghavul representative to collect their own tax. The former village head of Tangur (Ron) granted this request and appointed Musa Yenle (Mwaghavul) to collect tax from the Mwaghavul as from 1976. When the village head died in 1989 and a new one, Zakka Malau (Ron), was appointed, he saw the action of Mwaghavul as directed towards asserting their independence from the Ron of Tangur. In response, the village head refused to recognise Musa Yenle. He went further to appoint two Mwaghavul people to collect tax from their people who were under the two Ron clans. The Mwaghavul rejected the divide-and-rule tactics of the ward head, and took their tax directly to the district head of Bokkos (who accepted them), without reference to the village head of Tangur.[20] This tension later had a tremendous impact on the conflicts at Mushu.

There was also the personal ambition of some people who facilitated this conflict because they were interested in being appointed village heads and tax collectors by either of the district heads in the disputed areas. The most glaring example of this was the case of a Mwaghavul who in his ambition to become a ward head of Mushu, stirred trouble between the Ron and the Mwaghavul. He attempted to get the existing ward head deposed. When it failed, he incited the Ron against the Mwaghavul. In all the conflicts, he sided with the Ron against his "co-tribalists". He was thus spared by the Ron and lived in their midst. This contest over chieftaincy actually contributed a great deal in instigating the take-over of farmlands from the Mwaghavul by the Ron, and the violence that followed.

d)   Party Politics

Party politics created a gulf in the relationship between the Mwaghavul and the Ron people. Prior to the creation of Mangu

Local Government Council in 1976, the Ron and Mwaghavul were in Pankshin Division. They were both united, as minorities in Pankshin, in the struggle to split Pankshin into two, thus giving them their own local government council in Mangu, which materialised in 1976. As soon as the Mwaghavul and Ron came into Mangu Local Government Area, a new majority and minority situation emerged in the politics of the area.

With party politics, the Mwaghavul and the Ron were hardly on the same side. In the First Republic, the Ron teamed up with the Pyem as ethnic minorities in the local government area to support the Nigeria People's Party (NPP), as opposed to the Mwaghavul where a majority of the people were supporters of the National Party of Nigeria (NPN). During the Second Republic, the Ron, along with the Pyem, were firm supporters of the Social Democratic Party (SDP), while the Mwaghavul hovered between the ADP and the National Republican Convention (NRC). The supposed numerical terror of the Mwaghavul created some degree of tension among the key ethnic groups in the local government area.

As such, both the Pyem and the Ron felt that they deserved to be excised from Mangu Local Government into their own local government council. In 1982, the Solomon Lar government created Bokkos Local Government Council. This was reversed by the Buhari regime in 1984. However, the struggle for the creation of Bokkos Local Government Council was not lost by the people. The Pyem also embarked on a sustained campaign for the creation of Gindiri Local Government Council. Sadly, the Mwaghavul opposed the inclusion of certain parts of their land in the proposed Gindiri Local Government Area, thereby making it difficult to realise. These various local disagreements had an impact on the conflict between the Ron and the Mwaghavul communities.

e)   Creation of Bokkos Local Government Council

When Bokkos Local Government was eventually created in 1991, it became a great political and social relief for the Ron. The excitement coincided with perceived boundaries of the local government council. Thus, those Mwaghavul who lived in the boundary settlements found themselves physically in Bokkos Local Government Area.

As stated earlier, there was a sense in which the Ron felt quite marginalised while in Mangu Local Government Area. They therefore approached the boundary problems of places like Mushu with a degree of past frustration, on the one hand, and a feeling of liberation in the present situation, on the other. They would not, therefore, wish to allow the Mwaghavul any chance to do what they did to them while in Mangu Local Government Area. The exercise of authority over farms previously cultivated by the Mwaghavul became a small dimension of this newly-won independence.

f)   Government Handling of the 1992 Conflicts

The manner in which the Plateau State Government handled the 1992 conflicts was regarded by both the Mwaghavul and Ron communities as one of the factors that led to a repeat performance of the conflict in 1995. Following the 1992 fracas, the then governor, Sir Fidelis Tapgun, despatched the deputy governor and the Secretary to the State Government to visit the scene of the conflict and report to him. These officials, at the end of their visit, recommended the setting up of a panel of inquiry, which was promptly done by the government. The Justice Jummai Sankey Panel promptly completed and submitted its report to the state government. A draft white paper was also prepared by the government. However, the government later became slow, indeed reluctant, in implementing the White Paper and findings of the inquiry.

Two explanations were proffered for the failure of government to implement the decisions by releasing the white paper. The first was political. The Plateau State Government being a Social Democratic Party (SDP) regime, did not want to do anything that would jeopardise the solid support which the party enjoyed among the Ron (as the report of the inquiry put a large part of the blame on the Ron people), more so that election times were drawing close. The Mwaghavul support for the SDP was not as solid and consistent as that of the Ron. As such, the Government kept the white paper secret.

The second explanation was the fact that the government was unsure if releasing the white paper would not do more harm than good. It was assumed that each party felt so strongly about its various positions that an attempt to resolve the conflict by administrative means would escalate rather than resolve the conflict. In this case, it was left to time to heal the wounds and the issues. This also appeared to be the case with the results of the second inquiry set up in 1995 by the Plateau State Government on the same conflict.

It is, therefore, appropriate to submit that the inaction of government did not resolve the conflict at all. The repetition of this conflict in 1995 bore semblance to those in other Nigerian locations like Zangon Kataf, Tafawa Balewa, Wukari, etc., where either government inaction, indifference or incompetence in handling earlier conflicts led to their re-emergence on larger scales.

g) The Political Economy of the Bokkos Farm Project (BFP)

The Mwaghavul Community in their memo following the repeat performance of the conflict in 1995, contended that the conflict was fuelled by the Government of Plateau State as a means of dividing the Mwaghavul and Ron communities in order to go ahead with its plans of selling the Bokkos Farm Project unopposed. The argument was that if the two communities were at peace and in agreement over the farm, it would be difficult for the government to go ahead with its plans.

The Bokkos Farm Project was set up in early 1970s by the Benue-Plateau State Government as a successful venture in mechanised farming. The land used for the project was taken from the Ron and Mwaghavul communities cheaply by the Government. However, the Tapgun regime in Plateau State developed a reputation for selling government property to the rich. The multi-million naira BARC farms at Zallaki and Madara Limited (a dairy farm) had been sold to two separate retired army generals. Others like the Highland Bottling Company at Barkin Ladi and Quix Company were also sold. The attempts to sell Panyam Fish Farm were resisted by the local community and the Mangu Local Government Council. The Bokkos Farm Project was also on the line.

The hypothesis of the Mwaghavul community was that if the wealthy had bought the farm, they would have carted away all the equipment, which were themselves helpful to the local Ron and Mwaghavul communities.[21] In the words of the Mwaghavul community:

> BFP is one of the most famous ideas that has brought common benefits to Ron and Mwaghavul people... the best thing to do is to make Mangu

and Ron people enemies, thus succeeding through divide and rule,.... The equipment should have been given to, or acquired cheaply in recognition of the people who sacrificed the land for experimenting the mechanised farming. By inducing persistent quarrel between the Ron and Mwaghavul at Mushu, Government may decide to take over the land. This will give them a wide opportunity to sell the farm with ease.[22]

From this perspective, therefore, one of the causes of the conflict was the divide-and-rule tactics of certain government officials, aimed at creating the necessary conditions for government to allow the sale of state farms, including BFP, to bourgeois farmers. This practice promoted class interest.

h)   Petty Jealousy

The Mwaghavul, mainly, and a section of the Ron at Mushu/ Kwahasnat, farmed on a very rich marshy valley[23] which produced an enormous amount of rainy season and dry season crops like maize, Irish potatoes, coco-yam, tomatoes, pepper and assorted vegetables in the dry season. Both the Mwaghavul and the Ron, partly as a result of this, and due to other general agricultural activities, became relatively wealthy, albeit disproportionately. The evidence of this wealth was to be seen in the large family compounds built, the purchase of vehicles for private and commercial use, ownership of milling machines, roofing with zinc as opposed to thatched huts, etc.

Following this, the Ron requested for a large share of the land from the Mwaghavul, based on the notion that the Mwaghavul farmers were in-comers. The Mwaghavul farmers were not forthcoming on sharing the land with the Ron. Against the background that the Ron felt they were the original inhabitants of the area, this created anxiety among the two communities. This led to lack of confidence between the two groups. Property destruction and looting indicated that petty jealousies resulting from material acquisitions promoted conflicts.

Steps Taken so Far

This conflict which appeared to have defied most of the attempts to manage it, suffered from a lack of genuine effort by any group or individuals to resolve it. However, a number of efforts were made in the past, albeit quite inadequate.

a) The Samson Mashat Initiative

As chairman of Mangu Local Government Council, Samson Mashat (Ron) attempted to resolve the crisis, first on 31 August, 1991. The Ron people were reluctant. On 3 September, 1991, another meeting of both communities was held at the palace of the Bokkos district head. As the decision rested on sharing the fertile farmlands earlier described, a position the Ron had always maintained, the Mwaghavul declined to embrace the decisions taken. This continued as each side rejected the position of the other, until the conflict culminated in the 1992 carnage.

b)   The Mangu Local Government Peace Committee

As earlier mentioned, there was the committee headed by the district head of Langai, Mallam Iliya Yaktor. This committee achieved very little because it was at the early stage of the conflict. It was also overtaken by the violence of 1992.

The second effort was the committee of twenty set up by the Mangu Local Government Council, including the Mishkagham Mwaghavul, Mallam Ali Dapal Damiyal, the Saf Ron-Kulere, Mallam La'azarus Agai, the Deputy Police Commissioner, Area Commander of Police, etc. Again, this did not make any significant impact other than appealing to the conflicting parties for calm.

Thirdly, the Plateau State Government under Sir Fidelis Tapgun, sent a delegation headed by his deputy and including the then Secretary to the Plateau State Government, Mr. Sylvanus Lot, to examine the problem. This delegation paid visits to the conflict spots, and promptly advised the State Government to institute an inquest into the conflict and provide relief materials to the victims.

c)   The Justice Jummai Sankey Panel of Inquiry

The visits and recommendations above led to the establishment of the Justice Jummai Sankey Panel of Inquiry. The panel had three other members, namely, Mr. Peter Gurumpyen of the State's Ministry of Justice, Alhaji Ibrahim Egyegini of the Bureau for Social Development, and Mr. James Agbo of the Cabinet Office.

The terms of reference were to identify the remote and proximate causes of the disturbance, identify groups and individuals that were directly or indirectly behind the crisis and to determine the role of each individual/group in relation to the clash. Others were to ascertain the extent of damage and to recommend to government appropriate relief materials to acquire to reduce the burden on the victims, and to proffer solutions/suggestions that could assist the government in forestalling future re-occurrence.

The Panel promptly completed and submitted its report to the Plateau State Government. Sadly, the government swept the report under the carpet. Even though a white paper was drafted, it was never implemented or even made public. This remained the situation until the 1995 conflict broke out again. It had been earlier mentioned that the poor handling of the 1992 conflict partly caused the 1995 violence.

d)   The 1995 Administrative Committee on the Mangu-Bokkos Disturbances.

This was a second committee set up by the Plateau State Government under Col. Mohammed Mana following the violent upheaval of May 1995. The government was perhaps embarrassed that the violence erupted when it was yet to make public the findings of the Justice Sankey Panel. The Committee invited and received memoranda from all the parties in the conflict. Interestingly, the terms of reference were nearly a total duplication of the Justice Sankey's mandate. People wondered what fresh findings would be made by this panel. Yet government had to appear to be doing something, even if in reality that amounted to nothing. Close to four years after the conflicts, nothing was heard about the outcome of the investigations. There was the idea that the report would be treated in secrecy and neglect like the previous one.

e) Academic Associates PeaceWorks Education Workshops and Other Activities

In December 1997, Academic Associates PeaceWorks, a non-governmental organisation, conducted peace education workshops for secondary school teachers and CBOs in the conflict area. The schools were deliberately selected to represent the areas most affected by the conflict. The women CBO selected was the COCIN Women's Fellowship, because it was the most deeply entrenched group in the whole conflict zone. It was also the group that cut across the conflict divide.

The workshop was generally successful. It brought to the fore the fact that women could be empowered to be relevant in conflict avoidance, conflict management and peacebuilding. (A full report of the workshop is available with Academic Associates PeaceWorks). Follow-up activities continued to be sponsored by AAPW in Mangu-Bokkos for youth and the women groups. A leadership training programme was conducted for the women in 1998. A Youth Camp also took place under the auspices of AAPW at the Leadership and Citizenship Training Centre, Shere Hills, Jos, in April 1997. All of these activities were also aimed at inculcating leadership as well as conflict management skills in the trainees.

Stake Holders in the Conflict

This conflict, local as it should have remained, was fuelled by local elites and individuals who perceived a number of benefits ranging from prestige, grandeur, access to more farmlands, political advantages, access to traditional power. The following stake holders were easily identifiable, all of whom could play constructive roles, should they choose to, in resolving the conflict.

Mr. Robert Wood: He was the District Head of Bokkos and a Ron. He was in a position to broker peace if he chose. He did not help the chieftaincy tussle in the area when he accepted tax directly from the leader of the Mwaghavul at Kwahasnat (Musa Yenle), which should have, procedurally, been passed through the village head of Tangur. This deepened the traditional dimension of the conflict. Even though the Mwaghavul were trying to resist the divide-and-rule tactics of the village head of Tangur, he should have intervened as the partner in the traditional hierarchy.

Secondly, his position, along with that of the first chairman of Bokkos Local Government, T. S. Brown, to the effect that the Mwaghavul people should share their farms with the Ron as pre-condition for peace, did not help resolve the conflict. He went personally to Jos to secure the release of the Ron people arrested for mischief and trespass. His interest concerned the size of his territory and area of jurisdiction, volume of tax, prestige, the number of village areas under his domain, etc. Thus, the Justice Sankey Committee recommended that Mr. Wood should be cautioned to be a father to both groups in the conflict under his domain, and to restrain himself from being partisan.

Mr. T.S. Brown: The first executive chairman of Bokkos Local Government Area was Ron. As a politician, his role could perhaps be explained by the need to gain political acceptability among the Ron. He, along with the councillor for Tangur Ward in his government (Jeffrey Taylor), maintained the same position about the need to share the disputed lands as a pre-condition for peace. He ordered all farming activities to cease, pending a settlement. However, the farms continued to be tilled in defiance of his orders. The Plateau State Government in its White Paper noted that "Government hereby reiterates that it is constitutionally wrong for the local government to give directives that individual farmlands be shared."[24] Although out of government at that moment, Mr. Brown still commanded respect among the Ron people generally. He could contribute to resolving the issues.

Mr. Jeffrey Taylor: He was Ron, and a councillor in the T. S. Brown Council in Bokkos when the 1992 crisis occurred. He was perhaps the most fanatical character the conflict produced. He came from Tangur-Mushu and so had a close stake in the conflict. Thus, even as an elected councillor, he was accused of personally inspecting and leading the destruction of homes and property of his opponents. He repeatedly made uncomplimentary remarks, referred to them as settlers, and asked them to leave Mushu if they were not happy with the conditions given by the Ron.

Mallam John Smith: He was a former chairman of Mangu Local Government Council, and a Mwaghavul, born at Mushu but currently resided at Mangu town. He was accused of leading the Mwaghavul in Mushu, and of inciting them to reject peace plans proffered by the Ron people. However, these accusations were found to be baseless. He was, as a matter of fact, commended for his role by the Justice Sankey Panel and the government white paper that followed. His role was seen to be peaceful, mature and mediatory.

Mallam Richard Booker: He was Mwaghavul and an ex-service man from Mushu. He understood the conflict very well. He was one of the leaders of the Mwaghavul community, but deeply suspected by the Ron of Mushu. Thus, they rejected his membership of the Samson Mashat peace initiative on the grounds that he was an elite. Nothing linked him directly with the conflict, but he could positively contribute to resolving the conflict.

It was a positive development that the positions of the paramount rulers in the area, namely the Saf Ron Kulere and the Mishkagham Mwaghavul, were quite reconciliatory as opposed to being divisive. The conflict could have been made more complicated had it been abetted by any of them. They too could continue to play positive roles in the future.

The Church of Christ in Nigeria (COCIN) at various levels could also be considered as a factor relevant to any resolution of the conflict. For the avoidance of doubt, the church neither fuelled nor supported the conflict. It was mentioned earlier that their ministers brought about a cessation of fighting during the carnage. Most members of these communities belonged to the church.

The Women Fellowship of COCIN was perhaps the most relevant in this direction. Although, only the COCIN Church Mushu II had a combination of Mwaghavul and Ron women, Academic Associates PeaceWorks could work with women invited separately from the opposing churches, as a starting point for eventual co-operation.

Notes

[1] .These were names used differently by the Mwaghavul and the Ron to refer to the same settlements. Each side was of the opinion that the names of the settlements were changed by the other party in the conflict, having been allowed to settle by the 'landlord'.

[2] The Ron and Kulere are separate ethnic groups, but come under the same Chiefdom. Even though the memo was presented on behalf of the entire Chiefdom, it was worthy to note that the Kulere had little or nothing to do with the conflict. It was between the Ron and the Mwaghavul. Perhaps the involvement of the Kulere would have deeply complicated the conflict.

[3] See *Bauchi Provincial Report* No. 35, for the quarter ending 31st March 1908, dated 29th February 1908.

[4] This is probably an exaggeration. It makes more sense to argue that the Birom were displaced from some of the lands they previously occupied, as opposed to believing that the whole of the Mwaghavul districts were occupied by the Birom at some point in time.

[5] The period of this raid must have been between 1810 and 1834. It was probably after the defeat of the Pyem by Yakubu of Bauchi that an unsuccessful attempt was made to also overrun the Mwaghavul in the 1930s.

[6] See Hogben, S.J. and Kirk-Green, A.H.M. (1966): *The Emirates of Northern Nigeria* (London Oxford University Press).

[7] This position was confirmed by the District Head of Kombun, Alhaji G. Ibrahim.

[8] As a result of the ethnic cleansing following the conflicts of 1992 and 1995, the Ron and Mwaghavul communities became physically separated in such a way that the Mwaghavul totally abandoned the schools and churches which they previously shared,

as teachers, students and pupils. At the time of fieldwork the only church where Ron and Mwaghavul were found under the same roof was COCIN Church Mushu II. Mwaghavul children began to return to the Tangur Community Secondary School in small numbers.

9. See *Nigerian Standard*, 8th September, 1991.

10. Mwaghavul people who felt harassed often took their complaints to the Divisional Police Office in Mangu, as opposed to Bokkos, which had by now attained its own divisional command. This did not go down well with the Ron people, who interpreted it as an act of rebellion and insubordination to the authorities in Bokkos.

11. As such, the 1995 violence did not start at Mushu, but at new locations like Manja, Kombun Nting, Tim Nanle, etc. It spread to Mushu after a few days from its take-off location.

12. Good as the case for demarcation of boundaries would appear, it is far from the issue in this conflict. The conflict is not about boundaries. The Mwaghavul people did not claim to be living in Mangu Local Government. They had been paying their tax to the district head in Bokkos via the village head of Tangur. The 1992 and 1995 conflicts did not arise over boundaries, but farmlands. See *Government Views and Decisions on the Report of the Panel to Investigate the Ron-Mwaghavul Crisis at Mushu, Bokkos Local Government Area*, June 1993, p. 8, hereafter cited as *Government Views and Decisions on Justice Jummai Sankey Report*.

13. However, the role of Mushu women in stirring the 1992 crisis must be put on record. On four occasions in March 1992, Ron women were alleged to have led the destruction of farmlands belonging to Mwaghavul men at Mushu. They succeeded, on each occasion, in chasing away the men from the farm and thereafter, asserted their authority. See *Letter from Mwaghavul Community at Mushu to the Governor of Plateau State*, 14th April 1992.

14. It is necessary to repeat that even though the Memo came from the Ron-Kulere Chiefdom Development Association, the Kulere people were not a part of this conflict. Perhaps the conflicts would have been more complicated if they had been involved. It was purely between the Ron and the Mwaghavul people. The Kulere were a different ethnic group from the Ron, but both shared a Chiefdom and one paramount ruler.

15. See *Memoranda Submitted to the Administrative Committee on the Bokkos-Mangu Disturbances by the Ron-Kulere Community*, June 1995.

16. The exact number of the cases pending in court, or which have been completed, cannot be ascertained However, it is noted by the report of the Justice Sankey Committee that there are a number of such cases. See *Government's Views and Decisions on Justice Jummai Sankey Report*.

17. It is necessary to note that under the Land Use Act of 1978 which governs the use of all lands in Nigeria, the government is, in principle, the owner of all lands. Individuals are allowed to acquire an interest in land only for a particular period of time.

18. See *Government Views and Decisions on Justice Sankey Report*, p. 11.

19. One of our informants argued that the payment of tax to the district head of Bokkos had a history. It was argued that in the colonial period, the district head of Kerang was supposed to collect tax from the Mwaghavul at Mushu/Kwahasnat. He, however, declined on account of the distance. He reasoned that since the tax was going to the same colonial treasury in Pankshin, it did not matter whether it was the district head of Bokkos or Kerang that collected it. Although it was said to be sanctioned by the colonial Divisional Officer in Pankshin, there were no documents to this effect. Interestingly, the 1995 Memo of the Ron community to the Panel of Enquiry suggested the exact opposite with respect to Marish and Bandungang.

20. See *Government Views and Decisions on Justice Jummai Sankey Report*, p. 8.

21. See *Memorandum to the Administrative Committee on the Bokkos/Mangu Disturbance, by the Mwaghavul Development Association*. June 1995.

[22] ibid., p. 7.

[23] Although the valley is very narrow and may be considered by outsiders as too small to generate the amount of conflict it did, it is at the centre of the political economy of these two communities. Most of the people depend on it in the dry season, and make an enormous amount of money from activities there.

[24] See Government Views and Decisions on Justice Jummai Sankey Report, p. 17.

References

Bauchi Provincial Report No. 35 (for the quarter ending 31. 3. 1908 dated 29. 2. 1908).

Hogben, S.J. and A.H.M. Kirk-Green (1966). *The Emirates of Northern Nigeria*. London. Oxford University Press.

Sankey, J. (1993). *Report of the Panel to Investigate the Non-Mwaghavul Crisis at Mushu, Bokkos Local Government Area*. June 1993.

Ethnic and Religious Conflicts in Kano

INTRODUCTION

Kano, the most populated and industrialised city in northern Nigeria, is one of the hottest spots of ethnic and religious conflicts in Nigeria. The problems can be easily explained within the context of migrations into the city since its occupation by the British in 1903, especially by the Christian-dominated southern Nigerians. Before then Kano was an important Islamic urban centre in Western-Central Sudan playing active roles in pre-colonial trans-Saharan trade and also hosting many north African merchants and Islamic scholars. So much was the influence of the Muslim north Africans, and later of the Sokoto jihadists, on Kano that by the nineteenth century, it was a vibrant Islamic state with all the attributes of a typical Islamic city (Frishman 1986). With colonisation by the British in 1903 came "modernisation" or "westernisation" which opened Kano to different kinds of culture change and forced it to shed some aspects of its former self as an Islamic city. Some of the immigrants into Kano at this time were southern Nigerians who introduced Christianity to the city and now control sizable proportion of the city's informal economy. The practice of Islam also experienced dramatic changes as different sets of Islamic movements started establishing their presence in the city, especially in the colonial and post-colonial periods. All these have been major sources of conflicts.

Historical Background of Kano

Kano is one of the oldest indigenous cities in Nigeria. It was founded around the seventh century as a settlement of Abagayawa immigrants blacksmiths who came to mine iron ore from the iron stone outcrop of Dalla hill [Willet 1971: 368]. The Abagayawa were conquered by the Maguzawa [non-Muslim Hausa] led by Bagauda around the tenth and eleventh centuries. The city thus became a formidable political entity under the leadership of Bagauda and starting from this period, Kano began to experience rapid physical, economic and social development.

In 1095, Sarkin Gigi, who succeeded Bagauda as the Sarki [king] started the construction of the popular Kano city walls as a protective device against foreign invasion. The construction of the walls was completed in the twelveth century during the reign of Sarkin Yusa [Frishman 1977: 214]. In the fifteenth century, during the reign of Muhammadu Rumfa, the walls had to be extended by 54 per cent to accommodate the new immigrants streaming into the city especially from Bornu area as well as from north Africa. The motivation for this migration trend was the economic importance of Kano. It was a major centre of tran-Saharan trade in the pre-colonial period.

Islam was introduced to the city by some Wangara and Sharifai immigrants in the fourteenth century [al-Hajj 1963: 7-16] and it became the official religion during the reign of Sarkin Muhammadu Rumfa [1463-1499]. Before this period, the successive rulers of Kano were at best nominal Muslims [Paden 1973: 47] and it was Rumfa who played host to Al-Maghili, a radical north African Islamic scholar from Tlemcen who first introduced Kano to Islamic fundamentalism. His visit to Kano was motivated by the ideological conflicts that arose in the western Mediterranean and north Africa as a result of the colonial offensive of Portugal and Spain and the call by Pope Martin V and Pope Eugenius for Christian monarchs to eliminate Muslims, considered to be infidels, from their domains in the early fifteenth century.

Al-Maghili's visit to Kano, like the visit of many other Islamic scholars to different parts of Sahara and South equator, was to conquer the Christian propaganda and, on the other hand, make the Muslims see the Christians as infidels [*kafirai*].

The major task of Al-Maghili in Kano was that of confidence-building: he encouraged the Muslims to have more faith in their religion and established various frameworks upon which the true practice of Islam could rest in the city [*Yahaya* 1989]. As a result of Al-Maghili's visit, Kano because a major centre of Islamic civilisation in Africa. Shortly after this the traditional "animists", popularly called Maguzawa in the city were overthrown and eliminated from all state matters. The practice of the Islamic religion became more reinforced in Kano as a result of the Sokoto jihad which took place in the city in 1807 and consequently made Kano a complete Islamic urban centre.

The city was occupied by the British in 1902 at the end of a bloody resistance movement by the Kanawa who for the first time were "forced" to play host to people of other religions especially the Christians from southern Nigeria. The culture-shock resulting from this contract partly explains the present tide of ethnic and religious conflicts in the city.

Background to the Ethno-Religious Conflicts in Kano

The present-day ethnic and religious conflicts in Kano can only be clearly understood within the context of modern migrations into the city. Modern migrations are here meant to be the twentieth-century migrations of the christian - dominated southern Nigerian traders and public servants into the city. Though the Igbo dominate the present population of the southern Nigerians in Kano, the Yoruba were the first major southern Nigerian migrants to settle in Kano, in any substantial number immediately after the city was colonised by the British in 1903. This is not surprising considering the fact that it was from Yorubaland that the British colonialists fist recruited their personal staff: cooks, messengers, clerks etc. Those that were brought by the colonial administrators to the North were later joined by some traders who were so many that one of the British officials noted in 1904 that,

> A few years ago you might search the whole of the left bank of the Niger for a Yoruba trader, and not find one; now I venture to say that in every market town of northern Nigeria you will find them.

The official census conducted by the colonial administrators (NAK Kano Prof. 5/1, 5908) indicated that whereas there was a total of 1471 Yoruba people in Kano in 1921, the Igbo who now dominate the migrant population in the city were so few that no mention of them was made. The Yoruba population was surpassed by that of the Igbo immediately after the second world war. This was because of the colonial railway that then reached Kano from the Igbo-dominated eastern Nigeria and the rapid industrial development that Kano experienced at that time. The Igbo flooded Kano in search of skilled and unskilled jobs, and some of them became long-distance marketers of finished products of the newly established industries. Many others became permanent traders in the different Kano markets. To the "ubiquitous Ibo and other tribes from the distant south," as R.L. Maiden, one of the colonial officials in Kano noted in 1938, the city of Kano was "an El Dorado" (NAK KanoProf. %/1, 4292 p. 18).

By 1948, the population of the Igbo in Kano was 6,680 compared to that of the Yoruba which was 4,514. The Igbo population rose to 12,770 in 1955 while that of the Yoruba stood at 5,174. The superior numerical strength of the Igbo which made them to dominate the economic activities in Kano later worked against them as they were seen and frequently attacked physically as interlopers who came to "steal" what belonged to the Kanawa indigenes in order to develop eastern Nigeria from where they came.

From the inception of the colonial administration in Kano, the British could clearly foresee the hostility that would mark the relationship between the Kanawa and the southern Nigerian settlers in their midst. The first problem that revealed itself was religious. Kano was a predominantly Islamic urban centre very aversive towards western civilisation. On the other hand, the southern Nigerians who had had a long history of contacts with the Europeans and hence western civilisation were largely Christians. As early as 1901, Lord Lugard who led the occupation of northern Nigeria had promised the Sultan of Sokoto (who headed the Sokoto Caliphate of which Kano was a part) that he would not do anything that could hinder the practice of Islam (Lugard 1903: 164). In fact feared by the colonial officials that an uncensored interaction between the southern Nigerians and the Muslim Kᵕnawa could generate social stresses that could lead to violent revolt against the colonial system, Lord Lugard noted in his First Annual Report that the typical southern Nigerian "... is quite certain to give much trouble in his dealings with the natives and by his fondness for litigation" (Lugard 1901: 20). Although this idea was later dropped, the British first tried to limit the number of southern Nigerians coming to Kano and other northern Nigerians cities in other to solve this problem. The immigrant southern Nigerian traders who would have been victimised by such a policy were found to be desirable persons in terms of the boost they gave to the marketing of European goods among the different people with whom they traded and the amount of taxes paid. It was recommended that, "...every effort should be made to encourage natives of the protectorate (i.e. northern protectorate) to become small traders and collectors of local produce" (Lugard 1900-1901 p.20).

The British could only have wished that the Hausa-Fulani become effective small scale traders and collectors of local produce. But it was not possible for them to force their will on the reluctant Hausa-Fulani Kanawa; the Kanawa had little or nothing to do with the colonialists. They saw the colonial masters as a victorious Christian invader of a Muslim society. At the same time, the British were perceived by the Kanawa not too differently from the Christian immigrants that followed them to Kano in 1903 and thereafter. The two were simply referred to as Nasara (Christian) or Kafirai (infidels) with whom devoted Muslims should have no serious relationship. The capitalist strategy of accumulation and development that attended the British incursion into Kano was not well rated and hence it was not to be taken too seriously by the Kanawa. Therefore at the initial stage the Kanawa maintained safe distance from the British (Lubeck 1986: 137). This served as an incentive for more southern Nigerians to move into Kano to exploit the benefits of the booming formal and informal economy in the city.

The Kanawa realised that as long as the colonial authorities were in their midst, it was impossible to completely keep aloof from the capitalist economy. They had no paper qualifications that could make them play comfortable roles under the new dispensation. Yet they had to pay taxes to the Emir in British pounds under the indirect rule system of governance. This meant that as a matter of compulsion they had to search for some economic jobs for themselves under the colonial system. The Kanawa reluctantly did this at a very slow pace, moreso as the British frustrated their efforts to continue the trans - Saharan trade with north-Africans as done in the pre-conquest era. The British charged high tariffs on the north Africans products so that people could buy the good shipped in Manchester and Liverpool at cheaper prices (Yahusa 1990: 56-8) to encourage more people to go into the coastal trade in European goods.

As the Kanawa suffered under the new dispensation, the southern Nigerians in their midst experienced economic boom which naturally led to hostile dispositions towards the southerners by their Kanawa hosts. The strangers started to be looked upon as enjoying economic benefits that ought to have been reserved for their hosts.

The cultural difference between the Kanawa and their southern Nigerian "guests" was worrisome to the British colonial officials. To reduce the contacts between the two groups a segregated settlement named *Sabon gari* [pl. *Sabon garuruwa*] had to be established for these southern Nigerian immigrants around 1911, and their Hausa-Fulani hosts were restricted to the old walled city [*Birni*]. The *Sabon gari* in Kano was the first of such modern migrant settlements to be established in Nigeria. Other such settlements were established at about the same time in Zaria and Kaduna to serve a similar purpose. In 1914, the first *Sabon gari* in southern Nigeria was established in Ibadan [Albert 1993b].

The residential segregation between the Kanawa and the southern Nigerian Christians was strictly enforced in Kano: the southerners were segregated from their Kanawa hosts physically and the segregation also had political and legal dimensions. Whereas the *Birni* was put under the native authority system headed by the Emir of Kano, the *Sabon gari* was managed directly by the colonial authorities so that the two settlements could have little or nothing to do with each other. The strangers were completely forbidden from living in the inner city, *Birni*, reserved for the indigenous Muslim population (Albert 1994: 1996) and the Kanawa too were forbidden from living in the Sabon gari with the southerners. They were expected to respect a law signed by the governor - general in 1914 stating that:

> Any person who is directly subject to the Native Authority who should reside within a native reservation in the township should be guilty of an offence and on conviction shall be liable to a fine not exceeding five pounds (NAK, SNP 9/1 1774/1914).

The southern Nigerians did not allow the system of residential and political segregation to bother them. They lived at whatever place was dictated to them and devoted more of their energies and time to improving their economic status. By the late 1940s, a large proportion of the commanding heights of Kano's economy, whether in the formal or informal sector, was in the hands of southern Nigerians. They dominated the staff list of the commercial banks, post offices, the European trading houses, law firms etc. They were responsible for the importation of forest products into Kano and were the sellers of building materials and motor-spare parts, carpenters, plumbers, bricklayers, shoemakers etc. At a point they started selling imported praying mats and kettles to the Muslim population in Kano. The Sabon gari market which they established in 1918 greatly rivalled the traditional Kurmi market established several centuries ago and which played significant roles in the trans-Saharan trade of the pre-colonial era in the Birni. Because of its vibrancy, more people preferred to go to the Sabon gari market.

The southerners were able to control Kano's formal economy because they were better educated than their Hausa-Fulani host population in the western sense. Special qualifications which the northerners lacked were needed for the "office jobs". The southerners were also able to control the informal economy because they were more ready to co-operate with the colonial authorities and work closely with the European trading firms which imported foreign goods into Nigeria. The European firms did wholesales, while the southerners did bulk-breaking and retail sales. The different foreign firms were also ready to grant the southerners credit facilities which boosted their business.

The city of Kano became more industrialised in the early 1950s and attracted more southern Nigerians. The Igbo, as before, formed the largest percentage of the migrants and the Kanawa who seemed to have had enough of the southern Nigerians' incursion into their territory concluded that this new wave of migration was meant to facilitate the colonisation of the north by the Igbo and Yoruba (Paden 1973:36).

The fear of the Kanawa this time around was not only economic but also political. As early as 1947 when the Richards Constitution was passed, there had been political rivalries between the southern and northern Nigerians as they are today. Northern Nigerians feared the domination of the southerners who were considered more sophisticated politically, economically and educationally. The Kano migration was seen as part of the plans of the southerners to "colonise" northern Nigeria. Most of the ethnic and inter-religious conflicts experienced in Kano were the results of direct or indirect attempts to check the ascendancy of these southern Nigerians in the city. The first open hostility between the two groups was the 1953 riot.

Three Cases of Ethnic Conflicts

1. The 1953 Ethnic Violence:

The 1953 ethnic conflict was fuelled by the existing local grievances against the *Sabon gari* settlers in Kano. A motion was moved on the floor of the Federal House of Representatives Lagos by Chief Anthony Enahoro, a member of the Yoruba-dominated Action Group (A.G.) calling for Nigeria's independence in 1956. Members of the Hausa-Fulani dominated Northern People's Congress (N.P.C) opposed the motion claiming that Nigeria was not ripe for independence. The latter were openly insulted as stooges of the British in Nigeria not only by their colleagues in the Parliament but also by the Yoruba and Igbo people on the streets of Lagos and by those enroute to the north across various Yoruba towns.

By May 1953, members of the A.G. tried to take their campaigns for Nigerian independence in 1956 to the North. Kano was chosen as the first place to visit. The way the southern press promoted the proposed A.G. visit to Kano compounded the crisis. Different kinds of disparaging and inflamatory reports and editorials were written about the leadership of the Northern People's Congress [NPC], especially in the *Daily Service* owned by some southern politicians. The leaders of the NPC swore to disrupt the visit of A.G. leaders to Kano [see Albert 1997].

On 15 May, 1953 a mass demonstration broke out in Kano against the Chief Ladoke Akintola-led A.G. tour of Kano and the demonstrators went straight to *Sabon gari* when they believed the kinsmen of the Yoruba and Igbo collaborators could be found. Invaluable lives and property were lost during the crisis and by the time normalcy was restored on 19 May 1953, a total of twenty-one southerners had officially been declared dead while seventy-one others were wounded. The southerners also killed fifteen northerners and wounded 163 (NRG 1953: 21).

Most of those killed were Igbo, though the crisis was caused by a Yoruba political party (Albert 1993). The victimisation of the

Igbo during this riot was for two main reasons. Apart from dominating the economic system in Kano, the Igbo, unlike the Yoruba, had little or nothing to do with Islam, of which the local Kanawa people were strong adherents. The Igbo immigrants were Christians. They were therefore seen as complete strangers who were not prepared to integrate into their host community. The 1953 ethnic violence was followed by a "northernisation policy" which was aimed at retrenching the southerners from the northern public service and replacing them with northern Nigerians. The Igbo and Yoruba who were retrenched refused to return to the South but became small-scale traders or self-employed artisans. So strong was the economic aggressiveness of the immigrants who operated at the *Sabon gari* market that by 1965, they had succeeded in swaying buyers away from the traditional *Kurmi* market in the *Birni* controlled by the Hausa-Fulani. Most people preferred to do their shopping at the *Sabon gari* market. The Kanawa became more worried. Some of the Hausa-Fulani traders at *Kurmi* market had to abandon retail trade to commence wholesale trade in competition with the Europeans and Lebanese. Those who were not wealthy enough to compete with the Europeans and Lebanese started to accuse the Igbo of repatriating the profits made in Kano to develop eastern Nigeria. There were therefore calls for the repatriation of the Igbo strangers.

2.   The 1966 Crisis

On 15 January 1966, some young Igbo army officers led by Major Chukwuemeka Kaduna Nzeogwu organised the first ever military *coup d'etat* in Nigeria. As a result, some prominent Hausa-Fulani leaders including the prime minister, Alhaji Tafawa Balewa and the premier of the North, Sir Ahmadu Bello, were killed. General Aguiyi Ironsi, an Igbo man, consequently replaced Sir Tafawa Balewa as the Nigerian head-of-state. The Igbo in the North were thereafter accused of over-celebrating their "victory" over the Hausa-Fulani. This generated different degrees of hostility against the Igbo traders. There was a demonstration in Kano on March 29, 1966 against the unification decree which the new head of state promulgated. Between 100 and 200 Igbo people were killed at *Sabon gari* and by July that same year, some northern military officers staged another coup to avenge the death of their leaders in the January coup. A genocide against the Igbo in Kano also followed. Many were pulled out of their houses and killed. The survivors fled back to the East, leaving behind all their property and investments in Kano. This episode was followed by the Nigerian civil war of 1967 to 1970.

There is the need at this point to shed some light on why the 1953 and 1966 ethnic hostilities occurred in Kano. It was more against the Igbo than the Yoruba or any other group. The economic reasons for this were suggested earlier in this chapter. The Igbo dominated the economy of Kano and were the most easily blamed for the "colonisation" of the city's economy. To further complicate matters, the Igbo were found by their Kanawa hosts not to be receptive to Islam and the social practices that predominated in Kano. On the other hand, some of the Yoruba immigrants who were Muslims were easily disposed towards Hausa-Fulani socio-cultural practices. The northerners were also very careful with the Yoruba because it was through the Lagos sea-port that they received most of their imported goods. To this end, the Kanawa ensured that the Yoruba, especially the Muslims among them, were cautiously treated during inter-ethnic hostilities in Kano. And, in fact after 1966, things changed as ethnic conflicts between the Kanawa and their southern Nigerian guests became more religiously defined as we shall discuss later.

3.   **The 1995 Ethnic Disturbance at Sabon gari Market**

On May 30 1995, there was a simple fight between two persons along Hausa/Ibo Road by Russel Avenue around the Sabon gari market. Mr. Arthur Nwankwo, an Igbo man who had a shop within the vicinity sighted two thieves stealing a bag from the boot of a taxi. The thieves concealed the stolen bag near a car being guarded by Mallam Abubakar Abdu, alias Dan'Fulani, a Fulani man. The bag was later recovered from the thieves as a result of Mr Nwankwo's alarm. Trouble started when Mr. Nwankwo challenged Dan Fulani as to why he did not stop the theft. The latter replied that he was not interested in the theft because the affected car was not parked under his care. The thieves later went to Mr. Nwankwo to accuse him of unduly interfering in their "business" as the theft had little or nothing to do with his role as a shop owner in the area. They went away telling him of nat would be the repercussion of such an action in the future. Dan Fulani later returned to Mr. Nwankwo to engage him in a battle of words which developed into a scuffle. Dan Fulani hit Nwankwo with a stone on the head and the later hit Dan Fulani with a firewood. The latter was also pushed into a hot pot of vegetable oil. A free-for-all fight ensued with some Hausa-Fulani supporting Dan Fulani and some Igbo supporting Nwankwo. At the end of this "ethnic conflict", twenty five people were officially declared dead, "excluding the many unidentifiable charred remains recovered within Sabon Gari by the police/REDA/Fire Brigade." Ninety three persons were seriously injured [Official Report 1995: 11]. A total of thirty two vehicles, eighty-one motorcycles and forty-nine shops were vandalised by the rioters and the police arrested fifty-four persons for looting, arson, attempted murder, murder and other minor offences.

Religious Conflicts in Kano

There are two major kinds of religious conflicts in Kano. The first is that between the fundamental and orthodox Muslims [intra-religious conflicts], while the second is between the Muslims and Christians [inter-religious conflicts]. Each of these conflicts has had devastating effects on the peace and tranquility in the city and the factors responsible for the two are not the same. We shall therefore treat them separately focusing first on the Muslim-Muslim conflicts.

Intra-Religious Conflicts

(i) Maitatsine Riot of 1980

In the course of its historical development, Kano played host to different kinds of Islamic scholars, especially from north Africa and the neighbouring Cameroon and Chad Republics. A few of these scholars, especially in the colonial and post-colonial periods introduced Kano to fundamentalist religious activities which led to the development of several Islamic sects in the city. The Maitatsine riot of December 18-29, 1980 was the first in the series of popular denunciation of the activities of some of these fundamentalists Islamic teachers in Kano.

In 1980 when the Maitatsine riot occurred there were several Koranic Mallams in Kano representing different sects. The most articulate among these were Mohammed Marwa, M. Salih, Salisu Kofar Wambai, M. Damnakashi, IIIyasu Gwammaja, Musa Gwammaja and Uba Yakassai. Each of these Islamic scholars preached fundamentalist Islamic religion and often denounced those in Kano who belonged to the *Kadiriyya* and *Kabulu* sects as pagans.

In their own words there is no place in the Koran "where such nasty religious sects exist" [see FGN 1981:27]. As early as 1979, several reports were made to the police by the majority of Kanawa who belonged to these often attacked sects. All efforts to make the Mallams stop their illegal and conflict-prone religious activities failed. It was in the effort to forcefully check the activities of these mallams that Mohammed Marwa stuck his neck out as the most deviant of them all.

However, the 1980 Maitatsine riot which Marwa led cannot be clearly understood without taking a cursory look at the history of the man's life in Kano. He is believed to have emigrated from Marwa in nothern Cameroun to Kano as an Islamic scholar in 1945 [Tamuno 1991:175; Adamu 1993:16-7]. Kano had the reputation at this time of receiving any Islamic scholar with open arms. Marwa could therefore not have been turned back. But his true personality became known as he later declared himself a prophet of God and started engaging in several rituals and statements that the orthodox Muslims in Kano considered heretic. He challenged some contents of the Koran and preached against the prophethood of Prophet Mohammed [FGN 1981:15]. He preached against modernisation and branded as infidels all Muslims using wrist watches, motor cars, bicycles etc. He asked God to punish whosoever refused to accept his teaching ["Wanda bai yarda ba Allah ta tsine mishi"]. This was why he was also referred to as "Maitatsine" meaning "He who curses". His followers who had numbered up to between six and ten thousand in 1980 [Balogun 1989:67] were popularly known as "Yan tatsine" [The children or followers of he who curses].

On account of his fundamentalist religious activities Marwa was deported in the early 1960s by Alhaji Muhammadu Sanusi, the late Emir of Kano but quickly returned to Kano to continue his religious activities in 1965 consequent upon the former's deposition [Whitaker Jr. 1970: 279-82] in 1963. In 1973, he was convicted for threatening the peace of Kano and quietly sneaked back to the city after completing his jail terms at Markurdi prison. By the late 1970s he had become "a menace beyond the law of the land" [Adamu 1993: 16].

The first step to the 1980 crisis was probably taken by the government on 26th November 1980 when Marwa was asked by Alhaji Abubakar Rimi, the then governor of Kano State, to demolish some illegal structures he had built for his homeless followers. He was given fourteen days within which to complete his evacuation from the public land on which the structures were constructed. Marwa was also accused of being in possession of some illegal weapons which he was asked to submit to the government immediately. Marwa reacted by asking his followers to attack the "infidels" that had declared war on him and the targets of the Yan tatsine were the police and the orthodox Muslims. Over 500 people including Marwa himself lost their lives in this crisis and goods worth several millions of naira were destroyed by the fundamentalists. Similar riots were organised by the yan tatsine in other parts of northern Nigeria [Bulunkutu, Jimeta, Yola, Gombe and Funtua] between 1982 and 1987.

(ii)   **The Shiite Attacks of 1996 and 1997**

The Shiites formed another fundamentalist Islamic group that caused intra-religious conflicts among the Muslims in Kano. The base of the sect in Nigeria was Zaria under the leadership of Mallam Ibrahim El Zak-Zaky who was detained by the federal government on account of activities considered to be inimical to public peace and order in the country. The Shiites were generally believed to be supported from Sudan and Libya; it was a youth movement. The sect preached against political corruption and held anti-establishment views. They had a pathological hatred for the Nigerian judiciary and police all of whom were considered to be instruments of Satan. They particularly referred to the police as **Babbuque** meaning the "burnt ones" [Olugboji 1995: 6].

The Shiites in Kano broke away from their organisation in 1992. For some unknown reasons, they declared Mallam Zaky as their enemy and even had to physically assault him in 1994 while he was preaching at a mosque at Bayero University, Kano. Members of this sect in Kano were popularly known for indoctrinating their converts with "a mixture of anti-establishment rhetorics and threats against Muslims and non-Muslims that do not follow Shiite teachings." The major grievance of the people of Kano against the Shiites was not actually their anti-establishments activities but the way they blasphemed some Caliphs and faithfuls of Allah. Some of the things they said while preaching were considered by the orthodox Muslims in Kano to be heretic and insolent, and the physical violence between them and the other Muslims in Kano was often defined within this context.

Unlike the Marwa-led Yan tatsine, the Shiites consisted of well educated young men and their members spread round the ancient city of Kano. They were not concentrated in any specific quarters. When they were attacked or chose to attack any group, they did not employ the "fight to finish" strategy of the Yan tatsine; they tactically withdrew from areas of violent conflict when the occasion called for it and reorganised at some other places or time using new strategies. All these factors combined to make counter-insurgent policies against them to be less productive.

Kano's peace was threatened several times by the Shiites and two of these moments are quite outstanding in terms of their human casualties. The first was the clash between the Shiites and the *Yan tauri* in August 1996. The word *Yan tauri* in English means "the invulnerable". They were so called because of the belief that these young men had native medicaments which made it impossible for a knife to penetrate their bodies. The *Yan tauri* were a special category of street boys/youths in Kano. They engaged in different kinds of on-the-street hooliganism [see Albert 1997; Dawa 1996] and were popularly known for "buying" street fights from weak parties, thus helping to fuel simple disagreements into large scale civil disturbances.

The August 1996 disturbance was a result of the failed attempts orthodox Muslims around Adakawa quarters made to prevent the Shiites from operating in their area. In early August 1996, the Shiites had indicated their interests to mark the Id-El Maulud, the birthday of Prophet Mohammed, at Adakawa quarters. The people living around this area were worried that such a forum could be used by the Shiites to offend the religious sensibilities of other Muslims. They therefore asked the Shiites to keep away from the area. The fundamentalists however swore to carry out their programmes as scheduled, asking the members of the community to do their worst. It was at this stage that the Yan tauri threatened that the Shiites either obeyed the simple warning earlier given to them or risk a violent attack. The police also warned the Shiites to keep away from the area but they remained adamant. As they were defiantly holding their Maulud meeting on the 11th August 1996, the Yan tauri appeared on the scene asking that the gathering disperse immediately. This led to a free-for-all fight in which various kinds of dangerous weapons were used [Olorunfewa 1996: 10]. Supported by members of the Adakawa community, the Shites were however overpowered and the crisis did not last more than a few hours. The police also came to the scene so quickly that the civil disturbance could not spread round the city of Kano as experienced in the past.

The Shiites struck once again, in Kano, on the 7th February 1997 on the occasion of the annual Eid-el-Fitr prayers that was held at Kofan Mata, one of the popular quarters in Kano. The Shiites came before 7.30 am to the vicinity to "punish" the orthodox Muslims in Kano for their "lukewarm" attitude to the practice of "true" Islam. The Orthodox Muslims who started arriving at the Kofan Mata praying ground as early as 7.30 a.m. noticed the presence of the Shiite fundamentalists around the praying ground. The Shiites felt that a true Muslim should not have been as complacent about the political developments around them as the orthodox Muslims seemed to have been. They expected all true Muslims to have violently revolted against the political injustices and corruption in Nigeria. For failing to take arms against the government of the day, the Shiites saw the orthodox Muslims in Kano as accomplices of the Abacha regime. They therefore found it difficult to understand why Allah would not compensate whosoever waged war against such "infidels". Taking the law into their hands, the Shiites vowed to violently prevent the Muslims from saying their Id-el-Fitr prayer and blocked all entrances to the prayer ground. They started to make provocative statements about the political and religious leaders who in their own estimation misled their followers from practising true Islam in Kano. The police soon arrived at the scene and asked the Shiites to either join the prayer team or vacate the premises. The Shiites reacted by calling the police sheepish agents of a corrupt regime and when the verbal assault on the police did not yield the desired result, the Shiites started hawling stones and bottles at them. In the shoot-out that ensued four of the fundamentalists were killed and several others were wounded [*Weekend Times* 8th February 1997].

2. Inter-Religious conflicts

The first church in Kano was not established until 1911. The colonial urban development policies restricted the construction of churches to the Sabon gari as a way of reducing conflicts between the Muslims and Christians. Except Christ Church which was an example of where the Christians had to acquire land for constructing church outside the Sabon gari, the Christians tried as much as possible to restrict their activities to Sabon gari. Those of them who wanted to build churches were probably not able to acquire land for such purposes from their Kanawa host. This explains why there are more churches at Sabon gari settlement today than one would find in any similar settlement in Nigeria.

Up to the early 1980s, there was no open hostility between the Christians and Musilms in Kano beyond the often joking relationship of the Muslims referring to the Christians as *kafirai* (infidels) and the latter too referring to the Kanawa as *kulle-kulle* (meaning those who lock up their wives). The situation changed in the early 1980s as Nigeria opened up to fundamentalist Christianity. There was a rapid growth of Christian churches in Nigeria with many of their members professing "born again" theology. A recent survey by Albert [1997] in Kano indicated that there are now [averagely] more Christian churches in Sabon gari, Kano, than in many big southern Nigeria cities. When the result of this survey is critically considered along the historical circumstances of Christian growth in Kano, the basis for the present Muslim-Christian conflicts in the city becomes clearer. The fact is that Kano is now becoming more open to Christian influence.

The majority of Christians in Kano are not Kanawa, but rather indigenes of other places. The Kanawa are therefore sure of not injuring the feelings of their own people when any hostile policy is pursued against the Christians.

How Christians propagated their faith was sometimes

considered objectionable to the Muslims. For example, when preaching, the Christians usually presented Jesus as the only way to the kingdom of God. All other ways, including the Islamic way were considered to lead nowhere other than hell. In buses and market places, the Muslims were therefore daily enjoined by the Christians to "accept Christ into their lives". The Muslims considered this to be an act of provocation though the "born agains" who championed this kind of course were usually not violent in their activities [Bako 1996: 44]. This was regarded as a bad way of "avoiding conflict" [Albert 1997b]. What resulted from these were often "bottled up emotions". From time to time, the Christians organised public crusades some of which were advertised in manners that annoyed the Muslims. The most easily cited was the tradition of Christian preachers citing from the Koran to defend whatever interests they sought to pursue. The Muslims felt that the Christians had no right to use the Koran as they did. They also believed that the Koran was usually cited out of context. The Muslim-Christians conflicts in Kano were attempts to check the ascendancy of the Christian activities in the city as we shall discuss below.

(i)   **The 1982 Fagge Crisis**

There was a violent inter-religious conflict in Kano in October 1982. It was the first major violent reaction of the Muslims against the ascendancy of Christianity in the city. The problem started at Fagge [near the Sabon gari] where some Christians attempted to reconstruct a dilapidated "Christ Church". The Muslims living around the area felt that the old church was located too close to a mosque. Rather than reconstructing it, they felt the Christians should relocate the church elsewhere. They did everything within their power towards ensuring that the building plans for the new church were not approved by the government. But under police protection, the Christians soon started to reconstruct the church. The Muslims consequently reacted violently and in the disorder that followed three churches were burnt by the Muslims and several other churches were vandalised [see Chime 1985; Ekoko and Amali 1989: 121-2; Albert 1994]. The federal government resolved this issue by paying N75,000 as compensation to the Christian Association of Nigeria in Kano.

(ii)   Reinhard Boonke Riot of 1991

In 1991, the charismatic movement in Kano tried to organise a religious crusade to be addressed by a German preacher, Evangelist Reinhard Boonke, and some American preachers. This religious event was widely advertised by the Christians on the electronic media and newspapers. Several thousands of posters and handbills were distributed in Kano and the neighbouring communities. The publicity given to the event later attracted the attention of the Muslims who felt that the crusade must not be allowed to hold in Kano. First, the Muslims accused the government of double standards for failing to grant permission to one Sheikh Deedat from South Africa who had wanted to organise a religious revival for the Muslims in Kano. They asked why the same government should grant a licence to Reinhard Boonke to preach in Kano, an Islamic city.

The Muslims were also annoyed by the tone of the Christians' advertisement of the proposed crusades, especially the one carried by some posters saying "Jesus for all by the year 2000" [Mukhtar 1992: 17]. The messages on some of the posters and handbills were even written in *Ajami* [Hausa language written in Arabic letters] which the Muslims saw as something very provocative. More detested by the Muslims were photographs and art works on some of the posters and handbills. One side of the posters contained pictures of some blind men who, on the other side of the poster, were strolling away as they abandoned their walking sticks. This was supposed to be an open invitation to the blind men and women in Kano to accept Christ as a precondition to regaining their sight. The Kanawa saw this as something very provocative and resolved to stop the Reinhard Boonke's crusade from holding.

The first step taken by the Muslim was to protest to the government that the Christians should not be allowed to use Kano Race Course for the religious revival. Pressure was also mounted on the government to withdraw the permit earlier issued to the expected German preacher. But it was too late to withdraw Rev. Boonke's licence. The Christians therefore changed the venue of their programme to the compound of St. Thomas/St. Louis School in Sabon gari. The Muslims still resolved to use force in preventing the crusade from holding. As Rev. Boonke arrived Kano on 13

October 1991, violence broke out. The Christians living around Sabon gari, Rimi Kebe and Tudun Murtala suffered the greatest human and material losses. The Hausa-Fulani population that attacked the Sabon gari this time were not discriminatory in their killing but killed both Christians and Muslims as long as they were of southern Nigeria origin (Albert 1994: 219-27). The southerners co-operated with one another by constituting themselves into hit-squads and militia groups around their settlements and attacked their aggressors using modern firearms Several hundreds of people were killed on the two sides and properties worth several millions of naira were destroyed. The Kanawa devoted more time during the Kano riots to destroying the properties of southern Nigerians. In the past the southern Nigerians used to stand by as the Kanawa destroyed their properties but in 1991, they launched counter-offensives against the Kanawa thus inflicting great human and material losses on them also [*Daily Champion* 23 October 1991; *Newswatch* 28 October 1991: Albert 1993: 15-6].

(iii) **The Akaluka Incident of 1994**

In 1994 another round of religious-cum-ethnic violence took place in Kano. It started on December 6, 1994 when an Igbo man, Gideon Akaluka, accused by the Hausa-Fulani of having desecrated a leaflet of the Koran was beheaded by some Shiite fundamentalists at the Bompai prison where he was awaiting trial. In broad daylight, Gideon's head was stuck to a spear and taken round the city of Kano by the "victorious" Islamic faithfuls. This and the circumstances surrounding how the rioters could have so easily broken into a federal prison annoyed the southerners. The government of Kano however came out with apologies that later calmed the charged atmosphere [*Newswatch* 6 February 1995, *Weekend Vanguard* 18 Feb. 1995]. But up to the present time, the head of Akaluka is yet to be found by his kinsmen who claim it is an abomination in Igboland to bury their dead headless. As long as the "search" for Akaluka's head continues in Kano, the relationship between the Igbo and Kanawa will continue to be conflictual. Several other ethnic conflicts that took place, most especially in 1995, resulted partly from this "bottled-up" emotion.

Predisposing Factors of the Conflicts

We have discussed above three types of conflicts: inter-ethnic, intra-religious and inter-religious conflicts. Each of these was caused by some unique factors. Managing the conflicts would therefore require more than one type of instrument and before concrete suggestions could be made on how to manage the conflicts there is the need to clearly understand the issues involved in each of them. These are issues that interveners must understand.

[i]   Problem of Cultural Integration

The ethnic conflicts in Kano resulted from the nature of colonial migrations and the historical circumstance of the southern Nigerian settlers in the city. When a person migrates from his place of origin to another, he finds himself threatened or intimidated by the dominant social, religious, political and economic character of his new environment. As Samin Amin [1974:115] pointed out, such a migrant is left with three major means of survival: assimilation, pacific co-existence or animosity. Where the migrants refuse to assimilate or are denied assimilation they are bound to be treated with animosity, especially when efforts at pacific co-existence fail to produce the desired result due to social, economic and political problems. The southern Nigerian settlers in Kano were in constant conflict with the Kanawa because of their unwillingness to assimilate into the Hausa-Fulani cultural system. The historical circumstances of their settlement in Kano also did not make it easy for them to be assimilated into the systems of their host communities.

Though southerners have lived in Kano since the early twentieth century most of them saw themselves as strangers. The Kanawa also saw them as such. They resisted cultural assimilation. To be regarded as permanent friends by the Kanawa, the southerners were expected to get themselves "Hausanised" and the most important evidence of "Hausanisation", according to our informants, was the acceptance of Islam. It could also involve the persistent wearing of Hausa robes. The Igbo, more than the Yoruba, but like the Hausa-Fulani, have great respect for their culture and often resist external influences. They therefore find it difficult to be assimilated into the Hausa-Fulani cultural systems and openly reject the Islamic religion as well as consider the Hausa social systems as "feudalistic".

What our average Igbo informants in Kano would regard as "feudalism" was what Alhaji [Dr.] Maitama Sule explained as the "Philosophy of the Fulani herdsman" during the Second Republic. According to him, the cattle are subservient to the wishes of the Fulani herdsman because of the latter's love for his animals. The Fulani man never gives to his cattle any water that he himself cannot drink; he stakes his life against any wild beast that seeks to attack his cattle and therefore the animals "hold" the herdsman in high esteem. Alhaji Maitama Sule used this parallel to explain the subservience of the Hausa-Fulanis to their superiors and claimed it to be a major issue in the political integration of the north.

But the Igbo were diametrically opposed to this kind philosophy of life. For example Nnoli noted in one of his works that:

> ...Igbo society looked down on people who accepted superiors, depend on them, or relied on them for their progress. Subservience and unquestioning obedience signified weakness and lack of masculinity. It placed a premium, instead, on occupational skill, enterprise and initiative. The man who was respected, powerful and influential was the one who was sufficiently self-motivated to work hard and successfully compete with, and challenge the power and wealth of his superiors. His success was basically self-made rather than attained through climbing the socio-economic and political apron-strings of his superiors [Nnoli 1978:132].

A similar observation was made about the Igbo by Damachi [1972: 12] and within this framework the frictions between the Kanawa and the Igbo in Kano can be better appreciated. The Igbo were openly aversed to Hausa-Fulani cultural systems. Most of the ethnic and sometimes religious conflicts in Kano were therefore often targeted at the Igbo-speaking people in the city. The Kanawa saw them as "strangers" and the Igbo did not pretend to be indigenes. On the other hand, there were many Yoruba Muslims in Kano. Even those Yoruba in the city who were Christians felt comfortable with Hausa-Fulani cultural practices including their mode of dressing. They were more subservient to their superiors which partly explained why the Kanawa were more tolerant of the Yoruba than the Igbo in moments of ethnic or religious conflicts.

Some other factors made the attack on the Igbo to be regular. One of these, according to some of our informants, was the economic successes of the Igbo. The Igbo control a fairly large percentage of the big commercial houses in the city and control about eighty per cent of the business around the Sabon gari settlement. The Kanawa believed that the Igbo had different strategies for monopolising any economic activities in which they [the Kanawa] have interest. As testified by one Alhaji Saidu Adhama and A.G. Abdullahi before the panel that probed the 1995 disturbances at the Sabon gari market, the Igbo "discourage and intimidate other ethnic groups from setting up shops" in the Sabon gari market area and also pay higher rents to landlords as a way of depriving the local Hausa-Fulani people of access to such shops [KSN 1995:15]. The Kanawa also believed that the Igbo did not invest their profits in Kano but preferred to repatriate such profits back home for the development of eastern Nigeria. This issue generated resentment since the 1940s and, up to the time of research, had been a major problem in Hausa-Igbo relations in Kano. The Igbos were regarded as interlopers controlling the wealth that ought to have been in the hands of the natives and they did not use such wealth to develop Kano.

The relationship between the Kanawa and the southern Nigerians in Kano would probably have not been so bad had the British not introduced the Sabon gari policy [of residential segregation] around 1911. This policy of "separate development" forced the two peoples to live apart in manners that made it difficult for members of the ethnic groups to interact. As noted in the earlier part of this chapter, the colonial government made it punishable for anybody to live outside the area demarcated for people of his origin. Within a few years of its establishment, the settlement became formally stigmatised as an abode of Kafirai [infidels] and social misfits by the Kanawa. Muslim parents started to teach their children to see the settlement within this framework. This perception of the Sabon gari area of the town has to change if the mutual hatred is to be obliterated.

[ii] **Religious Intolerance and Fanaticism**

As already indicated, there is a high degree of religious intolerance in Kano and this explains the incessant intra-religious and inter-religious conflicts in the city. Religious intolerance cuts across all religious groups. Hence the Muslims are opposed to the Christains and the orthodox Muslims would have nothing to do with the members of the fundamentalist sects.

Most of our Christian informants alleged that the Muslims were intolerant of peoples of other religions. According to them, the Muslims would not want to see Kano cease to be an Islamic city while the Muslims made the same allegation against the Christains. The Kanawa considered the Christains to be intolerant of the Muslims who were supposed to be the "owners of Kano". Most annoying to them was the regular statement from the Christians that "Jesus is the only way". Our Kanawa informants were of the opinion that the Koran recognised the Christian as "People of the Book" [Alh lu' l-kitab] who were supposed to be Christians and Judaists [see Ali n.d. chap. 6 vs. 6]. The "People of the Book" were supposed to be tolerated by the Muslims but such a tolerance was not to be carried to the extent that the religion of Islam was brought to ridicule. The Muslims believed that the Christians tried to do this in a city that was supposed to be a centre of Islamic civilisation. They explained the occasional Muslim-Christian riots in Kano as reactions against the "excesses" of the Christians.

The Muslims would want the Christians to respect the Islamic religion as the Koran has enjoined the Muslims to respect the "People of the Book". However, such a mutual respect was lacking in Kano according to our Muslims informants. Christians openly preached to denounce the Islamic faith and often distributed "offensive handbills" when organising their crusades. This, according to most of our informants, was the main reason why the Reinhard Boonke crusade of 1991 was aborted. As long as Christians, like the Muslims fundamentalists, continued to use offensive language to disseminate their religious ideas, the Muslims felt that there would continue to be intra and inter-religious violence in Kano. The Christians, on the other hand, felt the constitution of Nigeria guaranteed them the right to practise their religion. How this was to be done should not be dictated by those whom they had the responsibilities to save from the impending wrath of God. Both Christians and Muslims considered themselves to be doing what was best in the sight of

God. This was the crux of the inter-religious conflicts.

(iii) **The Influence of Non-Nigerian Muslim Migrants**

The tolerance of the Muslim immigrants, especially from neighbouring African countries by the Kanawa was dangerous. Kano played host to different kinds of migrants from north Africa. Cameroun and Chad Republic. Some of these foreigners exploited this open door policy of the Kanawa to turn Kano into a breeding ground for many kinds of fundamentalists Islamic ideas.

The majority of those that broke into Kano prison and later got Mr. Gideon Akaluka beheaded were believed by the Kanawa to be non-Nigerians. Most of them came from Niger Republic. Only one out of the many people who were arrested for the 1995 disturbances was found to be an indigene of Kano State. Most of them came from neighbouring African countries. The same discovery was made by the Justice Aniagolu Tribunal which was constituted by the government to investigate the issues involved in the Maitatsine disturbance of 1980. The Tribunal noted, *inter alia*:

> From the evidence before the Tribunal...and arising from the visit to the border post of Kongolam on the Nigeria/Niger boder...we are of the view that so much laxity exists in the present procedure for the control of the entry of aliens which no doubt is of general application. There is also a total misconception of the provisions of the ECOWAS Protocol... It is sufficient at this stage to note that owing to the ease with which aliens of Niger Republic and other neighbouring African countries walk into and out of Nigeria..... our gates are wide open and therefore exposed to uncontrolled infiltration. If you had no card you just paid 100 Dallas, the equivalent of twenty Naira and you are in [FGN 1981: 36].

The panel that probed the 1995 disturbance came to almost the same conclusion: that the Nigerian borders were very porous [KSN 1995: 16].

The love of the Kanawa for Islam made it quite difficult for them to differentiate between genuine and fake Islamic teachers. The moment a person presented himself as an Islamic teacher he was considered to be of high moral integrity. This was why it took so long for the true identity of the [violent] religious fundamentalists in the city to be discovered. One wonders why and how Mohammadu Marwa found it so convenient to entrench himself in Kano for so long before being finally eliminated, "accidentally", during the 1980 riot.

[iv]　**Urban Poverty**

Poverty was important in explaining how religious fundamentalists and ethnic chauvinists in Kano recruited their members. Most of the people who fought on the side of the Maitatsine in 1980 and the bulk of the members of the Shiites were the urban poor and destitutes. Some of them were farmers who had lost their farmlands in the process of Kano's expansion as an administrative and commercial nerve centre of northern Nigeria. Umar [1989: 91] considers the Maitatsine in particular to be a revolt of the marginalised urban peasants. Most of these people who were displaced from their land had no official means of rehabilitation and so could only express themselves by joining any groups that were given to violence. Writing further, Umar notes:

> ...the resulting alienation has the effect of total estrangement of the Maitatsines from the society, to the extent that they came to view the society itself as too monstrous to be allowed to continue to exist. What seems like a simple correlation between the wretched socio-economic conditions of the Maitatsines and their violent disposition may in fact be a positive causal relationship. Since they cannot articulate their grievances because of their political marginalisation, they make resort to an aberrant brand of Islamic revivalism.

The report of the panel that investigated the 1995 Sabon gari market disturbances also included issues related to urban poverty as a factor responsible for the disturbance. It noted that there were too many unemployed youths in Kano who would earn their living from doing just anything:

> The first is the general poverty afflicting the generality of the public in the society. This is linked to misuse of resources, under-production, stagnant wages and galloping inflation. The general squeeze engenders further such negative indices like idleness, unemployment, exploitation and the contradiction of widening gap between the rich and the poor. In such an atmosphere, crime thrives particularly in the urban centres [KSN 1995: 13].

[v]　**Insurgents as Political Adventurists**

A careful look at the *modus operandi* of the *sYan tatsine* and the Shiites suggests that they were a misunderstood social movement against the present level of social injustice in Nigeria; they were simply reformist organisations expressing what were supposed to be popular grievances sbut using unpopular strategies. When testifying before the Aniagolu Tribunal, the Emir of Kano His

Royal Highness Ado Bayero, noted that though the desire to make money could explain some of the things Mohammadu Marwa did during his life time, the overriding agenda of his religious fundamentalism was political. According to the Emir, Marwa saw himself first and foremost as a reformer who needed political power to effect his reformation of the society [FGN 1981: 65]. Ekoko and Amadi [1989: 123] also note:

> The Maitatsine movement was anti-authority; they regarded every kind of authority as an idol... Maitatsinism incorporated certain kinds of people who felt a recurrent need to react violently against the existing order, to question the right of the existing authority to rule and to assert that all authority other than their own is unnecessary and evil. The movement had an enduring belief in the healing properties of violent destruction, a boundless optimism in the possibilities of an immediate and radical transformation of the society for the better and the building of a completely new order on the ruins of the old. These perceptions were reinforced by a sense of belonging to a secretive group operating clandestinely until the moment of open revolt arrived.

The attitude of the Shiites to authority was as insolent as that of the *Yan tatsine*. For example Yakubu Yahaya, a member of the top echelon of the Shiites once told a *Tell* Magazine reporter:

> We as Muslims, we don't recognise the authority of the federal government, state government, local government or any form of authority... We do not recognise them as our leaders. We are revolting against them. What is between us and them is enmity, eternal enmity, fight, war, forever until the day they will come to the book of Allah... We as Muslims, we have our own law which is the Koran and the Sunna, the traditions of Prophet Mohammed and we execute them under the leadership of Mallam Ibrahim El Zak-Zaky [*Tell* May 6, 1991].

The arrest of the leader of the Shiites in Nigeria, Mallam Ibrahim El Zak-Zaky, and his indefinite detention by the Nigerian federal government confirmed what Yahaya said above that they and those in authority in Nigeria were strange bed-fellows. Much of what the Shiites did were in reaction to the problems in the country. The violent methods they used however singled them out as an unpopular social movement.

[vi] **The Phenomenon of "Street Culture"**

Probably most of the riots in Kano would not have been as fatal as they were if there had not been the problem of street culture in the city. By street culture I mean "an abnormal situation in which an individual who has no home or workplace spends a disproportionately large part of his or her time on the street and consequently becomes liable to involvement in illegal or anti-social activities" [Albert 1997:286-7]. The streets of Kano are, at every hour of the day, overcrowded by many idle hands such as the *Almajirai* begging for alms, different categories of hawkers, street hooligans like the *Yan tauri* etc. This had great implication for the character of ethnic and religious conflicts in Kano. Because of the ever presence of these people on the streets those who wanted to start civil disorder were always assured of a large crowd at the slightest signal of a riot.

The *Almajirai* were successfully used by ethnic chauvinists and religious fundamentalists to champion their causes. These children from Islamic schools were constantly present on the streets begging for alms. As soon as there was any civil disorder they simply joined the rioters, looting, maiming and making difficult any preventive actions of the Police. Commenting on the role of this problem on the character of conflicts in Kano, the panel constituted to investigate the disturbances of May 30th 1995 noted, *inter alia*:

> The vulnerable, toddling and teenage "Almajirai" are enticed into moving to the big cities like Kano by "Mallam" teachers, some of whom are of dubious character, in the name of religious pursuit. These, and the teeming "young urchins"... and touts in and around Sabon gari, loitering in idleness, squatting, alms begging, street hawking, finally graduate into hooliganism, thievery and murder [KSN 1995: 11].

The same problem was mentioned in the report on the Maitatsine riot in Kano, and as long as the streets of Kano was overpopulated by too many idle hands, slight religious and ethnic disagreements would always be transformed into large-scale civil disturbances.

The *Yan tauri* were believed to be the most handy instrument used by anybody seeking to start any civil disturbance in Kano. For a small honorarium they, like the "area boys" of Lagos, are willing to throw the first stone or take the first step in ethnic or religious riots.

Impact of the Conflicts

During each of the ethnic and religious conflicts discussed above, several hundreds of lives and property worth millions of naira were lost. Such losses were suffered by both the local people as well as the stranger elements in their midst. As a result of this, the strangers in Kano were leaving the city in hundreds for fear of being attacked once again. Most of the Igbo and Yoruba elements who decided to remain were those having large investments in the city. They found it difficult to leave easily. This category of strangers consisted of two types. There were those who sent their wives and children to their respective home towns since the 1991 Reinhard Boonke crisis believing that this would ease their own escape if and when another crisis occurred. They lived in the Sabon gari settlement like bachelors. They travelled home regularly to see their repatriated family members. The second category of those who refused to leave Kano were those who believed that as Nigerian citizens they had the right to live in any part of the country. Such people resolved to fight whosoever challenged their stay in the city.

The various ethnic and religious conflicts in Kano divided the local people [the Kanawa] into two ideological camps. The majority believed that ethnic and religious conflicts were unwarranted, they were therefore not happy with those who perpetrated such evil acts. There was however a tiny minority that held strongly to the belief that Kano, being an Islamic city, should continue to pursue a hostile policy towards non-Muslims or those Muslims not practising the religion according to the dictate of certain sects.

The net effect of all these problems was that Kano might not be able to attract certain kinds of local and foreign investments given its present image as a city of violence.

Past Methods of Conflict Management

Over the years, the government favoured a "fire brigade" response to the conflicts. Going by the number of religious and ethnic conflicts witnessed in Kano since 1953, one would expect the political leaders to have vast experience on how to deal with urban insurgencies. The government often responded to every conflict as if the city had never experienced such happening before. Government's response often came after the conflict had escalated into violence. Although, soon after the disputants were reported killing one another, the government drafted the police to the scene and at times several of the rioters got killed or wounded, the ineffectiveness of this strategy was often obvious from how the rioters usually returned to the streets the following day to continue their violence. Almost all the ethnic and religious conflicts in Kano therefore took several days to control.

Although at the end of such violent conflicts, the government often set up a commission of inquiry, the reports of such commissions were never seen by members of the public before another violent conflict started. For political and religious reasons the suggestions in such reports were also never implemented [KSN 1995: 15]. This was the situation in Kano especially since the Maitatsine riot of December 18-29 1980. All the Reports of Commissions of Enquiry that we used in this study, except that of the 1953 crisis which was obtained from the National Archives in Kaduna, were never made public. We obtained them from some journalists who gained access to them through informal sources and risked being prosecuted by the government for being found with "classified materials".

This approach to conflict management itself compounded the conflict situation in Kano. The institution of every commission of inquiry was often held by the people as an evidence of the readiness of the government to establish the facts of the conflict and consequently put in place the necessary policies for preventing a re-occurrence. Some victims of the civil disturbances saw the Commissions of Inquiry as the body through whom their losses would be compensated for by the government. But the conflict situation always became more compounded when the findings of the Commissions were hidden away from the public after their submission to the governments. Rumour-mongers immediately went to work inciting the people that the report favoured one group or the other. This sometimes fuelled subsequent conflicts.

Suggested Interventions

The foregoing analyses demonstrated that the government was largely not able to generate sustainable resolution of the conflicts. There is therefore the need to discuss other options for managing the problems.

What the conflicts in Kano required was not mediation but facilitation of constructive dialogue between the several disputing parties in the city. Put in another language, the people of Kano needed peace-builders and not necessarily peace-makers. It has to be mentioned however that building peace in Kano might be more difficult in some spheres than in others. For example, achieving a constructive dialogue between the Muslims and Christians might be an easier task than facilitating peace between the orthodox and fundamentalist Islamic groups in the city.

The issues of contention between the Muslims and Christians were not as serious as some of the past riots in the city would suggest. Inter-religious conflicts were therefore not intractable. The desire of the Christians was to be left alone to practise their religion. The Kanawa also said at various times that they were not diametrically opposed to Christian activities in their city since Christians were recognised as "People of the Book". They, however, resented the practice of Christians trying to ridicule the practice of Islam in their efforts to propagate their own religion. To the Kanawa it was "undue provocation".

Facilitating Inter-Religious Dialogue and Harmony

The interests of the two parties can be reconciled and their goals achieved in two complementary spheres: [1] by forging a working relationship between Muslim and Christian religious leaders and [2] also by facilitating regular dialogue between the youths of the two religions. It is suggested that Kano should have a committee on inter religious dialogue which should consist of prominent Christian and Muslim leaders. The committee should meet from time to time to review the state of Christian-Muslim relations. In the course of its works issues that have led to conflicts previously could be openly discussed and resolved. It is also suggested that for the next decade, the Kano branch of the Christian Association of Nigeria should be led by Christian indigenes of Kano. With a sound knowledge of Hausa-Fulani cultural practices and willingness to defer to these traditions such a Christian leader might be better listened to at every meeting of the two religious leaders. At the end of the first ten years, after which a sound working relationship might have been established with the Muslim leaders, the leadership of CAN could now go round among the other Christians, if so necessary.

Most of the past religious riots in Kano were led by the youth.

To this extent it is necessary to facilitate a dialogue between Muslim and Christian youth in the city. There should be a permanent youth forum which will enable Muslim and Christian youth leaders to come together periodically to discuss religious issues. Two facilitators who have received various trainings locally and abroad, Imam Ashafa and Pastor Wuye, have already been commissioned by the British Council, Lagos to start something in this direction for youth leaders in northern Nigeria.

Establishment of a Committee of Community Leaders

To facilitate better inter-ethnic harmony in Kano, there is the need to establish a committee of community leaders which from time to time should, among other things, be charged with the task of reviewing the relationship between the Kanawa and the stranger elements in their midst. The work of this committee will be much assisted by the existing political structure. The city is presently divided into several wards, each of which is led by a ward head [*Mai ungwa*]. The southern Nigerians who live in the Sabon gari settlements are also well organised. They all belong to different ethnic and town unions. The Yoruba town unions are fewer. Each of the unions is led by a president who could be invited to become a member of the committee of elders. At the apex of the political system in the Sabon gari are two community leaders: the *Sarkin Igbo* and the *Sarkin Yorubawa*. These leaders are usually appointed with the approval of the Emir of Kano and can play prominent roles in the work of the community of elders in Kano. The community should meet from time to time to deliberate on how to improve the interaction between the Kanawa and the immigrant settlers in their midst. With sincerity of purpose, the committee should be able to avert several inter-ethnic conflicts in the future. Conflict management training programmes could be organised for the members of the committee from time to time.

Dealing with "Street Culture"

One of the ways by which inter-religious and inter-ethnic harmony can be promoted in Kano is by dealing with the problem of street culture. As a matter of urgency the government should deal with the *Almajirai* system by formally absorbing the Koranic schools which these children attend into the formal educational system in the country. Alternatively, Islamic scholars should be given government grants for the re-organisation of their schools according to modern standards. The pupils from these schools should be stopped from begging on the streets. If the *Almajirai* could be permanently kept off the streets of Kano, those who seek to cause religious or ethnic violence would not find enough people on the streets to support their mob action.

Methodological Appendix

At a time like this when the world is universally exchanging "cold war" for "hot peace", research projects on conflicts must be action-oriented and be geared towards informing policy making and facilitating constructive interventions. This concern informs not only how our field work was carried out but also how this report is presented. With a view to establishing how the conflicts in Kano [especially the conflicts between the *Kanawa* and non-indegenes] started, we consulted the colonial records at the National Archives, Kaduna. The files consulted included inter-departmental correspondences, intelligence reports, petitions and newspaper articles. The information derived from all these sources explains the south-north migrations into Kano in the period following the 1903 occupation of the north by the British, and the social economic and political base or some of the conflicts. We supplemented the archival data with interviews across different sections of the population and, believing that those resident in the city knew best on how their problems could be solved, we placed greater emphasis on approaches of conflict management. We sought to know from each informant how he or she thought ethnic or religious conflicts could be managed. The impression we got was that the people had a good knowledge of how to live harmoniously with each other but lacked any serious institution for galvanising their knowledge into concrete policies. Most of our informants believed that the conflicts were politically-motivated by the elites. In addition to the information collected from the archival sources, participant observers and interviews, we also used some data from existing literature on Kano.

We are also systematic in our report. We adopted a historic approach, systematically narrating and analysing what happened at different periods, and trying as much as possible to reduce the number of our value judgements. We deliberately adopted this method to enable those who want to use our data for intervention purposes to have a true picture of what happened rather than getting "misled" by our interpretations. Our analysis [interpretation] of the conflicts was done in the second part of the report with substantive and theoretical interpretation of what happened as well as their predisposing factors, and how the conflicts were managed in the past, especially by the government, and what future interveners could do.

References

Adamu, A. (1993). "Maitatsine. Act VI Scene VI", *Citizen*, Feb.1

Ade Ajayi, J.F. (1975). "The aftermath of the fall of old Oyo" in J. F. Ade Ajayi and M. Crowder (eds.), *History of West Africa* vol. 2 London: Longmans pp.126-66.

Akintoye, S. (1971). Revolution and Power Politics in Yorubaland, 1840- 1893: Expansion and the Rise of Ekitiparapo, London.

Albert, I.O. (1993b). "The growth of a migrant community in Nigeria: The Hausa Settlements in Ibadan, c. 1830-1979", *Ife: Annals of the Institute of Cultural* Studies, no. 4, pp. 2-17.

Albert, I,O. (1993). *Inter-ethnic Relations in a Nigerian City: A Historical Perspective of the Hausa-Igbo Conflicts in Kano.*(1953-1991), Ibadan: IFRA.

Albert, I. O. [1994]. "Urban Violence in Contemporary Africa: Some theoretical explorations", in I.O. Albert *et. al.* [eds.], *Urban Management and Urban Violence in Africa*, Ibadan: IFRA.

Albert, I.O. [1994b]. "Violence in Metropolitan Kano: A Historical Perspective", in Eghosa Oshagae *et al.*, *Urban Violence in Africa*, Ibadan: IFRA.

Albert, I.O. [1995]. "Ethnic residential segregation in Kano, Nigeria and its antecedents", *African Study Monographs*, vol. 17, no. 2, October, pp. 27-42.

Albert, I.O. [1996]. *Interface of Poverty and Urban Violence in Africa,* Discussion Paper no. 2, Abidjan: World Bank's Urban Management Programme Regional Office for Africa.

Albert, I.O. [1996b]. Women and Urban Violence in Kano, Nigeria, Ibadan: Spectrum Books.

Albert, I.O. [1997]. "Kano: Religious Fundamentalism and Violence", in G. Herault and P. Adesanmi [eds.], *Jeunes, Culture de la rue et Violence urbaine en Afrique*, Ibadan: IFRA and African Books Builders Ltd., 1997 pp. 285-325.

Albert, I.O. [1997b]. "The role of communication in the escalation of ethnic and religious conflicts in Nigeria", Communication, vol. 1, pp. 1-20.

Ali, Y. [n.d.]. *The Holy Quran: Translation and Commentary.*

Aluko, J.O. (1993). *Osomaalo: The Early Exploits of the Ijesa Entrepreneur*, Ibadan: African Books Builders.

Amin, Samin [1974]. "Introduction", in S. Amin (ed.) *Modern*

Migrations in West Africa, London: Oxford University Press, 1974.

Bako, S. [1992]. "The Maitatsine Revolt: A Study of the Formation and Struggle of Semi-proletariat in northern Nigeria, 1980-1985". Ph. D. Ahmadu Bello University Zaria.

Bako, S. [1996]. "Urbanisation and religious conflicts in Nigeria", in Antoinette Louw and Simon Bekker [eds], *Cities Under Siege: Urban Violence in South, Central and West Africa,* Durban: Indicator Press.

Bako, s. [1997], " Religious Conflicts in Nigeria: Sources, Impact and Management", Paper presented at the conflict management workshop organised by Academic Associates Peaceworks Lagos, at Ogere Conference Centre.

Balogun, S.A. (1989). "Islam in Nigeria: Its Historical Development", in *Nigeria Since Independence* vol. ix.

Chime, S.C. (1985). "Religious disturbances in Nigeria: Report on Kano/Kaduna Sector", Paper at the Nigerian Police Seminar on Religious Disturbances: The Maitatsine Experience, Jos 6-8 November.

Damachi, U.G. [1972]. *Nigerian Modernization,* New York.

Ekoko, A.E. and L.O. Amadi [1989]. "Religion and Stability in Nigeria", in *Nigeria Since Independence: The First 25 Years,* vol. ix, Ibadan: Heinnemann.

Federal Govt. of Nigeria (1981). *Report of the Tribunal of Inquiry on Kano Disturbance,* Fed. Govt. Press Lagos.

Frishman, A. (1977). "The population growth of Kano, Nigeria", in *African Historical Demography,* Proceedings of a Seminar at the Centre of African Studies, University of Edinburgh 29th and 30th April.

Frishman, A. (1986). "The impact of Islam on the urban structure and economy of Kano, Nigeria", *Journal of the Institute of Muslim Minority,* vol. 7, no. 2, July.

Hodder, B.W. and Ukwu, U.I. (1969). *Markets in West Africa,* Ibadan University Press.

Nnoli, O. [1978]. *Ethnic Politics in Nigeria.* Enugu: Fourth Dimension Publishers.

Northern Regional Government (1953). *Report on the Kano Disturbance 16th, 17th, 18th and 19th May, 1953,* Lagos: Government Printers.

Ottenberg, S. (1962). "The development of local government in a Nigerian township", *Anthropologia,* N.S. vol. 4, no. 1.

Paden, J. (1973). *Religion and Political Culture in Kano,* Berkeley: University of California Press.

Peel, J.D.Y. (1983). *Ijesas and Nigerians: The Incorporation of a Yoruba Kingdom, 1890s-1970s,* Cambridge University Press.

Kano State of Nigeria [KSN 1995], Report of the Panel of Investigation on the May 30th 1995 Sabon-gari Market Disturbances, Kano. Government.

Linekin, J. and Poyer, L. (1990). "Introduction" in Linnekin, J. and Poyer, L. (eds), *Cultural Identity and Ethnicity in the Pacific,* Honolulu: University of Hawaii Press pp. 1-16.

Lubeck, P.M. (1986). *Islam and Labour in Northern Nigeria,* Cambridge.

Mukhtar, R. Isa (1992). "The linguistic background of some religious crisis in Kano" *Al-Bayan: Journal of Islamic Research,* 1 (1) pp. 73-81.

Olugboji, B. (1995). Religious Uprising: Deadly, Divisive, Destructive," *Constitutional Rights Journal,* 5 (15).

Olorunfewa, A. (1996). "Bloody Riots", *Tell,* August 26.

Osaghae, .E.E. [1994]. *Trends in Migrant Political Organisations in Nigeria: The Igbos in Kano,* Ibadan: IFRA.

Tamuno, T.N. (1991). *Peace and Violence in Nigeria,* Panel on Nigeria Since Independence History Project, University of Ibadan.

Umar, M.S. [1989]. "Islam in Nigeria: Its concept, Manifestations and the role in Nation-building", in *Nigeria Since Independence,* vol. ix, Ibadan: Heinemann.

Whitaker, S.Jr. (1970). *The Politics of Tradition: Continuity and Change in Nothern Nigeria, 1946-1966,* Princeton University Press.

Archival References.

Lugard, F. *Annual Report for 1900-1901.*

Lugard, F. *Annual Report for 1903.*

Lugard F. *Annual Report for 1904.*

NAK (National Archives Kaduna), Kano Prof. 5/1, 4292, *Report on the Kano Native Reservation.*

NAK KanoProf. 5/1, 5908, *Tribal Population Statistics.*

NAK SNP 11/4 204M/1913...

NAK SNP 9/1 1774/1914.

Chapter 11

Akin Akinteye, J.M. Wuye and M.N. Ashafa

Tafawa Balewa Crisis: A Case Study

Background

July 1 1995 marked a turning point in the history of conflict in Tafawa Balewa Local Government Area of Bauchi State. This crisis which started in the form of road blockage by some Sayawa (ZAR) women in protest against a proposed reception in honour of the newly appointed commissioner for information, later developed into an armed conflict which claimed several lives. Much propei `.y was also destroyed. These crises have an historical origin dating back to the 1930s as we shall see later.

In early 1995, the Bauchi State Government decided to carry out a cabinet reshuffle in which the commissioner for education, Mr. J.K. Manzo, a Sayawa man from Tafawa Balewa Local Government Area, was dropped and Mr. Ibrahim Musa, an Hausa man representing the same Local Government Area, was appointed. Ibrahim Musa, according to information available to us, was an indigene of Gokaru in Alkaleri Local Government Area. Information has it that he came to Tawafa Balewa in 1959 with his brother who was a blacksmith, to settle in Tafawa Balewa town. His parents were still living in Gokaru village. The removal of J.K. Manzo did not go down well with the Sayawa in that the newly appointed commissioner was seen as an antagonist in the Sayawa' struggle for self-determination. J.K. Manzo was perceived as representing Sayawa interest in the government. With Manzo's removal, the Sayawa felt cheated and marginalised.

The indigenes of Lere district decided to organise a reception for the newly appointed commissioner in the local government headquarters - Tafawa Balewa Town. In pursuance of this, the indigenes of Lere district working with the local government council were levied, the levy being deducted from source. This action was repulsive to the Sayawa in the district. They protested against the levy to the local government authority who promptly stopped the deduction. By that time, tension had started mounting in the local government area especially among the Sayawa.

Knowing the vulnerability of the local government area to crises, some concerned individuals advised the councillors concerned to suspend the reception in order to avoid the looming crisis. This advice was ignored, and the reception plans continued.

On the 1st of July 1995, the reception day, guests were greeted at the entrance of Tafawa Balewa town with barricades mounted by Sayawa women preventing them from entering the town. This action forced the councillors to cancel the reception. The cancellation aggravated some Hausa youths who confronted the Sayawa women. In the process of escaping from the attack, the Sayawa women ran back home to their people who later went out to confront the Hausa youths. The latter had already taken over the streets. The fight which was initially between the Sayawa and the Hausa took a wider dimension to include members of other ethnic groups, mostly the Fulani and the Jarawa. At the end of crisis, over forty-four villages and hamlets were burnt. Several lives and properties were also lost.

Consequent upon this, the state government set up a special tribunal headed by Justice Ibrahim Zango to try those arrested in connection with the crisis. However, the tribunal could not conclude its assignment due to some legal and technical abnormalities in the edict which was challenged by the counsel to the Sayawa at the Federal High Court, Jos. The court stopped the proceedings of the Tribunal and released the accused persons on bail.

Causes and Sources of the Conflicts

Chiefdom/Self Determination - Historical Brief

Usman Dan Fodiyo, the leader of 1804 religious war (Jihad), established the Bauchi emirate system in 1805 under the leadership of Mallam Yakubu Bauche, his former student. Mallam Yakubu took the jihad movement further and conquered various villages and ethnic groups in Bauchi area except Ningi and Sayawa land. On the receipt of the victory message of Mallam Yakubu the Sayawa proceeded to sign a peace treaty with him in which they agreed to be loyal to him and always remit tax to the council. To further show their loyalty to the Emir, they voluntarily contributed 100 able-bodied soldiers to his army.

However, suspicion, fear and disrespect began to crop up in

1900. By this time, Bauchi had come under a new Emir, Mallam Umoru. The new Emir went to Bogoro to demand for slaves. He was however refused because of the peace treaty already signed with the Bauchi emirate council by the Sayawa during the reign of Yakubu I. However, enroute to Bauchi, the Emir captured Rugan Dole - a Sayawa village and enslaved the whole village. Furthermore, he attempted to enslave other villages but was dissuaded by one of his lieutenants - Chiroma Mu Allayidi. Umoru's act was regarded as a breach of trust committed against the Sayawa. He was later captured and imprisoned in Lokoja by the British and was succeeded by Allayidi as the Emir.

With the advent of the British colonisation came the introduction of the indirect rule system. This empowered the traditional rulers to control their people and make them obedient subjects to the King of England. In order to facilitate the collection of taxes and the production of cash crops as raw materials for exportation, the colonialists regrouped various ethnic groups into districts to include a certain number of villages and hamlets. The heads and rulers of such districts and villages were posted from the Bauchi emirate council regardless of differences in cultural and religious orientations. In 1906, Mallam Atahiru Aliyu I, a Fulani of the Ajiyan Bauchi family was appointed by the Emir of Bauchi as the first head of Lere district which was predominantly inhabited by the Sayawa.

The introduction of indirect rule and consequent appointment of district head to Lere district, and the method of tax collection which occurred without prior notice by the Emir's emissaries, brought about disaffection and dissent against the status quo. The intermittent collection of taxes in the form of farm produce, cash and animals among others and the dehumanising treatment meted out to the defaulters, made the Sayawa want to return to their self-governing traditional system; hence the renewed call for self-governance.

In addition, the introduction of the emirate judicial system presided over by the alkalis disempowered the Sayawa traditional judicial system. Prior to the introduction of the native court system by the colonial masters, the Sayawa used their local courts adjudication to resolve conflicts. Their punishments included banishment, ex-communication, and death sentences in the case of serious offences with the saying that "the masquerade (*dodo*) has transformed the person". The head of the judicial system was usually the chief priest in the locality known as *Sunkur*.

Consequent upon the establishment of the native court, cases were referred for adjudication at these courts. This phenomenon reduced the power of the traditional chiefs. The Sayawa chiefs protested against this system but to no avail.

In 1910, the missionaries arrived in southern Bauchi and by 1916 they were in Mwari village with the assistance of Mr. Yohanna Gowon the father of General Yakubu Gowon (rtd.) where they established an adult literacy class. Between 1920 and 1926, they established schools which exposed the Sayawa to formal education. The effect was the conscientisation of the Sayawa to the exploitative and manipulative administrative system of the emirate council.

The return of the demobilised second world war soldiers of Sayawa origin between 1945 and 1946 encouraged further, the quest for self-determination. These returnees strengthened the demand for self-rulership by the elders.

The year 1948 marked the first formal protest against the emirate council by the Sayawa local chiefs. The Sayawa chiefs gathered at Bogoro village on a market day and took a decision that the Emir should take away the district head and appoint an indigene to replace him. In a bid to arrest the chiefs by the native authority police (known as *dongari gwado*), a fight ensued and the village heads were arrested and detained in Bauchi prison. The Emir then replaced them with new village heads, with the exception of Mwari village which rejected the new appointee. These new village heads were Sayawa. In Mwari village, the people claimed that they were fully in support of the arrested chief and that the chief carried out their demands. Hence they rejected the new appointee from the Emir.

In continuation of the struggle for self-governance, the new chiefs, though appointed by the Emir, constituted a traditional council known as *Zauren Gwantu* under the leadership of Baba Peter Gonto, the first Christian convert who led the struggle from 1948.

The newly constituted traditional council took the challenge further by seeking alliance with other minority ethnic groups to form the Habe Tribal Union, a non-Fulani speaking union which later joined the defunct United Middle Belt Congress (UMBC), an opposition party to the defunct Northern Peoples Congress (NPC) which was believed to be under the tutelage of the northern emirate system.

In furtherance of the struggle for traditional governance, the UMBC in collaboration with the Action Group (AG) presented, in 1959, Baba Peter Gonto to contest an election against late Sir Abubakar Tafawa Balewa of the NPC. The latter won the election. This further widened the gulf of animosity between the Sayawa and the emirate council.

However, the late Sir Abubakar Tafawa Balewa and the late Sardauna of Sokoto, Sir Ahmadu Bello, brokered a reconciliation between the Sayawa and the emirate council. The reconciliatory agreement was that the Sayawa should join the NPC in order to be given an indigenous district head. By 1965, the Sayawa voted en mass for the NPC but unfortunately, the promise of an indigenous district head could not be fulfilled before the 1966 military coup in which Sir Abubakar Tafawa Balewa, the prime minister, and Sir Ahmadu Bello, the premier of Northern Region, were assassinated.

During the tenure of the late Lt. Col., later Brigadier-General, Hassan Usman Katsina as the first military governor of Northern Region, the Sayawa petitioned him in 1967 demanding for a indigenous district head which he promptly promised. While awaiting the fulfilment of his promise, twelve states were created in Nigeria and the current Bauchi State became part of the North Eastern State. The Sayawa carried their demand further to the governor of the state, late Brigadier-General Musa Usman, narrating their ordeal for self-rulership from 1944 to then. The petition was granted and in 1970 the first indigenous district head, Mallam Aliyu Wulumba Dadi, a Sayawa Muslim who was then a scribe in the emirate council, was appointed.

There was relative peace until 1976 when the district head was allegedly accused of misappropriation of public funds. He was consequently removed. The case was taken to court where he was discharged and acquitted but he was not reinstated. Another Sayawa man was appointed in his place in Oct. 1976. Not quite eight months after the appointment of this district head, Lere district was divided into two against the wish of the Sayawa.

This division resulted in the creation of Lere and Bogoro districts.

To the utter dismay of the Sayawa, the indigenous district head was posted to Bogoro district and a Fulani man was appointed to be the district head of Lere. This development was totally condemned by the Sayawa on the claim that Lere district was predominantly a Sayawa settlement and therefore should be ruled by them. This situation presupposed that the struggle against domination by Hausa and Fulani was exhumed. In protest against this appointment, the district head was assassinated in Sept. 1977, barely three months after his appointment.

A new district head was appointed through an electoral college set up by the emirate council. He was Mohammed Lulu - a Fulani man. The Sayawa reluctantly accepted the outcome of the election. They unequivocally claimed that the process was rigged. They thus refused to recognise the existence of the new district head. The Baba Gonto-led Council of Elders then assumed de facto powers in Lere.

Between 1977 and 1991, there was another relative peace in the history of Tafawa Balewa Local Government Area. Even though there were still agitations for self-government, these did not result in violence. The fragile peace that existed within this period did not indicate the absence of discontent among the Sayawa. In the latter part of 1991, there was an election that ushered in the first Sayawa man as the local government chairman.

Discontent in the LGA manifested itself later in a conflict over a piece of meat (*suya*). The conflict spread to several parts of Bauchi State claiming many lives and properties. This event led to a more intensified Sayawa struggle and demand for self-government. The incident also led to the formation of the Justice Babalakin Judicial Commission of Enquiry. In their submissions to the commission, the Sayawa changed their demand for a district head to an autonomous chiefdom to be carved out of the Bauchi emirate council. Among the recommendations of the commission was that of the Sayawa chiefdom which was approved by the federal government in a white paper released to the Bauchi State government. The delay in the implementation of this recommendation formed one of the major causes of the 1995 crises that completely changed the demand of the Sayawa from independent chiefdom in Bauchi State to a request for transfer to

Plateau State.

Tafawa Balewa Township Questions

The town Tafawa Balewa, Puji and Tafieri Baleiji, as it was called respectively by Hausa, Sayawa and Fulani was a name derived form a black rock situated at the south western part of the town. The actual origin of the town could not be determined; however, historical evidence has it that the town had existed long before the Usman Dan Fodiyo Islamic Jihad of 1804. However, it came into the limelight as a result of the proclamation of the 1916 Native Authority Ordinance by the colonial administration. The town was about eighty kilometres south west of Bauchi, the state capital.

Tafawa Balewa was the headquarters of Lere district and later became of Tafawa Balewa Local Government in 1976. It was the centre of economic and political activities in the locality and the home town of the first and only Nigerian prime minister, late Sir Abubakar Tafawa Balewa. Several ethnic groups lived in the town. These included the Sayawa.

The founding of the town was claimed by both the Sayawa and the Fulani, thus leading to conflict between them. These claims came out vividly in 1991 when the Sayawa requested for a chiefdom with the headquarters in Tafawa Balewa town during the proceedings of the Babalakin Commission of Enquiry. Each ethnic group presented historical and archaeological evidence and records to support their claims.

The Sayawa claimed that they had settled in Tafawa Balewa, then known in their language as Pus ji (later shortened to Puji) long before the Fulani came. The migration map approved by the Bauchi State Ministry of Land and Survey showed that the Sayawa migrated form the present Chad Republic through Ngazargamu, the then Borno Empire headquarters, between 9th and 13th century to settle in Puji and Bogoro. They were then living in hamlets and on the rocks and hills with their kinsmen, the Jarawa, who migrated from the same geographical area with them, and with whom they shared the same culture and tradition, but with different linguistic dialects.

In support of their claim to the town, they presented historical evidence that wherever the Sayawa lived, they had a culture of grinding cereals on the rocks and this normally formed troughs leaving permanent marks on the rocks till today. Several samples of these were seen in Tafawa Balewa town and other Sayawa settlements. Further to this claim, the 1952 census showed that if the Hausa and Fulani were in Tafawa Balewa town, their population was negligible whereas that of the Sayawa was above fifty thousand.

The Sayawa claimed further that in 1906 when the first district head, Mallam Atahiru I, was posted to Tafawa Balewa, the Chief of Bogoro, a Sayawa man, instructed their chief priest, Sunkur, to vacate his house for the visitor. They claimed that this would have been impossible if the said land belonged to the Fulani. Sunkur's house then became the house of district heads that ever lived in Tafawa Balewa town up till today. At the time of fieldwork the house was directly opposite Tafawa Balewa Central Mosque, and directly in front of it were the grinding troughs. To further make the district head feel more comfortable, the Chief of Bogoro directed all Muslim converts under his domain to settle and live with him. The chief also assisted the district head in collecting taxes which he (the district head) later took to the Emir. These people were later joined by the Fulani, Kanuri and Hausa who were mostly interested in trading.

The Sayawa claimed further that the Fulani always moved in and out of the place with their cattle. However, when they first came, they asked for the name of the town and its meaning and because they could not pronounce Puji, they called the town Tafieri Balieji meaning the same thing in Fulfulde. However, during the colonial rule, the town maintained Tafawa Balewa as its administrative name because the Hausa and Fulani were the administrative staff.

The Fulani and the Hausa, on the other hand, claimed that the town was founded by a Fulani man known as Abubakar Goje as a grazing field for their cattle because of its green vegetation all the year round and the availability of water at the foot of the rock. Hence the saying *"sha baki garin Goje"* meaning the town of Goje frequented by visitors. They claimed that due to their nomadic nature, the specific date and century their first parents settled there could not be ascertained. However, they claimed that Jawo was their ruler before the Kanuri took over. They claimed further that when Ajiya Atahiru I came to the town in

1906, he met the Fulani and the Kanuri and encouraged intermarriages between them and other ethnic groups in the area. In one of their memos to the Balalakin Commission, one of the elites also claimed that they had grinding troughs similar to those of the Sayawa where their wives ground maize and pepper.

Furthermore, reference was made to *The Right Honourable Gentleman* published in 1991 that the Fulani made permanent abode beside the rock which was a few kilometres to a "pagan' settlement, the Sayawa, in the 18th century. Reference was also made to another book titled *The Muhammedan Emirates* published by S.J. Hogbens in 1930 and the Colonial Resident, Mr. Howards' note of 1808 that the Sayawa headquarters was Bogoro.

Amidst these claims and counter-claims, the information available to us from independent sources said that the actual first settlers could not be ascertained. But one fact remained, that when the first district head arrived in the town, because the Sayawa went about half naked, covering themselves with leaves, they were not allowed to live in the town. Apart from the fact that the Sayawa were people of the hills, the statistics available to us from the local government chairman revealed that the Sayawa have the largest population in Tafawa Balewa town followed by the Jarawa, the Fulani and the Hausa in that order.

The Sayawa vowed to die fighting if their chiefdom was created without the headquarters in Tafawa Balewa town. The same went for the Hausa and the Fulani who did not object to the creation of Sayawa chiefdom but without the headquarters in Tafawa Balewa town.

Ethno-Cultural/Religious Differences

Tafawa Balewa Local Government Area is an heterogenous community consisting of about twelve ethnic groups. These were the Sayawa, Jarawa, Sigidawa, Fulani, Hausa, Angasawa, Barawa, Tabshinawa, Boyawa, Bijimawa, Dugurawa and the Badawa. The Sayawa and the Jarawa share the same origin. These ethnic groups shared the customs of circumcision, marriage and some festivals together. Their traditional modes of dressing were identical. On the other hand, the Fulani traditional marriage institution of flogging the potential bridegroom with sticks was not found in other groups.

There were three religious groups: Islam, Christianity and

traditional religions. The Hausa, Fulani and the Jarawa were predominantly Muslims while the Sayawa were predominantly Christians. As a result of this religious affinity, the Jarawa took after their Hausa and Fulani Muslim brothers, which automatically grouped them together against the Sayawa during the 1991 and 1995 crises. However, these ethnic groups still had a significant percentage of traditional religious worshippers. There were Christians among the Jarawa and Muslims among the Sayawa.

These cultural and religious differences determined the alliances in all crises and incidents as from the 1940s. However there were secret agreements between the Sayawa, the Jarawa and other minority groups in the locality. This was based on the reason that if the Sayawa were supported in getting their chiefdom with Tafawa Balewa town as political capital, positions would be shared fairly and the Sayawa would also support the other groups in attaining their own chiefdoms when desired.

Socio-economic & Political Differences

Inequality also existed in the distribution of socio-economic and political power in the local government area. This was another cause of the conflict in the area. The Sayawa and the Jarawa together with other ethnic groups were farmers and hunters. The Fulani were nomads; and the Hausa were traders and administrators. Therefore, the Hausa and Fulani had the economic and political edge over other ethnic groups in the local government area. In addition, the outdated colonial indirect rule type of administration appointing the Fulani from the emirate council to administer the districts became unacceptable.

Briefs on Actors and Interests

The following were the major actors in the Tafawa Balewa crises.
  Bauchi Emirate Council;
  The Sayawa;
  The Jarawa, Hausa and Fulani;
  Religious groups;
  The elites/individuals;
  The government: local state and federal;
  The Elders Council;
  The Youths.

The Bauchi Emirate Council

The Bauchi Emirate Council was formed by Yakubun Bauchi in 1805 after the success of Usman Dan Fodiyo's Islamic Jihad of 1804. The then emirate extended to Alkaleri, Toro, Daraso, Tafawa Balewa, Ganjua, Plateau province with river Benue as the boundary. The emirate was later divided into five traditionally independent districts, each with its own district head appointed by the Emir of Bauchi viz: Madakin Bauchi in charge of Ganjau, Wambain Bauchi in Charge of Kirfi, Galadiman Bauchi in charge of Zungur, Sarkin Yaki in charge of Lamy and Ajiyan Bauchi in charge of Tafawa Balewa. These five traditional title holders later became the kingmakers of the Bauchi emirate. Since that time the Ajiya family ruled Tafawa Balewa but did not reside there until 1916.

In order to understand the interest of Bauchi emirate council and its initial reluctance to grant the Sayawa their chiefdom, it is necessary to know that, during the fieldwork, Bauchi State was traditionally zoned into three divisions viz: Katagum, Gombe and Bauchi. The Bauchi emirate council ruled over the Bauchi division in which there were many ethnic groups seeking self-rulership independent of Bauchi emirate council. Apart form the Sayawa, there were Ganjua, Darazo and Duguri. This then presupposed that if the Sayawa was granted chiefdom, there would be no justification for the emirate council to withhold the request of others. The consequence of this therefore was that the emirate council's area of jurisdiction would be drastically reduced while some of their kingmakers might lose their constituencies and chances of becoming the Emirs. As a result, they maintained that the traditional status quo must remain. This point is better understood by the action of the emirate council in appointing village heads in some villages in the area and the district head in Bula district. This was after the state government had warned the emirate council to stay away from the local government area in 1992 after the release of a white paper on Babalakin Commission's recommendations.

The Sayawa

The Sayawa were said to have migrated with the Jarawa from Chad through the mountains of Borno to Ngazargamu - the headquarters of Borno empire and finally settled in Tafawa Balewa local government area between the 9th and 13th century. Their closest neigbours at that time were the Jarawa and the Fulani nomads who were scattered throughout the area.

Before the advent of indirect rule, the Sayawa claimed to have a well-organised traditional system of government. Their hamlets and villages were independent of one another. Each had her head and chiefs. The linkage between them was consultative meetings held to decide on ethnic matters and well-being apart from ethnic festivals and activities. Meetings were summoned by the chief priest and were rotated amongst the villages. At each meeting, a chairman was appointed to direct the affairs of the day's meeting. This directly pointed out to us that the Sayawa had a way of governing themselves but did not have a paramount ruler or a district head at that time.

With no reliable figures to validate these claims, the general consensus was that the Sayawa were the predominant group in Lere and Bogoro districts. These two districts constituted the agitated Sayawa chiefdom or "Sayawa land". They also formed the majority of the population in Tafawa Balewa town and its suburbs. Sayawa were mostly Christians while the rest were Muslims, Christians and traditional religious worshippers.

In compliance with the directives on the establishment of native authority courts in 1916 coupled with the movement of the district head to Tafawa Balewa town by the emirate council, especially form the Ajiya family, the Sayawa traditional chiefs' powers were usurped. The realisation of the loss of power, the acquisition of western education by expatriate Christian missionaries, and the exposure of the Sayawa to western way of life, motivated them to question the *status quo*, hence they demanded self-governance.

In pursuance of this, the Sayawa constituted a forum of elders whom they called "freedom fighters" (*Zauren Baba Gonto*) to explore ways of realising their demands. They used several methods among which were the writing of petitions, refusal to pay tax and homage to the emirate emissaries, violence, civil disturbances and belonging to any political party that could further their interests.

The Jarawa, Fulani and Hausa

The Jarawa are next in population to the Sayawa in the local government area. They were said to have migrated with the Sayawa from the East of Chad Republic and settled in Kardam, Wai and other hamlets in Lere district. These people spoke almost the same language (with differences in dialect) with the Sayawa. They are mostly Muslims like the Hausa and the Fulani, hence the religious affinity.

The Fulani being nomads, their origin before moving to Tafawa Balewa could not be ascertained. However, in one of their memos they claimed that they were in Tafawa Balewa town before the Jihad of Usman Dan Fodiyo in 1804. However, with the success of the jihad, they had a long record of rulership of the local government area, especially Lere district.

According to Oliver Haward (1908) one member of the ruling family of Zazzau, by name Biri, having lost the chieftaincy contest, asked his relations and followers to migrate with him to the present site of Lere village formerly ruled by the local chief of Rafawa. This marked the first settlement of the Hausa in the local government area. However, the 1952 population showed that the number of the Hausa and Fulani was negligible in Tafawa Balewa Local Government.

The Hausa and the Fulani, having tasted power but realising their weak population in the local government area, were unwilling to relinquish power to avoid marginalisation by the more populous Sayawa. The same reason of marginalisation, apart from religious affiliation, partly made the Jarawa to team up with the Hausa and Fulani to form a stumbling block to the creation of a Sayawa chiefdom that would include Tafawa Balewa town. As mentioned earlier, the Sayawa agreed with other groups to respect their rights if the chiefdom was created. Part of the agreement was the election of a Jarawa as the local government chairman in March 1996.

Religious Groups

The conflict which, from inception in 1948, had no religious connotation assumed a religious dimension in 1991 and 1995. The Jamatul Nasril Islam found themselves identifying with the Hausa, Fulani and Jarawa, these three groups being predominantly Muslims. They saw the demand of the Sayawa as one that would instal a Christian rulership over the Muslims, that is against Islamic injunctions. The Christian Association of Nigeria identified with the Sayawa - being a predominant Christian community. Hence the religious dimension to the crises got outside Tafawa Balewa Local Government Area itself. These inter-religious conflicts resulted in the destruction of churches, mosques, mission houses, hotels and houses on both sides. This was even extended to post-conflict relief activities when both parties were seen distributing the relief materials only to their religious followers who were affected by the conflict.

Individuals

Baba Peter Gonto

Baba Peter Gonto - a Sayawa prince and the oldest Sayawa political leader, was a symbol of the Sayawa struggle and inspiration for self-governance. He continues to be a reference point for Sayawa actions. He was leader of the 14-man committee of elders - the highest recognised ruling body by the Sayawa for the Sayawa. The body, though not recognised by the local and state governments, still commanded some respect from the government, especially when the district head of Lere was in self-exile in Bauchi even though he was still being paid.

Alhaji Adamu Tafawa Balewa - Ajiyan Bauchi

Alhaji Adamu Tafawa Balewa - a Fulani man - was the leader of Ajiya family of the Bauchi emirate council. He served as the 7th district head posted from Bauchi to Tafawa Balewa from 1956 to 1970. He was viewed by the Sayawa as the only obstacle to the creation of their chiefdom that would include Tafawa Balewa town. On the other hand he regarded himself as a lover of the Sayawa. He attributed his fame and current position to the love and assistance given to him by all the ethnic groups living in Tafawa Balewa, especially the Sayawa.

His family, being one of the king makers whose constituency was Tafawa Balewa, would definitely lose their constituency as district head of Lere district but would still retain their Ajiya title, should an autonomous chiefdom that included Tafawa Balewa town be created for the Sayawa. However, Alhaji Adamu Tafawa Balewa seemed to realise this when he pointed out in his memo to the Shehu Awak Committee that the Lere district head, his brother, who was chased out of Tafawa Balewa town during the 1991 crises, had not been allowed by the government to return to his duty post in Tafawa Balewa.

However, he supported the creation of a Sayawa chiefdom with the headquarters in Bogoro or Boi, but excluding Tafawa Balewa town. He advocated the creation of another chiefdom to be called Tafawa Balewa Chiefdom for all other minority groups, to include Tafawa Balewa town. He went further to suggest a chiefdom to be created in Bulla district with its headquarters in Bunumu. Finally, he suggested the creation of Bogoro and Bula local governments as another way out of the crisis. Thus, there would be three local governments within the present Tafawa Balewa Local Government Area.

However, some critics felt that these suggestions were not realisable because the government could not afford to create these suggested chiefdom, while the viability of Bogoro Local Government was considered doubtful.

The Elites

The elites in each group comprised powerful educated youths and elders who served in different capacities in the government. They included, among others, Mr. J.K Manzo, a former commissioner; Mr. Kefas Magaji, a legal practitioner; Alhaji Ibrahim Musa, commissioner for information and culture and Mr. Damazumi Musa a lecturer at Abubakar Tatari Ali Polytechnic. These men commanded respect among the youths in their ethnic groups and were capable of influencing them in the course of the struggle.

Some of these elites took commendable initiatives to either prevent or resolve the conflict. However, some of them were prepared to spill the last drop of their blood if one group's demand was conceded to the other group by the government. In addition to their utterances, some of them had some influence in and outside their community over government decisions. Some even prevented any unfavourable decision from seeing the light of the day.

The Government

The Local Government

Tafawa Balewa Local Government was created in 1976. In 1980, during the Shagari administration, Bogoro Local Government was created out of it, but was again merged with it in 1984 when the military took over. The local government council consisted three different districts namely; Bula, Lere and Bogoro districts. Bula district with its headquarters in Bununu, was occupied predominantly by Hausa, Fulani, Jarawa and other minority groups as enumerated earlier. Bogoro district with its headquarters in Bogoro, and Lere district with its headquarters in Tafawa Balewa town, were occupied mainly by Sayawa with other groups as Jarawa, Hausa, Fulani, and other minority groups.

The Tafawa Balewa Local Government Council recognised and interacted favourably with the district heads. On the other hand, the elders committee of the Sayawa was quasi-recognised but their interaction was informal, depending on the attitude of the local government chairman, and whether a Sayawa man was in control of the local government.

The local government council played a very important role in trying to prevent the 1991 crisis. It did this by sending security reports to the state government reporting the mounting tension immediately after the fight over a piece of roasted meat *(suya)* was partially resolved. They were able to control the situation for two days. It escalated when they took the corpses of the casualties from Tafawa Balewa to Bauchi.

However, the reverse was the case in 1995 when some of the local government councillors started the conflict. They did this by deducting from some workers' salaries money for a reception against their wish, ignoring all the warnings from Sayawa elites and elders of the local government council. In the end, the reception did not hold but there was armed conflict. On the other hand, the local government council took some post-conflict initiatives by setting up a peace and consultative committee to settle farmland disputes that could develop into armed conflict between the Sayawa on one part, and the Jarawa and Fulani on the other. The present chairman of the council and his councillors advised the new military administrator to implement the

Babalakin Commission's recommendations.

The State Government

Bauchi State was created in 1976 out of the North Eastern State with its headquarters in Bauchi. Since that time, the state inherited the Sayawa and Tafawa Balewa crises. The action and attitude of state government did not satisfy any side. Both groups accused the state government of taking sides at one time or the other.

However, the escalation of the 1991 crisis was seen as the result of the nonchalant attitude of the state government to heed the early warnings when the suya incident was first reported. In addition, the action of the state government by allowing the corpses of the victims of the crisis to be brought to the state capital did not help the situation. It was also claimed that while the crisis engulfed Bauchi city and other parts of the state, it took the government two days to move security agents into the scene to arrest the situation. It was not until the disputants called for the removal of the police and soldiers from the scene that the crisis subsided.

Later, the recommendations of the Babalakin Judicial Commission of Enquiry set up after the crisis was passed to the state government to implement. Out of all the recommendations in the report, the creation of Sayawa chiefdom was yet to be implemented by the state government. Instead, the Shehu Awak Committee was set up by the state government to work out the details for the creation of the Sayawa chiefdom. The Sayawa believed that the committee was set up to deceive them and delay justice.

However, this is not to say that the state government did not make some genuine moves towards resolving the conflicts. Under Governor Dahiru's administration, 1991-1993, the government called the elders from both sides to resolve the crisis. However, this effort could not yield any result due to the non-cooperation of the Hausa/Fulani group. The attitude of the group was later found to be a result of external influence of powerful non-residents of Tafawa Balewa town. These elites doubted the sincerity of the state government and thereby instructed their group not to attend the meeting again. The meeting was held three times before the

Hausa/Fulani group discontinued participation.

This same administration having received the federal government's instruction to create the Sayawa chiefdom, directed the excise of the area from the jurisdiction of the emirate council of Bauchi pending the determination of the extent of area of jurisdiction of the Sayawa chiefdom. To further monitor this directive to the core, the officer-in-charge of chieftaincy affairs in the state government ministry was suspended for conniving with the emirate council in 1993 in appointing a district head for Bula district area even though this was not part of Sayawa land.

Dahiru's successor, Wing Commander James Kalau, wanted to actualise the crucial recommendation but was suddenly removed. His successor, Capt. Raji, could not solve the problem before he was transferred to Sokoto. He was even accused of writing a letter of protest to the Attorney-General of the Federation questioning the power of the Jos Federal High Court in granting bail to the 1995 riot accused persons. In addition, he lifted the order which excised Tafawa Balewa from the emirate. The emirate council then went on to appoint hamlet heads in the local government area. This brought about tension which led to a protest letter to Capt. Raji on May 20th 1996 advising him to stop the emirate council from the continuation of the appointments. The governor then ordered the emirate council to stop the appointments.

The Federal Government

After the 1991 armed conflicts, the federal government set up a commission of enquiry under the chairmanship of Justice Babalakin. The commission made six recommendations which the federal government accepted and then issued a white paper to that effect. The federal government went further by releasing money for payment of compensations but this was considered inadequate by the state government and the disputants.

The state government in implementing the other recommendations, decided that in addition to the creation of the Sayawa Chiefdom, the federal government should create three local government areas from the present Tafawa Balewa Local Government. The federal government was yet to act on this recommendation.

The Sayawa Elders Council

The Sayawa constituted an elders council known as Zauren Baba Gonto under the leadership of Baba Peter Gonto in 1948. This council was formed to pursue Sayawa struggle for self-rulership. The council comprised one representative from each village, in Sayawa land. The council was formed as an aftermath of the event of 1948 when the Sayawa protested against the district head. The chiefs and other personalities who took part in the protest were arrested. Since the formation of this council, it has functioned in the forefront of Sayawa' struggle for self-rulership.

The council took binding decisions on behalf of the Sayawa. The Sayawa held this council in very high esteem to the extent that they did not embark on any action unless the council gave the go-ahead.

However, the attitude of the various tiers of government towards the traditional council was indecisive and sometimes confusing. After the 1991 crisis, the federal government emissaries visited the leader while the various committees set up by the government in relation to the crises accorded the council its due respect. However, at the state and local government levels, the relationship with the council depended on the administration's perspective of the dispute.

The Youths

In all the crises in the local government area so far, the youths were regarded as the instrument used to perpetuate the crisis to the extent desired by the elders. In some cases, the youths were used either to start crises or take over a crisis situation. At the end of each crisis, the youths thus formed the largest percentage of the casualties.

Mechanism for Crisis Management and Resolution

Several committees and commissions were set up to manage and resolve the Tafawa Balewa crisis. Among these were:
- The Justice Babalakin Commission of Enquiry;
- The Shehu Awak Committee for the Creation of the Sayawa Chiefdom;
- The Justice Ibrahim Zango Tribunal;
- The Peace and Reconciliation Committee.

Justice Babalakin Commission of Enquiry

This commission was set up by the federal government to look into the causes of the Tafawa Balewa crisis of 1991 and make recommendations.

In discharging its duties, the commission called for memos from all indigenes of Bauchi State. The commission met both in Bauchi city and Tafawa Balewa town. After its sittings, it made the following recommendations:

1. Dissolution of the Tafawa Balewa Local Government Council;
2. Punishment of the culprits of the crisis;
3. Payment of compensation to the victims of the conflict;
4. Building of separate abattoir for the Christians and Muslims;
5. Re-building of Tafawa Balewa township market;
6. Creation of Sayawa Chiefdom.

These recommendations were approved by the federal government and a white paper was released to that effect. The Bauchi state government was directed to ensure the implementation of the recommendations. All the recommendations were implemented except the sixth one. The council could have been created but for the dispute over the position and role of Tafawa Balewa town within or outside the Sayawa Chiefdom.

Shehu Awak Committee for the Creation of Sayawa Chiefdom

In pursuance of the directives of the federal government, the Bauchi state government set up this committee in 1992 to work out modalities and determine the area of jurisdiction for the Sayawa chiefdom. The committee which comprised five members also called for memos from all citizens of Bauchi State. The committee finally submitted its reports in the early part of 1994 to the state government. However, the state government's reaction to the report was being awaited at the end of fieldwork.

Justice Ibrahim Zango Tribunal

This tribunal was set up by the Bauchi State Government after the 1995 conflict to identify and punish the culprits. The tribunal however could not complete its assignment due to an order from the Federal High Court, Jos stopping the proceedings. The Tribunal was said to have been set up without following the legal procedures.

Peace and Reconciliation Committee

This committee was set up by the current chairman of Tafawa Balewa Local Government. The committee comprised ten representatives from each of the three districts in the local government area. It attempted to resolve the current farmland disputes among the Sayawa and their neighbours. The committee was doing well at the time of this study.

Conflict Resolution Initiatives

The Sayawa struggle for self-determination witnessed various stages of successes and failures. In 1948 when Sayawa chiefs first confronted the then district head, they were all arrested because their approach was confrontational. They then changed their strategy when they joined the Habe Tribal Union. In 1952, they massively joined the Yoruba-dominated Action Group with the hope of overcoming the Hausa and Fulani domination. Unfortunately, this political affiliation did not succeed as the party lost the elections. In 1965, they massively voted for the Northern Peoples Congress with the hope of getting a promised self-rulership. But, before this could materialise, there was a military intervention and the promise was not realised.

The fact was obvious to the Sayawa that they could neither use confrontation nor form any alliance with political parties. They continued to write petitions, make appeals, and hold consultations at opportune times. These activities yielded some dividends in 1970 when an indigenous district head was appointed to rule over Lere district.

However, confrontations re-occurred in 1991 and 1995 after twenty years of relative peace. Just as before, violence did not yield any result and the creation of Sayawa chiefdom was in the cooler. However, there was change in 1996. The elites of the communities soon realised the necessity to cooperate with other ethnic groups in the local government area. This made it possible for a Jawara to get the local government council chairmanship. Other arrangements included respect for other minority ethnic group demands and rights if they chose to live in the Sayawa chiefdom.

The Sayawa claimed that they were being discriminated against in Bauchi State. In addition, they believed that the local government area suffered in terms of development projects and other social amenities. They complained that they were abandoned because those at the helm of state affairs opposed the development of Tafawa Balewa Local Government Area. All these, put together, made them to opt for a merger with Plateau State where they hoped they would feel at home with other minority groups who shared the same culture and tradition with them. They also hoped to achieve a higher level of development under Plateau State.

The Babalakin Commission of Enquiry was seen to be balanced in terms of its composition. All the people, except the Hausa, Fulani and Jarawa, believed that the commission's recommendations were capable of putting the conflicts to rest.

However, the federal government did not take any follow-up action to implement the recommendations as expected, despite the vulnerability of the area to crisis. Thus, the re-occurrence of the crisis in 1995. This laxity was viewed by the Sayawa as a form of insincerity on the part of the federal government especially when the state government claimed to be waiting for orders from the federal government to act on the commission's recommendations. It was not clear to the public what orders the state government was still waiting for even after a white paper had been issued on the recommendations.

Frequent change of state governors did not allow enough time to study the intricacies surrounding the creation of Sayawa chiefdom to implement whatever plans they might have had regarding the crisis and the chiefdom. The Raji administration planned to take some initiatives regarding the crisis before he was reassigned by the federal government.

The Shehu Awak Committee, right from inception, was sharply criticised for its composition. It was held that since the proposed chiefdom was for the Sayawa, it was important for them to have a representative on the committee. Another shortcoming was the call for memos from all citizens of Bauchi State. This was viewed as inappropriate since the committee was working for a particular community within a particular jurisdiction. Therefore the call for memos should have been limited to this area and the parties concerned. In addition, the committee was not given any dateline to submit its report. Above all, the state government's reaction to the committee's report was still being awaited two years after its submission.

The state government was also accused of being influenced by an individual in Bauchi. Many Sayawa believed that the military administrator took orders, not only about the crisis, from this individual but also about issues that affected the whole state. This opinion could be assessed when the person's suggestions in his memos to both the Babalakin's Commission and Shehu Awak's Committee were compared with the state government's recommendations to create three local government councils in Tafawa Balewa Local Government Area. It was also assumed that the person influenced the non-implementation of the recommendation to create the chiefdom with Tafawa Balewa as part of it.

On the other hand, the Council initiative in setting up the Peace and Reconciliation Committee to resolve farmland disputes was successful. The committee succeeded in preventing many armed conflicts and provided an enabling environment for resolving land and other disputes.

Finally, the Justice Ibrahim Zango tribunal was stopped by the Federal High Court in Jos due to technical reasons in its set-up. It was discovered by the counsels to the Sayawa that the state government did not receive the permission of the federal government before setting up the tribunal. The conflict might not be easily resolved by the government because of ethnic and religious dimensions. In fact the former Administrator, Navy Captain Rasheed Raji, in an interview with *Tell Magazine*, said that the disputants needed to find a common ground in order to resolve the crises under a neutral, independent, non-governmental organisation.

Suggested Strategies for Resolution, Prevention and Management of Conflict

Disputants have to be made to know that conflict can be a learning process. It creates opportunity for people to understand each other better, and to live together tolerating and accommodating each other's strengths and weaknesses. Too strong attachment to positions by each group makes it difficult for them to satisfy each other's interests and needs. People need to come together to find a common ground. To this end there is the need to create an enabling environment for ethnic groups to consent to come together to find the common ground that can bring enduring peace to the area.

There were several solutions suggested by each party towards a permanent resolution of the conflicts in Tafawa Balewa: The Hausa/Fulani suggested the creation of Bogoro Local Government Area, excluding Tafawa Balewa town as was the case in 1980 during Shagari's administration. This could lead to the creation of three chiefdoms in the existing three districts of the local government area. A critical analysis of this option revealed that the problem would still remain because Tafawa Balewa town which was the key issue to the conflict would go to one side which would eventually mean success for one party, and failure for the other thereby prolonging the conflict.

Another option was the creation of Sayawa chiefdom with the headquarters in Tafawa Balewa town. This would be unacceptable to the Hausa/Fulani who also laid claim to the town. Another important factor was that the creation of the chiefdom would mean the rulership of christians over the Hausa, Fulani and the Jarawa. Surely this option would not resolve the problem.

In the same vein, the option of the Sayawa to move to Plateau State with Tafawa Balewa town was risky to the Sayawa because the federal government was capable of merging the part of the land excluding Tafawa Balewa town. This action was equally capable of causing another ethno-religious upheaval. The other option was to divide Tafawa Balewa into two between the Sayawa and the rest.

Harmony amongst the ethnic groups in Tafawa Balewa Local Government Area needed a highly conducive atmosphere for the representatives to engage in dialogue. There were other options available. Firstly, the Sayawa already had a council of elders in place. This council of elders could be widened in scope to include elders from other ethnic groups in the local government area. This council could be recognised by the government to resolve the existing conflict. The second option was to use the existing Peace and Reconciliation Committee. The terms of reference of this committee could be expanded to include non-farmland conflicts and to work with the expanded elders council in bringing about a lasting peace in the community. These two committees could utilise the promise of the Sayawa to give due recognition to other ethnic groups under them if the chiefdom was created. The future creation of a chiefdom was a possibility. In fact, the residents of Tafawa Balewa town, irrespective of ethnic origin, believed in the above option if the powerful intruders from the state capital and the emirate council were kept out of the matter.

Other outside organisations such as Academic Associates PeaceWorks could assist by providing the necessary training to strengthen the capacity of the two committees to create a "win-win" situation over a period of time prior to the creation of the chiefdom.

To enhance the capacity of the two committees, there is the need to impart skills to community and youth leaders, and the local government councillors and officials. These leaders would in turn form a conflict management network that would be working with the two committees in resolving the conflicts and preventing future disputes. Outside organisations could also devise and promote peace education in primary and secondary schools in the local government area to avoid mutual suspicion.

To break the barrier between the communities in the local government area, the council, the committees and NGOs must create interactive activities in form of sports, joint festivals and joint developmental projects apart from the peace-making efforts.

It is important to put post-workshop arrangements in place for regular follow-up activities to ensure that these structures are strengthened in the local government area.

References

Aliyu, W.D. (1993). *Memorandum submitted to Bauchi State Committee on Creation of Sayawa Chiefdom.* 14/9/1993.

Aliyu, W.D. (1991). *The Local Government Reforms and Autonomy: A Case Study of Tafawa Balewa Local Government of Bauchi State.* Project submitted to the Department of Public Enterprises and Management Studies, ASCON, Badagry, Lagos.

Aliyu, W.D. (1991). *Memorandum submitted to Justice Babalakin Commission of Enquiry into the Civil Disturbances in Bauchi State, 1991.*

Bukata, R.A. (1991). *The April 22nd Crisis in Tafawa Balewa: Remote and Immediate Causes.* Being a memo submitted to Babalakin Commission of Enquiry 8/7/91.

Bula District Indigenes Resident in Bauchi and Elsewhere. (1993).

Memorandum submitted to the committee on creation of Sayawa Chiefdom. 6/9/93

Christian Association of Nigeria. (1991). Press Release 20/5/91.

Crampton, E.P.T. (1952). *Nigeria Population Map according to Tribal Groups*

Dull Primary Health Centre, Tafawa Balewa. (1991). *Problems Confronting us in Dull village as a result of April 22nd crisis.* 18th June, 1991.

Eluwa, G.I.C. *et al.* (1988). *A History of Nigeria for Schools and Colleges.* Onitsha: Africana-FEP Publishers Limited.

Fate, S.S. (1993). *Memorandum on the Creation of Sayawa Chiefdom Submitted to the Committee on Creation of Sayawa Chiefdom. 30/8/93.*

Human Rights Monitor, (June 1996). *Legal Rights Monitor,* Vol. 1, No.2. Kaduna: Author

Hogben, S.J. (1924). *The Mohammedan Emirate of Northern Nigeria.*

Magaji, K. (1996). *Memorandum Submitted to the State Creation and Boundary Adjustment Committee on Merger of Tafawa Balewa Local Government to Plateau State.*

Mamman, M. (ed.) (1979). *The Effects of the 1976 Local Government Reforms in Dass Local Government.* Zaria: University Press

Musa, I. (1993). *The need to be wary of historical sources in determining the authenticity of the claims of various interest groups on the issue of the creation of Sayawa Chiefdom*

Musa, A. (1993). *Memorandum Submitted to Bauchi State Committee on Creation of Sayawa Chiefdom. 1/9/1993.*

Morgan, W. (1924). *The Historical and Ethno-geographical Notes on the Tribes of Bauchi Province.* Kaduna: National Archives. SNP. 9-2485/1924.

Oliver, H. (ed.) (1908). *Northern Nigerian Historical notes on Certain Emirates and Tribes.* London: Waterloo and Sons Ltd.

Omonoh N.W., Nkem, J. (1974). *The Role of Local Government in Nation Building, "The Nigeria Case".* London: Microfilm Xergraphy.

Paden, J.N. (ed.) (1986). *Ahmadu Bello, Sardauna of Sokoto. "Values and Leadership in Nigeria.* "Zaria: Hudahuda Publishing Company.

People of Kardam Ward. (1993). *The position and recommendation of people of Kardam ward in Lere District toward the creation of Sayawa chiefdom in Tafawa Balewa Local Government Area. 2/9/93.*

The Ajiyan Bauchi Family (1993). *The Ajiyan family's position and suggestions to Shehu Awak Committee on creation of Sayawa chiefdom. 3/9/93*

Tafawa Balewa, A. (1996). *Memorandum on the brief history of Ajiya house submitted to the Bauchi Disturbances Judicial Commission of Inquiry.*

Tseayo, J.J. (1974). *Conflict and Incorporation in Nigeria.* Zaria: Gaskiya Corporation.

Tribal Studies in Northern Nigeria. London: Kegan Paul, Trench Tubner and Company Limited.

Tell Publications. (1996). *Bauchi on time Bomb*. Lagos: *Tell*. 8/1/96.

Youth CAN, Bauchi State. (1991). *Report of Religious Riot in Bauchi City*. 22/5/91.

New Nigerian Newspaper 20/9/77.

New Nigerian Newspaper 1/1/96.

New Nigerian Newspaper 12/4/96.

New Nigerian Newspaper 6/8/96.

Oral Interviews

Hon. Alhaji Adamu Tafawa Balewa, Ajiyan Bauchi.

Hon. Aliyu Wulumba Dadi, Dallatun Bauchi.

Hon. Wakili Boyi Bar, Deputy Chairman, Zauren Gwanu.

Hon. Barrister Kefas Magaji, Counsel to the Sayawa Community.

Hon. Dan Azumi Musa, Lecturer, ATAP, Bauchi.

Bishop Chukwuma, Chairman CAN, Bauchi State.

Imam Muhammed, Ahmed Bala, former Secretary, Bauchi LGA.

Hon. J.K. Manzo, former Commissioner of Education, Bauchi State.

Mr. Dan-Maryam Baba, Secretary, Sayawa Dev. Youth Association.

Hon. Ibrahim Alilu, Chairman, Tafawa Balewa Local Government.

Alhaji Maikano Gori, Chairman Peace and Reconciliation Comm. TBLGA.

Mr David Malle, State Secretariat, Bauchi.

Rev. Kiyas Mailafiya, Theological Institute, Tafawa Balewa.

Pastor Jingirns Samu, Assistant Chairman, CAN, Bauchi State.

Pastor Ishaku Komo, COCIN Church, Kutaru Village.

Barrister James Auta, Deputy Registrar, High Court, Bauchi.

Mr. David Jaja, Tafawa Balewa.

Mr. Kennedy Misau, Y.M.C.A., Bauchi.

Chapter 12

Onigu Otite

Aspects of Conflicts in Theory and Practice in Nigeria

Reflections on Conflict

The contents of this book suggest that strong elements which contribute to conflicts are present in the social structures and the various spheres of formal and informal relations in societies characterised by multi-ethnicity and pluralism. Yet certain compelling social institutions that represent Parson's "strategic structural significance" (1951), by acting as instruments of social constraint, prevent the disintegration of such societies through various mechanisms of conflict prevention, resolution, transformation or management.

Thus it has been possible over the centuries to bring social thinkers and theorists together, each carving a niche for himself from the perspectives of conflict and, or consensus. A conflict may be regarded as a natural announcement of an impending reclassification of a society with changed characteristics and goals, and with new circumstances of survival and continuity. Conflict is a negative means not only of limiting people's desires and expectations, but also a way of promoting the happiness of individuals and groups in a plural society. In the final analysis, consensus and cooperation are viable parts or consequences of conflict.

The Nigerian society is a social system compounded by contested demands on access to scarce resources especially in the political and economic fields. It is a society defined by natural cleavages and man-made conflicts. Natural membership of ethnic groups and occupational specialisations threatened by the expanding interests of other multiple users in the same or adjoining ecological zones, surviving administrative attributes of colonialism, states and their political-administrative activities, religious practices and fanaticism, expected divergence in the identification and perception of the use of limited resources, etc., provide grounds for the emergence of conflicts. The scale and dimensions of conflicts vary according to the issues involved in relation to the cultures concerned. Nigeria has a typical socio-territorial space in which the elements of consensus, co-operation, and conflict, function to promote its continuity as a social system.

Models of Conflict Resolution, Transformation and Management in Nigeria

Pluralism in Nigeria embodies a co-existence of perspectives of conflict which require different approaches to their management. Three broad models of conflict resolution, transformation and management are evident: the indigenous, the modern-western, and the one with mixed procedures and processes

1. Traditional Model of Conflict Transformation

This consists of various forms:

(a) *The Elders' Council.* The symbolism of authoritative decisions associated with elders' cultural trusteeship and customary practices, has sustained conflict resolution and management in Nigerian societies. The constitution of King-in-Council or of village or town councils and their legitimacy of interventions in conflict situations, are well known events in Nigeria, especially in the rural areas.

The elders may not have physical power to enforce decisions, but they rely on leaders of the various age-grades or youth associations to bring about and monitor peace on the basis of the negotiated terms in particular conflicts, or of the known institutionalised forms of conflict management. Kings and chiefs of various designations and statuses practise their indigenous cultures admirably in resolving, transforming and managing conflicts within and between their domains. Yet, those who disagree with the verdict of these functionaries proceed freely to settle their conflicts in the modern westernised sector, for example, the magistrate courts.

Town councils are agents of conflict prevention, resolution, transformation, or management within and between their communities. The basis for this mode of intervention is the peoples' surviving confidence, trust, and reliance on culture as a means of rallying and mobilising people to behave in patterned ways, a condition which can thus be used to handle conflict problems at the ethnic or inter-ethnic levels.

The principles involved in the resolution, transformation and management of conflicts are associated with the customary systems of government and justice. Elias (1963), Schapera(1956) and Gluckman (1967) have shown how African societies in general use judgement and justice to resolve conflicts and disputes. In the process of sitting in council (with political roles) and turning it to court (with judicial roles), rulers target and achieve recompensation, restitution, and reconciliation. This practised life-style directed by the same key actors, and in which political authority strengthens judicial decisions, is an important way of pleasing and satisfying various parties in a conflict. These customary procedures and practices of conflict resolution and management are culture-based and have lasting effects. They have more interest in the equilibrium model of society, and less in the conflict model.

(b)   The intervention of the supernatural element

Traditional religious beliefs and practices are still strong even among practitioners of Islam and Christianity in Nigeria. The world of ancestors is an extension of the world of the living, and the supernatural beings are part of the Nigerian systems of thought. Ancestors and predecessors, royal and non royal, like other deities and shrines, are believed to impose decisive rightful verdicts in controversial issues of conflict within and between communities. When kola, drinks, food, etc are shared and prayers said to settle disputants in land, farm and feuding conflicts, participants from all the parties involved regard such disputes and conflicts to be finally settled with divine sanction. Such conflict settlement terms are generally accepted and obeyed for fear of negative sanctions such as deaths or affliction with bad and incurable diseases from the spirit world. Tempers are cooled and dangerous weapons, like cutlasses and local and modern guns, can be put aside in these circumstances of believed supernatural participation in conflict resolution and management.

2.   Westernised-modern Model of Conflict Resolution, Transformation and Management

This consists of very well known use of the Nigeria Police, the courts – from magistrate to the supreme court, for example in the Sapele Itsekiri – Urhobo land case (see Otite 1982: 261) and in inter-state boundry conflicts etc. There are also sectional provisions in government ministries such as the Ministry of Labour and Productivity where arbitrations in wage-labour disagreements, disputes, and conflicts are referred to such management devices as mediation, conciliation, industrial arbitration panel, and then to the national industrial court. Hence there is government provision for conflict resolution, transformation and management through known and clearly stated procedures, involving parties from both the public and private sectors. Courts of origination or of appeal are legitimate means of managing and settling conflicts between individuals and groups.

3. Model with Mixed Personnel and Procedures for Conflict Resolution, Transformation and Management

This model involves multiple but simultaneous use of elements from the indigenous and "modern" efficacious practices. Here the Customary and the Sharia courts in which kings and chiefs who function with Weber's traditional legitimate authority, co-exist with specialists exercising national-constitutional legitimate authority in one plural legal system. This model thus embraces the Magistrate Courts, the High Courts and their appelate system, to the Supreme Court. When Government panels and commissions of enquiry are set up, these may include traditional rulers and those with authority under the modern constitution. Sometimes the panels are separated in terms of personnel composition such as the 1997 royal (Oba Ashiru Tadese, Oluwo of Iwo-led) peace commission, and the 1981 Justice Ibidapo Obe judicial panel, both on the Ife-Modakeke crisis as described by Albert. These multiple approaches are a recognition of the potency of co-existing plural factors in contemporary Nigeria's social structure. Certain traditional rulers mobilise different categories of peace workers to resolve conflicts such as what the Sultan of Sokoto and other traditional rulers did when they intervened in the conflict between the Tiv and Junkun as described by Shedrack Best.

Adhoc and Informal Means of Conflict Resolution and Transformation

In addition to the above institutionalised mechanisms for conflict transformation and control, Nigerian societies have their own devices for conflict resolution and for ensuring social peace. Some of these are eclectic while others take the form of frantic fire brigade solutions (Also see Albert et al, 1995). The following are examples.

(1)   **Non-Governmental Organisations (NGOs).**

These organisations intervene on the notice of conflicts between groups. They make on the spot enquiries to find out the causes and courses of conflicts and attempt to reach some understanding and settlement. An example is Best's account of the Mangu-Bokkos conflict. Another well known example is the Legal Aid Council in Nigeria, established through the Legal Aid Decree No. 56 of 1976. It resolves conflicts out of court, or funds the financially disadvantaged people in seeking redress.

(2)   **Religious Organisations.**

Religious bodies such as those of Christians and Muslims, which are universalistic, often get involved in resolving conflicts among their members and between the groups of believers. The intervention by the Church of Christ in Nigeria (COCIN) in the Mangu-Bokkos crisis is a good example. This kind of intervention is particularly effective if members of the groups in conflict are also members of the same religious organisation.

(3)   **Social Networks and Pressures**

Social networks and points of social pressures are defined by kinship, descent, in-law or official relationships, old school Alma Mater ties, club membership, political party or work-place ties, etc. They are often activated and mobilised to exert social pressures in the negotiation of settlements. Persons holding particular positions in relation to the parties in conflict, are particularly useful and effective in pressing for the resolution or transformation of specific conflicts.

There are several other informal and voluntary local and national organisations devoted to identifying areas of conflict and intervening to restore peace. A good example is the Association of Arbitrators of Nigeria (See *The Guardian* of January 15 1999 p.4), the ethnic culture-based associations such as the Ijebu-Ode Development Association (IDA) (see Sina Kawonise 1997: 125 – 30), Urhobo Progress Union (see Otite 1982: 262-7), the Isoko Development Associaion, the Ijaw National Congress, and various nationality-ethnic associations, and elders fora in different parts of Nigeria.

Scope of Conflict Resolution, Transformation and Management

Four main levels of conflict are identified, requiring different approaches to their resolution or transformation. The first is the town level where conflicts may ensue between distinct sectors or wards of the same town such as Ife and Modakeke in Ile Ife.

There could also be inter-ethnic group conflicts, where, in the same environment, different categories of indigenous users, such as the Ijaw and the Itsekiri with their well defined social structures and ethnic cultural symbols, co-exist in Warri, Delta State. Futhermore, there are situations where one ethnic group is the recognised owner of the settlement and farmlands, and immigrants or strangers and indigenes come into conflict. In the case of Hausa's Kano. the Emir recognises the head of the immigrants, such as the Eze Ndi Igbo of the Igbo immigrants and the Seriki Yorubawa of the Yoruba, as authorities to mediate and settle conflicts arising from the daily interactions betwen the Muslim indigenes within Kano walls and markets, and the Christian immigrant-stranger settlers in Sabon Gari (see Otite 1998).

The second level is that of the local government area (LGA) consisting of various towns and villages, and in many cases, inhabited by members of several ethnic or sub-ethnic groups. Many of our case studies show this feature. Sources of conflicts at this level include uneven distribution of development projects such as markets and maternity homes, incumbency of the position of chairman of the local government council, local representations of the national political parties especially the party controlling the state or federal government, cross-border land conflicts involving two local government councils, etc. The resolution of such conflicts may involve the services of elders' forum, setting up of judicial or administrative panels or commissions, etc.

The third level is the State. We noted in chapter one that Nigeria developed into thirty-six states in 1996. These federal government creations led to inter-state boundary conflicts, and were confronted with several kinds of problems arising from the activities of local government functionaries and traditional rulers and political elite. Each state has to resolve, transform and manage conflicts in its area of jurisdiction. It has become usual in these circumstances to set up judicial enquiries such as that of Justice Ibidapo Obe to examine the Ife-Modakeke crisis, the Justice Jummai Sankey panel of enquiry as well as the various initiatives and the 1995 administrative committee on the Mangu-Bokkos conflict. The 1997 Delta State Justice Idoko Judicial Commission of Enquiry on the conflicts between the Ijaw and Itsekiri is another example of state government intervention to settle inter-ethnic conflicts. The Justice Nnaemaka Agu's 1993 Judicial Commission / enquiry and the Delta State Elders Forum were also set up to examine the communal conflicts in Warri.

The fourth level is that of the federal government. There is a strong element of political necessity and interest in federal government involvement in conflict resolution. By exercising its jurisdiction and constitutional powers ostensibly to benefit Nigerians, the federal government often inadvertently creates unintended areas of conflict which it is now attempting to solve in different parts of the country. As the only authority for the creation of states and especially local government councils, the government unintentionally caused conflicts through the location and relocation of capitals or headquarters, for example in Warri and Ile-Ife. The location or shifting of headquarters from one place to another to favour one or the other section of the community, has led to conflicts resulting in deaths and destruction of property in Warri and Ile Ife. Also, by defaulting through the uneven development of the country, the federal government created grounds for conflicts. In particular, by neglecting the development of the oil producing areas, and because of the perception of injustice by the indigenes of the areas, conflicts have been endemic in the Niger Delta, the oil producing area of Nigeria.

The conflicts are at two levels - between the ethnic groups such as the Ijaw and the Itsekiri over contested claims to territories where oil wells are located and from which royalty, social recognition, development programmes, and financial compensations are derived; and between an ethnic group, for example, the Ogoni or the Ijaw, and the federal government on the other hand, for daring to, or deliberately neglecting the development of the people and their territory. Lack of industries and employment facilities are part of the causes of conflict.

As both the cause and settler or manager of conflicts, the Federal Government set up, in the past, various kinds of interventions and negotiating commissions and panels such as the National Reconciliation Committee (NARECOM) as mentioned by Albert in the case of Ife-Modakeke crisis; the National Boundary Commission (NBC) which often coopts traditional rulers of the parties in conflict to resolve their differences over the ownership of territories; and the recent (January 1999) group of interveners-mediators which the Federal Government sent to examine the conflict in the Niger Delta.

Theoretical, Practical and Policy Implications

Conflict as a social phenomenon must constitute an aspect of the theory of peace and development. An understanding and appreciation of other peoples' cultures and divergent perceptions of resources and their uses is a prerequisite for successful conflict resolution, transformation or management. Although present in all societies at various stages of development, conflict varies in degree and forms of expression—physical, verbal or ideological. Changing demographic factors and densities of the population of competing multiple users of limited but valued resources, are important in assessing the prospects and problems of conflict resolution, transformation or management. Conflict must co-exist with co-operation and with an appreciable degree of peace for development to take place in society. Indeed, the phenomenon of conflict contains the seeds for its resolution, transformation and management. Physical and verbal expressions of conflict end ultimately in peaceful co-existence of people with diverse interests.

Yet, in practical terms from experienced social devastations, as opposed to the theoretical perspective of the positive contributions of conflicts, it is apparent that the more ethnic conflicts we have, the less the development we can achieve. Inter-ethnic conflicts are generally socially, physically and mentally destructive, leading to losses in human capital and material properties, visible scars and symbols of violent conflicts or wars such as deformities and ruins of buildings, and the legacy of mutual distrust and suspicion. Ethnic-government conflicts and systemic resistance may bring in some net development only after many lives and properties would have been lost on both sides. In all cases, the best path to development remains the prevalence of peace and socio-political stability through consensus building, negotiated settlements and the resolution of conflicts.

Stubborn issues generating conflicts in plural societies include disputed tenancy and landlordship strengthened by symbols and myths of migratory history and settlement, political jurisdictional overlordships, and overlapping issues of geographical-border boundaries especially those in which mineral deposits are found, crude petroleum exploited, and capital investment made. Thus although peace achieved at the end of conflict resolution may form a firm basis for development, the latter may be a source of conflict. Development brings about conflict when people struggle to benefit from it or when it is used by a group of people or political controllers to benefit unequally, different ethno-territorial units. This is because the development of a territory is often associated with the progress of its indigenous owners and landlords. Practical feelings and existential conditions which define individual and group life and survival in different political-economic environments must inform the development of conflict theories. Conflict may, in many cases, be seen theoretically, more as a positive phenomenon than as a factor of social destruction. Strategies of conflict resolution, transformation and management must therefore be developed to cope with various forms of conflicts as they occur in different contexts. Peace is a tranquilisation of conflict which itself leads to development and to peace. Practical experiences and theoretical formulations must recognise this developmental cycle of conflict, its resolution, transformation and management, peace, development and conflict.

The above discussions have some obvious policy implications. First, since self or group development is an expected and legitimate goal, the development of the human capital is an imperative government function. Investment in education is an important means of empowering individuals and groups intellectually to appreciate the symbols of different socio-cultural groups, the evaluation and perception of scarce resources, and the friendly co-existence of their different users in the same territorial region. Enlightened populations have the strongest chance of understanding and appreciating the factors generating conflicts, the complex issues involved in their resolution, transformation and management, and the restoration of peace in multi-ethnic and diverse institutional settings.

Second, because a majority of conflicts derive from unequal access to scarce resources for development, there must be an equitable development of the various ethno-territories – through the construction and distribution of roads, bridges, electricity, animal water spots, pastures and animal passages which avoid farmlands, canals, etc.

Third, government's formal agents of conflict resolution should be improved and maintained. For example, NARECOM and NBC should be strengthened. It is not enough to set up adhoc panels or commissions of enquiry; Government should study and implement promptly, those recommendations found appropriate in particular circumstances. It will be recalled that delays in the implementation of the findings and recommendations of panels and commissions exacerbated conflicts, for example in Best's Mangu-Bokkos case study.

Fourth, it is important to explore all traditional institutional provisions for the resolution, transformation and management of conflicts and disputes. Indigenous perceptions of their societies as equilibrium systems incline Nigerians fundamentally to the avoidance or resolution and management of conflicts. Most Nigerians are still culture-bound, and the phenomenon of shared symbols has an exhilarating effect on people's trust and confidence. The accepted authority of gerontocratic town councils and courts, kings-in councils, inter community affinal and economic ties, elders' fora etc. can be mobilised to mediate and settle conflicts. Government should promote the enshrined triple consensus-building and legal-political practices of recompensation, restitution and reconciliation which indigenous governments uphold in the settlement of disputes and the resolution of conflicts within and between communities. Also important in this connection is the position of such recognised mediators as the changing forms of the "leopard-skin" chief and the invocation of the supernatural controllers and deciders of conflicts, accompanied with commensality and kola hospitability, as instruments and evidence of agreed positive resolution of conflict.

Fifth, there should be a definite policy of youth education and development. Since 1966, Nigerian youths have been born into a military culture of violence, coups and counter coups, the use of guns and other weapons of war, and the destruction of human life. Nigerian youth constitute about 70% of the country's population and most of them fighting in the front of violent confrontations, are just under thirty-three years. Even those who are educated have no employment. Hence government should not only educate and train the youth academically, professionally, and technologically, but it should also provide employment facilities for them, especially in their own environments.

There is the hypothesis, for instance, that if the petroleum and other engineers in the oil companies in the Niger Delta were indigenes, they would be most unlikely to allow the destruction of the oil wells and equipment under their control. Such indigenes-employees would intervene quickly to prevent conflicts that would get them out of employment to the detriment of their families, dependants and local citizens, including those engaged in conflicts. Where such local employable labour is not available, they should be trained. The Niger-Delta conflict, and indeed most of those discussed in this book, were promoted by the engagement of the youth in physical aggression and violent killing, partly because of their unemployment.

The case of Kano youths is slightly different. Here, government should devise means of destroying "street culture". The youths should be kept off the streets. They should be educated and trained through the use of training workshops, and be economically-financially empowered to engage in self-employment, or get employed in the public and private sectors of the economy. In this way they cannot be easily mobilised as idle persons to participate in street and other (religious) forms of violent conflicts.

In some other cases, the creation of new local government

councils and their capitals are perceived as sources of employment, of local socio-political identity, and of local development. The relocation, especially of their headquarters, is consequently resisted. Such deprived peoples, including their youths, always find this as enough provocation to engage in conflicts with other "outgroup" communities, and the government. As a policy, Government should avoid improper and inappropriate decisions of the location and relocation of local government councils and their headquarters.

Sixth, there should be a deliberate pre-emptive policy for avoiding conflicts. A good example is peace education involving citizenship-political socialisation on the avoidance of conflicts and of the destruction of human life and property. The dignity and sanctity of human life must be appreciated. There should also be some form of "human remote sensing" for the discovery of tendencies of social pre-starters of conflicts, and for the necessary combination of factors which precipitate inter-group conflicts.

Seventh, there should be government's standing preparedness to encourage non-governmental organisations (NGOs) to intervene promptly to resolve conflicts. Government's management of conflict through this "delegated" form permits it more freedom and ability to handle the more elusive problems of the maintenance of peace and social development. On the other hand, NGOs can initiate and undertake conflict resolution, transformation and management programmes, such as the many conflict management training workshops undertaken by AAPW in Ife-Modakeke (see chapter 2), and those by other NGOs in the central and north-eastern parts of the country (see chapter 7 for instance). The training and functions of the community-based orgnisations (CBOs) should also be part of the programme.

Eighth, friendly competitions should be developed to displace conflict inclinations and relationships. This conversion of conditions can be done through traditional sports or economic programmes involving members of groups in short-term or long-term collaborative endeavours. Football competitions between schools, clubs or groups of youths from the communities in (perennial) conflict should be arranged. The spirit of sportsmanship, and the concept of a zero-sum game should be explained and appreciated. Also agricultural shows and festivals where conflict is exchanged for healthy competition for various kinds of prizes, can also be arranged to achieve win-win outcomes. Such overlapping programmes can be perceived as theatres for acting out conflicts and anger in a competitive spirit.

Ninth, government and non-governmental organisations should establish inter-ethnic and inter-community lines of communication and dialogue through leading leaders, including traditional rulers, for constant surveillance over conflict and for negotiated settlement of thorny issues. Such committees of community leaders should be given or should , on their own, take up the responsibility to sniff out areas and possible occurrence of conflict, using traditional and, or new "modern" means.

The Future of Conflict Resolution, Transformation and Management in Nigeria

Societies, such as Nigeria, maintain their systemic continuity because conflicts involving various individuals and groups do not attack the basic foundations of their collective existence. Despite the endemic nature of conflicts there is an overall compelling necessity for the co-existence and inter-dependence of multiple users and exploiters of commonly valued economic and political resources. For many societies in general, "peace and feuding, conflict and order are correlative. Both the cementing and the breaking of the cake of custom constitute part of the dialectic of social life" (Coser 1968). This statement is applicable to Nigeria of today and tomorrow.

As new political and economic development continues to create new resource areas of conflict, there is an obvious need to intensify and diversify national and local institutional and adhoc devices for the solution and management of conflicts.

In this respect the issue of government is important at the local and national levels. In the first place, government must be democratic, involving freely elected representatives of the people. Decisions on the creation of new political units must be based on research findings. Level fields should be provided for all eligible and competent competitors for political positions such as those of the local government councils. This is one way of avoiding sectional agitations against government and other groups sharing the same environment. The provision for popular participation in local and national government is another viable way for creating grounds for mutual trust and collaboration in the same micro or macro society.

Regardless of where the key government functionaries come from, they must be transparent in the management of the common treasury and other resources, and must develop their areas equitably. Once all the ethno-territorial areas of the state are treated equally, the main basis for oppositions and conflicts with government and other groups of people would have been reduced, or even prevented.

Increase in population at the present Nigerian rate of 2.83% per annum is bound to increase demands on resources by eligible multiple users. There is need to improve on the quantity and quality of land and pasture resources through government-sponsored research. Although it may not always be possible to increase the limited political positions and other resources created through expanded bureaucratisation and differentiation of political and administrative roles, access to the available ones must be openly and freely contested for by those qualified and interested in the various sections and ethnic-territorial units of the society. The structure and processes of government and its mode and degree of efficiency of resource management, are critical factors in reducing the occurrence of conflicts, based on ethnic, class, gender, religion, and other factors.

References

Albert, I.O.,T. Awe., G. Herault and W. Omitogun (1995). *Informal Channels for Conflict Resolution in Ibadan Nigeria.* Ibadan, IFRA.

Coser, L. (1968). *Conflict Social Aspects in the International Encyclopaedia of the Social Sciences* (ed) D.L. Sills. New York. The Macmillan Co. and The Free Press.

Elias, T.O. (1963). *Government and Politics in Africa,* London: Asia Publishing House.

Gluckman, M. (1967). *Custom and Conflict in Africa.* Oxford. Basil Blackwell.

Kawonise, S. (1997). "Civil Society in a Mixed Urban and Rural Area: Ijebu-Ode, Ogun State" in Adedeji and Otite (eds)

Nigeria, Renewal fron the Grassroots. The Struggle for Democratic Development, London: Zed Books.

Otite, O. (ed) (1982). *The Urhobo People*, Ibadan Heinemann.

Otite, O. (1998). "Perspectives in National Integration in Multicultural Societies: A Nigerian Overview". Paper prepared for the Symposium on Dimensions and Dynamics of Ethnicity, organised by the committee on Ethnic Relations under the panel on Multicultural Education. Fourth Congress of the Authropological and Ethnological Sciences. Williamsburg, Virginia, USA. July 26 - Aug. 1, 1998.

Parsons, T. (1951). *The Social System.*

Schapera, I. (1956). *Government and Politics in Tribal Societies,* London: Watts.

Appendix

States and Local Government Areas of the Federal Republic of Nigeria.

States	State Capitals	Local Government Areas	Number of Local Government Areas
1. Abia	Umuahia	Aba North	17
		Aba South	
		Arochukwu	
		Bende	
		Ikwuano	
		Isiala-Ngwa North	
		Isiala-Ngwa South	
		Isuikwuato	
		Obi Ngwa	
		Ohafia	
		Osisioma Ngwa	
		Ugwunagbo	
		Ukwa East	
		Ukwa West	
		Umuahia North	
		Umuahia South	
		Umu-Nneochi	
2. Adamawa	Yola	Demsa	21
		Fufore	
		Ganye	
		Gombi	
		Girei	
		Guyuk	
		Hong	
		Jada	
		Lamurde	
		Madagali	
		Maiha	
		Mayo-Belwa	
		Michika	
		Mubi North	
		Mubi South	
		Numan	
		Shelleng	
		Song	
		Toungo	

| | | | Yola North | |
| | | | Yola South | |

3. Akwa Ibom	Uyo	Abak	31
		Eastern Obolo	
		Eket	
		Esit Eket	
		Essien Udim	
		Etim Ekpo	
		Etinan	
		Ibeno	
		Ibesikpo Asutan	
		Ibiono Ibom	
		Ika	
		Ikono	
		Ikot Abasi	
		Ikot Ekpene	
		Ini	
		Itu	
		Mbo	
		Mkpat Enin	
		Nsit Atai	
		Nsit Ibom	
		Nsit Ubium	
		Obot Akara	
		Okobo	
		Onna	
		Oron	
		Oruk Anam	
		Udung Uko	
		Ukanafun	
		Uruan	
		Urue	
		Offong/Oruko	
		Uyo	

4. Anambra	Awka	Aguata	21
		Anambra East	
		Anambra West	
		Anaocha	
		Awka North	
		Awka South	
		Ayamelum	
		Dunukofia	
		Ekwusigo	
		Idemili North	
		Idemili South	

Ihiala
Njikoka
Nnewi North
Nnewi South
Ogbaru
Onitsha North
Onitsha South
Orumba North
Orumba South
Oyi

5. Bauchi	Bauchi	Alkaleri	20
		Bauchi	
		Bogoro	
		Damban	
		Darazo	
		Dass	
		Gamawa	
		Ganjuwa	
		Giade	
		Itas/Gadau	
		Jama'are	
		Katagun	
		Kirfi	
		Misau	
		Ningi	
		Shira	
		Tafawa-Balewa	
		Toro	
		Warji	
		Zaki	
6. Bayelsa	Yenegoa	Brass	8
		Ekeremor	
		Kolokuma/Opk	
		Uma	
		Nembe	
		Ogbia	
		Sagbama	
		Southern Ijaw	
		Yenegoa	
7. Benue	Makurdi	Ado	23
		Agatu	
		Apa	
		Buruku	
		Gboko	

Guma
Gwer East
Gwer West
Katsina-Ala
Konshisha
Kwande
Logo
Makurdi
Obi
Ogbadibo
Oju
Okpokwu
Ohimini
Oturkpo
Tarka
Ukum
Ushongo
Vandeikya

8. Borno   Maiduguri   Abadam   27
Askira Uba
Bama
Bayo
Biu
Chibok
Damboa
Dikwa
Gubio
Guzamala
Gwoza
Hawul
Jere
Kaga
Kala/Balge
Konduga
Kukawa
Kwaya Kusar
Mafa
Magumeri
Maiduguri
Marte
Mobbar
Monguno
Ngala
Ngaanzai
Shani

9. Cross River	Calabar	Abi	18
		Akamkpa	
		Akpabuyo	
		Bakassi	
		Bekwarra	
		Biase	
		Boki	
		Calabar Municipal	
		Calabar South	
		Etung	
		Ikom	
		Obanliku	
		Obubra	
		Obudu	
		Odukpani	
		Ogoja	
		Yakurr	
		Yala	
10. Delta	Asaba	Aniocha North	25
		Aniocha South	
		Bomadi	
		Burutu	
		Ethiope East	
		Ethiope West	
		Ika North East	
		Ika South	
		Isoko North	
		Isoko South	
		Ndokwa East	
		Ndokwa West	
		Okpe	
		Oshimili North	
		Oshimili South	
		Patani	
		Sapele	
		Udu	
		Ughelli North	
		Ughelli South	
		Ukwuani	
		Uvwie	
		Warri North	
		Warri South	
		Warri South-West	
11. Ebonyi	Abakaliki	Abakaliki	13
		Afikpo North	
		Afikpo South	

Ebonyi
Ezza North
Ezza South
Ikwo
Ishielu
Ivo
Izzi
Ohaozara
Ohaukwu
Onicha

12. Edo	Benin City	Akoko-Edo	18
		Egor	
		Esan Central	
		Esan North-East	
		Esan South-East	
		Esan West	
		Etsako Central	
		Etsako East	
		Etsako West	
		Iguegben	
		Ikpoba-Okha	
		Oredo	
		Orhionmwon	
		Ovia North-East	
		Ovia South-West	
		Owan East	
		Owan West	
		Uhunmwonde	

13. Ekiti	Ado Ekiti	Ado Ekiti	16
		Aiyekire	
		Efon	
		Ekiti East	
		Ekiti West	
		Ekiti South-West	
		Emure	
		Ido-Osi	
		Ijeto	
		Ikere	
		Ikole	
		Ilejemeji	
		Irepodun/Ifelodun	
		Ise/Orun	
		Moba	
		Oye	

14. Enugu	Enugu	Anieri	17
		Agwu	
		Enugu East	
		Enugu North	
		Enugu South	
		Ezeagu	
		Igbo-Etiti	
		Igbo-Eze-North	
		Igbo-Eze-South	
		Isi-Uzo	
		Nkanu East	
		Nkanu West	
		Nsukka	
		Oji-River	
		Udenu	
		Udi	
		Uzo-Uwani	
15. Gombe	Gombe	Akko	11
		Balanga	
		Billiri	
		Dukku	
		Funakaye	
		Gombe	
		Kaltungo	
		Kwami	
		Nafada	
		Shomgom	
		Yamaku/Deba	
16. Imo	Owerri	Aboh-Mbaise	27
		Abiazu-Mbaise	
		Ehime-Mbano	
		Ezinihitte	
		Ideato North	
		Ideato South	
		Ihitte/Uboma	
		Ikeduru	
		Isiala Mbano	
		Isu	
		Mbaitoli	
		Ngor-Okpa'a	
		Mjaba	
		Nwangele	
		Nkwerre	
		Obowo	
		Oguta	

Ohaji/Egbema
Okigwe
Orlu
Orsu
Oru East
Oru West
Owerri-Municipal
Owerri North
Owerri West
Unuimo

17. Jigawa	Dutse	Auyo	27
		Babura	
		Birnin Kudu	
		Biriniwa	
		Buji	
		Dutse	
		Gagarawa	
		Garki	
		Gumel	
		Guri	
		Gwaram	
		Gwiwa	
		Hadejia	
		Jahun	
		Kafin Hausa	
		Kaugama	
		Kazaure	
		Kiri Kasamma	
		Kiyawa	
		Maigatari	
		Malam Maduri	
		Miga	
		Ringim	
		Roni	
		Sule-Tankar-Kar	
		Taura	
		Yankwashi	
18. Kaduna	Kaduna	Birnin-Gwari	23
		Chikun	
		Giwa	
		Igbabi	
		Ikara	
		Jaba	
		Jema'a	
		Kachia	

Kaduna North
Kaduna South
Kagarko
Kajuru
Kaura
Kauru
Kubau
Kudan
Lere
Makarfi
Sabon-Gari
Sanga
Soba
Zangon-Kataf
Zaria

19. Kano Kano Ajingi 44
Albasu
Bagwai
Bebeji
Bichi
Bunkure
Dala
Dambatta
Dawakin Kudu
Dawakin Tofa
Doguwa
Fagge
Gabasawa
Garko
Carum Mallam
Gaya
Gezawa
Gwale
Gwarzo
Kabo
Kano Municipal
Karaye
Kibiya
Kiru
Kumbotso
Kunchi
Kura
Madobi
Makoda
Minjibir
Nassarawa

Rano
Rimin Gado
Rogo
Shanono
Sumaila
Takai
Tarauni
Tofa
Tsanyawa
Tudun Wada
Ungogo
Warawa
Wudil

20. Katsina   Katsina   Bakori   34
Batagarawa
Batsari
Baure
Bindawa
Charanchi
Dandume
Danja
Dan Musa
Daura
Dutsi
Dutsin-Ma
Faskari
Funtua
Ingawa
Jibia
Kafur
Kaita
Kankara
Kankia
Katsina
Kurfi
Kusada
Mai Adua
Malumfashi
Mani
Mashi
Matazu
Musawa
Rimi
Sabuwa
Safana
Sandamu
Zango

21. Kebbi	Birnin Kebbi	Aleiro	21
		Arewa-Dandi	
		Argungu	
		Augie	
		Bagudo	
		Birnin Kebbi	
		Bunza	
		Dandi	
		Fakai	
		Gwandu	
		Jega	
		Kalgo	
		Koko/Besse	
		Maiyama	
		Ngaski	
		Sakaba	
		Shanga	
		Suru	
		Wasagu/Danko	
		Yauri	
		Zuru	
22. Kogi	Lokoja	Adavi	21
		Ajaokuta	
		Ankpa	
		Bassa	
		Dekina	
		Ibaji	
		Idah	
		Igalamela-Odolu	
		Ijumu	
		Kabba/Bunu	
		Kogi	
		Lokoja	
		Mopa-Muro	
		Ofu	
		Ogori/Magongo	
		Okehi	
		Okene	
		Olamaboro	
		Omala	
		Yagba East	
		Yagba West	
23. Kwara	Ilorin	Asa	16
		Baruten	
		Edu	

Ekiti
Ifelodun
Ilorin East
Ilorin South
Ilorin West
Irepodun
Isin
Kaiama
Moro
Offa
Oke-Ero
Oyun
Pategi

24. Lagos	Ikeja	Agege	20
		Ajeromi-Ifelodun	
		Alimosho	
		Amuwo-Odofin	
		Apapa	
		Badagry	
		Epe	
		Eti-Osa	
		Ibeju/Lekki	
		Ifako-Ijaiye	
		Ikeja	
		Ikorodu	
		Kosofe	
		Lagos Island	
		Lagos Mainland	
		Mushin	
		Ojo	
		Oshodi-Isolo	
		Shomolu	
		Surulere	
25. Nassarawa	Lafia	Akwanga	13
		Awe	
		Doma	
		Karu	
		Keana	
		Keffi	
		Kokoma	
		Lafia	
		Nassarawa	
		Nassarawa-Eggon	
		Obi	
		Toto	
		Wamba	

26. Niger	Minna	Agaie	25
		Agwara	
		Bida	
		Borgu	
		Bosso	
		Chanchaga	
		Edati	
		Gbako	
		Gurara	
		Katcha	
		Kotangora	
		Lapai	
		Lavun	
		Magama	
		Mariga	
		Mashegu	
		Mokwa	
		Muya	
		Paikoro	
		Rafi	
		Rijau	
		Shiroro	
		Suleja	
		Tafa	
		Wushishi	
27. Ogun	Abeokuta	Abeokuta-North	20
		Abeokuta-South	
		Ado-Odo/Ota	
		Egbado North	
		Egbado South	
		Ewekoro	
		Ifo	
		Ijebu East	
		Ijebu North	
		Ijebu North-East	
		Ijebu Ode	
		Ikenne	
		Imeko-Afon	
		Ipokia	
		Obafemi-Owode	
		Ogun Waterside	
		Odeda	
		Odogbolu	
		Remo North	
		Shagamu	

28. Ondo	Akure	Akoko North-East	18
		Akoko North-West	
		Akoko South-East	
		Akoko South West	
		Akure North	
		Akure South	
		Ese-Odo	
		Idanre	
		Ifedore	
		Ilaje	
		Ile-Oluji	
		Okeigbo	
		Irele	
		Odigba	
		Okitipupa	
		Ondo East	
		Ondo West	
		Ose	
		Owo	
29. Osun	Osogbo	Aiyedade	30
		Aiyedire	
		Atakumosa East	
		Atakumosa West	
		Boluwaduro	
		Boripe	
		Ede North	
		Ede South	
		Egbedore	
		Ejigbo	
		Ife Central	
		Ife East	
		Ife North	
		Ife South	
		Ifedayo	
		Ifelodun	
		Ila	
		Ilesha East	
		Ilesha West	
		Irepodun	
		Irewole	
		Isokan	
		Iwo	
		Obokun	
		Odo-otin	
		Ola-Oluwa	
		Olorunda	

Oriade
Orolu
Osogbo

30. Oyo Ibadan Afijio 33
Akinyele
Atiba
Atisbo
Egbeda
Ibadan-Central
Ibadan North
Ibadan North-West
Ibadan South-East
Ibadan South-West
Ibarapa Central
Ibarapa East
Ibarapa North
Ido
Irepo
Iseyin
Itesiwaju
Iwajowa
Kajola
Lagelu
Ogbomosho North
Ogbomosho South
Ogo-Oluwa
Olorunsogo
Oluyole
Ona-Ara
Orelope
Ori Ire
Oyo East
Oyo West
Saki East
Saki West
Surulere

31. Plateau Jos Barikin Ladi 17
Bassa
Bokkos
Jos East
Jos North
Jos South
Kanam
Kanke
Langtang-North

		Langtang-South	
		Mangu	
		Mikang	
		Pankshin	
		Qua'an Pan	
		Riyom	
		Shendam	
		Wase	
32. Rivers	Port-Harcourt	Abua/Odual	23
		Ahoada East	
		Ahoada West	
		Akuku Toru	
		Andoni	
		Asari-Toru	
		Bonny	
		Degema	
		Emuoha	
		Eleme	
		Etche	
		Gokanna	
		Ikwerre	
		Khana	
		Obia/Akpor	
		Ogba/Egbema/Ndoni	
		Ogu/Bolo	
		Okrika	
		Omumma	
		Opobo/Nkoro	
		Oyigbo	
		Port-Harcourt	
		Tai	
33. Sokoto	Sokoto	Binji	23
		Bodinga	
		Dange-shuni	
		Gada	
		Goronyo	
		Gudu	
		Gwadabawa	
		Illela	
		Isa	
		Kware	
		Kebbe	
		Rabah	
		Sabon Birni	
		Shagari	

Silame
Sokoto North
Sokoto South
Tambuwal
Tangaza
Tureta
Wamakko
Wurno
Yabo

34. Taraba Jalingo Ardo-kola 16
Bali
Donga
Gashaka
Gassol
Ibi
Jalingo
Karim-Lamido
Kurmi
Lau
Sardauna
Takum
Ussa
Wukari
Yorro
Zing

35. Yobe Damaturu Bade 17
Borsai
Damaturu
Fika
Fune
Geidam
Gujba
Gulani
Jakusko
Karasuwa
Machina
Nangere
Nguru
Potiskum
Tarmua
Yunusari
Yusufari

36. Zamfara Gusau Anka 14
Bakura

Birnin Magaji
Bukkuyum
Bungudu
Gummi
Gusau
Kaura Namoda
Maradun
Maru
Shinkafi
Talata Mafara
Tsafe
Zurmi

FEDERAL CAPITAL TERRITORY, ABUJA
AREA COUNCILS IN THE TERRITORY

37. Federal Capital
Terrotory, Abuja.   Abaji   6
                              Bwari
                              Gwagwalada
                              Kuje
                              Kwali
                              Municipal Area
                              Council.

Total Number of Councils = 774

Source: *Federal Republic of Nigeria Official Gazette No. 72 Vol. 83, Lagos. 30th Dec, 1996.*

Index

371